Adventure Guide

The Italian Riviera

San Remo, Portofino & Genoa

Amy Finley

D1415946

HUNTER

HUNTER PUBLISHING, INC,
130 Campus Drive, Edison, NJ 08818
☎ 732-225-1900; 800-255-0343; fax 732-417-1744
www.hunterpublishing.com

Ulysses Travel Publications
4176 Saint-Denis, Montréal, Québec
Canada H2W 2M5
☎ 514-843-9882, ext. 2232; fax 514-843-9448

Windsor Books
The Boundary, Wheatley Road, Garsington
Oxford, OX44 9EJ England
☎ 01865-361122; fax 01865-361133

ISBN 1-58843-577-6
© 2006 Hunter Publishing, Inc.
Manufactured in the United States of America

*This and other Hunter travel guides are also available as e-books
through Amazon.com, NetLibrary.com and other digital partners.
For more information, e-mail us at
comments@hunterpublishing.com.*

Cover photo: *Portofino*, by Greg Schaefer
Spine photo: *Fresco detail from Chiesa di San Bernardo, Paigna*
Back cover photo: *Apricale* (www.apricale.org)
Interior color photographs by Greg Schaefer,
unless otherwise indicated.

Maps by Toni Carbone, © 2006 Hunter Publishing, Inc.
Index by Jan Mucciaroni
1   2   3   4

Contents

Where to Eat

Dedication

To Greg, who taught me to travel and who makes life on the
road a reality.

Introduction

The scent of herbs and pines, the startling blue of the sea. The brilliant white of cliffs tumbling into the depths, the bronze of suntanned skin. The sound of pounding surf, the chiming of church bells. The sight of mountain peaks that break the clouds, the chill of an alpine breeze. All this, and more, is the Italian Riviera.

Pinned between the mountains and the sea, on a steeply-sloped crescent of land stretching from the French border to Tuscany, the people of the Italian region of Liguria – commonly known as the Italian Riviera – developed a unique character and way of life. The area is small – only 170 miles long and a mere 23 miles wide at its widest point. Some historians and sociologists have theorized that the geography of Liguria had a profound psychological impact on the people who lived there. They reason that the limited landmass – with the sea on one side and daunting mountains on the other – had an "island effect," compelling the Ligurians to take to the sea as fishermen, traders, explorers, and sailors. To be sure, among their number is perhaps the most famous explorer of all time, Christopher Columbus.

This predilection for seafaring and commerce enabled Liguria's principle city, Genoa – once capital of the Republic of Genoa – to amass unparalleled riches and astonishing political power between the 12th and 18th centuries. An old saying states that "Gold is born in the Americas, passes through Spain, and dies in Genoa." The city's fascinating history is filled with intrigue as its leading families used murder, marriage, might, and manipulation to secure their personal fortunes and the global ascendancy of the Republic they ruled as oligarchs.

More than half of Liguria is protected park land and the coastal areas are carefully and deliberately stewarded. Each town of the Riviera is an actor in a larger drama that has been playing for centuries. In the past the storyline centered on the prestige and ambition of the Genoese Republic and its influence in the world. Today, the people are working to reap the rewards promised by global tourism, while maintaining their identity and integrity.

How to Use this Book

Every traveler has a different definition of adventure. Some seek adrenalin-pumping thrills or to push their physical limits. Others find challenge enough in the goal of relaxation and leaving the stress of daily life behind. Then there are those for whom the pursuit of new knowledge and experience is the ultimate reward and the ultimate adventure.

It will quickly become apparent that I'm a bit of a history junkie. I find places all the more fascinating when I understand how they came to be as they are. A ramshackle building comes alive when you know the tale of its former glory, the scenes and passions that transpired within its walls. Genoa is like that. And the story of Genoa is all-important to understanding how the other villages evolved and how they knit together.

To travel on the Italian Riviera is to pass through a region that was once the unlikeliest power center of all Europe. A tiny fragment of coastline, it logically should never have become the player it became. But its intrepid sailors and shrewd power mongers – not to mention the hearty common folk who literally hewed a livelihood from the inhospitable soil of a thousand cliffs – gathered wealth and prestige for Liguria. Consider that the entire country of Italy had five Maritime Republics (though history remembers only four), and that two of them – Genoa and Noli – were located on the Riviera, so close together you can now travel from one to the other in less than an hour by car.

When I'm traveling, I spend a great deal of time trying to understand where I am by understanding the area's history. But, once I've nailed down a context, I'm ready to have a good time, and for me that generally involves activity of some kind. I take lots of long walks to look at things and to pop in and out of the shops (shopping definitely qualifies as activity in my book). If I'm on the coast, I go to the beach where I like to be in or under the water. I love hiking and exploring the natural environments around me. I find the Italian Riviera to be the ideal vacation spot. Loads of history, urban and natural environments, beauty, activity. Every day is an adventure.

The Italian Riviera has something for every kind of traveler, and this book aims to help you get the most out of your experience. The presentation of each town follows the same format.

- Introduction and History (to help set your perspective).
- Getting There (practical information about transportation).
- Resources (websites you might want to check out and location of the tourist office).
- Being There (a quick orientation both to physical layout and atmosphere, followed by detailed descriptions of the most important sites and their significance).
- Only In... (what's special here that you might not encounter elsewhere and what's nearby that you shouldn't miss?).
- For Active Travelers (what you can do here, and what you need to do it).

Websites

Almost every commune (town) in the region maintains a website with both civic information for residents and useful info for potential tourists. In addition, the various provinces have their own websites, including tourist websites that aim to help travelers put together their trip itineraries. Then there are the websites specifically for promoting tourism to Liguria, and those of individual businesses, museums and hotels.

You get the point. There's a lot out there. Some are very useful and I've included links for those in this book. But even among them there's a lot of variation, especially when it comes to language. Some have excellent English-language versions. Some have English translations so bad you're better off pulling out the Italian dictionary and muddling through the Italian content.

When that's the case, I generally either use the Babblefish translator provided by AltaVista, or the Google translator. Both produce sloppy and almost incoherent translations, but it gets you a step closer and sometimes close enough to find that nugget of info you were looking for. Try to enjoy it and not get frustrated. It's good preparation for the actual experience of traveling in Italy.

To give you an idea of some of the many options the Italian Riviera has to offer...

The Top 10 Adventures

(in no particular order)

- Maxing out your credit card (and celebrity spotting) while shopping in Portofino.
- Imagining knife-wielding assassins prowling the medieval streets of Genoa while wandering the caruggi, the narrow streets, of the Centro Storico, then marveling at the palaces on the Via Garibaldi before heading to the aquarium on the Porto Antico.
- Hiking the Alta Via dei Monti Liguri, the beautiful hinterland trail that runs from one end of Liguria to the other.
- Languishing on the sandy beaches of the Western Riviera.
- Hiking the ancient mule-tracks linking the five charming villages of the Cinque Terre.
- Sampling troffie a la genovese, farinata, and other Ligurian specialties.
- Diving to the Cristo degli Abissi off the Portofino Promontory.
- Gambling with the high-rollers at the casino in San Remo.
- Sailing on the Bay of Poets.
- Having a glass of Rossese di Dolceacqua after exploring the hilltop villages of the Val Nervia.

Whatever you do, I know you'll have a fantastic time exploring the Italian Riviera. Have a wonderful trip. Ciao!

Practicalities of Travel

■ When to Go, Where to Go

Once you've fallen in love with the idea of vacationing on the Italian Riviera, it's time to do your homework and nail down all the practicalities. When to go, where to go, and settling the issue of trans-

portation (including deciding how you're going to get from place to place) are the first steps in planning your trip, and it's always good to have some basic information about things such as currency and banking, language, customs, etc.

When to Go

The high and low travel seasons along the Italian Riviera follow the weather, which is, on the whole, quite mild (and what drew the first proper tourists – Brits fleeing the wet winter – to Liguria). As the thermometer goes up, so do the crowds, with the height of the high season peaking in July and August (high season is offi-cially mid-June to mid-September). In the summer months you may find yourself elbow-to-elbow on the beaches, stuck in traffic on the Via Aurelia, or waiting – and waiting – for a table at a restaurant. On the plus side, everything is open and there's a party atmosphere as the towns and villages of Liguria host numerous festivals and special events (see the calendar, below). It's hard not to love the Riviera in the sum-mer, all hassles aside.

If you don't want to deal with crowds, April, May, and late September – the shoulder seasons – are an excellent time to visit. The weather is warm (averaging 70°F), rain is rare, and the crowds are at bay. Room rates are generally cheaper dur-ing the shoulder season as well, though you should, of course, verify with your hotel at the time of booking. Easter week does bring crowds, but the festive atmosphere surrounding this important Italian holiday (Catholicism is the predominant religion in Italy) offsets any nuisances.

Once upon a time it wasn't uncommon for hotels and restaurants along the coast to close from October to February, but this is becoming more and more rare. Most of the Riviera is now open year-round, though museums and shops might have limited hours during the off-season. Information about closures and odd hours is provided in the individual listings of this book. The rainy season falls during October, November, and December. Liguria doesn't get a lot of rain, but when it does it can cause havoc on the narrow, curvy inland roads. Some of the mountain towns get snow during the winter and Liguria has a sprinkling of ski resorts and numerous locales for cross-country skiing and other winter activities.

Airfare from North America to Europe also follows the seasons. Generally, the best fares are available during the "off-peak" months, from mid-October to mid-May. The summer months, following supply and demand, bring the most expensive airfares. However, between miles rewards programs, ticket consolidators, tour operators and packagers, and the web, it's still possible to find a reasonable fare for travel during the summer.

Italians love a good festival, and the calendar along the Riviera is packed with events that bring locals to the piazzi for food, revelry, and commemoration. Tourists are not only tolerated, they're welcomed with the warmth and spirit typical of Italy. You might want to plan your trip to coincide with any of the following:

- **January:** To celebrate the Feast of St. Sebastian on January 20th, the townspeople of **Dolceacqua** and **Camporosso** carry laurel trees decorated with colored communion wafers through the streets. At the end of the month, **San Remo** hosts the Italian Festival of Popular Songs.

- **February:** The Festa dei Fulgari, held in mid-February, commemorates the defeat of Saracen pirates at **Taggia**, a coastal city famous for its olives, citrus, almonds and figs.

- **Easter:** The most important holiday on the Catholic calendar is celebrated all over Liguria with feasts, processions, and festivals. The most famous are the Black Thursday and Good Friday processions in **Ceriana**, and the Good Friday processions in **Savona** and **Triora**.

■ **May:** Though landmines dotted the seas off **Camogli** during WWII, the fishing fleet made it back to shore safely. Their return is commemorated each second Sunday of May with a festival featuring a giant frying pan and hundreds of fish, which are cooked and freely distributed among the revelers.

■ **May/July:** The Regatta of the Maritime Republics takes place alternately between Genoa, Amalfi, Pisa, and Venice. Dating from Renaissance times, only men born in the respective cities can compete in the boat race, though anyone can watch. Also during the summer months, the Ligurian towns of **Chiavari** and **Sestri Levante** participate in the Maritime Palio, a series of races and events on the sea similar in origin to the Palio horse races in Siena.

■ **June:** Seven weeks after Easter, Whit Sunday is celebrated in **Baiardo** with the Festa delle Barca, which has nothing to do really with the apostles or the tongues of flame. Instead, villagers – and festival-goers – dance around a decorated pine tree in recreation of what is thought to be an ancient pagan ritual. Also in June, on the Sunday following the feast of Corpus Christi, the towns of **Diano Marina** and **Sassello** host a unique celebration in which artists create ephemeral masterpieces on the pavement using only flower petals. In **Genoa**, the Festival of St. John – the city's patron saint – is celebrated the on 24th with a street procession and city-wide party.

■ **July:** Fireworks explode over **Rapallo** as part of Nostra Signora di Montallegro. The lovely village of **Cervo** hosts the International Festival of Chamber Music near the end of the month in the square outside the Baroque church of San Giovanni Battista.

■ **August:** The first Sunday of the month is festival time in several villages. **Camogli** hosts Stella Maris, a beautiful boat procession. In **La Spezia**, there's a regatta and fireworks for the Palio del Golfo. See villagers in period costume participating in the procession as part of Corteo Storico in **Ventimiglia**. August 13-14, the town of **Lavagna** cuts a giant cake and hosts tournaments and a procession to commemorate medieval fieschi weddings as part of Torta dei Fieschi. At the end of the month (August 23), the heart of the Cristo degli Abissi festival off **San Fruttuoso** is the descent of divers to the ocean floor where a wreath is laid at the feet of a bronze statue of Christ.

■ **September:** Feast on delicious snail dishes as part of the Sagra della Lumaca, or Snail Festival, in **Molini di Triora**. The second Sunday of the month, a regatta and procession is held in **Noli** for the Regatta dei Rioni.

■ **December:** Most towns and villages hold various events for the Christmas season, including nativities, craft fares, and processions. Santa Lucia (December 13) in **Toirano** features a candlelit procession, and in **Dolceacqua**, a bonfire is lit on Christmas Night.

Where to Go

The Italian Riviera stretches from the French border in the west to the region of Tuscany in the east. Thin and crescent-shaped, Liguria is predominantly coastline (only 23 miles wide at its widest point) and is backed by the Apennine Mountains that stretch northward into the Italian region of Piedmont. This inland section – sometimes referred to as the hinterland – is filled with small villages that dot the hillsides, perch on mountain peaks, and line the floor of valleys that cut through the terrain. Liguria is classically divided into two sections, dubbed the *Riviera di Ponente* (in the west, for where the sun sets) and the *Riviera di Levante* (in the east, for where the sun rises).

Riviera di Ponente

The western Riviera is home to the coastal cities of Bordighera, San Remo, Alassio, Albenga, Noli, Varazze, and others. Inland you'll find Dolceacqua, Pieve di Teco, Sassello, and other hilltop villages. Generally speaking, the coast of the western Riviera is characterized by broad, sandy beaches, especially around the resort towns of Alassio, Varigotti, and Varazze. (Possibly the best sand beach of the Riviera is at Varigotti.) Keep in mind that what the Italians consider sand may be vastly different from what you consider sand. It's coarser and pebblier than many travelers might be used to, but quite different from the pebble beaches that characterize the eastern Riviera.

The inland towns of the western Riviera are some of the most interesting in Liguria, both for their history and their gorgeous settings amid the forests, valleys, and peaks of the Apennine Mountains. The hiking here is also fantastic, and the trails are frequented as well by mountain bikers and riders on horseback.

All of Liguria is divided into four provinces, and two – Imperia and Savona – are found in the eastern half of the region. The province of Imperia (which stretches from Ventimiglia to Cervo) is also colloquially referred to as the *Riviera dei Fiori*, or Riviera of the Flowers (www.rivieradeifiori.com). While this summons up visions of blooming hillsides, in reality the hillsides are covered in greenhouses, which gives them somewhat of an industrial look. Imperia *is* the flower-growing province of Liguria, and you *can* visit a bustling flower market in San Remo, but it doesn't translate into quite the picturesque setting that the moniker implies.

Everyone has their favorite destinations, for their own reasons. The following are some places not to miss when you're on the Riviera of the Flowers.

Don't Miss on the Riviera dei Fiori...
■ Busana Vecchia (otherworldly)
■ Dolceacqua (for the *Rosesse* and the walk to the castle)
■ Apricale (for the artistry)
■ Imperia (for the olive oil)
■ Alassio (for the beach)

The other half of the Riviera di Ponente is composed of the province of Savona, running from Andora to Urbe and colloquially referred to as the *Riviera dei Palme* (www.inforiviera.it). The nickname here is a bit more fitting. The seaside towns uniformly boast palm-lined promenades where people congregate at night for the *passegiata* (an early evening stroll where friends and neighbors are greeted, children are admired, and a lot of flirting goes down). The name also refers to the palms that grow among the olives and Mediterranean maquis on the hillsides. (However, legend holds that the first palm seed in Liguria came ashore in the fourth century at Bordighera, on the Riviera dei Fiori.)

Don't Miss on the Riviera dei Palme...

- Albenga (for the medieval city)
- Varigotti (for the beach)
- Noli (for the beach and the ambiance)
- Albisola Marina (for the ceramics)
- Sassello (for the *amaretti* and the Beigua Regional Park)

Riviera di Levante

While the western Riviera is lovely, the eastern Riviera is really, really amazingly beautiful and has many of the towns that are the best known outside of Liguria. In addition to Genoa – which some will love and some will hate but which is poised to be the Prague of Italian tourism – you'll find the gorgeous coastal cities of Camogli, Santa Margherita Ligure, Sestri Levante, and Portovenere, *plus* the enchanting Cinque Terre and the Eden that is Portofino. There are some interesting inland towns as well, but the coast is so magnificent you'll have a difficult time tearing yourself away.

It's not really the beaches that make the coastal villages of the Riviera di Levante so spectacular – they're generally pebbly or (as in the case of the Cinque Terre) nonexistent. Instead, it's the general environment; a combination of the village architecture and ambiance, the lush verdure of the hillsides, and the savage beauty of the shoreline where rocky cliffs plunge into turquoise water. The Portofino Promontory is the Beverly Hills of Liguria, and the presence of the beautiful people and their splendid toys help make it a standout.

The Ligurian provinces of the eastern Riviera are Genoa and La Spezia, but the nicknaming doesn't so neatly follow the provinces as it does on the western Riviera. The province of Genoa spans from Cogoleto to Moneglia, but only the stretch from Genoa to Mongelia is called the *Riviera di Tigulio* (www.portofinobayarea.com, for the Bay of Tigulio that wraps around the eastern section of the Portofino Promontory). I have a lot of personal favorites here.

Don't Miss on the Riviera di Tigulio

- Genoa (becoming a destination for hip travelers, plus loaded with history and culture)
- Portofino (exclusive and gorgeous)
- Santa Margherita Ligure (more laid-back than Portofino, but still sophisticated)
- Sestri Levante (deserving of its fairy tale reputation)

The last stretch of the Riviera di Levante, from Deiva Marina to the Tuscan border, coincides with the province of La Spezia and goes by the moniker *Cinque Terre and the Riviera dei Poeti* (www.aptcinqueterre.sp.it). As the name implies, this part is largely dominated by the *Parco Nazionale delle Cinque Terre* nestled within which are the "Five Lands" (*Cinque Terre*) of Monterosso al Mare, Vernazza, Corniglia, Manarola, and Riomaggiore. Little visited before the 1990s, Cinque Terre is now one of the most popular spots in Liguria for American tourists. To a degree this diminishes their charm, as in summer you hear more English on the trails and the piazza than you do Italian. But there's no denying the uniqueness of the towns, which perfectly preserve their fishing village layout, style, and ambiance, and that are surrounded by hillsides artfully and painstakingly terraced with dry-stone walls over the course of millennia. Hiking the trails between the villages is a wonderful experience, and it's hard to believe that anyone could leave the Cinque Terre disappointed.

Beyond the Cinque Terre, the Bay of La Spezia earned the name Bay of Poets thanks to Byron and Shelley, who lived and wrote here in the 19th century (and in the case of Shelley, died here). Lined with small villages and the large town of La Spezia, it's an azure pool popular with boaters and windsurfers. What shouldn't you miss on this part of the Riviera?

Don't Miss on the Cinque Terre & Riviera dei Poeti

- The hiking trail between Monterosso and Vernazza
- Vernazza (for its tiny beach and lively piazza)

- Portovenere (for posh shopping and dining and Byron's Grotto)
- Montemarcello (for seclusion and the *Parco Naturale Regionale di Montemarcello-Magra*)
- Sarzana (for antique shopping)

Setting the Stage

The Italian Riviera has always been a magnet for artists and writers, and so it shows up a lot in various artistic forms (movies, books, paintings). To set the stage before you go, you might want to check out any or all of the following:

- Read *Pictures from Italy*, by Charles Dickens, in which he talks about his travels on the Riviera and in particular his impressions of the town of Camogli.

- Watch *The Barefoot Contessa*, 1954, directed by Joseph Mankiewicz and starring Humphrey Bogart and Ava Gardner. The movie was filmed and takes place in Portofino.

- Listen to *Love in Portofino*, by Fred Buscaglione. You'll hear this, the unofficial anthem of Portofino, played a million times on every imaginable instrument on the town's piazetta.

- Read *The Cat in the Rain*, by Ernest Hemingway. It was inspired by his 1923 visit to and set in the town of Rapallo.

- Read *The Cantos of Ezra Pound*, by Ezra Pound. Written in Rapallo while the author was living there between 1925 and 1945.

- Read *Extra Virgin: A Young Woman Discovers the Italian Riviera, Where Every Month is Enchanted*, by Annie Hawes. A nonfiction work that describes her time living in a villa near Chiavari, growing olives, and learning the particular ways of Ligurians.

- Read and/or see *Exodus* (book by Leon Uris, film by Otto Preminger and starring Paul Newman). In the years immediately following the Holocaust, La Spezia earned the name "The Port of Zion" for its role in transporting survivors to Palestine. The ships *Faith* and *Exodus* were secretly furbished in La Spezia and set sail in 1946 and 1947, respectively, but not before enduring great trials. The Jews aboard declared a hunger strike after originally being denied permission to embark on their journey.

■ Read *Byron: Life and Legend,* by Fiona MacCarthy. The Romantic hero spent a great deal of time on the Gulf of La Spezia, in particular in the towns of Portovenere and Lerici.

■ Read *Enchanted Liguria*, by David Downie. Excellent photographs of the picturesque Italian Riviera, plus recipes for some of its famous cuisine.

■ Listen to *Sound of Festival San Remo*, available on CD.

■ How to Get There

Web-savvy travelers will appreciate the technological investments Liguria has made to help facilitate trip planning. In addition to the general travel information below, see www.orriotrasporti.regione.liguria.it, which has schedules, routes, connections and travel times for trains, buses, and metro transportation throughout Liguria.

By Plane

Liguria has two airports, but only the **Aeroporto Internazionale Cristoforo Colombo** in Genoa (see www.airport.genova.it, where an English version is available) supports international travel. The airport at **Villanova d'Albenga** on the northwest limit of the Albenga plain is served by AirOne – flights to/from Rome – and AirVallee – flights to/from Sardinia.

A modern airport on a man-made peninsula jutting out into the sea, Cristoforo Colombo is located six km (four miles) from the city center, but there are no direct flights from the United States to Genoa. Instead, **Alitalia** has connection service from Milan and Rome and **British Airways** provides connection service from London. **Crossair** provides connection service from Zurich and **Air France** has connection service from Paris.

If you hope to fly direct from the United States to Genoa, you'll need to disembark at Milan's **Linate and Malpensa** airports (www.sea-aeroportimilano.it, two hours northeast), or the **Aeroport Nice Cote D'Azur** (www.nice.aeroport.fr) in Nice, France (2½ hours west).

If you're arriving at Cristoforo Colombo you'll take either a taxi or bus into the city center – the taxi station is just outside the exit doors and to the right. Past the taxi station is the **Volabus** stop. Volabus makes the trip to the city center every 30 minutes, with stops at Stazione Brignole, and Stazione Principe at the Piazza Acquaverde. The first trip originating from the Genoa airport is at 6:15 am, and the last of the day is at 11:45 pm. For the reverse trip, the first Volabus leaves Stazione Brignole at 5:30, and the last at 11 pm. Tickets are on sale on the bus and cost around €3.

By Train

 Trenitalia is the Italian Railway and runs all train travel within the country. Italian train service has been improving in recent years, though it's still not uncommon for lines to be shut down by strikes, especially in the month of May, though throughout the summer travelers might encounter this inconvenience. On the Trenitalia website (www.trenitalia.com) you can find schedules and make reservations and it's very useful for planning your movement around the region. Note that on maps and in this book the station is marked by the letters *FS*, standing for *Ferrovie de Stato* (meaning state rail line).

If you're heading to Liguria from elsewhere in Europe or Italy your destination will be Genoa, the principle city of the region. Trenitalia participates on Eurail (www.eurail.com), linking Genoa to other large European cities. If you're aiming for the eastern Riviera, you can also book your train travel through La Spezia.

Things to Know
About Train Travel in Italy

A ticket grants the right to travel on the train, not necessarily to have a seat. The only way to assure a seat is to make a reservation for a seat at the time you purchase your ticket. This is not generally an issue for short hops between the close-together cities of Liguria, but if you're traveling a longer distance you'll want to be explicit about this at the ticket office. On the village-to-village trains (mostly InterRegional,

Regional, or Diretto trains – see below) it's not uncommon for commuters to save seats for other passengers – always ask before moving someone's newspaper to sit down.

There are several different types of trains, dependent on the number of stops they make and the caliber of the train cars themselves. It's most useful to know these when deciphering train schedules posted at the station. Each destination will be marked with a symbol identifying which type of train provides service there and the timetable of arrivals/departures. An additional legend explains special circumstances and exceptions (arrival/departure times that are only valid on weekends and holidays, for example). The important trains to know are:

- IC – InterCity (travels between major and important Italian towns and cities; has first and second class compartments)

- IR – InterRegional (village to village travel; no reservations required)

- R – Regional (village to village travel; no reservations required)

- D – Diretto (village to village nonstop; no reservations required)

You must validate your ticket before boarding the train. Do this at the small orange machine beside the platform. Insert your ticket and wait for it to make a stamping noise, and then remove the ticket. Your ticket is not valid for travel until the machine has stamped it. (The conductor may assess a fine for unstamped tickets.)

By Car

 Thanks to the *autostrada* (highway, see www.autostrada.it) that runs from one end of Liguria to the other, traveling by car on the Italian Riviera is very fast and easy. It isn't, however, free, as these are toll roads managed by the *Autostrade per l'Italia* company. From Ventimiglia to Genoa drivers travel the A10; from Genoa to La Spezia the A12. Road signs pointing the direction to the autostrada are in green and white.

The autostrada is simple to use. You'll receive a ticket when you enter the highway. When you exit at your destination you'll insert your ticket into a machine that will read the distance traveled and indicate the fee to be paid. You can do this with cash or by credit card. There is no fee to pull off at any of the convenience stops along the highway selling gas or food. (Eating at the *Autogrill* is sort of a cultural rite of passage for travelers in Italy.)

Off the autostrada the state and provincial roads are all free. In Liguria, the most prominent of these is the SS1, also known as the *Via Aurelia*. With a few breaks it traverses the length of the region, often passing through the middle of the coastal cities on or just off the waterfront (where its name might change until you reach the other end of town). Indicated by blue signs, the Via Aurelia is very scenic, but can be extremely crowded during the summer months, especially on the eastern Riviera.

Car Rental

The following companies rent cars in Italy and have service booths at the airport in Genoa.

Avis, www.avis.com, ☎ (39) 010.650.7280

Hertz, www.hertz.com, ☎ (39) 010.651.1191

Budget, www.budget.com, ☎ (39) 010.651.2467

Sixt Rent-a-Car, www.e-sixt.com, ☎ (39) 010.651.2716

Europcar, www.europcar.com, ☎ (39) 010.650.4881

Things to Know About Driving in Italy

- Speed limit on the Autostrada is 130 kph (kilometers per hour).
- Speed limit on other highways is 110 kph.
- Obey posted speed limits in towns.
- On the autostrada, you're supposed to drive with your lights on.
- Seat belts are mandatory.
- You are legally supposed to carry an International Driver's Permit (IDP) *and* your US driver's license while driving in Italy. (You can get an IDP through AAA and it's valid for one year.) You might need to show an IDP to rent a car in Italy. You will be asked to show an IDP if you are pulled over for a traffic violation.

- Parking lots are indicated by a blue and white sign with a large "P" and are generally on the outskirts of the villages. Parking is usually limited and can be quite difficult to find along the coast during the summer. Always inquire at your hotel whether parking is included in the room rate and if they provide parking.

■ Getting Around

Trains are the most popular method of transportation within Liguria. They're fast, cheap, and run largely on time (though they only service the coastal cities). If you want to penetrate the hinterland, you'll need to rent a car or make use of Liguria's excellent bus services (see individual *How to Get There* entries in this book for carrier information). Using the buses between towns in Liguria is quite straightforward. Buy a ticket at any *tabacchi* (newsstand), wait for the bus at the green bus stop marker, and validate your ticket when you get on. In addition to transport between cities, the larger towns (Genoa, La Spezia, Savona, Albenga, etc.) have service within the city limits. The same usage guidelines apply, but you'll need to consult the schedule posted at bus stops to determine which bus lines travel to which destinations.

Ferries run regularly between major coastal cities, especially on the eastern Riviera where taking the boat around the Portofino Promontory or between the villages of Cinque Terre and Portovenere is very popular and a pleasure not to miss. Individual entries in this book feature information about ferry services and carriers.

If you're planning on **boating** between towns on your own steam, you'll want to inquire at the individual marinas regarding berthing requirements. There are 61 marinas in Liguria, but the most interesting (and beautiful) ports of call are at Alassio, Bordighera, Camogli, Finale Ligure, Genoa, La Spezia, Monterosso, Portofino, Portovenere, San Remo, Santa Margherita Ligure, Sestri Levante, and Vernazza. Contact the tourist offices of these towns after docking requirements for their marinas.

■ Practical Details

It's a good idea to be familiar with the requirements of travel on the Riviera. The following information should be useful.

Travel Documents

Visitors from the United States must hold a valid passport. A Visa is not required. If you're interested, the State Department posts travel advisories for every country of the globe. Find them at www.travel.state.gov/travel_warnings.html. In case of emergency or disaster, the US Embassy is located in Rome (☎ 06.46.74.1) and there are Consulate offices in Florence (☎ 02.29.03.51) and Milan (☎ 055.26.69.51).

Money & Banking

Since 2002 Italy has been on the euro (currency symbol "€"), though this doesn't mean that the shops have stopped listing prices both in euros and lire (mostly to accommodate elderly Italians who still fear they're being gypped). In addition, prices for things like museum entrance seem to have been directly translated from lire to euros, resulting in fees like €2,07 or €6,48. (Note that a comma is used in place of a period when writing out prices in Italian.) Consequently, you're wise to hold on to even your smallest coins: You'll use them in Liguria.

Euro notes come in denominations of 5, 10, 20, 50, 100 and 500 euros. Coins are in 1 and 2 euros (the €2 coin is about the size of a quarter, the €1 coin just slightly smaller), and 1, 2, 5, 10, 20, and 50 cents.

The conversion rate is €1=$1.25 or £.69

So long as you have a 4-digit PIN number you can use your ATM card at any *Bancomat* cash machine, and most shops, hotels, restaurants, museums, and ticket offices accept Visa, Mastercard, and American Express credit cards.

Tipping

A service fee is often included in a restaurant bill (*servizio compresso*), but even so it is polite to leave a few coins (€1-€2) as a tip. You should tip around the same amount to taxi drivers and porters and chambermaids at hotels.

Telephone

So you don't awaken anyone unnecessarily, Italy is one hour ahead of Greenwich Mean Time, which means six hours ahead of US Eastern Standard Time and nine hours ahead of Pacific Standard Time. Daylight-savings time starts on the last Sunday in March and clocks are moved ahead one hour. Clocks are set back one hour on the last Sunday in September. (Don't forget this when trying to make a train!)

To make a local telephone call within Italy you will generally require a prepaid telephone card, which is available in €5, €10, and €20 denominations at *tabacchi* and newsstands around the country. Local calls are charged by time. To use the card, rip off the marked corner and insert into the slot on the phone.

The city code is always required, even when making a local call within the same city. For example, to dial a phone number in Genoa from Genoa, you still begin with 010, the city code. When dialing from one city to another, dial the city code then the local number. Italian phone numbers vary in number of digits (there is no standard). In this book, phone numbers are listed as you would dial them within the country: They begin with the city code and then the local number.

To Dial Italy from the US or Canada

- Dial 011 (the international dialing prefix for the US and Canada)
- Dial 39 (the country code for Italy)
- Dial the city code for the city you wish to call. If the city begins with 0, drop the 0
- Dial the local number

To Dial the US or Canada from Italy

- Dial 00 (the international dialing prefix for Italy)
- Dial 1 (the country code for the US and Canada)
- Dial the area code for the city you wish to call
- Dial the local number

Cell phones are ubiquitous in Italy and several tourist-oriented types of businesses (dive shops, boat rentals, etc.) use cell phones as their primary contact number. If you plan on using yours while traveling, inquire with your service provider in advance regarding fees or updates you can make to your plan to avoid astronomical charges.

Emergency Phone Numbers

- Police: ☎ 112
- Fire, Doctor, Ambulance, Police (Emergency Service): ☎ 113
- Emergency Medical Assistance: ☎ 118
- Breakdown Service: ☎ 116

Holidays

 Most religious festivals are public holidays in Italy, and shops, restaurants, and cultural attractions are generally closed on these days. Annual closures include:

- January 1: New Year's Day
- January 6: Epiphany
- Easter Sunday, Easter Monday
- April 25: National Day of Liberation
- May 1: Whit Sunday
- August 15: Feast of the Assumption
- November 1: All Saints
- December 8: Feast of the Immaculate Conception
- December 25, 26, Christmas

Stamps & Post Offices

Post offices are generally open at least from 8 am to 1:30 pm, and later in bigger towns. You can buy stamps and post a letter at the post office, or you can buy stamps from tabacchi or newsstands and mail letters from any red post box using the slot marked *"Per tutte le altre destinazioni."* Letters should be marked *"par avion"* or *"posta prioritaia"* for airmail service. To send a postcard to the US you'll need a Zone 2 stamp, which costs €0,52. A standard letter (20 g) sent via airmail to the US should cost €0,77.

Voltage

Bring your adaptors. Italy generally runs on 220 v, but sometimes on 110 v. Buy an adaptor before you leave the States; they're hard to find in Liguria.

Language

Though you'll get by decently with English, you'll have an easier time managing the Italian Riviera with a little Italian. (Italians are gracious to non-Italian speakers, but don't count on them being able to speak English themselves.) Here are some words and phrases that will be most helpful. At the very least, learn to say please and thank you. In any language they're the words most likely to earn you a little goodwill and consideration.

Yes	**Sì** (see)
No	**No** (no)
Okay	**Va bene** (va baynay)
Please	**Per favore** (pehr favoray)
Thank you	**Grazie** (graatseeay)
Thank you very much	**Mille grazie** (meelay graatseeay)
Hello/Hi	**Salve/Ciao** (saalvay/chaao)
Good morning	**Buongiorno** (bwon jorno)
Good afternoon	**Buonasera** (bwona sayra)
Good evening	**Buonasera** (bwona sayra)
Good night	**Buonanotte** (bwona nottay)
Goodbye	**Arrivederci** (arreevaydehrchee)
Excuse me! (to get someone's attention)	**Scusi!** (skoozee)
Excuse me (to get past someone)	**Permesso** (pehrmehsso)
Do you speak English?	**Parla inglese?** (parla eengglaysay)
I don't speak Italian	**Non parlo italiano** (non parlo eetaleeaano)
Please write it down	**Lo scriva, per piacere** (lo skreeva pehr peeachayray)
Where is it?	**Dov'è?** (doveh)
Where is the bathroom?	**Dov'è la toilette?** (doveh la toehlehteh)
When will the train arrive?	**Quando arriva il treno?** (kwando areeva eel trayno)
How much is that?	**Quanto costa?** (kwanto kosta)
Check, please! (in a restaurant)	**Il conto, per favore!** (eel konto pehr favoray)

■ Cuisine of the Italian Riviera

Ligurian Specialties

If you've fantasized about eating your way across Italy, you might consider attempting the same feat in Liguria. Its manageable size and diverse cuisine – not to mention the healthiness of the diet – makes the Riviera a gourmet's paradise.

With an extensive coastline and not a lot of land suitable for cultivation, the Ligurian diet consists primarily of seafood. This is augmented by a variety of vegetables, grown either on the plain of Albenga or in numerous small terraced gardens throughout Liguria. The scarcity of land on the coast meant that little could be spared for raising pigs or cattle, so neither beef nor pork features in the diet. Although chickens could be raised, poultry is basically absent also (although eggs are used in the preparation of fresh pastas). In the hinterland, wild game is plentiful and the dishes there often make use of wild boar, game birds, and sometimes goat or venison.

Olive oil is the foundation of all Ligurian cooking. It's the only oil used in food preparation, and is also used as a dressing and flavoring. The DOP-certified oil of Liguria is made of Taggiasca olives and has an acidity of .8%. Yellow or yellow-green in color it has a fruity taste with sweet tones.

 To be classified as truly extra virgin, olive oil must have an acidity of under 1%, though many oils Americans are familiar with are closer to 1% than the Taggiasca oil at .8%, The lower the acidity, the more the flavors and aromas of the oil can be experienced. So the Taggiasca oil is especially flavorful, a bit fruity and sweet, especially later in the harvest.

As elsewhere in Italy, **pasta** is an important part of the Ligurian diet and particular varieties are native to towns of the Italian Riviera. You'll find *trenette*, a slender noodle, and also *trofie*, a short, spiraled noodle, appearing on almost every menu in Liguria. Other specialties include *pansotti*, a type of ravioli that might have a variety of fillings but that is most authentic when it's stuffed with a mixture of chopped wild greens and herbs. Wild greens and herbs – which could be harvested wild or grown beneath the olive trees – are an important component of Ligurian cooking. They're also a large part of why the cuisine is so healthy. Chard is a typical green, and basil, parsley, rosemary, marjoram, thyme, chervil, and chicory all feature in the herb blend. The sauce for pansotti is usually somewhat creamy and made of walnuts (*salsa di noci*). Absolutely delicious.

In parts of Liguria you'll find *corzetti* (and possibly the stamps used to make them), a small, disk-shaped pasta that is impressed with an image while fresh and before cooking. Then there are *picagge*, which are rather like lasagna noodles, and *mandilli de saea*, or "silk handkerchiefs," which are like elegant rags of fresh pasta.

Pastas in Liguria – which are found on the menu, as the *Primi Piatti*, or first courses – are served simply dressed and in small portions. They might be tossed simply with olive oil and presented with fresh parmigiano-reggiano cheese for sprinkling, or adorned with a condiment like salsa di noci or – even more commonly – *pesto*, which is *the* sauce of the Italian Riviera and originated in Genoa. It's made of fresh basil, garlic, olive oil, cheese (either parmigiano or pecorino), and pinenuts ground together (traditionally) with a mortar and pestle. Fragrant and colorful, it's a favorite not only on pasta but also slathered on fresh *fococcia* or *farinata* (or layered into American-style sandwiches at some establishments) and drizzled into the Genovese *minestrone*.

Fococcia is no doubt familiar to anyone who's ever bought a gourmet sandwich in the United States, but farinata is probably a mystery and *fococcia al formaggio* may be assumed to be little more than bread with cheese. In fact, **farinata**, a kind of pancake made with chickpea flour and olive oil, is Ligurian fast food (but much healthier for you than grabbing a burger). When it's made with onions in the batter and fried it's less healthy and goes by the name *panissa*. You'll find shops all over the Riviera selling farinata and fococcia and maybe, depending on how many tourists the town is used to, slices of pizza. (On the other hand, *pizza dell'Andrea* is a native dish that has little in common with Neopolitan-style pizza. Named for Andrea Doria – it was his favorite – it's a savory snack made with onions, garlic, tomatoes, black olives, and anchovies or sardines.)

Along with the standard fococcia, slick with olive oil and sprinkled with coarse salt, you'll find thin pieces of fococcia al formaggio. At its best, the sheets of "bread" are pasta thin and held together with a gooey layer of flavorful, slightly pungent, melted *prescinsêua* cheese. The dish originated in Recco (and you'll find the best examples of it there), possibly at the restaurant *Manuelina* where the proprietor's grandmother claims to have developed it to feed hungry neighbors returning to Recco after a night at the Genoa opera. Another version of the genesis story has the recipe originating in the 16th or 17th century, when citizens of Recco fled to the hills in advance of Saracen pirate raids. They brought with them flour, salt, and oil and made a bread that they traded with local shepherds for cheese, which was then incorporated into the refugees' dish. At these same shops you'll probably find *torta pasqualina* and *torta verde*, two savory pies made with vegetables, and possibly *torta marinara* made with fish.

Is your mouth watering yet? *Piatti secondi* – second courses, served after the pasta or soup (but never order soup and pasta together) – revolve around **fish** or **shellfish** on the coast, served simply grilled, sautéed, or fried (*frito misto* is a menu staple). In addition to standard-sized fish – usually locally caught – in Liguria you'll find dishes composed of tiny anchovies and sardines. Particularly tasty is *gianchet*, which are very small fish stuffed with parmigiano and herbs and then coated in bread crumbs and fried. Shrimp, scallops, lobster, clams, mussels, octopus, and squid are all on the menu. Jumbled all together they might be served as *frutti di mar* – the fruit of the sea. In a delicious stew, fish and shellfish come together to make the delicacy *ciuppin*, said to be the dish from which San Francisco's *cioppino* derived.

Around the Riviera, and certainly in Genoa, you'll find dishes made with *stoccafisso* – air-dried cod. You might also see the odd-looking white planks hanging from hooks or piled into barrels in gourmet markets around Liguria. It's reconstituted in water as a first step in the preparation, and then commonly served with a sauce that has some acidity. Surprisingly good. The smell of the dried fish can be a bit ripe, however.

Meat dishes are more common in the inland areas than on the coast. Again, the meat might be simply presented and ordered with a *contorno* or side dish. If a *piatto secondo* is listed without any garnishes, then it has none, and you'll want to order a *contorni* if you'd like to have an accompaniment. There are also some special preparations. *Cima ripiena* is a piece of veal rolled around a filling of eggs and cheese and topped with vegetables; there are other rolled veal filets called *tomaxelle*. Tripe – the lining of an animal's, usually a cow's, stomach – is braised or used as a component in a hearty stew. Rabbit and wild boar are common on the menus of hinterland *osteria*, where you'll also find dishes made with the wild mushrooms that grow abundantly in the shade of the forests.

On the sweet side there are *baci*, little confections made from hazelnuts and chocolate, and *amaretti*, anise-laced cookies perfected in Sassello. *Pandolce* might be familiar to travelers as a Christmas-time treat. The best versions use abundant amounts of jewel-like candied fruit, which you'll find for sale in some of the better candy shops of Genoa and the Riviera.

Wine & Cheese

The few cattle that are raised in Liguria are often used for milking, and there are a handful of cheeses that are native to the region. They tend not to travel far, and you're most likely to find certain cheeses used in the dishes of – or sold in the shops of – the towns from which they hail.

Bruzzu is a soured and fermented ricotta cheese you'll find in Triora, Molini di Triora, and some of the towns of the Valle d'Arroscia. Made from ewe's milk, it is creamy in body with an ivory-white or brownish-white color. Also from Triora is *formaggio d'alpeggio di Triora*, a pasteurized cheese made of cow's milk that is aged for around three months (or longer for more complex taste) until a firm, golden yellow cheese is produced.

In towns nearby you'll find *formaggetta della valle argentina*, made by nearly every farmer in the area inland of Savona and Imperia but with a different flavor from producer to producer dependent on where the cattle were grazed. Generally eaten fresh, it's white, firm and soft, but it might also be matured until it's straw-colored with small, evenly-distributed eyes. When it's three months old it might be used as a grating cheese for pesto or vegetable pies.

Another cheese from the area of Savona, *formaggetta savonese*, is a fresh cheese made from hand-salted curds of cow's milk. A variation, *formaggetta di Stella* is made only in that municipality and is 90% goat's milk and 10% cow's milk.

Prescinsêua, the cheese of focaccia al formaggio, is found around Genoa and might be served at breakfast sprinkled with sugar (it resembles yogurt). From the Val d'Aveto comes *San Sté*, a brine-soaked, mature cheese made from cow's milk. And finally, from the Val di Vara near La Spezia comes *stagionato de Vaise*, a firm but supple straw-yellow cheese similar in taste and texture to the French *tomme* from the Savoie region.

Liguria's cheese pairs well with its wines, the most famous of which is the *Rossesse of Dolceacqua*, which is produced not only in that small village but throughout the Val Nervia and immediately surrounding area. It's a red wine with notes of blackberry, red currant, and pine resin. The Nervia Valley also produces the white *Vermentino*, characterized by a delicate, fruity flavor. From the Arroscia Valley comes *Pigato*, another white, with an intense perfume and a slight taste of almonds.

Between Imperia, San Remo, and Ventimiglia there are vineyards producing *Ormeasco*, a dry, deep-red wine with blackberry and cherry flavors that goes well with the stewed and roasted meats of hinterland cuisine. In the area around Finale Ligure you'll find a white wine billed under a variety of names – *Lumassina*, *Mataosso*, or *Buzzetto*.

This whole section needs more headings to break up.On the eastern Riviera, the most celebrated wine is undoubtedly the *Sciaccetrà* of the Cinque Terre. The terraced vineyards that give the Five Lands its unmistakable beauty are on very rocky soil, forcing the vermentino, bosco, and albarola vines to work very hard and to produce small grapes of intense sweetness. Picked when ripe, the grapes are then left to wither on special grates until late autumn. The wine made from these raisins, *sciaccetrà*, is amber-colored, sweet and alcoholic. It's also quite rare, as the grapes yield very little of the concentrated juice when pressed. A bottle is an excellent souvenir or gift from your travels in the Italian Riviera.

Slow Food

In 1996, Carlo Petrini founded the Slow Food movement in Italy (www.slowfood.com), and it's gradually gathered momentum to become a multinational force. The guiding principle is the preservation of culinary traditions and their ties to cultural identities, though this philosophy has expanded to encompass both the manner in which food is enjoyed – and thus the protection of small, regional cafés and restaurants where you can linger over a meal – and in which food products are produced, favoring organic, sustainably-grown or harvested and locally-sourced items.

To help promote their mission, Slow Food invites restaurants around the world that subscribe to their philosophy to become members, and allows them to display a special symbol that identifies them as part of the movement. They've also extended membership to food shops that carry regional specialties, and put out several guides to the eateries and boutiques where you can find meals and items in sync with the concept of Slow Food. On the Slow Food website you'll find several shops, restaurants, and wine boutiques in Liguria that have been accepted to display the Slow Food snail.

Going Metric

To make your travel a bit easier, we have provided
this chart that shows metric equivalents for the measurements
you are familiar with.

GENERAL MEASUREMENTS

1 kilometer = .6124 miles
1 mile = 1.6093 kilometers
1 foot = .304 meters
1 inch = 2.54 centimeters
1 square mile = 2.59 square kilometers

1 pound = .4536 kilograms
1 ounce = 28.35 grams
1 imperial gallon = 4.5459 liters
1 US gallon = 3.7854 liters
1 quart = .94635 liters

TEMPERATURES

For Fahrenheit: Multiply Centigrade figure by 1.8 and add 32.
For Centigrade: Subtract 32 from Fahrenheit figure and divide
by 1.8.

Centigrade	Fahrenheit
40°	104°
35°	95°
30°	86°
25°	77°
20°	64
15°	59°
10°	50°

San Lorenzo, Genoa

Above: Piazza Ferrari, Genoa

Below: Porto Antico, Genoa (Amy Finley)

Steep alleyways in Genoa's Centro Storico

Genoa

■ History

Two marble-carved lions crouch flanking the stairs leading to the entrance of Genoa's monumental cathedral of San Lorenzo. Their proud features are marred by graffiti – cartoonish scribbles rendering their expression more pathetic than fierce. They're an apt metaphor for the city of Genoa itself, which can be a challenging one for tourists. During two millennia of tumultuous history, Genoa has seen its fortunes rise and fall. At its pinnacle, the city – center of the Genoese Republic – had unparalleled wealth and economic and political power. French historiographer Fernand Braudel wrote of the city, "If ever a diabolically capitalist city can be said to have existed before the capitalist age in Europe and the world, then it is Genoa, opulent and sordid at the same time."

From these heights Genoa would plunge over successive centuries, losing hegemony, then autonomy, and finally prosperity. Today, in a region fabled for pristine beauty and the authenticity and persistence of old-world ambiance, Genoa stands apart as gritty and modern. But it is a city in the grip of evolution. There is much that is decrepit and shabby, and much that exemplifies the worst attributes of modernity. But there are also the heralds of a renaissance both economic and cultural. The lion that is Genoa may be blemished and humbled, but there is every evidence that with attention and caretaking it is regaining – if not its former brilliant grandeur – at least its dignity and relevance on the world stage.

Perhaps that's why Genoa is particularly poignant, and important for travelers who hope to leave Liguria with a greater understanding of the region – both what it was, and what it is becoming. Some will leave dispirited; others hopeful. It is impossible to leave Genoa unimpressed and without an opinion.

Ascendance of a Port Town

Genoa is – and has been for millennia – a port town, and the nature of a port is to facilitate trade via access to both sea and land routes. The geography of Liguria is characterized by mountains that plunge steeply into the sea, and that are criss-crossed by deep valleys. Genoa – which sits at the near middle of Liguria's great land crescent – is not only at the epicenter of what, from above, appears as one giant harbor. It is also at the crossroads of land routes that made use of these deep valleys to cut across the Apennines to northern Italy and the rest of Europe.

Trade involves both goods and services and the trade of ideas and influences, so port towns are natural melting pots. Genoa percolated over several centuries, absorbing and incorporating into its indigenous culture influences from the Etruscans, Greeks, Phoenicians, Celts, and Romans that passed through. Roman influence was particularly strong, as the city allied itself with Rome during the Second Punic War, was destroyed by the Carthiginians in 205 BC, and was promptly rebuilt and incorporated into the Empire by the Romans, who recognized the potential of its strategic harbor.

Roman domination of Genoa persisted until the fall of the Empire some seven centuries later. It would take several more centuries, and the defeat of the Saracens in 1148, before Genoa would arise as an independent power. It would also take the Crusades and the start of trade with the Orient, which brought immense wealth to the ruling families of Genoa, and general prosperity up and down the coasts of Liguria. The Genoese dominated the seas, defeating Pisa at the Battle of Meloria off Livorno in 1284 and the Venetians in a battle off the coast of present-day Croatia in 1298. By the start of the 14th century, Genoa's reach into the Orient was long, with trading posts, harbors, and storage depots in Constantinople, the Black Sea, Armenia, Syria, and North Africa. It also owned Corsica and part of Sardinia.

Through various means and with mixed success – the western Riviera was much less easily dominated than the Eastern – Genoa was also expanding its territory throughout Liguria. As its influence spread, the city continually upgraded and expanded its system of defensive walls. Ninth-century walls were replaced in 1155, and between 1320-1346 the Mura Vecchie – a third ring of walls – were built. Within these barricades, the medieval city grew not so much through demolition as through the repurposing of older buildings, which contributes to the character of today's Centro Storico and its honeycomb maze of *carrugi* – narrow alleyways.

This first golden age of Genoa collapsed during the 14th and 15th centuries. Trade had enriched the leading families, but wealth and power – and the greater game of global politics – had also sewn the seeds of division. The Fieschi, Montalto, Grimaldi, and Guarchi families, collectively known as the Guelphs, supported the Pope, while the Doria, Fregoso, Adorno, and Spinola families – identified collectively as the Ghibellines – allied with the Holy Roman Emperor. For 20 years, internal war raged within the Republic, and in 1339 the first *doge* was imposed by an anti-noble movement. Factions within Genoa appealed for foreign aid, and between 1353 and 1499 Genoa, always preserving nominal independence, would in turn be ruled by Milan and France. A Genoa stripped of many of its previous overseas holdings – Sardinia, Corsica, and the eastern Mediterranean – was subjugated to France until 1507.

Importantly, Genoa and its wealthy families continued to amass wealth and to be leaders in trade throughout these periods of political tumult. Their vast experience in international business transformed them from merchants to bankers and experts in contract negotiation. It was at this time that Andrea Doria – a legendary figure in the history of Genoa – entered the scene.

Having secured his fortune and naval credentials in the first years of the 16th century,

Andrea Doria, 1526, by Sebastiano del Piombo

helming his own independent fleet and vanquishing the Barbary Corsairs on the Western Mediterranean, Doria was appointed governor-general of the galleys of France by Francis I, who was at war with the Hapsburg Emperor Charles V of Spain over control of territory in Italy, Navarra (Spain) and Burgundy (France). For nearly five years he served the interests of France and Clement VII, a Medici Pope who had aligned with the French king against the Empire. But in 1528 he abruptly changed sides and entered the service of Charles V. In exchange for inclusion in Spain's political and economic system, Doria won for Genoa assurance of the Republic's autonomy and territorial integrity, and was himself appointed doge. A social constitution was created wherein the old and new nobility were incorporated into a system of 28 *alberghi* led by the main families, a move which effectively passified opposition and strengthened the Republic.

With this switch in loyalty came an upswing in the fortunes of Genoa. Poised with the establishment of the *Banco di San Giorgio* in 1408 to become a world financial center, the Republic now became bank to the Spanish kings, helping them to finance activities in the New World.

> *Gold is born in the Americas, passes through Spain, and dies in Genoa.*
> ~ 17th-century saying

Thus began Genoa's second golden age. Wealth from trade paled in comparison to the riches accumulated through finance, and money poured into a variety of public and private projects. Doria – whose rule until his death at

Palazzo del Principe

the age of 93 was undisputed, save for a conspiracy by the Fieschi family that was (brutally) suppressed in 1547 – built the *Palazzo del Principe*, the closest thing to a royal palace ever constructed in the history of the Genoese Republic. Other leading families of the day petitioned to create a private district away from the cramped medieval city center, and in 1551 the *Strada Nuova* (today's Via Garibaldi) was initiated. The palaces were constructed and sold between 1558 and 1583, with proceeds from the sale used to finance a variety of public works, including new roads and squares.

Other projects from this period include reconstruction of the 14th-century walls (now the 'Old Walls'), the redesign of the dome and presbytery of San Lorenzo, the renovation of Palazzo San Giorgio, construction of the Palazzo Ducale, and erection of the "New Walls" along the mountain ridges and shoreline from the Lanterna to the Bisagno River. Around the city, private villas were constructed, many of which were deemed elegant enough to participate in the *Rolli*, a system adopted by the Senate in 1576 to provide hospitality on the occasion of state visits.

Genoa, with its character and opulence, attracted visitors from all over Europe, including the Dutch artist Peter Paul Rubens, who was particularly enamored of the palazzi of the Strada Nuova. He undertook a collection of reliefs, drawings, and plans, published in 1622, that were intended as models for the construction of similar residences in the thriving commercial cities of Holland.

Inevitable Decline?

Like so many empires and cities of magnificence before it, Genoa eventually fell from its rarified position. Or, perhaps it's more useful to characterize its political decline as part of a cyclical redistribution of power and influence. In Liguria's fragmented history, individual valleys, villages, and towns were under control at any given time by an assortment of commissaries, feudal lords, military captains, and *podestàs* (local administrators appointed by the Republic). Some were Italian in origin, some from nearby realms. The unification of so many areas during the second golden age of the Genoa Republic was unusual.

The winds of change were blowing during the 17th and 18th centuries. In France, Louis XIV, the *Roi Soleil* (Sun King), ascended the throne and inaugurated his doctrine of Absolute

Monarchy. With it came expansionist intentions that ran up against the might of the Genoese navy on the Mediterranean. Initially, the French pressured Genoa to dismantle its fleet, but when it refused, a bombardment ensued between May 18 and 28 in 1684. Overwhelmed by the strength of French opposition, Genoa capitulated and successive decades would find the city increasingly under the influence of France.

Close on the heels of the American and French revolutions of 1776 and 1789, Genoa broke the rule of the doges and aristocracy, proclaiming itself the Democratic Ligurian Republic in 1797. But this period was short-lived. Witnessing the meteoric rise of the Emperor Napoleon, probably sensing the futility of resisting the tug of the growing Empire, and perhaps expressing affinity for his roots (Napoleon's ancestors had originally hailed from Sarzana, and Corsica had once been a Genoese possession), Genoa and its territories accepted annexation in 1805. This would be profitable, above all, for La Spezia, which became an important naval base and saw its population and prosperity increase steadily.

The cycle of power redistribution quickened its pace, and Napoleon's rule came to an end in 1815 following the defeat of his army by the crushing strength of the Russian winter. Genoa then joined the Kingdom of Piedmont-Sardinia as the Duchy of Genoa, but not without internal opposition. As a movement for Italian independence grew, Genoa became a center for activism that was spreading through Liguria. The freedom fighters Giuseppe Mazzini, Giuseppe Garibaldi, Goffredo Mameli and Nino Bixio – names immortalized in Italy – were Ligurians. Following the establishment of the *Risorgimento* between 1849 and 1859, Garibaldi waged a campaign to overthrow the Bourbons in Sicily and Southern Italy, and in 1861, Liguria entered the Kingdom of Italy under Vittorio Emanuele II. The era of powerful states, versus independent city-states, had begun. Genoa would cease to be independently powerful, its fortunes now tied to development and events that were involving the whole of the country.

A Modern City

It was during this time that Liguria first came to the attention of European – at first, primarily British – travelers. In 1855, Giovanni Ruffini, an Italian writer, published (in English) *Doctor Antonio*, a novel set primarily in the peaceful, flower-scented western Riviera city of Bordighera. This view of the Ligurian coastline, with its mild winters and balmy summers, flowers, vineyards and olive orchards, enchanted wealthy Britons. Fleeing the wet, cold English winters, they flocked to the seaside villages. Many built, or bought, the sumptuous villas and gardens that are now so characteristic of the region.

Concurrently, the Industrial Revolution brought change to Genoa. A regional railway system was inaugurated, connecting Genoa to the neighboring northern city of Milan, to Ventimiglia on the French border, and to the harbor city of La Spezia in the east. Just as once before the development of a road network increased the value of the port, so now the easy transport of goods to Genoa via the railways did the same. Between 1872 and 1882 the port was extensively expanded and renovated to handle the boom in trade. Increased trade meant more job opportunities and a swell in population. The city grew, annexing six coastal communities to the municipality.

Fought on battlefields that were relatively far away, the First World War, which Italy entered in 1915 on the side of France and Britain, did not have a massive impact on Genoa. But in its aftermath, the region as a whole saw significant population shifts as immigration to the United States began in earnest. Genoa became a city of farewells, the most important point of embarkation for ships traveling to America. For many émigrés, their parting memory of *Italia* was of the Lanterna lighthouse standing proud over the port of Genoa. The immigration drain still affects Liguria, especially its mountain cities which were steadily depopulated due to a dearth of

employment opportunities. Job seekers moved to the coast, or caught the boat to the US.

Throughout their history, Ligurians have behaved independently. The region's long history of geographic isolation, and Genoa's political moderation (a byproduct, perhaps of worldly exposure thanks to its trading history), created a temperament to challenge the status quo. This would be important in the years after WWI, when Fascism was sweeping the country. In Genoa, there was organized opposition, which gained momentum after Mussolini pledged allegiance to Hitler and joined WWII on the side of Germany in 1940. The resistance hardened after the 1941 bombing of Genoa by the British, and probably saved the city after Italy changed sides in the war and joined the Allies. A fighting infrastructure was already in place and could quickly respond to the German army, which attempted to destroy the port's shipyards and other industrial installations – the backbone of Genoa's economy – in 1943. In April of 1945, the Genoese Resistance launched a successful uprising against the German garrison in advance of the arrival of Allied troops.

Since the end of the War, changes in Genoa have been primarily cosmetic, economic, and cultural. The Cristoforo Colombo International Airport was inaugurated in 1962, followed by massive work on the Ligurian highway network, including the infamous elevated stretch that mars the waterfront. By the 1970s, Genoa was in marked decline. Though the port – the most important in the country – retained prominence and solvency, ensuring jobs for thousands of workers and underpinning the city's economy, Genoa as a whole was falling into an advanced state of disrepair. The carrugi (narrow streets) of the Centro Storico were crime-ridden, the honeycomb of streets and decrepit old buildings a hive of illicit and malicious activity. Whole segments of the city were abandoned by those of even moderate means, and the truly wealthy ensconced themselves in exclusive districts and developments on the periphery of the city. Visitors to Genoa were few and far between, put off by the city's nefarious reputation.

In part, it was the Doria family that again came to Genoa's rescue. They were at the forefront of a movement to revitalize the city and broaden its appeal to tourists; logical, since tourism was and remains the bulwark of the Italian Riviera's economy, but with 80% of tourism dollars going to the small coastal cities. The year of the 500th anniversary of Christopher Columbus's discovery of the Americas, 1992 was chosen as the target date for the unveiling of a host of improvements and renovations to be made to the *Porto Antico*. The waterfront as we see it today – with its restaurants, hotels, cultural attractions, and Europe's most widely-acclaimed aquarium – is the fruit of nearly a decade of planning and hard labor, begun in 1984.

Genoa

Many Genoese feared a sort of cartoonish, Disneyland-like exploitation of the port's history and charms. But the Porto Antico is now a source of pride. And it has certainly had a positive impact on tourism to the city. Newly reawakened in the consciousness of Europe and the world, Genoa began to be singled out for the types of events and honors that, before, generally fell to modern capital cities. In 2001, it hosted the G8 summit – admittedly, with mixed success (violence erupted between police and protesters and the police forces were later widely criticized for their harsh suppression of protest activities). But even this notoriety was advantageous. Genoa was in the news in live, living color and people all around the world marveled at how beautiful the renovated port and its backdrop of palaces and princely architecture were. In 2004, Genoa, along with Lille in France, was named the European Capital of Culture. With the distinction came funds from the European Union, which have been reinvested in renovation projects all around the city. Buildings are being scrubbed clean, pedestrian-only streets cordoned away from traffic, public transportation improved.

Is Genoa on the eve of a third golden age? Quite possibly. The fortunes of such magnificent but once-crumbling cities as Prague and Budapest have been reversed by the tide of tourism and the money that follows. And Genoa, with its aura of mingled intrigue and prestige, its glorious palaces, beautiful port, and proximity to the spectacular Riviera coastline, is well situated to be a tourism magnet.

In the meantime, Genoa is confronting itself, its newfound prominence and its ancient role as a crossroads for cultures and peoples in flux. Visitors will notice the Africans and Asians peddling goods on the waterfront and pocketed into nearly homogenous communities along such streets as the Via Pré. They'll see the long-distance centers where cheap rates are posted for calls to the Middle East, South America, Southeast Asia, Eastern Europe, and Africa. They'll wonder, as Genoa is wondering, how and whether it will incorporate these people – and these languages, tastes and customs – into a new Genoa that is as inclusive, unique, and proud as La Superba has been at the height of its glory.

■ Getting There

By Plane: Genoa is home to the **Aeroporto Internazionale Cristoforo Colombo**, conveniently located on a man-made peninsula four miles from the city center (see www.airport.genova.it). There are no direct flights to Genoa from the United States, however. If you're looking to fly direct from the US to Europe, you'll need to use **Milan's Linate** and **Malpensa** airports (two hours northeast, connection to Genoa by train or commuter airline, see www.sea-aeroportimilano.it), or the **Aeroport Nice Côte D'Azur** in France (2½ hours west, connection to Genoa by train or commuter airline, see www.nice.aeroport.fr).

By Train: Genoa has two main train stations, and trains departing or ariving will generally stop at both stations. **Genova Piazza Principe** (GE P.P. on the trenitalia.it website) is in the historical center opposite the Palazzo del Principe and handles the bulk of

Genoa's train traffic. **Genova Brignole** (GE BRIG on the website) is located in the modern, eastern section of town. Departures from Brignole station might require a change of train at Principe before continuing on to your destination. For more information, see www.trenitalia.it.

 By Car: Genoa is easily reached by car. Arriving from the western Riviera, drivers travel the A10 autostrada. From the Eastern Riviera, the A12.

Resources

- www.genovatouristoffice.com
- www.apt.genova.it
- www.genovatouristboard.net
- **Tourist Offices: Porto Antico**, Ponte Spinola, ☎ 010.248.711, fax 010.246.76.58; **Stazione Ferroviaria Principe**, Piazza Acquaverde, ☎ 010.246.26.33; **Aeroporto C. Colombo**, Genova-Sestri Ponente, ☎ 010.601.52.47

Genoa

■ Being There

So crammed with palaces, cathedrals, and other medieval dwellings that the buildings sport trompe l'oeil frescoes rather than stucco embellishments, Genoa at first seems to have too much of everything – people, traffic, trash, noise – crammed into too little space. Especially if you're arriving after a sojourn in one of the peaceful coastal villages, Genoa is an assault on the senses. It's one of the (many) reasons why tourism to the coast is so popular – where do you think the Genoese go when they need a break from the city's bustle?

That being said, Genoa is poised to give the opulent rediscovered Eastern European cities of Prague and Budapest a run for their money. As layers of grime are, literally and metaphorically, cleaned away, Genoa is emerging as a hip destination for in-the-know travelers.

Retain perspective and take it slow at the beginning. One excellent advantage of the **Porto Antico** is that it is tailor-made for tourism. There is very little to offend here, and much to enchant. But don't confine yourself to the port – use it as an oasis of calm, a place to regather your energy for excursions into the heart of the city.

The **Centro Storico** is by turns gritty and grandiose. It's also where the process of gentrification has taken hold as artists and students, drawn to the formerly rough and tumble neighborhood for its cheap rents, reinvented the spaces around them and drew new businesses to the area. It is bounded by the streets Via Balbi, Via Cairoli, Via Garibaldi, Via XXV Aprile, and Via San Lorenzo, and fronted by the Ripa, the colonnaded waterfront. Within these confines are enough riches and wonderments to satisfy the most avaricious of admirers. The warren of narrow streets, some so slender that neighbors could reach out their windows and shake hands, were also the scene for centuries of intrigue and chicanery, artistry and innovation.

Beyond the historical center lies **modern Genoa**. Here you'll find refined residential districts and *creuze* – cobbled lanes – leading uphill toward 16th-century villas and convents. This urbanized quarter also contains contemporary museums and other cultural attractions and is the hub for the smart set.

Museum Pass

If you're planning on visiting many museums in Genoa – and you should, both for the collections themselves and for the magnificent buildings that house them – invest in a Museum Card. It shaves a few euros off the admission to 20 of the city's best museums, plus gives discounts at the Rinascente department store on Via Ettore Vernazza, 1, and at participating book and record stores (for a complete list, see www.museigenova.it/museiconvenzionati.asp). The Card also provides discounts on shows at the Teatro Carlo Felice, Teatro dell'Archivolto, Teatro di Genova, and Teatro della Tosse in Sant'Agostino.

The 24-Hour Museum Card is €9; for €10 the Museum + Bus Card is good for 24 hours of discounted museum admission plus free bus circulation during the same period. A Three Day Pass is available for €15, an Annual Pass for €30. Students can buy an annual pass for €15. Cards are available for purchase at participating museums, the Genoa Information Kiosk in Piazza Matteotti, ticket offices in Liguria's main train stations, Club Eurostar locations in Genoa's Brignole train station, and at the main AMT public transportation sales booths. Participating museums include:

- Museums of Strada Nuova - Palazzo Rosso, Palazzo Bianco, Palazzo Tursi
- D'Albertis Castle - World Cultures Museum
- Diocesan Museum
- Edoardo Chiossone Museum of Oriental Art
- Felice Ippolito National Antarctic Museum
- Frugone Collection
- Giacomo Doria Museum of Natural History
- Giannettino Luxoro Museum
- Ligurian Academy Museum of Fine Arts
- Ligurian Museum of Archeology
- Modern Art Gallery, with works of The Wolfson Collection
- Museum of Agricultural History and Culture
- Museum of S. Agostino
- Naval Museum, Pegli
- Palazzo del Principe
- Palazzo Reale Museum
- Palazzo Spinola National Gallery
- Risorgimento Museum
- Treasures of the San Lorenzo Cathedral Museum
- Villa Croce Contemporary Art Museum
- Galata - Sea Museum

Admission to all of Genoa's civic museums (Palazzo Bianco, Palazzo Rosso, Museo Sant'Agostino, and seven other minor museums around town) is free on Sunday.

Porto Antico

The mid-1980s found Genoa at a pivotal moment. Changes in technology, demand, and common practices threatened to render shipbuilding and the other heavy industrial activities of the port obsolete. Meanwhile, at the same time as tourism was bringing money and exposure to the coastal cities, Genoa was languishing under its reputation for crime and disorder. The city – once the most powerful, wealthy, and magnificent on the Mediterranean – was on the edge of irrelevancy. An infusion of vision and hope was required.

The port had once been the key to Genoa's success, the feature that enabled trade and communication with the world. The Genoese turned to the port again, entrusting its transformation to architect, and native son of Genoa, Renzo Piano, who is perhaps best known for the Centre Pompidou in Paris

The redevelopment plan aimed to restore the blend of waterfront with urban area – no small task thanks to the monstrous overhead highway that neatly divides the port from the city like a city wall. The highway remains, but pedestrians

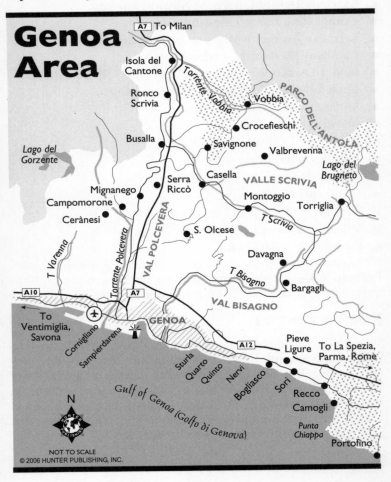

NOT TO SCALE
© 2006 HUNTER PUBLISHING, INC.

skirt traffic via several well-controlled crosswalks. The port area itself is now clean and calm, an inviting place for a stroll. Several attractions – namely the aquarium – reunite the city with the sea. Others repurpose historical buildings from various eras and appropriate them to illuminate Genoa as a center for learning and leisure. There are also ample restaurants and pizzerias, movie theaters, a library – even an ice-skating rink.

Acquario Genova

From the outside, Europe's largest aquarium and Italy's third most-visited monument is svelte and modern. Visitors arriving with a chip on their shoulder about the impressive aquariums of the United States – Monterrey Bay, Boston, Sea World – might even think it small and scoff at the likelihood of such a facility rivaling these grand dames.

Prepare to be floored. The flow plan zigzags you upward, past gleaming tanks with all variety of aquatic creatures, including dolphins, sharks, eels, and a stunning reef complete with jewel-toned fish and a slow, graceful sea turtle. The jellyfish exhibits are surreal, like living modern art. Each new level brings another awesome surprise, and English translations are provided for the engaging reading material. Especially interesting are the exhibits on whaling and the ecology of the Ligurian coastline. Obviously, it's heaven for kids – even small ones. Parents will probably appreciate that there's also a good café, and that the gift shop is small and unassuming. (☎ 010.234.56.78, www.acquariodigenova.it; open Monday-Wednesday 9:30 am-7:30 pm, last entrance at 6 pm; Thursday 9:30 am-10 pm, last entrance at 8:30 pm; Friday 9:30 am-7:30 pm, last entrance at 6 pm; Saturday and Sunday 9:30 am-8:30 pm, last entrance at 7 pm. Holidays open 9:30 am-8:30 pm, last entrance at 7 pm. Holiday eves follow Saturday schedule. Official holidays January 1st, Easter Monday, April 25th, May 1st, June 2nd, June 24th, August 15th, November 1st, December 8th, December 25th, December 26th; entrance fee adults €13, children 4-12 €8, children under four free.)

Genoa

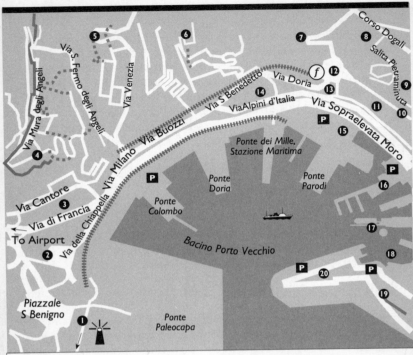

Genoa

La Città dei Bambini

Located on the third-floor of the Old Cotton Warehouse, this hands-on discovery and play center is a collaboration between the Genoese consortium Imparagiocando and the Cité des Sciences et de l'Industrie in Paris. Guided exploratory routes are aimed at visitors aged three to five and six-14, and parents will be impressed with the attention paid to details (colorful furnishings, specialist helpers) that children find generally inviting. As at the Paris site, age-appropriate exhibits, games, and activities coax expanded comprehension of natural and scientific phenomena. (☎ 010.247.57.02, www.cittadeibambini.net, cdibimbi@split.it; open Tuesday-Sunday 10 am-6 pm; entrance fee €4,13.)

Bigo

The Bigo rises out of the harbor like some gigantic alien-spider-sea creature. Tourists hitch a ride in a suspended glass cage, rising to a height of 40 m/120 feet and taking in a panoramic view over the port, harbor, and city as it tumbles down the hillside to meet the waterfront. Very touristy, but exciting all the same. (Closed November, December, February, last three weeks of January and Mondays. Open 10-5, 10-6 and 10-8, depending on season; entrance fee €3; children four-12, military, seniors +65 €1,50.)

Biosphere

Created for the occasion of the G8 summit in 2001, the Biosphere recreates a pluvial forest environment with tropical trees and flowers. A naturalist expert leads interactive tours. (Open Tuesday-Sunday 9:30 am-sunset; entrance fee €4, children under 12, €3.)

Palazzo San Giorgio

Reduced to banal functionality as the home of the Port Authority, the Palazzo San Giorgio is nonetheless interesting for its history. Built in the 13th century, the building was the

Town Hall until 1262, and
tradition erroneously maintains that Marco Polo was
imprisoned here in 1298
and dictated his *Il Milione*
to a fellow prisoner while in
captivity. The Venetian was
actually held at the Palazzo
Criminale, now part of the
Palazzo Ducale that houses
the Genoa archives. Argu-
ably its greatest historical

significance, however, is as the seat of the Banco di San
Giorgio, which it became in 1451. Famed French historian,
Fernand Braudel, claims of the bank – which was notorious
for its cupidity – that it was so powerful, and so deep were its
ties to several state apparatuses, that it discreetly dominated
the whole of Europe during the 16th century. Thus derives the
17th-century saying, "Gold is born in the Americas, passes
through Spain, and dies in Genoa." Treasures of the palace
are to be found in the Salone delle Compere (Buying Room),
where avarice is transformed into virtue through such propa-
gandistic works as *St. George of the Genoese and the Bank's
Emblem* (Luchino da Milano, 1444), and *Symbols of Justice
and Fortitude* and the *Genoese Coat of Arms* by Francesco de
Ferrari (1490-1491).

La Lanterna

Heading west beyond the Porto Antico around the great crescent of the harbor (you can also take a boat from the Porto
Antico) you find *La Lanterna*, symbol of Genoa. The current
lighthouse – which is still functional today – was built in
1543, but documents from the 12th century mention a tower
in existence at the time on the same spot. The first lamp,
fueled with olive oil, was installed in 1326; electrification did
not occur until 1936. Over the centuries many men and their
families have lived in the lighthouse, responsible for maintaining the fires and polishing and cleaning the glasses. One
of these was Antonio Colombo, paternal uncle of Christopher
Colombus, who was appointed to the position in 1449.

In 2004 a 10-year restoration of the Lanterna was completed, creating a visitors' complex that includes a Museum and 800-m/2,400-foot Promenade linking the Lanterna to Terminal Traghetti. This is the launching point for ferries to destinations across the Mediterranean. Visitors to the Lanterna can climb 172 steps to the first terrace, the highest level accessible to tourists, and take in an awesome panoramic view over the harbor. (☎ 010.910.001 or 010.549.94.69; www.provincia.genova.it/lanterna, fasciolo@provincia.genova.it; Lanterna and Museum – open weekends and holidays 10 am-7 pm, 10 am-6 pm in winter, also by appointment; Promenade is open every day from 8 am-sunset; entrance fee includes admission to the first terrace of La Lanterna and the Museum, €6; children seven-14 €4; under seven free; Promenade admission is free.)

Centro Storico

Bordered by the streets Via Balbi, Via Cairoli, Via Garibaldi, Via XXV Aprile, and Via San Lorenzo, and fronted by the colonnaded waterfront of the Ripa, the Centro Storico encapsulates medieval Genoa. Moving through the narrow, twisting streets is an activity that transports the visitor back in time – in most modern European cities, these ancient honeycombs have been long since paved over. Here, they are peppered with palaces, marked by Madonnas, and peopled with all walks of Genoese life.

Palazzo del Principe

The audacious maneuvering of Andrea Doria ushered in a gilded age, during which the city was liberally speckled with palazzi built by the leading families. His, however, was the first and set the standard for opulence up and down the Ligurian coast.

Following his strategic but surprising (to the French) allegiance with Spain in the midst of the Franco-Spanish war, Doria was proclaimed Prince for life by Emperor Charles V. Requiring a suitable residence in which to receive the Emperor (who visited for 12 days), Doria undertook the exaltation of an existing property he'd acquired in Fassolo (at the time outside the city walls). Not naïve to the tribulations of statecraft, Doria chose the location for his royal residence in part because it was wedged between the daunting Granarolo hill and a private harbor in which to anchor his personal fleet. These were dangerous, turbulent times. Doria, however, would rule uncontested – save for one rebellion, brutally quelled, by the Fieschi family in 1547 – until his death at age 93.

For the decoration of the palace, Doria commissioned Perino del Vaga, a student of the artist Raphael, who'd refined his stucco and fresco work while collaborating on the Vatican Logge in Rome. For Doria, Perino embarked on a mission of artistic propaganda, wherein allegorical figures and depictions relate the meteoric rise of Doria and his auspicious rule. Perino's work on the palace and the school he formed during his brief sojourn in the city (1528-1536) would make a lasting impact on artistic decoration in Genoa, launching the Mannerist style. The reverberations are to be seen in the palazzi constructed along the Via Garibaldi.

Until recently, these frescoes resisted the ravages of time better than the rest of Doria's palace. By the late 17th century, when Giovanni Andrea Doria III married Anna Pamphili and moved the family's main residence to the Pamphili palace in Rome, the Palazzo del Principe was falling into disrepair. In the 19th century the parts of its garden scaling the Granarolo were appropriated by the State to make way for the rail line, and construction of the Stazione Marittima severed the once all-important access to the sea. Thus it now sits squarely in the middle of Genoa's urban environment. Visitors who arrive via Genoa's Principe railway station might find it's the first monument to greet them.

But as Genoa recovers its former splendor and prominence, so too is the palace being reborn. The current heirs to the Doria estate – Princess Gesine Doria-Pamphili and Prince Jonathon – undertook restoration of the palazzo and its grounds in 1995. Visitors are now treated to a tour that includes the Atrium (where Perino's name and the date 1530 is emblazed on the ceiling's central rosette), the grand staircase leading to the loggia of the Gallery of Heroes (where Doria's ancestors are depicted clad as warriors), the Roman Charity Room, the Hall of the Giants, and the four private apartments of Andrea Doria, named for their frescoes – the

Room of the Sacrifices, the Zodiac Room, the Room of Perseus, and the Room of Cadmus.

The Hall of the Giants is considered the apogee of the palace. Signed with Perino's monogram, the frescoes depict Jupiter – King of the Gods, an allegory for Doria's benefactor Charles V – heaving thunderbolts at the Giants who dared to attack Mt. Olympus – an allegory for the Empire. The prominence of Jupiter in this western room was once echoed by a depiction of Neptune – God of the Sea, standing in for Doria – on a panel in the grand room on the palace's east side. Unfortunately this painting, in which Neptune calmed the seas after the ship-wreck of the Aeneas, was painted over in the 19th century during the renovations by Annibale Angelini.

The gardens are currently under restoration to return them to their 16th- and 17th-century form. Nestled among them are the *Fountain of the Triton* by Montorsoli (a student of Michelangelo), the *Fountain of Neptune* (Taddeo Carlone, 1599) and the *Fountain of the Dolphins* (Silvio Cosini). The references to Neptune again evoke the image of Doria as Lord of the Seas, a reference to his naval prowess and the sea bat-tles that assured his ascendancy to the seat of power. Visitors wishing to channel that maritime legacy can now voyage to the Palazzo by sea aboard the *Doria Frigate*, a vessel built according to 16th/17th-century designs that sails between the palace and the Acquario di Genova. (☎ 010.255.50.9, www.palazzodelprincipe.it/uktour.asp, info@palazzo-delprincipe.it; entrance fee Museum + Audioguide, €6,20 adults, €4,65 reduced fare with Museumcard. Museum + Doria Frigate, €11,36 adults, €9,30 reduced fare with Museumcard.)

San Giovanni di Prè

Working from the model of the Hospital of Saint John estab-lished during the Crusades in Jerusalem, the Knights Hospitaller of Saint John, later known as the Knights of Malta, built a hospital complex on the site of the church of Saint Sepulchre in Praedis in 1180. Praedis, the origin of the current Prè, was at the time on the outskirts of Genoa, the port of which was an important point for transit to and from the Holy Land. Thus, knights, travelers, and pilgrims could seek shelter and medical attention at the hospital according to its papal charter. Inside, a series of passageways, doors and staircases served to facilitate access to religious services for the sick and wounded. The lower church features vaults decorated by the different confraternities who quartered here, while the monumental upper church boasts a form that, while unusual for Genoese Romanesque architecture, is nonetheless attributed to Magistri Antelami (works by whom are sprinkled up and down the Ligurian coast).

The central altar of the right-hand side nave is dedicated to Saint Hugh Canefri, a 13th-century Hospital Knight who is said to have wrung water from stones to provide for those in his care. Above the saint's altar, behind the shrine with his relics, an early 18th-century altarpiece by Lorenzo de Ferrari depicts the miracle. Saint Hugh's feast day is celebrated at San Giovanni di Prè on October 19. (☎ 010.265.48.6.)

Via Garibaldi

The close, narrow streets had been the site of murderous 14th-century intrigue between the factions of Guelphs and Ghibellines, and as Genoa entered its second golden age in the 16th century these wealthy families petitioned the city to construct their own exclusive residential district on the steep hillside just outside the medieval city. Originally the street – named *Strada Nuovo*, or New Street – dead-ended at its western point with a monumental fountain and nymphaeum. It wasn't until the 18th century, when the *Strada Nuovossima* (today Via Cairoli) was laid out, that it was incorporated into the city's street network, joining the Via Balbi (where the Durazzo palaces, today's Palazzo Reale, are located).

The finest of everything in Genoa could be found in the private palaces lining the Via Aurea – or Golden Way, as it was

Via Garibaldi

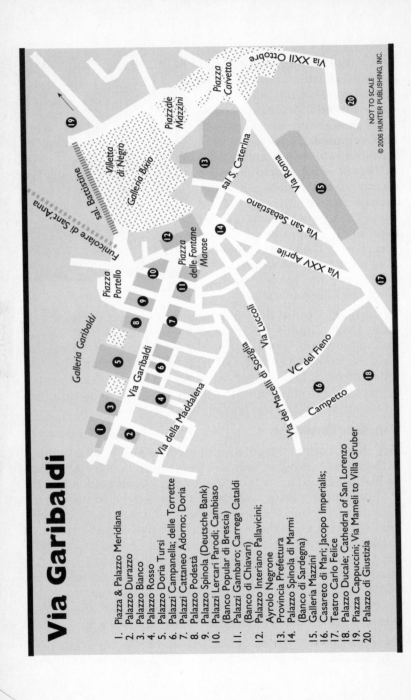

1. Piazza & Palazzo Meridiana
2. Palazzo Durazzo
3. Palazzo Bianco
4. Palazzo Rosso
5. Palazzo Doria Tursi
6. Palazzi Campanella; delle Torrette
7. Palazzi Cattaneo Adorno; Doria
8. Palazzo Podestà
9. Palazzo Spinola (Deutsche Bank)
10. Palazzi Lercari Parodi; Cambiaso
   (Banco Popular di Brescia)
11. Palazzi Gambaro; Carrega Cataldi
   (Banco di Chiavari)
12. Palazzo Interiano Pallavicini;
   Ayrolo Negrone
13. Provincia Prefettura
14. Palazzo Spinola di Marmi
   (Banco di Sardegna)
15. Galleria Mazzini
16. Casareto di Mari; Jacopo Imperialis;
17. Teatro Carlo Felice
18. Palazzo Ducale; Cathedral of San Lorenzo
19. Piazza Cappuccini; Via Mameli to Villa Gruber
20. Palazzo di Giustizia

nicknamed. Each was constructed with two *piani nobili*, or principle floors; one to accommodate the family, the other for the official guests (everyone from princes to ambassadors) they would receive as part of their participation in the *Rolli*, a system of hospitality necessitated by the Republic's lack of a royal residence. In some instances, however, both piani nobili were occupied by the family, as with the Palazzo Rosso, built for two brothers in the late 17th century. The palaces themselves were a feat of engineering. Features like monumental indoor staircases and terraced gardens masked the uneven terrain and the hill's steep drop toward the valley.

Lest anyone forget how important international finance was to the fortunes of Genoa's leading families, many of the palaces are now the Genoa headquarters of various banks. However, some rooms of these remain open to the public.

This description of the palaces of the Via Garibaldi proceeds from east to west, with the palaces listed by street number, name and the side of the road where you'll find each one, presented in the order you would encounter them as you walk along the street. The eastern terminus of the Via Garibaldi is marked by the Piazza delle Fontane Marose, where the Palazzo dei Marmi (now a bank) is located. The western end of the street is home to the Palazzo Doria-Tursi (today's City Hall) and the Palazzi Rosso and Bianco, which today house some of the finest art collections in Genoa. For more informatioon, see www.stradanuova.it.

1. **Palazzo Cambiaso** (north)

Now the Banca Popolare di Brescia, the palace was built in 1558-60 for Agostino Pallavicino, a prominent member of the Republic's government, and became the property of the Cambiaso family during the mid-18th century (the Cambiaso family's heraldic coat-of-arms can be seen in the atrium). The building was designed by Bernardino Cantone, and stylistic similarities suggest the involvement of Galeazzo Alessi, the architect behind Milan's Palazzo. The piano nobile is open to the public and boasts frescoes (*Banquet of the Gods*, *Apollo and the Muses*, and *Rape of the Sabine Women*) by Andrea and Ottavio Semino.

2. **Palazzo Gambaro** (south)

Now the Banco di Chiavari della Riviera Ligure, the palace was built in 1558-64 for Pantaleo Spinola, with work begun by Bernardo Spazio and completed by Pietro Orsolino. The otherwise simple façade is enlivened by a marble portal featuring two reclining figures by Orsolino representing Prudence and Vigilance. On the ground floor, Biblical frescoes by the brothers Giovanni Carlone and Giovanni Battista were painted in the early 17th century. The Art Nouveau glass compass dates from 1923. Other 17th-century works on the piano nobile include the vault fresco, featuring a mythological scene depicting the offering of the keys of the temple of Janus to Jove, by Domenico Piola and Paolo Grozzi.

3. **Palazzo Lercari Parodi** (north)

Commissioned by Franco Lercari in 1571, the palace is today owned by the Parodi family, who purchased it in 1845. It's current form differs dramatically from its original composition: the upper floors once featured open loggias, which were later enclosed with glass panes and then walled-in during the early 19th century. This loggia complemented the courtyard preceding the building proper, an innovation of Galeazzo Alessi that was the first of its kind in Genoa. The Lercaris were enriched by trade, and two aspects of the building's artworks remind current visitors of how hard-won those gains were. A vault in the hall of the second piano nobile has a fresco by Luca Cambiaso depicting Franco Lercari's ancestor Megollo Lercari's enterprise – the construction of trade warehouses that enabled trade with the Genoese colonies along the Black Sea. Going back to the building's façade, the mutilated noses of the male figures holding up the pillars of the palace portal recalls how that same ancestor tortured prisoners taken after an uprising in the colony of Cyprus.

4. **Palazzo Carrega Cataldi** (south)

This palace, now the Chamber of Commerce, was completed in 1561 for Tobia Pallavicino and constructed by Giovanni Battista Castello with the assistance of Barolomeo Riccio, Domenico Solari, and Antonio Roderio. At the beginning of the 18th century, after transferring ownership to the Carrega family, the palace was raised by one floor and two perpendicular wings were added, in addition to modifications made to the rear of the building and its façade overlooking Piazza del Ferro. Sixteenth-century decorations include Castello's frescoes of *Apollo* and *Musicians* in the vestibule, in addition to the numerous stuccoes and grotesques of the piano nobile. The chapel decorations are 18th-century, credited to Loreno de Ferrari, as are the door medallions depicting the Annunciation and Nativity. Ferrari also executed the Rococo golden gallery, which blends golden stuccoes, mirrors, and frescoes.

5. **Palazzo Spinola** (north)

Giovanni Spinola, the Republic's Ambassador to Spain and banker to Emperor Charles V, commissioned the palace in 1558, but died before its completion in 1576; final works were overseen by his son Giulio, who is also credited with leveling the hill behind the building and expanding the palace's courtyard and garden. Frescoes by the Calvi brothers on the palace façade were under restoration in 2004 as part of Genoa's distinction as European Capital of Culture. These – along with the frescoes in the atrium – honor the Spinola dynasty, depicting various family members dressed as Roman condottieri. A fresco by Andrea Semino on the upper floor depicts the palace's original appearance as seen from the side facing the mountains. The building currently houses the Deutsche Bank.

6. **Palazzo Doria** (south)

The façade of this palace, originally constructed in 1563 for Giovanni Battista and Andrea Spinola by the architect Bernadino Cantone, was considerably damaged during the bom-

Palazzo Doria

Palazzo Doria, interior

bardment by the French fleet in 1684. During reconstruction the palace façade acquired its current form. The Doria family purchased the palace in 1723; their heraldic eagle crowns a large pensile lantern in the atrium, which leads to the colonnaded courtyard and hanging garden. In a parlor on the upper floor, the Dorias established the picture gallery that today remains in its original configuration. Elsewhere, other artistic works evoke the Spinola dynasty, including frescoes on the vaulted drawing room ceiling. The drawing room features five 16th-century Flemish tapestries depicting the Story of Abraham.

7. Palazzo Podestà (north)

The Podestà family, whose ancestor Andrea Podestà served several terms as mayor of Genoa between 1866 and 1895, owned the palace from the mid-19th century until recently, when it was acquired by the Bruzzo family. It was built between 1559 and 1565 by Giovanni Battista Castello and Bernardo Cantone for Nicolosio Lomellino, and traded hands several times, belonging to the Centurione family in the 17th century, and later to the Pallavicini and Raggi families. The façade is notable for its stucco decorations in the Mannerist style. Inside, an open courtyard is enclosed by the palace's hind wings and an 18th-century nymphaeum is flanked by terraces that open into the garden extending toward the hills. Lorenzo de Ferrari created the stuccoes and frescoes depicting divinities on the gallery vault. In the room decorated by Aldovarandini, a series of canvasses with Stories of the Goddess Diana are by Marcantonio Franceschini.

An artistic treasure has recently come to light at the palazzo. In 1623, while the property was in the hands of Luigi Centurione, Bernardo Strozzi – perhaps Genoa's most well-known artist, and former Capuchin friar – was commissioned to create a series of frescoes. An argument occurred between the two men over payment, and Strozzi plastered over his work, which was then forgotten for 400 years. Under the guidance of painting historian Mary Newcome Schleier, these lost works have been uncovered and restored. This is particularly significant, as few of Strozzi's frescoes have survived the ages.

8 & 10. **Palazzo Cattaneo Adorno** (south)

The twin portals on the palace façade denote that this building is actually two distinct, symmetrical residences, originally commissioned by the cousins Lazzaro and Giacomo Spinola between 1583 and 1588. The interior decorations thus vary. At No. 10, the hall of the piano nobile features a fresco by Lazzaro Tavarone depicting the meeting between Urbano VI and Doge Antoniotto Adorno in Genoa.

9. **Palazzo Doria-Tursi** (north)

The largest palace on the street was built in 1565 by Domenico and Giovanni Ponzello for Nicolo Grimaldi, banker to King Phillip II of Spain and himself nicknamed "The Monarch" for the number of aristocratic titles he held. The palace was constructed on three adjoining plots of land, though the immense gardens and colonnaded loggia were added in 1596 after the property's purchase by Giovanni Andrea Doria, who bought it for his son Carlo, Duke of Tursi. The façade alternates pink stone from Finale Ligure with grey-black slate and white Carrara marble, and the portal is crowned with Genoa's coat-of-arms. The clock tower was added in 1820. From 1848 until recently the palace served as Genoa's City Hall, and between 1960 and 1965 architects Franco Albini and Franca Helg added the Public Offices on the side facing the Castello hill. Though the Palazzo Tursi now serves as an extension of the Palazzo Bianco Art Gallery, the Mayor's staterooms have been maintained and are available for visit. (☎ 010.557.2193,

Genoa

www.stradanuova.it, museopalazzotursi@comune.genova.it; open Tuesday-Friday 9 am-7 pm; Saturday-Sunday 10 am-7 pm; entrance fee €7 full fare; €5 reduced.)

12. Palazzo Campanella (south)

Thanks to the architectural drawings of the palazzi of the Strada Nuovo produced by Rubens, it is known that this palace once featured a fake architectural fresco decoration and was crowned by a monumental open loggia. Today, only the sculpted portal by Taddeo Carlone has retained its original appearance; the building was badly damaged during the French bombardment of 1684 and the 1942 air raids. The palace was built in 1562 for Baldassare Lomellini, and was in turn owned by Cristoforo Spinola and Domenico Serra before its purchase by the Campanella family, who still own the property.

14. Palazzo Torrette (south)

Named for its two small towers, the palace is the newest on the street, built in 1716 by Giacomo Viano for Giovan Andrea Doria, Duke of Tursi. Its sole purpose was to glorify the majestic Palazzo Doria-Tursi it faces, in part by concealing the crumbling medieval buildings behind it.

18. Palazzo Rosso (south)

A latecomer to the street, the Palazzo Rosso was built in 1670 for the brothers Ridolfo and Giovanni Francesco Brignole-Sale, the grandsons of Giovanni Francesco Brignole, an upwardly-mobile merchant-entrepreneur in the wool and silk industry whose family originally hailed from Rapallo. The elder Giovanni married strategically and well, taking as his bride the only child of Giulio Sale, a member of the Genoese nobility. The birth of their first son, Anton, in 1605 assured the inheritance of

Palazzo Rosso

the family name, title, and estate, a town residence, a villa in

Albaro, and the family fortune. But no home on the Strada Nuova.

In the open nobility of Genoa – which could be entered into by wealth – the flaunting of riches was a means of conveying economic and thus political and social power. In 1627, Giovanni Francesco commissioned the esteemed Dutch artist Van Dyck to paint monumental portraits of his wife Geronima and daughter Aurelia, as well as those of his son Anton Giulio and his wife Paolina Adorno. Eight years later, Gio Francesco was elected to the office of Doge, and died just days before the end of his term in 1637.

The family's ambitions for a residence on the Golden Way were realized in 1647, when son Anton – who owned three adjacent houses at the western end of the Strada Nuova – petitioned the local magistrates to close off the alleys running between them so he could build one large house on the piece of land. The request was granted, but three years later Anton was widowed and took religious vows, entering the Company of Jesus. It was thus his sons who would undertake the building, hiring architect Pietro Antonio Corradi to design the structure and Matteo Lagomaggiore to direct the construction. The colloquial moniker "Rosso" derives from the building's red stone three-dimensional exterior motifs.

Two piani nobili were constructed, one for each brother, but Ridolfo died suddenly in 1683 leaving no heir, and thus Giovanni became the sole owner of the property and established his family residence on the second floor. He undertook the first period of decoration and acquisition, purchasing the Van Dyck portraits of his parents from his niece Paola, wife of Carlo Spinola, and commissioning fresco works for the second-floor rooms. Today, this piano nobile – with its frescoes by Domenico Piola, Gregorio De Ferrari, and Paolo Gerolamo Piola –

San Paolo,
Bernardo Strozzi

Genoa

preserves the original ambiance of the family apartments.

Giovanni Francesco died in 1694. His eldest nephew Giovanni Francesco II Brignole-Sale became sole owner of the palace and its collection, which now included the Van Dyke portraits, paintings by Guido Reni, Guercino, Mattia Preti, and Bernardo Strozzi, as well as several 16th-century Venetian works (including paintings by Palma the Elder and Veronese) that had been added by his aunt, Maria Durazzo, after their inheritance from her father Giuseppe Maria Durazzo.

Several of the most important works in the Palazzo Rosso collection were added under Giovanni Francesco II, including the *Four Apostles* by Giulio Cesare Procaccini, the *Portrait of a Young Man* by Van Dyck, and *Charity* by Bernardo Strozzi. Portraits of himself and his wife were commissioned to Hyacinthe Rigaud, official court painter to the French aristocracy, during Gio's diplomatic mission to Paris from 1737 to 1739. Then, in 1746, he undertook the redecoration of the façade of the palace and the adjacent

St Sebastian, Guido Reni, 1615-16

"Palazzetto," adding the lion statues over the second floor windows, which bear the Brignole coat of arms. The political ascent of Giovanni Francesco II mirrored that of his ancestor and namesake, and on the heels of this program of artistic endeavor he was elected Doge of the Republic of Genoa in 1746.

In 1874, Maria Brignole-Sale De Ferrari, Duchess of Galliera, donated the Palazzo Rosso to the Commune of Genoa, stipulating that its furnishings and decorations remain intact and serve as a living museum (and monument to the Brignole-Sale dynasty). Today, the Palazzo Rosso has the city's largest art collection, and the frescoes and furnishings are considered to represent the best of the Genoese school. (☎ 010.247.63.51, www.museopalazzorosso.it, museopalazzorosso@comune.genova.it; open Tuesday-Friday 9 am-7 pm;

Saturday-Sunday 10 am-7 pm; entrance fee €7 full fare; €5 reduced.)

11. **Palazzo Bianco** (north)

Ten years after her bequest of the Palazzo Rosso to the Commune of Genoa, Maria Brignole-Sale De Ferrari donated the Palazzo Bianco, another Brignole-Sale residence, to the city, stipulating that it be used as Genoa's first civic art museum. The Duchess also stipulated that some property income was to be used for increasing the gallery holdings. Over the years several bequests, donations, acquisitions, and the vagaries of history (various 18th- and 19th-century laws transferred large numbers of works from religious bodies to the civic authorities) have resulted in a significant collection, rich in Flemish art – including several by Van Dyck and Rubens – and 17th- and 18th-century Genoese works.

The property's original building actually predates the Strada Nuova, constructed between 1530 and 1540 for Luca Grimaldi. Of modest form, however, it was not included among the sketches of the Strada Nuova published by Rubens in 1622. In 1711, after having passed to the De Franchi family some 60 years previously, the property was ceded to Maria Durazzo Brignole-Sale, the De Franchi family's main creditor. It was demolished and rebuilt in 1712 by Giacomo Viano, who based the design on the Palazzo Doria-Tursi. Today, two statues of Jupiter and Janus dating to 1585 are the only visible remnants of the original residence.

Much of the building was destroyed in the air raids of 1942, and was rebuilt in 18th-century style. This also provided an opportunity to reorganize the collection. When the museum reopened in 1950, with an interior layout and design by the rationalist architect Franco Albini, its modernity created an international cultural sensation. In addition to the spare, formal presentations on the piani nobili, a storage area was created of the upper mezzanine floor. Here, in 14 rooms that make ingenious use of nontraditional surfaces to display some 200 works, visitors can view paintings currently under study or awaiting restoration, or merely out of rotation from the main galleries. (☎ 010.557.21.93; www.museopalazzobianco.it, museopalazzobianco@commune.genova.it; open Tuesday-Friday 9 am-7 pm; Saturday-Sunday 10 am-7 pm; entrance fee €7 full fare; €5 reduced.)

Via Balbi

The success of the Strada Nuova persuaded another wealthy Genoese family to undertake construction of their own palatial street. At the turn of the 17th century the Balbi family – enriched originally by trade in silk and wool, and later by their multifaceted banking activities – petitioned the government to create their own district in what was, at the time, the suburbs. Over a period of 20 years (1602-1622), seven sumptuous palaces were built under the architect Bartolomeo Bianco, all for the use of members of the Balbi family.

In a city and at a time famous for conspicuous displays of wealth, these were ostentatious almost beyond belief, an assertion of power and influence by the Balbi clan that would not go unnoticed (or indeed, unpunished) in the political world of Genoa. During the tumultuous decades of the 1630s and 1640s, as the Republic's alliance with Spain faltered under that nation's growing debt and a series of disastrous military campaigns, Gio Paolo Balbi undertook to deliver the Republic to French rule. His plan was unearthed and he was condemned for treason and subsequently spent several years in exile. His maneuverings even ran him afoul of the Spanish Inquisition, which by some reports made seven separate, but failed, attempts on his life.

Palazzo Reale

Among the palaces was that of Stefano Balbi, the Palazzo della Corona. But the Balbi's ownership of the gorgeous property was brief, as it was sold to the Durazzo family in 1679. In 1824 it was sold to the House of Savoy when the Congress of Vienna delivered all of Liguria to the Kingdom of Sardinia and Genoa became a duchy. Suitably opulent, it became the royal residence and acquired its current name, the Palazzo Reale. Today it is owned by the state and houses the Galleria Nazionale di Palazzo Reale and the Falcone Theater.

The first piano nobile of the Palazzo houses the apartments of Luigi Amedeo of Savoy, Duke of the Abruzzi, a famous 19th-century explorer, navigator, mountain climber, and

Palazzo Reale courtyard

admiral. Painstakingly preserved, they present art, furnishings, and objects from the era to recreate the opulent royal lifestyle of Genoa under Savoy rule.

Galleria, Palazzo Reale

The second piano nobile commences the art collection of the Galleria Nazionale. Priceless works are displayed in gilded and frescoed rooms that once served royal functions. Among the most astonishingly beautiful is the Gallery of Mirrors, modeled after Louis XIV's palace at Versailles. Here, four statues by Filippo Parodi (*Hyacinthus, Clizia, Amor* – also known as *Narcissus* – and *Venus*) and a marble group (*Rape of Proserpina*) by Francesco Schiaffino are the stars.

Several grand-scale works by Van Dyck can be found throughout the Galleria, underscoring the important relationship between Flemish artists and Genoese patrons during the Second Golden Age of the city. Van Dyck, a student of Reubens – who famously sketched the palazzi of the Via Aurea so that the wealthy mer-

Adonis, by Filippo Parodi, 1680s

Genoa

chants of Antwerp might model their homes after them – spent six years (1621-1627) in Genoa doing the portraits of the rich and famous. His *Portrait of Caterina Balbi Durazzo* hangs in the Audience Chamber, and a *Crucifixion* hangs in the King's Bedchamber. (☎ 010.217.02.36, www.palazzorealegenova.it; open Tuesday-Wednesday 9 am-1:30 pm; Thursday-Sunday 9 am-7 pm.)

Caterina Balbi Durazzo, Anthony Van Dyck, 1623

Palazzo dell'Universitá

Higher education was an organized activity in Genoa as early as the 13th century, with colleges conferring degrees in Law, Theology, Medicine, and Arts. In 1569, the existing colleges were incorporated into the schools run the Jesuits by a decree of the Senate. Just under a century later, the religious Balbis helped the Jesuits settle onto the Via Balbi, creating the College of the Jesuits. Today known as the Palazzo dell'Universitá, the building is now the main premises of the Universitá degli Studi di Genova. Architect Bartolomeo Bianco based the plans for the site on the Palazzo Doria Tursi on the Strade Nuove, borrowing its atrium concept to cope with the slope of the Via Balbi. Construction began in 1634 and the complex was in use by 1640.

Other buildings on the Via Balbi now in use by the Universitá include that of Giacomo and Pantaleo Balbi, today the **Palazzo Balbi Senarega**, which is the seat of the university's Literature and Philosophy faculty. The courtyard with its beautiful loggias is open to the public. The University Library is located in the former **Church of Saints Gerolamo and Francesco Saverio**. At the foot of the Via Balbi, close by the Piazza della Nunziata, is the **Palazzo Durazzo Pallavicini**, the only palace on the street still privately owned.

Galleria Nazionale di Palazzo Spinola

Two opposing entrances lead into this splendid palazzo, which was donated to the State by the Marquis Spinola in 1958.

Constructed in 1593, the building was designed to separate the Piazza Inferior and Piazza Superiore di Pellicceria near the waterfront at the foot of the Via della Maddelena. Ironically, it was constructed as a residence for the Grimaldi clan – archrivals of the Spinola since the days when they led the murderous factions of the Guelphs and Ghibellines, respectively.

Loyalties aside, the Spinola eventfully inherited the property in 1734 – the Genoese tradition of strategic marriage for the sake of wealth and status often produced such strange bedfellows. It has two piani nobili to accommodate family and prominent guests, and these have been preserved according to the Spinola proviso that the palazzo remain untouched and be converted into a public museum. Today it is the National Gallery. The only architectural modifications made have been to the upper two floors, which were badly damaged during the air raids of WWII. These once constituted the bedrooms, private rooms, and servants' quarters.

Remaining are the public rooms of the piani nobili, which offer a glimpse of how this rarified environment appeared to the eyes of prominent guests in the 17th and 18th centuries. The first piano nobile boasts frescoes by Lazzaro Tavarone, brilliantly restored in 1993, depicting Francesco Grimaldi's distinguished participation in the conquest of Lisbon. The art and furnishings of this floor reflect the mid-17th century, when Ansaldo Pallavicino took possession of the palazzo from Tommaso Grimaldi, brother of his wife Dorotea. In the second *salotto* hangs a lovely Van Dyke portrait of the child Ansaldo Pallavicino.

The second floor presents a decorative arrangement from the 18th century, reconstructing the placement of furnishings and art according to a meticulous record left by Maddalena Doria, wife of Nicolò Spinola, who inherited the property in 1734. The layering of riches here conspires to make the salons of the first floor – as beautiful as they are – seem actually austere. Captivating frescoes by Lorenzo de Ferrari adorn the ceilings and rich, red velvet draperies grace the doorways. Particularly decadent is the Gallery of Mirrors, a gleaming hall lit by crystal chandeliers and the golden glow of gilded stucco work.

Genoa

An incomplete itemization of major works in the Gallery's impressive collection, placed throughout the rooms of the piani nobili, begins with a *Resurrection* attributed to Tintoretto, followed by local hero Bernardo Strozzi's *Portrait of a Nun* and the *Journey of Abraham* by Il Grechetto. On the second piano nobile, Van Dyck is represented by the four paintings of the Evangelists in the *salotto de Ferrari*.

His master, Peter Paul Rubens, is evoked on the third floor, where his masterful *Equestrian*

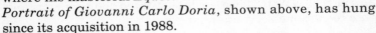

Portrait of Giovanni Carlo Doria, shown above, has hung since its acquisition in 1988.

The painting is an eloquent product of the relationship between Rubens and Gio Carlo, who was perhaps the greatest art collector of his time. Also included here is the *Ecce Homo* by Antonello de Messina, shown at left.

The elegant period décor of the piani nobili transitions smoothly to the clean, minimalist environment of the third and fourth floors, where black and white marbled floors echo the slate and marble used traditionally as a mark of nobility. After viewing the textiles and ceramics displayed on the fourth floor, step outside to the widow's walk, from which there is a commanding view of the city. (☎ 010.270.53.00, ticket office 010.253.04.54, www.palazzospinola.it, galspinola@libero.it; open Tuesday-Saturday 8:30 am-7:30 pm; Sundays and holidays 1-8 pm.)

Piazza Banchi

Modern financiers can come here to venerate – or bemoan – the institution known as "the bank", so named for the counters (*banchi*) employed by 13th-century moneychangers that give this piazza, and banking, its name. The square itself dates to the 10th century, when it sat on the outskirts of the city center, but close by the port and its warehouses. This convenient location lured merchants from all over the world, who met here to transact business. In the 13th and 14th centuries this included money lending, but the activity was officially barred from the square. It would take the transition of the Genoese economy from trade to finance – and the inclusion of the city's prominent families into the profession – before banking earned respect and a home on the piazza.

This came in the late 16th century, when the **Loggia dei Mercanti** was constructed, probably by the architects Lurago or Vannone. The loggia – which has a fresco on the rear wall by Pietro Sorri and side panels featuring reliefs of helmets, shields, and war trophies by Battista and Taddeo Carlone – replaced a structure that had been erected in the early 15th century after a fire (some say set by the Ghibellines) destroyed much of the square and the old church of St. Pietro in 1398. A rebuilt church in

Loggia dei Mercanti

the original location continued to serve the congregation until the close of the 15th century, when the Lomellini family acquired the property and built a residence.

A significant number of Genoese must have viewed the plague of 1579 as a form of divine retribution for the ascendancy of merchantry. During the pestilence, a public vote was made to construct a new church on the piazza. The Lomellini donated a building, but rather than evict the merchants from the ground floor, architect Taddeo Carlone instead designed a church rising from the first floor, surrounded by a balustrade in marble. Today, the **Church of San Pietro in Banchi** (1572-1585), still perched over merchant stalls, has newly restored frescoes on its façade by Giovanni Battista Bairardo.

 A final quirk of the piazza. Though the practice was officially prohibited by the ecclesiastic authorities, a market of sorts for priests took place here during the 18th century. The errant clerics would provide services in the private chapels of the richest families for a price, which, in true open market tradition, changed daily according to demand.

Just around the corner from the birthplace of banking is, suitably, a place where the wealthy from the Strade Nuove would go to spend their money. The **Via degli Orefici** (Street of the Goldsmiths) was and is populated by jewelry makers. On the corner formed with the Piazza Campetto is one of the Centro Storico's many votive shrines to the Madonna, this one commissioned by the corporation of goldsmiths.

Casa di Mazzini

Giuseppe Mazzini is to Italians as Thomas Jefferson or George Washington is to Americans. He is often called the Father of United Italy, and it was in a three-room apartment on the first floor of this building in the Maddelena neighborhood that he was born on June 22, 1805.

A political youth (his father was a Jacobin) and somewhat of an academic prodigy, Mazzini studied law at the University and joined the Carbonari, a secret society that was dedicated to the promotion of political freedom. At the time, Genoa was a duchy of the Kingdom of Piedmont-Sardinia, and Italy had not been a single political unit since the fall of the Roman Empire in the fifth century. As a contributor to *L'Indicatore Genovese* – a publication masquerading as a literary review – Mazzini advocated for the political unification of Italy. His subversive writings earned him exile, and from Marseille he organized Giovine Italia (Young Italy) in 1831. The movement was dedicated to the creation of a "single, independent, free, and republican" nation, and quickly gained a following. In response and in absentia, Mazzini was condemned to death by the Piedmont government.

The revolution of 1848-49, during which the brief Rome Republic was proclaimed, represented the climax of the first, "romantic" phase of the Risorgimento, the name given to the collective movement for Italian unification. Mazzini was summoned to Rome from exile to assist in creating a government and an army, but the popular revolution failed – pulled apart by internal and dynastic divisions and pressed by the overwhelming military might of their opponents, foremost among them Austria. A decade-long period then followed wherein nationalists rallied around Victor Emmanuel II of Sardinia and his minister Cavour, who sought military alliances with France and Britain to wrest away Austria's Italian holdings. In 1859-60, battles, diplomacy, and Garibaldi and The Thousand's famous conquest of the Two Sicilies resulted in a union of all but two Italian states – Venetia and Rome – with Sardinia that became the Kingdom of Italy under Victor Emmanuel II in 1861. Venetia became part of the Kingdom in 1866, and Rome in 1870, geographically creating the Italian state that we recognize today. Mazzini, the most radical of the revolutionaries, died in Pisa in 1872. He famously felt the true goal of the Risorgimento – a republican state – had failed.

The Casa di Mazzini today houses the Museum of the Risorgimento, a part of the Mazzini Institute. The collection, housed in 11 rooms arranged chronologically to convey the development of the movement for Italian unification, includes documents and curios pertaining to Mazzini and the Risorgimento, including original manuscripts, weapons, uniforms, and flags. (www.istitutomazziniano.it, museo-risorgimento@comune.genova.it.)

San Siro

Until the late ninth century, when it was displaced by San Lorenzo, San Siro was the cathedral of Genoa. After the ascendancy of San Lorenzo, however, it retained eminence as an Abbey, and is richly decorated with several important works of art. It also continued to host important functions, including in 1339 the election of the first *doge* of Genoa, Simone Boccanera.

Today, no remnants exist of the Romanesque church built by the Benedictines after 1006. The last vestige – a bell tower – was cleared away in 1904 after it was declared unsafe. The structure we see today came into being between 1585-1619, after a fire in 1580 destroyed the church basilica. The façade is even more recent, redesigned in 1821 by Carlo Barabino.

The interior is majestic, largely the product of a 17th-century period of decoration that included frescoes by Giovanni Battista Carlone, gilded stuccowork by his brother Tommaso Carlone, and the black marble and bronze high altar by Pierre Puget. An earlier version of Orazio Gentileschi's masterpiece *Annunciation* hangs in the first chapel on the right-hand side of the cathedral. The rich colors of the piece reflect the influence of the Flemish painters Rubens and Van Dyck, who were working in Genoa at the time and whose work could be viewed in several prominent collections in the city.

Albergo dei Poveri

As famed as Genoa is and was for its palaces and noble families, the truth is that most of its citizens weren't Dorias, or Spinolas, or Brignoles. While the wealthy merchant and banking classes lived in luxury, the human flotsam and jetsam of the port existed in dire poverty. In the 17th century, as remunerative relations with Spain floundered under that nation's growing debt, the situation of the poor would prove untenable. The climate was ripe for rebellion – or worse – and some among the wealthy realized their own survival was tied to the fortunes of the poorest of the city. In 1652, with major funding from Emanuele Brignole, construction began on the Albergo dei Poveri, a hospice for the destitute. Construction was deferred in 1656 when the fear of disease born of squalid living conditions materialized: Plague claimed 40,000 Genoese lives. Construction resumed a decade later, with further renovations and additions made in 1689, 1702, and 1835. These were paid for by donations from wealthy patrons, and their

Albergo dei Poveri

munificence was rewarded with the statues that today adorn the network of courtyards. Other benefactors are represented in portraiture in the picture gallery. Included here are the images of Giovanni Andrea de Ferrari, Orazio de Ferrari, and a depiction of Emanuele Brignole – who is also buried here – by Giovanni Bernardo Carlone.

In addition to providing services for the indigent, the building, which has a grand, 175-m/525-foot façade, served as a refuge for the population at large during the French bombardment of 1684. The treasures of San Lorenzo cathedral and the ashes of St. John the Baptist – the city's holiest relic – were also brought here for safekeeping during that bombing campaign. Today, the Albergo dei Poveri houses the Political Science department of the University.

Cathedral of San Lorenzo

The mismatched towers of Genoa's cathedral fit perfectly within the city's architectural stew. Its current, mainly Gothic, appearance arose in the early 1300s, when the black-and-white Tyrrhenian bands were crafted. These were layered over a 12th-century Romanesque structure, shown today by the side door of San Giovanni next to the baptistery and that of San Gottardo opening onto Via San Lorenzo. That was itself a modification to the original ninth-century church building. The taller of the two towers culminates in a 16th-century bell tower, completed at the same time as the cathedral dome by Galeazzo Alessi. The shorter north tower is capped by a loggia that was completed in the 14th century, at the same time as the central rose window over the grand portal.

Below the window and just over the great door is a decorative motif featuring Christ surrounded by the symbols of the four Evangelists. Just under

Cattedrale di San Lorenzo

Christ's feet is the figure of man lying on what appears to be some sort of grate. This is St. Lawrence, Archdeacon of the Roman Catholic Church, martyred in Rome in 258, who, tradition maintains, was roasted alive on a gridiron. The grisly story of his death is repeated in splendid color on the vault ceiling, painted by Lazzaro Tavarone in 1622-24. On the semi-dome is St. Lawrence pointing to an assembly of the poor and crippled. This relates to the circumstances prior to his execution. The Roman Emperor Valerian – in the midst of a purge of Rome's Christians – ordered Lawrence, archivist and librarian of the Church, to bring all its treasures to the imperial palace. The saint arrived with a motley crew of diseased, orphaned, and crippled Christians. "These," he said, "are the treasures of the Church."

The treasures of the cathedral are found in the basement. Inaugurated in 1956, the **Museo del Tesoro di San Lorenzo** exists in four excavated spaces that were designed by Franco Albini specifically to showcase the venerated objects and works of art accumulated over eight centuries. Set against dark grey walls of local calcareous stone are various gilded and jeweled pieces, superbly lit to accentuate their beauty.

Perhaps most interesting among these is the *sacro catino*, a green glass basin that was believed by 12th-century Genoese to be the Holy Grail, Christ's cup from the Last Supper, cut

Cross of Zechariah

from a single emerald. Now it is believed to be a stunning example of ninth- century Islamic art. Also of note is the Cross of Zechariah, a Byzantine reliquary in gold leaf with Oriental gemstones and pearls containing what are traditionally believed to be fragments of Christ's cross. From the 14th century, when it came to Genoa, it was used to bless the doges of the city. Finally, there is the golden ark containing the ashes of Saint John the Baptist, patron saint of Genoa. It is still carried in procession through the city streets on the saint's feast day, June 24. (☎ 010.247.1831, www.museo-sanloreno.it, info@arti-e-mestieri.it; open Monday-Saturday 9 am-12 am; guided tours 3-6 pm; entrance fee €5,50; reduced fare €4,50 for students and seniors.)

Sacro Catino

Piazza San Matteo

This small piazza to the northeast of San Lorenzo was the Doria family's private square. Here, in 1528, Andrea Doria announced the constitutional changes crafted to quell the fractious disputes between the city's leading families. Noble titles were banned, all citizens were declared equal, and an oligarchy of 28 clans of *nobili cittadini* with approved surnames and equal rank was created. It was the beginning of the crafty hyphenation scheme (even the modern descendants of Doria, the Doria-Pamphili, are hyphenates) that to this day is a hallmark of Italian aristocracy.

Around the square are various former residences of the Doria. At no. 17 is the **Palazzo di Andrea Doria**, given to Doria by the Senate in thanks for his service to the Republic. (He, however, preferred to live outside the city walls in the monumental Palazzo del Principe). Over the door is a carved plaque with winged cherubs and the coats of arms of Genoa and of the Doria, commemorating the donation of the palace in 1528. At no. 15 is the **Palazzo di Lamba Doria**, which had been given to Andrea's ancestor in the 13th century, thanking him for his instrumental service in the defeat of the Venetians at the pivotal Battle of Korcula. The **Palazzo di Domenicaccio Doria** is the banded 13th-century building at no. 16. The entrance to the **Palazzo di Branca Doria** has an entrance at no. 1 Vico Falamonica.

Andrea Doria is buried in the crypt of the **Church of San Matteo**, commissioned in 1125 by Martino Doria to be the family's private chapel. The exterior gained its characteristic black-and-white Tyrrhenian stripes during a 1278 remodel; in 1310 the square cloister was built. The Doria had a long tradition of military service, and two elements of the church celebrate their exploits: the façade, which has an epigraph relating the family's many victorious undertakings, and the bell, seized as war booty from a Venetian bell tower.

Andrea had the church rebuilt in the 16th century, keeping the outside decorations but refurbishing the interior. It is richly decorated with frescoes and stuccowork executed by Giovanni Angelo Monorsoli, Giovanni Battista Castello (aka 'il Bergamasco'), and Luca Cambiaso.

Church of Saints Ambrogio & Andrea

Sitting on the corner of the Via di Porte Soprano and the Piazza Matteotti, this Jesuit church, rebuilt in 1589 by Giuseppe Valeriani, is known to the Genoese as the Chiesa del Gesù. Inside are Baroque frescoes by Giovanni Battista Carlone, but art lovers come to gaze upon two works by Peter Paul Rubens. *Circumcision* hangs above the high altar, and *St. Ignatius Healing a Woman Possessed* is in the north transept chapel.

St. Ignatius, by Rubens, 1615-20

Palazzo Ducale

For four centuries the seething political world of Genoa was officially presided over by the *doge*, a ruler originally elected by the public and, after the reforms imposed by Andrea Doria in 1528, by members of the oligarchy through the Gran Consiglio. During a doge's reign he resided in the Palazzo Ducale, an imposing palace on the Piazza Matteotti. After languishing for years, the building was the object of Europe's largest restoration project in the 1990s, and reopened to the public for the Christopher Colombus celebrations in 1992. Since then it has become the center of cultural affairs in the city, ideally situated as it is in the heart of the carrugi (alleyways), close by the Piazza dei Ferrari, the area of the old city that has undergone the greatest gentrification.

Construction of the palace began at the close of the 13th century, when the *Capitani del Popolo* (People's Leaders) Oberto Spinola and Corrado Doria bought all the houses located between the churches of San Lorenzo and San Matteo. They next acquired a neighboring palazzo from the heirs of Alberto Fieschi, razed it, and built the nucleus of the palace, called then the Palazzo Popolo. It was renamed the Palazzo Ducale after the installation of the first Genoese Doge, Simon Boccanegra, in 1339.

Despite the appointment of Andrea Doria as "leader for life," the office of the doge persisted. (Doria declined the privilege, preferring instead his own official title, *Liberator et Pater*

Palazzo Ducale with Grimaldina Tower at left

Patriae – Liberator and Father of His Country.) Andrea did, however, have Vannone modernize the building beginning in 1591, adding a grand covered hall and two courtyards. The double staircase leading to two of the palazzo's standout artistic attractions: the *Salone del Maggior Consiglio* (Great Council Hall) and *Sala del Minor Consiglio* (Minor Council Hall). Both are also attributed to Vannone. The other, the Chapel, was decorated by Giovanni Battista Carlone in 1653-1655. A fresco on the vault here glorifies the Virgin Mary on the occasion of her 17th-century proclamation as Queen of Genoa. On the side wall, trompe l'oeil frescoes celebrate civic virtues.

Upon the construction of the Piazza de Ferrari in the early 20th century, architect Orlando Grosso created a new façade on the eastern side of the building. During those renovations he developed a theory that the Grimaldina Tower – a lofty feature of the palace – was not built earlier than 1298, though others have postulated it was hastily built in the 11th or 12th century as part of a town wall. Regardless of its actual origin, the Tower remains interesting for its history as a prison. Several prominent artists – feuds between workshops often became violent – were imprisoned here in the 17th century, and their graffiti in the form of frescoes still adorns some interior walls.

Today, the Palazzo Ducale is a cultural hub, drawing crowds for exhibitions and special events associated with its jazz, photography, and cinema institutes. There are also cafés and restaurants catering to the intellectual crowd. On the first weekend of every month (except for July and August), a small antique market is held in the gardens. (☎ 010.557.40.00, www.palazzoducale.it, palazzoducale@palazzoducale.genova.it; palace open daily, Tuesday-Sunday 9 am-9 pm, ticket office closes at 8 pm.)

Basilica di Santa Maria di Castello

This unassuming 12th-century Romanesque-style church sits in Genoa's most historically important neighborhood. Legend has it that Janus, the Roman god of beginnings who lends his name to the month of January, founded the city of Genoa by constructing an ancient fortification upon the Castello Hill. Fortifications did indeed exist here prior to Roman times. The city's first fortified citadel was here, and in the Middle Ages this area of strategically important high ground was the site of the bishop's palace.

Nymphaeum, Palazzo Podestà, Genoa

Castello Brown, Portofino

A yacht leaves the harbor, Portofino (Amy Finley)

Above: The harbor and Piazzetta, Portofino

Below: Portofino's Piazzetta

The basilica dedicated to the Virgin incorporates Roman columns and capitals from the second and third centuries, and is known for the Sale dei Ragusei. This was a series of rooms used by 16th- and 17th-century merchants from Dubrovnik (in present-day Croatia), a port town formerly known in Italian as Ragusa. There you will find a *Madonna and Child* by Barnaba da Modena and a *Coronation of the Virgin* by Lodovico Brea.

A museum is located in the former convent associated with the church. It has 12 rooms exhibiting reliquaries, illuminated manuscripts, silverware and sculptures, marble portals, vestments, and paintings. These were taken from other convents and monasteries in the area after their repression by Napoleon's republic in the early 19th century. (☎ 010.254.95.11; open daily 9 am-12 pm, 3:30-6 pm, and on request.)

Embriaci Tower

In 1296 a law was introduced declaring that no building could stand higher than 80 hands. At 41 m (about 403 hands or 120 feet), the 12th-century Embriaci Tower was an allowed exception to the rule. The name derives from the Embriaci family, powerful enough in the Castello neighborhood of the Middle Ages to have had a family member occupy its Bishop's seat. The tower honors the deeds of Guglielmo Embriaco, conqueror of Jerusalem in 1099. Though renovated in 1927, the tower is closed to the public and must be admired from below.

Sant'Agostino

A complex composed of the convent and deconsecrated church of Sant'Agostino houses the **Museo di Architettura e Scultura Ligure** (St. Augustine Museum of Ligurian Architecture and Sculpture). Here rest treasures representing 10 centuries of artistic development in Genoa.

Genoa

The church itself, formerly used as a theater but soon to be incorporated into the expanding museum's exhibition space, dates to 1260 and has a series of fascinating *trompe l'oeil* chapels parading down its left side. Its 13th-century bell tower – attributed to Pietro Bono, Magister de Antelamo, 1282 – has unusual green, black, brown, and white polychrome majolica tiling reminiscent of the tower at San Giovanni di Pré.

The museum occupies the space of the convent and its two restored cloisters, a late medieval triangular-shaped one (highly unusual in Genoa), and another 17th-century square-shaped one erected where the garden was once found. Sculptural works span the 10th to 18th centuries, and include remnants from the cloister of the monastery of San Tommaso (late 10th century) and 17th-century Baroque sculptures by Pierre Puget (*Rape of Helen*, *Madonna with Child*); and Antonia Canova's 18th-century *Penitent Magdalene*. There are paintings and detached frescoes (eighth to 18th centuries) by Carlone, Lorenzo de Ferrari, and Jan Roos, an assistant to Van Dyck during his Genoese period.

The pride of the collection are Giovanni Pisano's sculptures for the funerary monument of Queen Margherita of Brabante, shown at right. She died in Genoa in 1312 on her way to Rome for the coronation of her husband, Henry VII of Germany, as Holy  Roman Emperor. (☎ 010.251.12.63, www.museosant-agostino.it, museoagostino@comune.genova.it; open Tuesday-Friday 9 am-7 pm; Saturday-Sunday 10 am-7 pm; entrance fee €4, free for Museum Card holders, under18s and seniors over 65.)

Porta Soprana

Foes entering Genoa via this door, which links the Roman road and the 12th-century city walls, were warned by its inscription – *"If you come in peace, you are welcome; but if you*

*bring war, you will leave
dejected and defeated.*" The
Porto Soprana offers no such
admonishment today, as it
beckons global visitors from a
legion of postcards, posters,
and travel publicity. It has
become a recognizable symbol
of reborn Genoa, sitting at the
intersection of historical and
modern Genoa.

The fortification is twinned by
the Porta dei Vacca across town
on the waterfront adjacent to
the Porto Antico. It has two
crenellated keeps and overlooks the Piano di Sant'Andrea,
where the Porta Soprana Association maintains the **Casa di
Colombo**. Not actually where Christopher Colombus lived,
it's a 17th-century merchant's home. It does, however, sit on
the site where detailed historical research indicates
Colombus lived in a house with his father Domenico and his
mother Susanna Fontanarossa. That building was destroyed
during the French naval bombardment of 1684. Columbus
receives little homage in this, his home town, but he did have
to leave Genoa after all to find funding for the voyage that would
change the course of world history. (☎ 010.246.53.46 for Porta
Soprana Association that maintains both monuments;
portasoprana@libero.it; open Saturday-Sunday 9 am-12 pm;
2-6 pm; by arrangement; entrance fee €3.)

Modern Genoa

Crossing over the boundaries of the Centro Storico you enter
modern Genoa. The streets broaden and straighten, displaying that 19th-century penchant for the thoroughfare that was
part of a new social development, urban planning. Genoa had
a burgeoning middle class that needed accommodation, and
these new neighborhoods offered mixed residential and commercial uses. They also offered entertainments with shopping
arcades, parks, theaters, and museums. Climbing the hills as
it does, modern Genoa has panoramic scenic vistas and

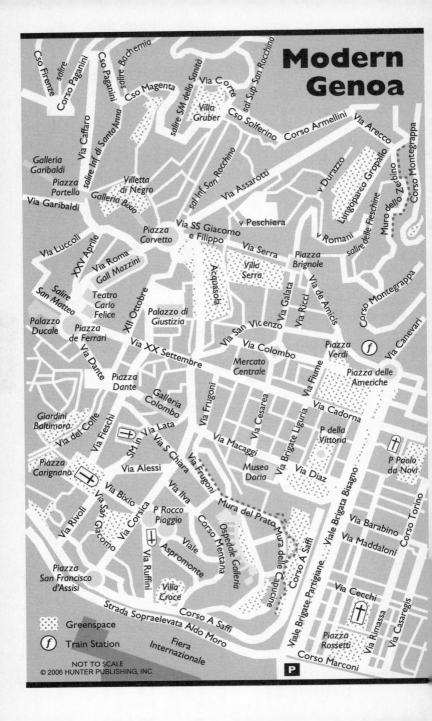

Modern Genoa

NOT TO SCALE
© 2006 HUNTER PUBLISHING, INC.

Greenspace

(f) Train Station

charming villas that over time were encircled by the encroaching city. The heart of the new city is the Piazza de Ferrari, laid out between 1899 and 1923, which sits just on the edge of the Centro Storico behind the Palazzo Ducale.

Teatro Carlo Felice

A decade at the turn of the 19th century witnessed the brief Democratic Republic of Liguria (1797-1805), which replaced the aristocratic governmental structure that had ruled the city for centuries. Short-lived (all of Liguria was annexed

to the French Empire as Napoleon swept through Europe), it nonetheless psychologically defined a time during which the thrust for a public theater began. Genoa's two existing theaters, the Falcone and Sant'Agostino, were considered too small and inelegant (the Falcone at the Durazzo family palace also had deep ties to the just-shrugged-off oligarchy). Modern civic life required a modern cultural hub.

In 1799, architect Andrea Tagliafichi submitted a plan for a theater that was widely supported by the city's population. It wasn't until 1825, however – by which time Genoa had, for good it turns out, lost its independence, becoming the Duchy of Genoa in the Kingdom of Piedmont-Sardinia – that a plan was approved. Carlo Barabino's construction, the Teatro Carlo Felice, was inaugurated on April 7, 1828, with a performance of Vincenzo Bellini's *Bianca e Fernando*.

That theater was destroyed during WWII by an incendiary bomb that fell on August 8, 1942. It would take 50 years for the theater to fully reopen, redesigned to match the footprint of Barabino's structure exactly and incorporating the extant pronaos, or entrance portico, and west porch of the original theater, but with a high-tech animated stage tower that is widely considered the most modern in Europe. The new Carlo

Felice achieves the elegance for which Piaggio pined, with exteriors of stone, plaster, and iron, and interiors decorated in marble and wood. There is also a luminous glass pyramid that runs the entire height of the building, rising through the roof like a spire, allowing sunlight to penetrate deeply and lighting up the night sky when the theater is open in the evenings.

The Carlo Felice is the venue for the opera, ballet, and symphony in Genoa, with a packed calendar full of choice offerings for which tickets are available online through the Ciaoticket service (www.chartanet.it; available in English). If you're hoping to catch a performance at the last minute, 30 half-priced tickets go on sale one hour before each event. There are standing tickets available for sold-out shows, offered 10 minutes before the start of the performance. (☎ 010.589.329, 010.591.697; fax 010.538.13.35; ticket sales by phone with Amex and Diners, 010.570.16.50 [service only available Tuesday-Friday, 2-5 pm], www.carlofelice.it, biglietteria@carlofelice.it; open Tuesday-Saturday 11 am-6 pm; Sundays with performance 10 am-3 pm.)

Palazzo & Museo dell'Accademia Liguistica di Belle Arti

While constructing the Teatro Carlo Felice, Carlo Barabino also designed and executed the Palazzo dell'Accademia Liguistica di Belle Arti (1826-31) that shares prominence on the Piazza de Ferrari. It's the home of the Academy of Fine Arts, founded in 1751 and still training students in the sculptural and painterly arts today.

The Palazzo also houses the Museo dell'Accademia Liguistica di Belle Arti, the picture gallery of the Academy with a collection of figurative art spanning five centuries. Specializing in Ligurian artists, the museum is particularly proud of its works by Bernardo Strozzi – a native of Genoa who in 1632 became a fugitive from the Papal Court after refusing to rejoin the Capuchin order he'd left in 1610 (he painted before, during, and after his tenure with the monastics). His seminal work, *The Cook*, hangs in the Palazzo Rosso, but a rare fresco fragment (*Head of John the Baptist*) and a sketch (*Paradise*) for frescoes executed in the apse of San Domenico (demolished in 1820) are here, as is the painting *Lamenting the Dead Christ*.

Other prominent works in the collection are Perin del Vaga's *Polyptych of St. Erasmus*, Giovanni Andrea de Ferrari's *A Saint Raises a Fallen Mason from the Dead* and *Adoration of the Shepherds*, as well as *The Animals Entering the Ark* by Il Grechetto. (☎ 010.581.957, www.accademialigustica.it, info@accademialigustica.it; open Tuesday-Sunday 3-7 pm.)

Via XXV Aprile

This shop-lined street, renamed for the official day that Italy was liberated from the Nazis (it was previously called Strada Carlo Felice), is part of the network of grand streets that was intended to connect the Savoy Palace (the Palazzo Reale) with the Carlo Felice opera house, the cultural hub of the 19th-century city. From that perspective, the route starts on the Via Balbi, proceeds through the Piazza della Nunziata to the Via Cairoli, down the Via Garibaldi, and through the Piazza delle Fontane Marose to the Via XXV Aprile, which terminates at the Piazza de Ferrari. The side porches of the Carlo Felice were designed to accommodate horse-drawn carriages that would unload privileged passengers – such as members of the House of Savoy – directly at the theater doors. The street was laid out between 1825-28, just 10 years after the city became the Duchy of Genoa.

Museo d'Arte Orientale Edoardo Chiossone

The life of Edoardo Chiossone embodies a sort of epic romanticism that Westerners – indoctrinated through such movies as *The Last Samurai* or novels like *Shogun* – have come to associate with the Orient of the 19th century.

Born outside Genoa in Arenzano in 1833, Chiossone – an artist and engraver trained at Genoa's Accademia Liguistica di Belle Arti – traveled to Japan and became, in time, the portraitist of the Meiji court. As the engraver of Japan's first banknotes, he is inextricably linked with the development of the island

nation into a Western-style
economy. And yet, his
greatest contribution to
Japanese culture, perhaps,
was as a preservationist.
His collection of more than
15,000 objects, culled from
the vast number available
on the antiquities market
in the years just after the
fall of the Tokugwa sho-
gunate, is displayed at the
Museo d'Arte Orientale
Edoardo   Chiossone,

housed in the Villeta di Negro in the Parco Pubblico di Villeta
di Negro.

Chiossone arrived in Japan on January 12, 1875, just eight
years after the ascension of 15-year old Prince Mutsuhito –
who took the title "Meiji," meaning 'enlightened ruler' – to the
throne as the 122nd emperor of Japan. An aggressive process
of Westernization was underway as the Meiji court pursued
bummei kaika, 'civilization and enlightenment.' Working
with the government printing bureau under the directorship
of Tokuno Ryohsuke (who would become a lifelong friend),
Chiossone trained the Japanese in printing techniques,
designed official papers and stamps, and taught the art of
making printing ink and watermarked printing paper.

Even while participating in the 'modernization' of Japan,
Chiossone designed banknotes that relied artistically on traditional themes (such as Daikoku, god of wealth, depicted on
the one-yen note). Perhaps this expressed his affinity for the
nation's tremendous artistic heritage, which he copiously documented in sketches and photography while traveling Japan
in the early 1880s. It was this cultural sensitivity that no
doubt endeared him to the Meiji court, winning him the honor
in 1888 of producing the official state portrait of the Emperor.
Chiossone would later make portraits of the Empress, the
future Emperor Taishoh, and several prominent and important members of the court.

In the modern setting of the Villeta – rebuilt by Mario Labò in 1971 (the original was destroyed by allied bombing in 1942) – the museum displays Japanese works from various epochs. There are paintings from the 11th to 19th centuries, arms and armors, enamels, ceramics, porcelains, polychrome prints, musical instruments, theater masks, costumes and textiles, and bronzes. There is also an extensive range of large sculptures from Japan, China, and Siam (modern-day Thailand), including an impressive collection of depictions of the Buddha. The entire collection was willed to the Accademia on Chiossone's death, in Japan, in 1898. He left his treasures to the city that gave him his education, but his heart remained in the East. He is buried in the Aoyama cemetery in Tokyo. (☎ 010.452.285, www.museochiossonegenova.it, museo-chiossone@comune.genova.it; open Tuesday-Friday 9 am-1 pm; Saturday-Sunday 10 am-7 pm; entrance fee €4 regular rate, free for under 18s, over 65s and for holders of Museum Card.)

Via XX Settembre

This colonnaded thoroughfare proceeding east from the Piazza de Ferrari is one of the standout works of Cesare Gamba, 19th-century urban planner and engineer. The straight, level street diverted traffic from nearby narrow and dangerous passages, but numerous homes and buildings had to be taken apart or demolished to make way for its construction (including the ancient Porta Pila, which was later rebuilt on the Via Montesano, beside Gamba's own house). The naming of the street – after an important date in the history of a unified Italy, on which Italian troops entered Rome in 1870 breaking the ancient hold of the Catholic Church on the Eternal City – was also controversial, especially among the city's devout Catholics.

Once the district for theater and movies, today the Via XX Settembre has returned to its original role as a shopping street. In addition to fashion boutiques, there is the **Mercato Orientale**, a sprawling indoor food market heralded as the best in the city and featuring olives, herbs, cheese, fruits and vegetables, and Ligurian specialties. The market is held Monday through Saturday 7 am-1 pm and 3:30-7:30 pm. Entrances are on Via XX Settembre and Via Galata.

The **Ponte Monumentale** crosses over Via XX Settembre just past the church of Santo Stefano. Designed by Gamba and Riccardo Haupt, it offers a bird's-eye view over the 20th-century buildings of modern Genoa.

Museo Civico di Storia Naturale Giacomo Doria

Natural history buffs owe a debt of gratitude to Giacomo Doria, the founder and director of Genoa's Natural History Museum inaugurated at the Viletta di Negro in 1867. Doria's passion for the natural sciences helped the museum quickly outgrow its original location (he contributed several personal collections, acquired others, and led exploratory voyages with the Italian Geographic Society that yielded numerous specimens). In 1912 it moved to the Via Brigata Liguria, built specifically for the purpose after the engineer and architect conducted a survey of Europe's leading museums. The first two floors house public exhibitions, including Italy's largest entomology (bug) collection, and a nearly-intact *Elephas antiquus italicus* skeleton presiding in the newly restored Paleontology Hall. (☎ 010.564.567 or 39.010.582.171, www.museodoria.it, museodoria@comune.genova.it; open Tuesday-Friday 9 am-1 pm; Saturday-Sunday 10 am-7 pm; entrance fee €4; free for under 18s, over 65s, and Museum Card holders.)

Museo d'Arte Contemporanea di Villa Croce

Surrounded by a leafy park on the edge of the Carignano district, the 19th-century Villa Croce houses Genoa's Contemporary Art Museum, inaugurated in 1985. A core of more than 3,000 works traces developments in artistic representation from the 1930s to the current day. Ligurian artists have their own special place within the permanent collection, which includes paintings, drawings, sculptures, graphics, photographs, and collages. The museum has earned a reputation for mounting cutting-edge temporary exhibitions exploring national and international themes in the arts and culture.

(☎ 010.580.069, 39.010.585.772, www.museovillacroce.it,
museocroce@comune.genova.it; open Tuesday-Friday
9 am-7 pm; Saturday-Sunday 10 am-7 pm; entrance fee €4;
free for under 18s, over 65s, and Museum Card holders.)

Castello d'Albertis

Perusing Genoa's lineage of seafaring eccentrics, in the 19th
century you find Captain Enrico Alberto D'Albertis, the
explorer, writer, and aristocratic collector who had this
neo-Gothic palace constructed at the close of that century to
house his vast inventory of ethnographic objects. The founder
of the Italian Yacht Club in 1879, D'Albertis traveled around
the world three times and circumnavigated Africa once. In
1893, using nautical instruments that he made himself modeled after those of his predecessor, he recreated Christopher
Columbus's voyage to San Salvador.

The Captain brought home innumerable souvenirs of his
travels, and these were artfully displayed throughout the
grand residence built by Alfredo D'Andrade atop the
Montegalletto hill on the ruins of late-medieval fortifications.
In 1921, *La Gazzetta di Genova* wrote, "This great assemblage
of objects, of such widely disparate origins and character, con-
veys the essence of a cultivated mind alive to all manifesta-
tions of beauty and science." This theme was seized upon
when the Castle, now home to the Museum of World Cultures,
underwent a recent restoration. It becomes a metaphor for
Genoa, inspired and enabled by the sea and soaked in exotic
influences. Visitors amble through the Columbian room, the
Gothic room, the fabulous Turkish sitting room, the Cabin,
and the Nautical room, viewing treasures from peoples as far
flung as Oceania, Africa, and the Americas.

The Castle is best reached by bus 33 (from the port, Piazza
Corvetto, or the Principe train station); stop at Corso Firenze.
(☎ 010.272.38.20, 010.272.34.64, www.castellodalbertis-
genova.it, castellodalbertis@comune.genova.it; closed
April-September, open Tuesday-Sunday 10 am-6 pm; October-March, open Tuesday-Sunday 10 am-5 pm; entrance fee
adults €6; children four-12 €5; under 3s and Museum Card
holders free.)

Genoa

Only in Genoa

Via di Prè

The Via di Prè, a porticoed street running just below and parallel to Via Balbi, is a study in contrasts to the prosperity of the palace districts. Women in traditional costume sit holding babies and selling cigarettes and bundles of herbs to their mostly North African neighbors and the streams of newly arrived immigrants lodging here. Halal butcher shops are packed in between *trattorie* and *friggitorie*, putting a face to the meshing of cultures that characterizes modern Genoa. It's a thought-provoking walk best undertaken in broad daylight, especially as numerous overhead construction projects block the little sunlight that penetrates, reinforcing the ramshackle air.

Greenery & Views

After visiting the Chiossone museum, spend some time in the **Parco Pubblico Villetta di Negro**, one of Genoa's loveliest urban parks, with exotic gardens laid out in the 18th century by Ippolito Durazzo. Fragrant camelias and grand trees surround a late 19th-century statue dedicated to Giuseppe Mazzini, and there is a fish pond and Chinese pagoda atop the hill; a nice place for resting between excursions. The park adjoins the **Piazza Corvetto**, where you can catch Bus 33 to tour the **Circonvallazione a Monte**, a zigzagging route along the hillside heading west and roughly parallel to Via Garibaldi and Via Balbi far below. In addition to lovely views, there are several interesting stops, including the late-Renaissance **Villa Pallavicino delle Peschiere** (now home to a brokerage firm), likely designed by Galeazzo Alessi and with terraced gardens by Giovanni Battista Castello. Further along, the 16th-century **Villa Grüber** has a park and gardens that are open to visitors.

Cable Cars, Lifts & Electric Trains

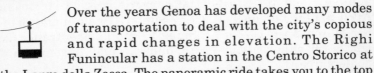 Over the years Genoa has developed many modes of transportation to deal with the city's copious and rapid changes in elevation. The Righi Funincular has a station in the Centro Storico at the Largo della Zecca. The panoramic ride takes you to the top of Monte Righi, climbing to more than 900 feet above sea level

in just under a mile. The Ascensore Portello-Castelletto, an Art Nouveau elevator, departs from the Piazza Portello and lands at the Belvedere Montaldo. Or, from the Piazza Manin at the top of Via Assarotti (in Modern Genoa) you can catch the Genova-Casella railway, now largely a tourist train that whisks you into the hinterland behind Genoa. During a journey of less than an hour you'll watch the landscape transform from the urban environment of Genoa to one of forests and meadows.

Staglieno Cemetery

Fans of Père Lachaise in Paris will be interested in this monumental complex located in the Bisagno Valley inland from eastern Genoa, reachable by bus from the city center. Built during the 19th and 20th centuries, it sprawls through a hilly, wooded area with fine, sculptural tombs peeping through greenery to give it an appearance of ramshackle splendor.

Nervi

This suburb to the east of Genoa bears little resemblance to its larger, more urban, and grittier neighbor. It more closely approximates San Remo, or another of the large seaside towns, complete with villas and parks. Along the waterfront is the **Anita Garibaldi Promenade**, a seafront walk hewn into the cliffside extending from the harbor. Waves crash below as you walk along taking in views down the coast toward Portofino.

Nervi's greenbelt is the park formed of the grounds of the Gropallo, Serra, and Grimaldi villas that extend along much of the promenade's length. Landscaped in English garden style with plenty of palms, it's the site of the **Galleria d'Arte Moderne** that houses a collection of works by 19th- and 20th-century Ligurian artists.

Boat Tours

 One of the best ways to see Genoa is from the sea. **Battellieri del Porto di Genova** (www.battellieri-genova.it) does narrated, 45-minute tours of the port departing from the Porto Antico. First sailing is at 9:30 am, €6. The same ship line does night trips for special events (July fireworks at Rapallo, Festo del Cristo degli

Abissi, September fireworks at Recco) with departures from the Calata Zingari Stazione Marittima. (Advance booking required, ☎ 01.026.57.12.)

During the summer months (June-September) Battellieri also provides ferry service between Genoa and Portofino, Cinque Terre, and Portovenere with departures from the Calata Zingari Stazione Marittima. A cooperative relationship with **Servizio Marittimo del Tigullio** (the transporter for that part of the Riviera) allows you to use the Tigullio boats for connections to San Fruttuoso from Portofino, or to visit the other villages of Cinque Terre from Monterosso. The ticket to Portovenere gets you onto the boats for Cinque Terre as well as a tour of Palmaria Island. (Genoa-Portofino, €15; Genoa-Cinque Terre, €23; Genoa-Portovenere, €25.)

For Active Travelers

Swimming

On the waterfront adjacent to the Magazzini del Cotone (former cotton warehouses), the **Piscina Porto Antico** is a public pool with sunbathing areas and a café. On summer evenings the location hosts musical activities. Open June through September. For more information, ☎ 010.251.3819.

Ice Skating

From December to March there is ice skating under the awnings of the Piazza delle Feste, next to the Bigo. (Hours: Monday-Friday 8 am-11:30 pm; Saturday 10 am-2 am; Sunday 10 am-11 pm.)

Hiking the Castle Walls

You'll need a car to traverse the entirety of the vast network of defensive walls that previously guarded Genoa. But there are several walkable segments that combine for quite a hike and, besides, the walls are just one feature of the **Parco Urbano delle Mura**, the largest green space in Genoa just 10 minutes from the city center. The park – which occupies over 2,000 acres – has chestnut trees, cluster pines and vast, rolling stretches of grass. The walls that traverse the park – the New Walls, built during the 17th century and refurbished in the 18th and 19th centuries – are dotted with fortresses, not all of which were constructed in the same period as the walls. Among them, one of the most interesting is the **Forte Castellacio**, a Guelph bastion in the 14th century and a soldiers' barracks during Andrea Doria's rule in the 16th century. The **Forte Sperone** at the top of Mt. Peralto was transformed into a citadel in the 19th century and is today used as a venue for theatrical performances in the summer. **Forte Begato** is the headquarters for the City Wall Park and site of the Visitor's Center where you can pick up information on hiking and walking tours within the park.

Genoa

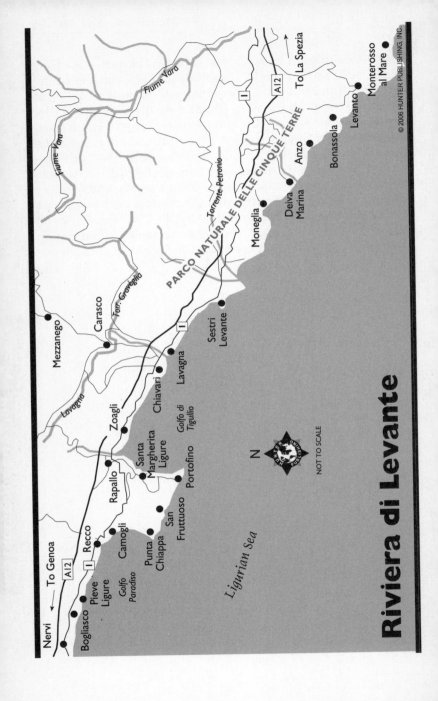

Riviera di Levante

Riviera di Levante

■ Portofino Promontory

East of Genoa lies the Portofino Promontory, an outcrop of land separating the Golfo Paradiso and the Golfo del Tigúllio. On the otherwise smooth arc of eastern Liguria it is an anomaly jutting out into the blue sea, capped by the heights of Mt. Portofino. A thick network of trails criss-crosses the landmass, passing through perfumed Mediterranean maquis on the southern slopes and crossing into woods of ash, chestnut, hazelnut, and maple in the northern hinterlands.

Tucked among the crags of its western flank is the town of **Camogli**, which Dickens once declared "the saltiest, roughest, most piratical little place." The hardened sailors of Camogli were sought after as mercenaries, and in the 18th century the Camogli fleet rivaled that of its powerhouse ally Genoa. Today, the sons and daughters of Camogli are still drawn to the sea – many graduating from the village's academy for the merchant marines – and it's not uncommon to hear a ship blast its horn as it passes by the captain's birthplace, bound for the ports of Genoa.

Leaving Camogli, the cliffs are tortuous, inaccessible, and largely barren until you reach the small bay of **San Fruttuoso** on the southern side. It was here in the eighth

Portofino Peninsula

1. Basilica Santa Maria Assunta; Castle Dragone; Museo Marinaro Gio Bono Ferrari
2. Abbey of San Fruttuoso di Capodimonte; Tonnare (tuna nets); Cristo degli Abissi; Doria Tower
3. Church & Castle of San Giorgio; Church of San Martino; Oratory of Nostra Senora Assunta
4. Park & Villa Durazzo; Villa del Nido; Villa San Giacomo; Oratory of Sant'Erasmo; Basilica di Santa Margherita d'Antiocha; Parco del Flauto Magico
5. Castello; Lungomare Vittorio Veneto; Cathedral SS Gervasio e Protasio; Chiesa di San Stefano; Civic Tower; Parco Casale: Villa Tigullio, Museo del Merletto (lace museum), Biblioteca Internazionale Città di Rapallo
6. Sanctuary of Nostra Signora di Montallegro

© 2006 HUNTER PUBLISHING, INC.

To Genoa

Recco

Camogli

San Rocco di Camogli

Golfo Paradiso

Ruta

San Lorenzo da Costa

Portofino Vetta

Monti di Portofino

Chiappa

San Fruttuoso

Ligurian Sea

Autostrada Genoa-Livorno

Torrente Boate

San Maurizio di Monti

Parco Regionale di Portofino

Oneto

Léivi

Torrente San Francesco

Zoagli

San Michele di Pagana

Rapallo

Santa Margherita Ligure

Nozarego

Parco Regionale di Portofino

Paraggi

Portofino

Punta Portofino (Punta del Capo)

Gulf of Tigullio

A12

N

2KM

1.2 MI

century that Prospero, Bishop of Tarragona, fleeing Spain to escape the Moors, founded a chapel to house the ashes of St. Fructuosus. Later, the Doria would finance an abbey in exchange for burial rites. Eight tombs were installed between 1275 and 1305. There are still no roads across the promontory to San Fruttuoso. The only way to visit is by boat or by foot, and in summer its miniscule pebble beach is dense with day-trippers who sojourn here from their hiking, or arrive on the ferries from Camogli or Portofino.

Though today it is the consummate yachting destination, picturesque **Portofino** started out as just another sleepy fishing village, albeit one surrounded by some of the most glorious verdure of the Italian Riviera. Its harbor is nearly hidden, which gave it great advantage against attack during the piratical centuries when seaside towns were regularly forced to fend against marauders. "Discovered" by English tourists in the late 19th century, in 1901 a former abbey was made over to become the Hotel Splendido, forever associated with the height of Hollywood glamour on the Riviera.

The promontory's only coastal road begins – or, you could rightly say, ends – at Portofino, and jogs past private villas to reach **Santa Margherita Ligure**, another elegant seaside town made popular by the English in the late 19th and early 20th centuries (as evidenced by its Art Nouveau hotels). Being much larger than Portofino, it is less exclusive but no less posh and a favorite of boaters who launch here to explore the marine sanctuary that wraps around the promontory.

Finally, on a crescent bay where the promontory rejoins the coastline, is **Rapallo**, a resort town with one of the oldest (and loveliest) golf courses in Italy. The most populous town on the Golfo del Tigúllio, it's a genteel place to unwind while enjoying tennis, riding, or boating, and many travelers make it their home base while exploring the nearby towns.

Camogli

Relics testify to a small pre-Roman settlement near the site of present day Camogli dating to the 12th century BC, but little is known of Camogli before the 11th century, when it begins to appear in trading documents from Genoa, its ancient ally. By

Portofino Promontory

that time, it had turned away from the land — the ancient settlers were hunters and kept livestock — and was a growing village on an *isola* (tiny island) surrounded by a small natural port. In the 12th century, the island was connected to the mainland by means of a pontoon bridge that could be pulled from the water to thwart invaders. (Today the strip of sea that once separated island from shore has been filled, forming the Piazza Colombo.)

By the 13th century Camogli, enriched by trade, was growing in power, but it retained its ties to Genoa and both towns profited from the relationship. The men of Camogli were excellent sailors, and offered themselves in support to *La Superba* as it conquered new trading posts across the Mediterranean. (The constant absence of men is the source for one translation of the name *Camogli* – "city of wives.") In exchange, the vessels of Camogli could fly under the Genoese insignia, and a few took advantage of their stronger neighbor's protection to engage in lucrative private piracy, thereby establishing the town's notorious reputation. But in the 14th century, it was diplomacy, not piracy, that distinguished the men of Camogli, as it sent ambassadors to both the Pope and the court of the Holy Roman Emperor, seeking to intercede and bring a peaceful solution to the war between Guelphs and Ghibillines that threatened to destabilize the Republic of Genoa. When war was unavoidable, the sailors of Camogli put themselves at the disposal of Pagano Doria on the side of the Ghibillines.

Ultimately, it was under the leadership of another Doria – Andrea – that Genoa entered its Golden Age during the 16th and 17th centuries. With its ally at peace and embarking on a campaign of redevelopment and architectural beautification, Camogli – its coffers enriched from centuries of legal and illicit wealth – undertook its own civic improvements. With the seas safe and quiet, the citizens decided to construct a wider, safer port than the natural one (which was the heart of village life) and to direct their attention to trade and building a domestic economy based on textile production. From the harbor, ships sailed toward Sicily and Africa, importing coal from Marimba. Others carried velvets and brocades made in Camogli to the ports of Provence.

With the annexation of Liguria to the French Empire under Napoleon in the early 19th century, Camogli was included in the system of ports of call on the Ligurian coast, organized to improve trading, and further improvements to the pier were made for that purpose. Camogli was evolving into the world's first powerhouse navy contractor, even as Italy was moving toward national unification. The ship owners of Camogli won contracts to transport mines, army baggage, and food provisions when the French pushed toward Algiers, and by 1839, the ship owners of Camogli controlled one third of the Sardinian mercantile fleet. During the Crimean War in the 1850s, Cavour (the minister to Victor Emmanuel II of Sardinia, who was working toward unification of the country under Piedmont-Sardinia), remarked, "If the supplies for the Sardinian army succeeded it is due to those devils of a people from Camogli, who gave Piedmont a real mercantile navy." The daring sailors of Camogli exploited the cover of fierce storms to evade naval blockades and deliver supplies to their allies, the French and English armies.

Centuries of daring exploits engendered both a deep respect for the sea and thankfulness to the Holy Family who watched over sailors. Walking through Camogli it is impossible not to notice the number of shrines erected to the Virgin Mary invoking protection for ships at sea. In 1954, the most poignant and unusual shrine was consecrated in the deep waters off nearby San Fruttuoso. A bronze statue of Christ the Redeemer was submerged 56 feet below the surface. Each year victims of the sea are remembered with wreaths laid at the feet of the underwater memorial.

Getting There

By Train: The **FS** station is south of the beach near the tourist office. For schedules, see www.trenitalia.it.

By Bus: Bus service is provided by **Tigullio Trasporti** (☎ 0185.288.835, www.tigulliotrasporti.it).

By Car: A12 motorway from Genoa-Livorno, exit at the tollbooths for Recco. S1 along the coast from Genoa is slow, but scenic. Parking within the town is extremely limited. Travelers are advised to park in one of the marked lots outside the village and then proceed on foot. Be forewarned – Camogli is known for steep flights of stairs.

By Boat: In the summer months there is boat service connecting Camogli to Genoa (Porto Antico and Nervi), Recco, Portofino, Santa Margherita Ligure, Cinque Terre, and Portovenere, operated by the **Trasporti Marittimi Turistici Golfo Paradiso** (www.golfopardiso.it, ☎ 01.85.772.091).

Resources

- www.camogli.it
- www.portofinocoast.it
- **Tourist Office:** Via XX Settembre 33, ☎ 0185.771.066 (Mon-Sat 8:30 am-noon and 3-7 pm, Sun 9 am-1 pm).

Being There

Camogli is perhaps the most authentic of the towns that dot the Portofino promontory, which makes it particularly comfortable for travelers. Life is being lived here by families that can trace their village roots back generations, and the atmosphere is welcoming and hospitable (unless you're trying to get a parking place in summer). There are a few sites, but the real pleasure of Camogli is just participating in the daily rituals of everyday life – café in the morning, watch the fishermen mend their nets, something to eat, a rest, a walk, more to eat, talking, laughing, drinking wine, watching the sunset, sleeping. Small enough to explore on foot, Camogli is also on the network of land and sea trails that grant access to the other delightful nooks and crannies of the promontory.

Basilica of Santa Maria Assunta

The reverent and wealthy citizens of Camogli were generous benefactors of their parish church, erected in the 12th century when the village still clustered on the *isola*. Today the church looks onto Piazza Colombo, created of concrete fill where once a straight of water separated the island from the promontory. The neoclassical façade is a 19th-century renovation, and features three niches with statues representing some of the building's patrons.

The Baroque interior is richly decorated with marble and gilt stuccowork and the vault of the central nave is decorated with 19th-century frescoes by Niccolò Barabino and Francesco Semino. In 1988, Pope John Paul II conferred the title of minor basilica on the church in recognition of the steadfast devotion of the townspeople of Camogli.

Castle Dragone

The castle was important to the protection of the village when it clustered on the isola. It is known that the walls of the island have existed since 1130, and that refortifications were made in the 15th and 16th centuries. The castle tower was restored in the 1950s and until 1998 housed the Tyrrhenian Aquarium.

Museo Marinaro Gio Bono Ferrari

This nautical museum's namesake was born in Camogli and published *La Città dei Mille Bianchi Velieri* (Town of the Thousand White Vessels) in 1935. Inside are paintings, artifacts, models, and other seafaring minutia, much of it donated by the families of Camogli. Remnants from history include part of the German torpedo that sank the English steamship *Washington* in the Camogli gulf, and pieces of the English frigate *Croesus* that in 1855 ran aground in the bay of San Fruttuoso after catching fire. If you're one of those who are always been fascinated by miniature ships in bottles, there are several here, including one that perfectly depicts the seaside houses of Camogli.

Only in Camogli

Sagra del Pesce

Since 1952, Camogli has been celebrating the feast day of San Fortunato, patron saint of fishermen, with a feast of which he would have approved. Tens of thousands of fish are fried in the world's biggest frying pan, then distributed to the partying crowds. The event begins a few days before the second Sunday in May with community awards, music, and food stands on the waterfront. On Saturday there is a procession, music, and fireworks, then on Sunday the fish and frying pans are blessed before the all-day party commences.

San Rocco, Punta Chiappa & the Tonnare

A half-hour's hike from Camogli is the village of San Rocco, where you can stop to admire the view and munch a slice of *galletta del marinaio* (sailor's flatbread, purchased from the Panifico Maccarini) before continuing on toward Punta Chiappa on the southwestern tip of the Portofino promontory. The last *tonnare* of the northern Mediterranean is enacted here from March to September. Six-man crews working from small boats net bluefin tuna as they migrate from the cold North Atlantic to the warm waters of the Mediterranean. The Cooperative Pescatori Camogli arranges guided visits (☎ 0185.772.091 for more information). On the first Sunday in August, 10,000 candles are lit and set afloat from Punta Chiappa in the celebration of Stella Maris. They drift on the currents, mingling with 10,000 more set adrift from Camogli.

For Active Travellers

Hiking

Trails from Camogli head up, over, and around the Portofino promontory, and hiking the well-marked and maintained paths is a popular activity with visitors. The ultimate destination is Portofino, on the promontory's southeastern tip, but potential routes to get there can include stops at the villages of Ruta, San Rocco, or Punta Chiappa, at the abbey of San Fruttuoso, or on the mountain's peak at Portofino Vetta.

Diving

Diving in the protected marine reserve is strictly regulated. To respect the rules, it's best to go on a guided dive with an authorized diving center. **B & B Diving Centre** is one (☎ 0185.772.751, fax 0185.770.254), or contact **San Fruttuoso Diving** (☎ 0185.774.413). Both lead dives to the Cristo degli Abissi off San Fruttuoso.

San Fruttuoso di Capodimonte

Competing legends describe the monastic origins of San Fruttuoso, tucked away on its small bay on the southern coast of the Portofino Promontory. Some maintain that the followers of Fructuosus (Fruttuoso in Italian) the martyr brought his relics to this tiny fishing village from Spain in the third century. Others (and this is perhaps the most popular telling of the tale), that they were brought by Prospero, Bishop of Tarragona, in the seventh century as he fled an invasion by the Moors. Still another school of thought maintains that the saint's remains came to the promontory as late as the 11th century.

Regardless, for centuries the Benedictine monks of the monastery complex were stewards of the area, in part responsible for the populating of nearby Portofino. Yet after its monastic use, for a period before the intercession of the Doria family in the 13th century, the village was a haven for pirates. Over several centuries the Doria made renovations and improvements to the abbey, including the construction of a family tomb (eight Doria are buried here) and the defensive tower that is one of the first elements of the village to come into view when approaching by sea.

Eventually, the village was abandoned and, in 1915, a flood destroyed much of the bay and the abbey's west wing. The property was donated by the Doria-Pamphili to the Fondo per l'Ambiente Italiano (FAI, the Italian Trust) in 1983. Extensive restoration has taken place since, and today the abbey complex is an important cultural and tourist

Cristo degli Abissi

attraction. Throughout the year (and especially in the summer months) the site hosts concerts and artistic exhibitions, and each July it is front and center as the Cristo degli Abissi (Christ of the Deep) is venerated in a nighttime ceremony on the Bay of San Fruttuoso.

Getting There

By Boat: Year-round you can reach San Fruttuoso from Camogli on the Golfo Paradiso ferries (schedules available at www.golfoparadiso.it), which depart nearly hourly from the harbor. During the summer months, Golfo Paradiso also offers a romantic three-hour night excursion (departures from Recco and Camogli) to San Fruttuoso.

Servizio Marittimo del Tigullio (www.traghettiportofino.it) runs ferry service between Rapallo, Santa Margherita, Portofino, and San Fruttuoso. Check the website for schedules. There is always at least one boat to and from daily, with several boats running the route from May-September.

By Foot: The hiking trail to San Fruttuoso from Camogli (about 90 minutes) or Portofino (about 90 minutes) is marked by two red dots.

Resources

■ www.fondoambiente.it

Being There

Most visitors to the area take a daytrip to San Fruttuoso, either hiking the trail from Camogli or Portofino, or enjoying the ferry ride over sparkling blue water. In the summer months, expect crowds and don't be squeamish about spreading your towel side-by-side with a stranger's – small pebbled beaches make for strange sunbathing-fellows. When the tide comes up the beach, such as it is, can be pretty well obliterated. That's a good time to make for the cool recesses of the abbey, or to *Da Giovanni* for a cool drink or gelato.

The Abbey

The monastery complex is accessed by a dimly lit tunnel from the pebble beach. The first church was constructed here by Greek monks in the middle of the 10th century. The inner dome of the current church reflects these Byzantine origins. The entrance portion of the complex also dates to that time, but much of the rest is from the 13th-16th centuries, the work of the Doria family. Notable among their additions is the black-and-white banded family tomb, located in the crypt off the lower cloister. Eight Doria were laid to rest here between 1275 and 1305. The upper cloister, originally constructed in the 12th century, was almost entirely rebuilt by Andrea Doria in the 16th century and features Roman and Romanesque capitals and columns. A 10th-century Romanesque loggia at the rear looks down into the Museum, located in 13th-century portion of the abbey on the seafront. The Museum documents the history of the abbey and the life and times of the monks, in addition to seasonal exhibitions. A path leads away to the Doria Tower, a defensive structure built in 1562 by Giovanni Andrea and Pagano Doria, heirs of Andrea Doria. The tower facades facing the sea feature the imperial eagle of the Doria family.

Cristo degli Abissi (Submerged Christ)

The last Sunday in July is the evening set aside for the official veneration of the submerged statue of Christ the Redeemer. The ceremony includes the blessing of the waters of the Bay of

San Fruttuoso, a torchlight procession, the laying of a laurel wreath at the feet of the statue, and mass celebrated on the shoreline. For the people of the promontory, the event remembers loved ones lost to the sea, the source of their livelihood.

Conceived by Duilio Marcante after his friend and fellow diver Dario Gonzatti died in the Bay in the 1940s, the bronze statue – made of melted down bells, cannons, ship parts, and sailing and athletic medals donated by local citizens – was crafted by Guido Galetti and submerged in 1954. It's a popular destination for divers from all over the world, but at a depth of just 56 feet it can also be viewed (from well above) by adept snorkelers.

For Active Travelers

Hiking

Stand on the pebbled beach and peer up the steep cliffs behind the abbey and you'll understand why San Fruttuoso is most popular as a hiking destination from Camogli or Portofino. If you're determined to forego the ferry, the first half-hour or so of the hike to either destination is a rigorous ascent.

● San Fruttuoso - Camogli

Take the most farthest west trail uphill. Once you've reached the top the trail winds along the cliffs to the **Batterie** – a left-over German anti-aircraft armament from WWII – before proceeding to **San Rocco**. The original village church here was built sometime before the 15th century, but destroyed in 1863 to make room for the bigger building you see today. Inside, a marble statue representing the glory of the angels dominates the high altar. After San Rocco it's down a series of staircases before the trail ends at the village of Camogli.

● San Fruttuoso - Portofino

The steep ascent leading east leads to the top of the ridge (Base "O"), with a view over the cove. The trail turns inland past villas and gardens and the small villages of **Prato**, **Olmi**, and **San Sebastiano** before turning to paved road that descends steeply into Portofino.

Portofino

If your objective on the Riviera is to sip from the rarified cup of *la dolce vita*, then Portofino is your destination. Once dubbed *Portus Delphini* ("Harbor of the Dolphins") by Pliny the Elder, today it might be known as Harbor of the Yachts for the fleet of pleasure craft moored here while their rich and powerful owners take in the scene on the waterfront piazzetta.

Perhaps because its present is so illustrious, Portofino's past is vague and scarcely documented. The sheltered, nearly hidden harbor and abundant verdure of the mountainside were attractive to ancient settlers, and relics have been found here dating to Roman times. By the 10th century, the town of fishermen was dependent on the nearby abbey of San Fruttuoso for protection and spiritual service, but in the 12th century that role passed to Genoa.

Until the mid-19th century, the local economy was based on fishing and lace production, a handicraft still practiced today by the older women of the village who vend their wares on the tiny piazzetta in the midmorning and early afternoon. Everything changed around 1867, with the arrival of Montague Yeats Brown, honorary British consul in Genoa. Taken with the loveliness of the locale – a turquoise cove surrounded by colorful dwellings, backed by a mountain of rippling green and brightly flowering vines – he purchased the hilltop Castello di San Giorgio (now commonly known as the Castello Brown), a fortress constructed by the Genoese in the 16th century as part of their coastal defense scheme.

As Brown entertained other wealthy English travelers at his panoramic villa, the word of this idyll spread. Another member of the peerage, Baron Baratta, purchased an abandoned four-story monastery on the opposite hillside overlooking the harbor and converted it into a family summer house. In 1901, he sold it to Ruggero Valentini who would become known as the pioneer of tourism at Portofino after he converted the estate into the Hotel Splendido.

In the 1950s and 60s, the hotel was *the* rendezvous point for the rich and famous, setting the standard for international

Hotel Splendido

chic. The who's who of guests, recorded in the hotel's Golden Book, begins with the Duke of Windsor and Wallis Simpson, who stayed in 1952. Close on their heels were other icons of the time, Humphrey Bogart and Ava Gardener (filming *The Barefoot Contessa* on location), Groucho Marx, Prince Ranier and Princess Grace of Monaco (who stayed soon after their marriage in 1956), Marcello Mastroianni, Jean Cocteau, Elizabeth Taylor and Richard Burton (1967).

Visiting moguls drop anchor in the harbor or park the Ferrari (vehicle of choice) in the Piazza della Libertá, the village's only public parking. Days are spent cruising the couture boutiques, working on the tan (preferably poolside or deckside), or day-tripping to Santa Margherita and Camogli. At night, the action is on the piazzetta, which is transformed into one large party for cocktail hour before everyone adjourns to their respective waterfront restaurants for dinner (Puny's is the coveted reservation). The village's miniscule scale all but ensures that any visitor (with a ready wallet) gets an inside seat on the glamour, personal fortune or screen credits notwithstanding.

Getting There

By Train: The closest **FS** stop is at Santa Margherita. For schedules see www.trenitalia.it. From there, take a taxi (queue at the station) or bus.

By Bus: Blue Tigullio buses ply the lovely coastal route between Portofino, Santa Margherita, and Rapallo. Stops are marked by green signs on the side of the road. (☎ 0185.288.834, www.tigulliotrasporti.it.)

By Car: Exit the A12 at Rapallo and take the Aurelia coastal road through Santa Margherita and Paraggi to Portofino. During summer, traffic on this – the only route to Portofino – can slow to a crawl. The only parking garage is at Piazza della Libertá where the road ends (☎ 0185.267.475). Expensive rates (approximately €5/hour or €20/day) may be included in your hotel room rate if you're staying in town (ask when booking).

 By Boat: If you're dropping anchor, mooring areas are in Zone C, 100 yards away from shore between Punta Pedale and Punta Caicca (north of the harbor opening) and Punta del Coppo and Punta Portofino (south of the harbor opening). See www.riservaportofino.it for maps and detailed information, or see page 109.

Ferry service from Camogli (and, seasonally, from Recco and Genoa) is on Golfo Paradiso (☎ 0185.772.091, www.golfoparadiso.it). From Santa Margherita and Rapallo (and seasonally from Chiavari, Sestri Levante, and Lavagna), service is by **Servizi Marittimi del Tigullio** (☎ 0185.284.670, www.traghettiportofino.it).

Resources

- www.comune.portofino.genova.it
- www.riservaportofino.it
- www.apttigullio.liguria.it
- **Tourist Office:** Via Roma, 35, ☎ 0185.269.024.

Being There

There are a few sites in Portofino, but the real attraction is in being *seen*. Dressed stylishly but casually, well-heeled visitors cruise the boutiques or take long lunches at one of the numerous cafés or restaurants ringing the piazzetta. Walking paths southwest of the piazzetta head uphill to the pretty church and castle, then onward toward the lighthouse and trail network leading to San Fruttuoso. Crossing the Via Aurelia in front of the parish church of San Martino, walkers find a gentle, lush trail that hugs the coastline all the way to Santa Margherita Ligure.

Portofino Promontory

Chiesa di San Giorgio

Sailors returning from the Crusades brought with them the supposed relics of St. George, enshrined here in the oft-reconstructed Chiesa di San Giorgio. Once the site of a Roman temple to the Persian god Mithras, the church has a commanding view over the harbor and surrounding bays. The saint's feast day is celebrated on April 23rd with the **Fato di San Giorgio**, a ritualistic bonfire on the piazzetta fueled by the trunk of a forest tree and the accumulated detritus thrown in by Portofino's citizens. Sparks drifting over and falling on the sea foretell good fortune in the coming season.

Castello Brown

Continuing up the same path from San Giorgio you reach the Castello Brown, built in the 17th century as part of Genoa's coastline defense system. Purchased in 1867 by Montague Yeats

Castello Brown

Brown, British consul in Genoa, it was renovated and furnished as a private villa and became the seed for modern tourism in Portofino. The castle remained in Brown's possession for more than 80 years, eventually passing over to the commune which maintains it today as a venue for historical and art exhibitions. Brown's stamp remains in the terraced Mediterranean gardens of flowers and pergolas. Two towering pine trees were planted to commemorate his marriage. (☎ 0185.267.101, www.portofinoevents.com, info@portofinoevents.com; open daily; May-September 10 am-7 pm, October-April 10 am-5 pm; entrance fee €3.50.)

Santa Maria Assunta Oratory

This 15th-century building, founded in the 14th century by the Confraternity of the Disciplinanti, houses an interesting collection of immense crucifixes (some weighing more than 220 lbs) carried in the processions marking the festival of St. George (April 23rd). The lunette over the entrance features the Madonna with the Infant Jesus surrounded by figures in traditional costumes representing the donors of the confraternity.

For Active Travelers

Beaches

Sadly, there's not much of a beach in Portofino, just a small strip of pebbles across the harbor from the piazzetta. Guests of the Hotel Piccolo have access to the hotel's private beach (on a gorgeous cove north of town, heading toward **Santa Margherita Ligure**), but everyone else takes the bus toward Santa Margherita Ligure, stopping at **Paraggi** (expensive, but beautiful) or one of the several beach clubs around **Punta Pedale** (between Paraggi and Santa Margherita). See entries under *Beaches* for Santa Margherita Ligure.

Sailing/Boating

The springtime Zegna Trophy is the most prestigious event on the sailing calendar for Portofino, with races on the Tigullio and side events around town. For more information, see www.yci.it or contact info@yci.it.

Want to pilot yourself? During the summer season **Giorgio Mussini** has seven boats available for charter by the hour, day, or weekend, and will send a captain along if you want a tour guide/someone to skipper the boat. (www.giorgio-mussini.com; info@giorgiomussini.com, ☎/fax 0185.269.327; Calata Marconi, 39, on the harbor.) **Motormarine Tigullio** also does rentals (www.motormarine.com, ☎ 0185.269.182, fax 0185.269.227; Calata Marconi, 13, on the harbor.)

Bikes/Scooters

Garage Portofino Motonoleggio rents scooters and mountain bikes – an excellent means of transportation along the coast. (☎ 0185.269.039, fax 0185.269.668; Piazza della Liberta, 27.)

Hiking

The trail leading to San Fruttuoso starts just past the Castello Brown. A long but lovely hike through Mediterranean maquis ends with the steep descent to the bay at San Fruttuoso. For more information, see *Hiking* in the section on Parco Portofino. Relax on the pebbled beach or see the abbey, then catch the ferry back to Portofino. For more information on hiking trails, see *Parco Portofino*.

Only in Portofino

Shopping Like a Superstar

If you've seen it in *Vogue*, you'll find it in Portofino. The biggest names are represented with their own storefronts – Celine, Dolce & Gabbana, Giorgio Armani, and Louis Vuitton (to name just a few) have shops here – while independent boutiques have a well-edited selection sure to please the discriminating clotheshorse. Got a shoe fetish? **Ming**o (Via Roma, 9) has bohemian-chic leather sandals made in Portofino. **Orizzonte** (Calata Marconi, 24) has uber-stylish housewares, while **Baccerini** (Via Roma, 7) has lovely and evocative hand-painted ceramics. The best deals in town, though, are found on the street. The elderly *signoras* of Portofino make and sell embroidered tea towels, hand-knit baby booties, and other precious items.

Tying the Knot

If the romance of the Riviera inspires you to take the plunge, **Just Married in Portofino** can coordinate all the details of your Italian fairytale wedding. Possible locations in Portofino include Castello Brown and the Hotel Splendido, or the Villa Durazzo up the coast in Santa Margherita Ligure. (www.just-marriedinportofino.com; info@epatrimoni.it, ☎ 0185.282.685, fax 0185.281.860.)

Santa Margherita Ligure

Little in low-key but stylish Santa Margherita Ligure hints at the divisions that once riveted the seaside town. Today, its citizens are united in their dedication to preserving not only a village atmosphere – no sprawling resorts or towering condo complexes here – but also the traditional activities of a fishing hamlet. Considering Santa Margherita's size and the amount of tourism each year (it's the second largest town on the promontory and receives 1.5 million visitors annually), it's a marvel that their efforts are successful. But indeed they are, as a stroll through the evening fish market or an afternoon in the park or piazza will attest. There is true community spirit here.

Artifacts date the original settlement to Roman times, and it's known that for much of its medieval history the town was constantly besieged by Saracen pirates. The Fieschi – one of the ruling families of Genoa – acquired the land as an estate in the 12th century, at which time it appears in the records under a single name, "Santa Margherita Pescino." By the 16th century, however – when the area was under dominion of the Republic of Genoa, who built a castle here as part of its coastal fortification scheme – the land was two disputing villages, Pescino and Corte.

This remained the state of affairs through the 16th and 17th centuries, even while the wealthy of Genoa were building lavish summer estates for themselves up and down the coast, including the Villa Durazzo atop Santa Margherita's San Giacomo di Corte hill.

The first friendly record between the two towns dates to 1800, and 12 years later they would be unified under the Empire and renamed Porto Napoleone (only to be renamed again, Santa Margherita di Rapallo, two years later with the dissolution of the Empire in 1814). In 1863 a royal decree by King Vittorio Emanuele II gave the current name, Santa Margherita Ligure.

Santa Margherita Ligure

Corso Niccolo Cuneo

Genoa
30 km

Parco

Corso E Rainusso

Salita S Agostino

Corso Giacomo Matteotti

Via Roma

Via Palestro

Via Gramsci

Via Pagana

BELVEDERE

Rapallo
3 km

Via Fratelli Arpe

Via Dògali

Gulf of Tigullio

SAN
GIACOMO

Corso Marconi

Via Favale

SANTA
BARBARA

Capitaneria di Porto

Ligurian Sea

Via Maragliano

MONTEBELLO

Via Milite Ignoto

Portofino
5 km

N

1. San Giacomo di Corte
2. Park & Villa Durazzo;
   Villa del Nido, Villa San Giacomo,
   Oratory of Sant'Erasmo
3. Santa Margherita d'Antiochia
4. Church of the Cappuccini;
   Castle ruins
5. Port; Ferry dock
6. Parco del Flauto Magico
7. RR Station (ferrovie)

200M

650 FT

Tourism was firmly established here by the British in the late 19th and early 20th centuries, as evidenced by several fine Art Nouveau hotels and the rambling English garden of the Villa Durazzo. Today the waterfront is a linchpin of tourist activities, with its broad and picturesque promenade, ferry service to nearby destinations, boat and kayak rentals, and congregation of divers who explore the marine sanctuary wrapping the coast.

Getting There

 By Train: The **FS** station in Santa Margherita Ligure is on the east side of town near the Piazza Nobili. For schedules, see www.trenitalia.it.

 By Car: Exit the A12 at Rapallo and take the Aurelia coastal road to Santa Margherita Ligure.

 By Boat: Santa Margherita is serviced by the **Servizi Marittimi del Tigullio** (☎ 0185.284.670, www.traghettiportofino.it), connecting it year-round by ferry to Portofino and Rapallo, and seasonally to Chiavari, Sestri Levante, and Lavagna.

You can moor a boat in the Santa Margherita Ligure harbor. Contact the **Maritime Authority** (☎ 0185.285.728 or 0185.287.029) for more information.

 By Bus: Blue Tigullio buses ply the lovely coastal route between Portofino, Santa Margherita, and Rapallo. Stops are marked by green signs on the side of the road. (☎ 0185.288.834, www.tiguilliotrasporti.it.)

Resources

- www.comune.santa-margherita-ligure.ge.it
- www.apttigullio.liguria.it
- www.parcoportofino.com
- **Tourist Office:** Via XXV Aprile, 4, ☎ 0185.292.91, fax 0185.290.222, infoapt@apttigullio.liguria.it.

Portofino Promontory

■ **Portofino Park Authority:** Viale Rainusso, 1, ☎ 0185.289.479, fax 0185.285.706, info@parcoportofino.it; trail maps and information on the Nature Reserve.

Being There

An excellent home base while exploring the Portofino promontory, Santa Margherita Ligure is at once gracious and chic. You'll still spy plenty of customized scooters – the basket-bedecked transportation of choice for the wealthy while vacationing at their villas in the area – but the vibe is less pretentious than Portofino. The old town streets surrounding the church of Santa Margherita, especially Via Palestro, are filled with shops and eateries friendly to the wallet of the Average Giovanni. On the waterfront promenade, lined with imported palms, you'll find groups of old men feeding pigeons while groups of young men admire the passing females.

Villa Durazzo

Surveying the bay from the San Giacomo hill is the Villa Durazzo, a 16th-century building attributed to Galeazzo Alessi and built for the wealthy and powerful Durazzo family of Genoa as a summer estate. The interior features period furnishings, decorations, and a collection of 17th-century paintings by Ligurian artists, including Domenico Piola, Giovanni Andrea de Ferrari, and Luciano Borzone. The family chapel in the Sala Belvedere is also noteworthy. The villa hosts classical music concerts on Fridays during the summer season (May-September).

The loveliest aspect of the villa are the grounds, converted to a public park in 1973 after the entire property was purchased by the town. The Italian garden, styled to complement the villa's formal architecture, is famous for its diverse collection of palm trees. The English garden mimics rambling woodlands with a small citrus orchard, paths, and fountains.

There's a café, popular with locals, ideally situated for the view. Elsewhere in the park you'll find a portion of the yacht *Elettra*, upon which Guglielmo Marconi carried out some of his Nobel Prize-winning experiments with radio waves in the Bay of Tigullio. (☎ 0185.205.449, 185.293.135; Villa – May-September, Tuesday-Sunday 9:30 am-6:30 pm; October-April, Tuesday-Sunday 9:30 am-4:30 pm; Park – May-September 9 am-7 pm; October-April 9 am-5 pm. Villa – €5,50 adults, €3 children. Park – free.)

Basilica di Santa Margherita d'Antiochia

This Baroque parish church with an 18th-century façade and a 17th-century interior is the subject of local legend. The story involves the pre-17th-century church on the same site, to which a medieval sailor brought a statue of the Virgin Mary holding a rose, to this day kept in a tabernacle over the main altar. During construction of the current building in 1672, a vial of scented water with miraculous powers was found under that altar, and its origins and properties entwined with the story of the Madonna della Rosa.

The reputed relics of Santa Margherita d'Antiochia – commonly represented leading a dragon – are kept in an urn in the chancel. Other church treasures include works on canvas by various Ligurian artists (including Giovanni Andrea de Ferrari) and a chalice and monstrance inlaid with pink coral gathered by the sailors of Santa Margherita.

The Piazza Caprera in front of the church is a hub of activity in the old town. On most days a few artists and other vendors can be found selling their wares – including lovely decoupage-decorated objects – from stalls here.

Portofino Promontory

Castle

Few events could motivate the rapid construction of an immense, and expensive fortification like Santa Margherita's waterfront castle. But in 1550 the infamous pirate Dragut laid waste to the town, not the first time this coastal region encountered such murderous marauders. The townspeople of Corte and Pescino (predecessors of united Santa Margherita Ligure) appealed for protection to Genoa, and the Doge issued a decree for the castle's construction. It was completed in a record six months. Today it is used for special events and has a small museum.

Oratory of Sant'Erasmo

The protector of fishermen and patron saint of sailors is venerated with this small church. Inside, the motif of storms and shipwrecks commemorates the saint's divine intercession on behalf of his followers. Outside there is a lovely black-and-white pebble mosaic *parvis* or courtyard executed with a maritime theme.

For Active Travelers

Beaches

 Santa Margherita has several beach clubs, with the nicest beaches found south of town heading toward Portofino. Try **Gio' E Rino Beach** (between Santa Margherita and Paraggi on Lungomare R. Rossetti, ☎ 0185.281.748). Near the train station (east side of town), the **Bagni Metropole** has pedal boat rentals (☎ 0185.286.134). The beach at **Paraggi** is gorgeous (see *Only in Santa Margherita Ligure*), but the clubs fill up quickly and are very expensive (around €25/person/day). Two to try are **Bagni Paraggi** (☎ 0185.289.961) and **Bagni Le Carillon** (☎ 0185.286.721); call ahead to reserve spots.

Diving

 Portofino Divers is a recreational and technical dive center, offering classes, certification, and guided dives at locations in the Portofino National Marine Reserve. (www.portofinodivers.com, info@portofinodivers.com, ☎ 0185.280.791, cell 348.150.8600, fax 0185.291.161, Via Jacopo Ruffini, 47 – on the waterfront by the wharf at Calata del Porto.)

In addition to guided scuba dives, **D&WS Scuba Service** leads snorkel trips to locations in the Portofino National Marine Reserve. (www.dws-scubaservice.com, info@dws-scubaservice.com, ☎ 0185.282.758, fax 0185.292.482, Via Jacobo Ruffini 2/A – near the wharf at Calata del Porto.)

Sailing/Boating

 One look at the harbor quickly confirms that Santa Margherita is a town for sailing enthusiasts. The Santa Margherita Ligure Sailing Club (Circolo Velico Santa Margherita Ligure) is the co-organizer of the Carlo Negri Cup, a celebrated regatta held each spring and featuring several days of racing and a rich schedule of side events. For more information see www.yci.it or contact info@yci.it.

The **Circolo Velico Santa Margherita Ligure** are the people to see for information regarding sailing instruction and boat rentals. (☎ 0185.280.485, fax 0185.280.485, Calata del Porto, 20.)

Only in Santa Margherita Ligure

Fish Market

Reprising a ritual as ancient as the town itself, on weekdays the fishing boats unload their catch at the Mercato del Pesce, the colonnaded building on Via Marconi, just past the castle. Locals arrive well in advance of 4 pm (traditional market time), as the catch of local octopus, famed Santa Margherita shrimp (a large, flavorful variety), anchovies, and other miscellaneous fish goes quickly and largely to restaurants in the area; find them on the evening's menu.

Parco del Flauto Magico

Conceived by fantastical and award-winning Genoese artist Lele Luzzati, this charming playground is animated by characters from Mozart's opera *The Magic Flute*. Travelers with young children will enjoy the colorful decorations and age-appropriate attractions (two-12 years).

Paraggi

Geographically and economically closer to Portofino, but part of the commune of Santa Margherita, this small hamlet on the water has the nicest and most expensive beach in the area. The castle on the hill is now privately owned, giving you an idea of with whom you're rubbing shoulders when sipping chilled Prosecco at the beach club.

Rapallo

In pre-Roman times, Rapallo was the home of the Liguri Tigulli, who gave their name to the Golfo de Tigullio. In our modern age, Rapallo has lent its name to a derisive term in Italian slang – *rapallizzazione* – meaning to ruin a charming place through overdevelopment. Hardly a good introduction to Rapallo, and not entirely fair. But it does point to a cultural phenomenon that is very real along the coast. Ligurians want to ensure that tourism is properly managed, so that regional integrity is maintained and the villages remain a good place to live and work, not just a lovely place to visit on vacation.

Long before it became a fashionable tourist destination, Rapallo took advantage of its protected point on the gulf to earn wealth from trade and to develop a domestic economy based on lace-making and other handicrafts. With money and a large population – it's still the most populous town in the Tigullio area – it was a player (albeit a minor one) on the world stage. Legend maintains that Hannibal crossed the medieval bridge here during the Second Punic Wars, and a few centuries later the city offered refuge to a flock of Milanese bishops fleeing the Lombard invasion.

Throughout the 11th and 12th centuries the free commune of Rapallo was at war with Pisa, and in 1229 swore allegiance to Genoa to gain the stronger power's protection. But that didn't shield it from a devastating pirate invasion in 1549, in response to which the waterfront castle was built by order of the Genoese Doge. In the 20th century, Rapallo's name would be affixed to a post-WWI treaty between Germany and Russia establishing recognition of the USSR, though that treaty was technically signed in Santa Margherita Ligure at the Imperial Palace Hotel.

The romance of the region has made Rapallo a favored spot with writers, including Ernest Hemingway and Friedrich Nietzsche (who found inspiration for *Thus Spake Zarathustra* while on a walk from Rapallo to Zoagli). The controversial Ezra Pound lived above the waterfront Café Rapallo from 1925 to 1945 and hosted several literary guests, including W.B. Yeats,

Ezra Pound

who described Rapallo in *A Packet for Ezra Pound*, and William Faulkner, who wrote about the city in an unfinished novel, *Elmer*.

Today, Rapallo is known for its beautiful golf course – considered one of the finest in the world – and for its seafront promenade, which is the heart of the town. It is ideally situated for exploring both the Portofino promontory and the seaside villages stretching towards the Cinque Terre.

Getting There

By Train: Rapallo's **FS** station is located near the center of town, by the Piazza Molfino. For schedules, see www.trenitalia.it.

By Car: Take the Rapallo exit from the A12.

By Boat: As the big town in the area, Rapallo is serviced by the **Servizi Marittimi del Tigullio** (☎ 0185.284.670, www.traghettiportofino.it) connected to most all the neighboring villages, including Genoa and Monterosso, Vernazza, Riomaggiore, and Portovenere in the Cinque Terre.

By Bus: Blue Tigullio buses ply the lovely coastal route between Portofino, Santa Margherita, and Rapallo. Stops are marked by green signs on the side of the road. (☎ 0185.288.834, www.tiguilliotrasporti.it.)

Portofino Promontory

Resources

- www.comune.rapallo.ge.it
- www.apttigullio.liguria.it
- **Tourist Office:** Lungomare Vittorio Veneto, 7, ☎ 0185.230.346, fax 0185.630.51.

Being There

The old town of Rapallo is arranged behind the waterfront crescent of Lungomare Vittorio Veneto, the seafront promenade. The southwestern tip of the arc ends at an inlet. A golf course is upstream of the inlet. On the opposite bank, off the Corso Cristoforo Colombo, is the medieval Ponte di Annibale, reputed crossing site of Hannibal. Heading farther south is the harbor. The eastern end of the promenade terminates at the town's castle, where sunbathers can be found on the rocks during the summer season.

Castel

A walk along the waterfront promenade ends opposite the 16th-century castle, a grim reminder of the terror that pirates wrecked along the Ligurian coast. On July 4, 1549, the town was ransacked in a surprise attack by the

pirate Dragut (who later lay waste to Santa Margherita Ligure). More than 100 men and women were taken captive, destined for the slave trade. The citizens of Rapallo appealed to Genoa for assistance, and a tax was authorized to raise funds for the castle's construction, completed by builder Antonio Carabo in May of 1551.

Cathedral of SS. Gervasio e Protasio

Rapallo says it owes the construction of the Collegiate Church of the Saints Gervasio and Protasio to the presence of the Milanese bishops, who first arrived in the town in the sixth century after fleeing the Lombard invasion. The church was constructed some 600 years later, consecrated in 1118, and was remodeled in the 17th and 20th centuries. The interior is richly decorated and the exterior marked by its noticeably leaning bell tower.

Church of Saint Stefano and the Civic Tower

The small black-and-white banded church of Saint Stefano is also known as the Oratory of the Blacks, and stands in the old

town near the 17th-century Oratory of the Whites (the colorful names suggest the color of capes worn by members of the respective confraternities). Documents date the church to 1155, but the present structure is the result of a 17th-century remodel. Abutting the oratory is the Civic Tower, constructed in 1473 to symbolize unity at a time when Rapallo was in serious social turmoil, the population split over government allegiances.

Museo del Merletto

Past the castle on the far eastern waterfront is **Casale Park** and the **Villa Tigullio**, built as a summer residence in the 17th century for the Furnace family, eventually passing to the Doria and then Spinola families. In the early 20th century it was ceded to the commune of Rapallo. Surrounded by lush gardens, the villa is now home to the Museo del Merletto (Lace-Making Museum), which documents Rapallo's history with the traditional handicraft. In addition to a modern lace panel designed by Lele Luzzati to represent the dramatic arts, there are couture lace gowns and other costumes and adornments – some 1,400 pieces in all, plus patterns and drawings – dating from the 16th through the 20th centuries. (☎ 0185.633.05; Tuesday, Wednesday, Friday and Saturday open 3-6 pm; Thursday open 10-11:30 am; entrance fee €3 adults; €1 children six-18; under six and over 70 free.)

For Active Travelers

Golf

The **Rapallo Golf and Tennis Club** (Circolo Golf e Tennis Rapallo) has one of the oldest, and most beautiful, golf courses in Italy. Open to the public, it has 18 holes spread over beautiful scenery, including the signature hole 7, backdropped by the ruins of the Monastero di Valle Christi. The course is a par 70 (par 36 for the front 9, par 34 for the back 9) with abundant trees and several water hazards imposed by the water inlet running from the harbor. (Via Mameli, 337, ☎ 0185.261.777, fax 0185.261.779, www.golfetennisrapallo.it, golfclub@ifree.it; closed Tuesdays; closed mid-January to mid-March and Christmas day.)

Tennis

Bring your racquet to the **Rapallo Golf and Tennis Club** (Circolo Golf e Tennis Rapallo) for play on three hard and three synthetic grass courts. Open to the public daily from 8 am-9 pm. (Via Mameli, 337, ☎ 0185.261.777, fax 0185.261.779, www.golfetennisrapallo.it.)

Fishing

Charter Pesca Rapallo leads fishing expeditions (casting, drifting, and trolling) on the gulf. Company owner Fabio Grassi says August and September are the best months for the sport, but year-round there is something to be caught using one or another technique. (☎/fax 0185.663.38, www.charter-pescarapallo.com, info@charterpescarapallo.com.)

Biking/Scooters

Rent a bike or scooter from the **GM Motor Center** and set off to explore the roads and nearby trails of the promontory. (Via S. Anna, 5, ☎/fax 0185.261.591, cell 328.868.5691.)

Only in Rapallo

Sanctuary of Nostra Signora di Montallegro

Just eight years after the town was ransacked by the pirate Dragut, when the townspeople were still in deep mourning, the Virgin Mary appeared before a peasant on this spot high above Rapallo and promised her protection. Luigi Rovelli oversaw construction of the neo-Gothic building, completed in 1557. Legend maintains that the church's Byzantine icon of the Virgin flew here on its own accord from Dalmatia, and that it delivered the town from several plagues over the course of the centuries. Reach the sanctuary by *funivia* (aerial tram) from Via Castagneto on the east side of town (☎ 0185.273.444, scontrol@tin.it), take the bus from the train station, or drive out of town along the Via Fratelli Betti, turning right after the small village of San Maurizio

di Monti. You can hike from the sanctuary uphill to the summit of Monte Rosa.

The miracle of the Madonna di Montallegro is evoked each July with a celebration held the first three days of the month. The icon is carried in procession through the streets and there are tremendous fireworks displays, including the mock burning of the castle.

San Michele di Pagana

Southwest of town is the hamlet of San Michelle di Pagana, a fishing village that has foregone development and its maintained colorful seafront houses. Above the village is the parish church of San Michele di Pagana where you'll find Van Dyck's painting *Crucifixion*. Between the village and the beach at Prelo is the **Punta Pagana tower**, part of the 16th-century coastal defense scheme against pirate invasion. It's been recently restored by the FAI, but is not currently open for visits.

■ Zoagli - Levanto

Between the Portofino Promontory and the Cinque Terre is a straight stretch of coastline spotted with fishing and resort towns of varying sizes. Settlement in the area depended on the vagaries of available terrain. Zoagli, a small fishing village, is nearly isolated, backed by the eastern stretch of the Parco Portofino, but nearby Chiavari sits on the Entella River estuary at the confluence of the Graveglia, Fontanabuona, and Sturla Valleys. Its proximity to the valleys – traditional crossing routes through the mountains to the regions beyond Liguria – helped Chiavari become the largest town in the area, separated only by the Entella river from its neighbor Lavagna, stronghold of the Fieschi clan. Farther down the coast, **Sestri Levante** and **Moneglia** were fishing villages that have embraced tourism but retain their ancient charm. Moneglia sits at the far northwestern reach of the Parco Nazionale delle Cinque Terre, and **Levanto** – within the park's scope – is nearly as isolated as the famous five villages of that region. It sits on the opposite side of the Punta del Mesco from Monterosso al Mare, the first town of the Cinque Terre.

Zoagli

The ruins of a pre-Roman castle here establish Zoagli as one of the oldest settlements on the Tigullio. Its reputation was made, however, centuries later, when its craft workshops began weaving silk velvet and damask cloth of unparalleled beauty and quality. The handicraft was already firmly established by the 11th century, when the region became a fief of the Fieschi family.

As with most of the towns in the area, Zoagli eventually came under the dominion of Genoa, in part to secure the protection of the stronger power against the frequent invasion of Saracen pirates. Two defensive towers remain on the waterfront. The town's relationship with the Republic helped the weaving trade expand – the cloth was favored among Europe's royalty – and today the craft is still practiced using traditional techniques. Silks from Zoagli are a sought-after souvenir.

There are two pebbled beaches here and numerous rocky shoals where sunbathers congregate in the summer. The village rings around the waterfront Piazza XXVII Dicembre, and is characterized by the narrow alleys typical to Liguria's fishing villages.

The Via Aurelia passes through the town, which can create a traffic nightmare during the crowded summer months.

Above: The Hotel Piccolo's private cove, Portofino (Casey Finley)

Below: Yachts in Portofino (Casey Finley)

Above: Approaching San Fruttuoso (Casey Finley)

Below: Private villas, Portofino (Amy Finley)

Above: The grounds at Villa Durazzo, Santa Margherita Ligure
Below: Villa Durazzo, Santa Margherita Ligure

Above: Piazza Caprera and the Basilica di Santa Margherita d'Antiochia, Santa Margherita Ligure (Amy Finley)
Below: Vegetable stand, Santa Margherita Ligure (Amy Finley)

Getting There

By Train: Zoagli's **FS** station is at the Piazza della Stazione, on the waterfront east of the Piazza XXVII Dicembre. For schedules, see www.trenitalia.it.

By Car: From the A12 autostrada, exit at Rapallo or Chiavari then take the Via Aurelia toward Zoagli. The coastal highway runs through the town.

Resources

- www.apttigullio.liguria.it
- **Tourist Office:** Via L. Merello, 6A, ☎/fax 0185.259.127.

Being There

Zoagli is a destination for those seeking a calm holiday: It has none of the bustle of nearby Rapallo. There are two pebbled beaches, a romantic walk cut into the sheer cliff face, and hiking trails that wind through Mediterranean vegetation to isolated parish churches of ancient beauty. The town itself shows the scars of heavy World War II bombing, but still manages to be lovely, with tall, colorful buildings typical of the region.

Madonna of the Sea

Mimicking San Fruttuoso's *Cristo degli Abissi* but with a feminine twist, in 1996 the sculptor Marian Hastianatte created the *Madonna del Mare*. The statue of the Virgin, which invokes protection for Zoagli's seamen, is sunk at a depth of nine meters/27 feet in the waters in front of the Grand Terrace (part of Zoagli's promenade). On August 6 the statue is venerated in a beautiful nighttime ceremony.

The Promenade

Though it lacks a long coastline like the resort towns of Rapallo or Santa Margherita Ligure, Zoagli still has a promenade. Starting up the cliff face, the walk unfolds in switchbacks that wind past the central beach, ending at the Grand Terrace. Illuminated at night, it is a popular gathering place.

Sem Benelli Castle

A landmark of sorts on the coast east of the town center, the castle was built by Sem Benelli, an Italian playwright born in the neighboring region of Tuscany. Most famous for his play *La Cena delle Beffe*, Benelli had plays performed by such illustrious actors as the Barrymore brothers and Sarah Bernhardt at the height of his popularity in the early 20th century. He died in the castle in 1949.

Only in Zoagli

Silk Workshop

In the 16th century the silk velvet woven in Zoagli was in demand among Europe's royalty and the aristocracy of Genoa. By the late 19th century, of the 1,236 looms in use along the Eastern Riviera, 1,200 of them were found here. The tradition is upheld today by the Seterie di Zoagli Cordani, a workshop founded in 1924 in a 19th-century villa painted with colorful trompe l'oeil decorations. The Seterie is the only remaining manufacturer of silk velvet, and their looms also produce a variety of other materials that are crafted into ties, scarves, stoles, dresses, and furnishing fabrics, all available for sale at the villa. A tour of the facility includes a look at the looms, some dating to the early 19th century. An onsite seamstress takes custom orders, including for bridal gowns, which have become something of a house specialty. (Via San Pietro, 21, ☎ 0185.259.141, www.seteriecordani.com.)

For Active Travelers

Hiking

A hike of the Five Bell Towers departs from the Piazza XXVII Dicembre, next to the pharmacy. Marked by a rectangle divided into two triangles – the upper one white and lettered "5C," the lower one solid red – the path takes about 3½ hours to complete and passes through the hamlets of San Pietro di Rovereto, Semorile, and San Ambrogio (where Ezra Pound once lived). The trail forms a ring looping back to Zoagli, passing through terraced olive groves and Mediterranean maquis, and throughout boasts magnificent views of the coast.

Diving

Zoagli Divers leads trips to nearby sites (including the marine sanctuary and shipwrecks along the gulf), providing boat transport and equipment rental. Courses are available for first-time divers with professionals. Walk-in dives from the beach visit the Madonna del Mare. (Via Piazza San Martino, 7, ☎ 0185.258.514; fax 0185.250.828, www.zoaglidivers.com, info@zoaglidivers.com.)

Tennis

If you're looking to swing a racquet, there are public courts available to all levels and ages, with an on-site pro for individual lessons. (Via Cristoforo Colombo, ☎ 333.909.7063.)

Chiavari

Chiavari's position on the Entella river estuary at the confluence of the Graveglia, Fontanabuona, and Sturla Valleys – crossing routes through the high mountains that lock in most of Liguria – strategically positioned it for settlement. Indeed its early name was *Clavarium*, meaning "key to the valleys." In 1959 an Iron Age necropolis was found here dating to the eighth century BC. Early in its history (1167) it came under the dominion of the Republic of Genoa, who sought to contain the powerful Fieschi and Malaspina families – much of the surrounding areas were Fieschi fiefs – through a policy of eastern expansion. The Genoese lay the physical foundation for the city as we experience it today. A grid-patterned layout was decreed, and four residential streets were constructed running parallel to the sea, cut at right angles by four smaller streets. Originally there were defensive walls ringing the city, but these were demolished in the 18th century.

Chiavari was quickly and permanently populated, and as it grew so did its influence. In 1332 it gained the Bishop's seat for Eastern Liguria, and in 1648 was given the title of city by Genoa. In recent years there has been talk of creating another province in Liguria with Chiavari as its capital (it is currently part of the province of Genoa).

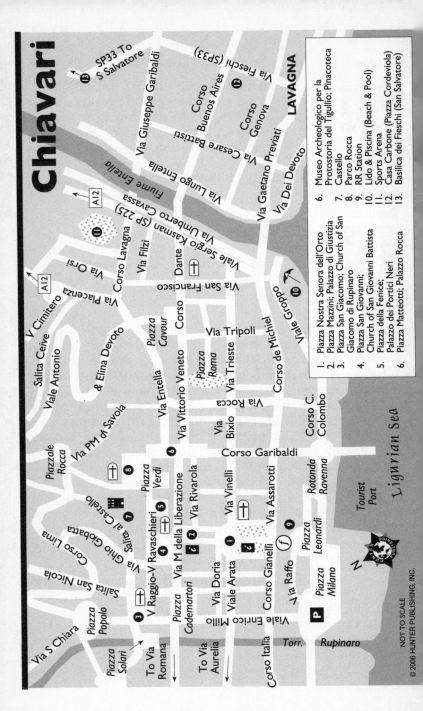

Chiavari

SP33 To S Salvatore

Via Giuseppe Garibaldi

Corso Buenos Aires

Via Cesare Battisti

Corso Genova

Via Fieschi (SP33)

Via Gaetano Previati

Via Dei Devoto

LAVAGNA

Via Lungo Entella

Fiume Entella

Viale Sergio Kasman (SP 225)

Via Umberto Cavassa

A12

Corso Lavagna

Via Filzi

Dante

Via Orsi

V Cimitero

Via Piacenza

A12

Salita Ceive

Viale Antonio

& Elina Devoto

Via San Francisco

Piazza Cavour

Corso

Via Tripoli

Piazzale Rocca

Via PM of Savoia

Via Entella

Piazza Roma

Via Trieste

Via Vittorio Veneto

Via Rocca

Corso de Michiel

Corso C. Colombo

Piazza Verdi

Corso Garibaldi

Via Bixio

Via Rivarola

Via Vinelli

Via Assarotti

Rotonda Ravenna

Corso Lima

Corso San Nicola

Salita al Castello

Via Ghio Giobatta

Via Raggio–V Ravaschieri

Piazza M della Liberazione

Piazza Cademartori

Via Doria

Viale Arata

Corso Gianelli

Via Raffo

Piazza Leonardi

Piazza Milano

Viale Enrico Millo

Via S Chiara

Piazza Popolo

Piazza Solari

To Via Romana

To Via Aurelia

Corso Italia

Torr. Rupinaro

Tourist Port

Ligurian Sea

P

N

HUNTER PUBLISHING, INC.

NOT TO SCALE

© 2006 HUNTER PUBLISHING, INC.

1. Piazza Nostra Senora dell'Orto
2. Piazza Mazzini; Palazzo di Giustizia
3. Piazza San Giacomo; Church of San Giacomo di Rupinaro
4. Piazza San Giovanni; Church of San Giovanni Battista
5. Piazza della Fenice; Palazzo dei Portici Neri
6. Piazza Matteotti; Palazzo Rocca

6. Museo Archeologico per la Protostoria del Tigullio; Pinacoteca
7. Castello
8. Parco Rocca
9. RR Station
10. Lido & Piscina (Beach & Pool)
11. Sports Arena
12. Casa Carbone (Piazza Cordeviola)
13. Basilica dei Fieschi (San Salvatore)

Chiavari's urban atmosphere is tempered by a large water-front and the beauty of the old city, which remains the heart of the town. The predominant industry here is also old world. The production of quality wood furnishings grew from the traditional crafting of *Campanine* chairs, known for their delicate and decorative spindle backs.

Getting There

By Train: The **FS** station is on the waterfront behind the Piazza Leonardi. If you're trying to cross into town from the waterfront, you'll need to cut through the train station or take Corso Garibaldi, which goes under the tracks. Otherwise, these form a barrier preventing you from accessing the center of town. For schedules, see www.trenitalia.it.

By Car: Exit Chiavari from the A12 autostrada.

By Boat: There is ferry service seasonally between Chiavari, Santa Margherita Ligure, Rapallo, Portofino, and Sestri Levante, provided by **Servizi Marittimi del Tigullio** (☎ 0185.284.670, www.traghettiportofino.it.)

By Bus: Bus service in Chiavari is provided by **Tigullio buses** (www.tiguilliotrasporti.it.)

Resources

- www.comune.chiavari.ge.it
- www.apttigullio.liguria.it
- **Tourist Office:** Corso Assarotti, 1, ☎ 0185.325.198, fax 0185.324.796.

Being There

Owing to its regular grid layout, the town is easily walkable, in part because Chiavari – unlike some of its neighbors – is built on flat land. The harbor (which has a lovely fountain along the length of its promenade), the train station, the cathedral, and the Piazza Mazzini, notable for its colorful trompe l'œil decorated buildings, form a straight access heading inland and intersecting Via Martiri della Liberazione, the old porticoed street that is the center of commerce.

Cattedrale di Nostra Signora dell'Orto

The cathedral complex in the center of town includes the 17th-century church and 19th-century Bishop's palace and seminary. The cathedral was built between 1613-1633 to house a venerated image of the Madonna that reputedly saw the city through plague in the 15th century. Befitting its importance as a Bishop's seat it is richly decorated with marble and gilt stuccowork. In addition to a painting of *Saint Joseph* by Orazio de Ferrari (in the third chapel on the right) and three wooden sculpture groups by Maragliano found in the south transept, its art treasures include many 18th-century works brought to the cathedral from monasteries following the French Revolution. The Bishop's Palace is now the home of the Diocesan Museum, displaying treasures of the church and open Wednesdays and Sundays from 10 am to noon.

Piazza Mazzini

The oft-photographed heart of Chiavari was home to an early 15th-century citadel that played an important role in the defense of the city against the Fieschi, ensconced across the Entella River in Lavagna. The citadel was razed in the late 19th century to make way for the Palazzo di Giustizia, but a single tower was preserved. It sits between the Palazzo and the Town Hall behind it. The piazza is the site of the town market, held every morning except Sunday.

San Giovanni Battista

The high altar of this parish church has a *Crucifix* by Anton Maria Maragliano and two paintings by Orazio de Ferrari. Its founding in 1182 coincides with Chiavri's annexation by the

Republic of Genoa. The church was rebuilt in 1623 by Bartolomeo Bianco and Andrea Vannone, and the wooden choir dates from that time.

Palazzo Rocca

Bartolomeo Bianco, who redesigned the parish church of San Giovanni Battista, received the commission to build a residence for the Costaguta marquises (art dealers to the Genoese aristocracy) in 1629. The palace, today the Palazzo Rocca, was enlarged in the 18th century when it was acquired by the Grimaldi family. Further changes were made in the early 20th century when it was acquired by the Rocca who used it as a luxurious private residence. The magnificent Parco Rocca, which tumbles down the Castello hill in a series of staircases, fountains, and a nymphaeum, was laid out at that same time.

Today the palace hosts the Civica Galleria, an art gallery, with a large collection of 17th- and 18th-century paintings from the Genoese school. The works are displayed through the parlors of the top floor amid porcelain objects and furniture typical of the late 19th century. The former stables of the pal-

Bernardo Strozzi, Le Tre Parche (Galleria Civica di Palazzo Rocca)

ace have been converted to house the *Museo Archeologico per la Preistoria e Protostoria del Tigullio*, where remains from the Iron Age necropolis unearthed in the 1950s are displayed.

(Civica Galleria – ☎ 0185.308.577; Museo Archeologico – ☎ 0185.320.829; Civica Galleria – musei@comune.chiavari. ge.it; Museo Archeologico – museochiavari@libero.it; Civica Galleria – open Saturday, Sunday, and holidays from 10 am-noon and from 4-7 pm; Museo Archeologico – open Tuesday-Saturday from 9 am-1.30 pm; every second and fourth Sunday of each month from 9 am-1:30 pm; both museums have free entrance.)

Only in Chiavari

Antique Market

On the second Sunday of each month the *centro storico* is the site of Chiavari's *Mercato dell'Antiquariato*, a flea market specializing in antiques. More than 120 stands are arrayed along the Via Martiri della Liberazione, Via Vittorio Veneto, Via Bighetti, and Via Vecchie Mura.

Campanino Chairs

Named for their inventor Gaetano de Scalzi – an early 19th-century craftsman nicknamed *Campanino* – Chiavari's famous chairs are delicate (weighing only three lbs) and made of olive or walnut wood. Check out the handmade chairs at the workshop **Fratelli Levaggi**. (Via Parma 469, ☎ 0185.383.092).

Macramé

Of equal importance to Chiavari as an artisan center was the production of macramé lace. See a demonstration of the art and purchase pieces at **Laboratorio Milu** (Via Entella, 169, ☎ 335.778.61.32) or **Venzi Elena** (via Remolari, 9, ☎ 0185.301.557).

Sanctuary of the Madonna delle Grazie

Northwest of town (take the Via Aurelia in the direction of Zoagli and follow the signs five km/three miles out directing you toward Bacezza), the Sanctuary of the Madonna delle Grazie has a panoramic view stretching from Portofino to Sestri Levante. Inside the early 15th-century church is a fresco series entitled *Scenes from the Life of Christ*, painted by Teramo Piaggio, a native of Zoagli active on the Eastern Riviera in the 16th century.

Valle d'Aveto

Inland from Chiavari the altitude increases dramatically – approaching 1,800 m/5,600 at the peaks of the Ligurian Apennines – and the terrain takes on an almost Nordic appearance. There are beech and coniferous forests, pastures where cattle graze contentedly, glacier-fed lakes, and snow in the winter months. Much of the territory is incorporated into the Parco Naturale Regionale dell'Aveto, and hiking paths wind throughout (see www.parks.it/parco.aveto for itineraries). Around the park's perimeter are several rural villages of great interest. **Borzonasca**, cloaked in chestnut woods, has an intact medieval church. A brief detour up the road toward Prato Sopralacroce arrives at a silent valley where the **Borzone Abbey** sits, retaining its 13th-century form (which is in the style of the Lombard school). Just past the village of Magnasco a small road leads to the **Lago delle Lame** – a glacier-fed lake – and its surrounding wetlands. Finally, near the border with Emilia-Romagna, is **Santa Stefano d'Aveto**, an inland retreat popular with the Genoese who cross-country ski in the winter and horseback ride through the picturesque alpine setting come summer. The 13th-century castle, now in ruins, belonged to the Malaspina family, who ruled the town for four centuries. One of the most powerful of the inland feudal clans, they were succeeded in ownership by the Fieschi, then the Doria.

From Chiavari, take SS225 to Carasco, then SS586 to Val d'Aveto. If traveling by train, debark at Chiavari then take a Tiguillio bus to the Val d'Aveto. The towns mentioned above form a clockwise ring around the heart of the park, beginning at "6" and ending at "2." For more information, see www.parks.it/parco.aveto. Tourist office in Santa Stefano d'Aveto located at Piazza del Popolo, 6, ☎ 0185.880.46.

For Active Travelers

Beaches

Several beach clubs are located on the pebbly beach in front of **Corso Valparaiso**, adjacent to the porto turistico. Farther west, near the mouth of the Entella River, the **Lido beach** (☎ 0185.325.134) has received a coveted Blue Flag by the

European organization of the same time, which gives awards based on water quality, environmental management, safety, and services.

Pool

Looking to get in a few regulation-length laps while on holiday? The Chiavari community pool (*piscina comunale*) is open Monday 7:45 am-2:30 pm and 7-10 pm; Tuesday 7:45 am-12:30 pm and 8:30-10 pm; Wednesday 7:45 am-2:30 pm and 6:30-8 pm; Thursday 7:45 am-2:30 pm and 8:30-10 pm; Friday 7:45 am-2:30 pm and 7-10 pm; Saturday 9 am-1 pm; and Sunday 9 am-12:30 pm. (Via Entella, ☎ 0185.364.855.)

Biking/Scooters

Mare Foto Alba rents bikes and mountain bikes for adults and children, and also has 2- and 4-seater rickshaw bicycles for sightseeing. (Corso Valparaiso, 126, ☎ 0185.314.974). **MultiEuro Noleggio** has scooters for hire. (Corso de Michiel, 34, ☎/fax 0185.324.328).

Tennis

The public courts at Tennis Club Chiavari (four outdoor, one indoor) are open every day from 8 am-10 pm. (Via Preli, 20, ☎ 0185.304.471.)

Boating

The **Yacht Club Chiavari** hosts regattas in the area and is the place to inquire about boat rentals. (Porto Turistico, ☎/fax 0185.310.150, www.ycc.it, info@ycc.it.)

Horseback Riding

Two stables in Santa Stefano d'Aveto lead trips through the countryside. Advance booking is required. (Cavallie e Natura di C. Giovagnoli – Strada per Rocca d'Aveto, ☎ 335.536.4630; Le Due Querce – Loc. Casoni D'Amborzasco, 42, ☎ 0185.899.006.)

Lavagna

Separated only by the Entella River from Chiavari, Lavagna is forever associated with the Fieschi, once the most powerful family in Eastern Liguria and the counts of Lavagna. Among their numbers were two Popes – Innocent IV and Adrian V – and a saint, Catherine Fieschi Adorno. For centuries the ambitious clan was tolerated by Genoa, and largely by the Doria, arguably the most powerful family in the Republic. Genoa's policy of eastern expansion, intended to contain the Fieschi, included annexation of Chiavari in the 12th century. Thus they could keep an eye on their ambitious neighbor.

In the 16th century – when the legendary Andrea Doria was installed in Genoa, ruling with the protection of Spain and the Holy Roman Empire – Gian Luigi Fieschi hatched a conspiracy to overthrow Doria's Republic and return it to the French as a protectorate (something the reigning Pope desired). The plot failed miserably, Gian Luigi drowned, and Doria extracted revenge against the family, wresting Lavagna from their control.

The imprint of the noble family remains in the Basilica dei Fieschi and the celebration of the Torta de Fieschi, which re-enacts the 13th-century wedding feast of Count Opizzo Fieschi and Bianca de' Bianchi with medieval pageantry and a 3,300-lb cake.

Lavagna has one of the largest harbors in Europe and shares proximity to the Valle d'Aveto with Chiavari. Nearby, the suburb of Cavi di Lavagna is primarily a bathing resort.

Getting There

 By Train: The **FS** station is on the waterfront to the east of the yachting marina. For schedules, go to www.trenitalia.it.

 By Car: The Via Aurelia passes through town. From the A12 autostrada, exit Lavagna.

 By Bus: Bus service in Lavagna is provided by **Tigullio buses** (www.tigulliotrasporti.it).

Resources

- www.apttigullio.liguria.it
- www.comune.lavagna.ge.it
- **Tourist Office:** Piazza dell Liberta, 48/a, ☎ 0185.395.070.

Being There

Lavagna has a medieval grid layout and the Via Aurelia runs through it, right on the waterfront. North of the autostrada is the suburb of San Salvatore dei Fieschi, home to the Basilica. The town was once a rural neighbor, but building has blurred the distinction between it and Lavagna.

Basilica dei Fieschi

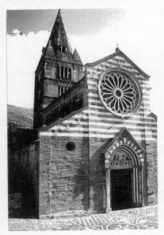

The Fieschi Pope Innocent IV began construction of the church in 1245, but it was completed seven years later by his nephew Ottobono (who would become Pope Adrian V). The façade is striped in white marble and the grey slate for which Lavagna and the nearby Fontanabuona Valley are famous (*lavagna* became the Italian word for blackboard). The Gothic portal is topped with a fresco, attributed to Barbagelata, in which Innocent IV and Ottobono Fieschi appear at the foot of the cross with the Madonna and St. John. Across the street is the **Palazzo Comitale**, constructed by the Fieschi in 1252 but badly damaged during a Saracen attack in the 16th century.

Casa Carbone

Formerly the residence of the Carbone family, who donated it to the Fondo per l'Ambiente Italiano, this early 20th-century home preserves the domestic environment of a middle-class Ligurian family at the turn of the century. Displayed through the rooms are art objects, ceramics, fin-de-siecle furniture, and 17th-century paintings from the Ligurian School. (Via Riboli, 14, ☎ 0185.393.902; open March-October Saturday and Sunday from 10 am-1 pm and 2-6 pm; entrance fee €2 adults, €1 children.)

Only in Lavagna

Torta dei Fieschi

Celebrated each August 14, the festival is held in San Salvatore dei Fieschi on the piazza in front of the Basilica dei Fieschi, the most enduring monument of this powerful family. Participants wearing medieval dress recreate the wedding feast of Count Opizo Fieschi (older brother of Sinibaldo, who would become Pope Innocent IV and initiate the building of the basilica in 1245) and Bianca de' Bianchi of Siena, who married in 1230. For the celebration of his marriage the Count purportedly wanted a cake big enough to be shared by the village. This is the foundation for the festival's spectacle – a 3,300-lb wedding cake. To claim a slice you must first participate in a game wherein males and females search for their soul mate (the holder of a ticket bearing the same "fantasy name" as theirs). Find your mate, then have your cake (and eat it, too).

For Active Travelers

Diving

 Several operators provide instruction and lead dives to the Portofino marine sanctuary and sites around Sestri Levante and the Punta Manara. Try **Tigullio Sub Service** (Corso Mazzini, 28, ☎/fax 0185.392.217) or **Odissea Sub** (Porto Turistico, 108, ☎/fax 0185.324.170, www.odisseasub.it).

Boating

 Lavagna has one of the largest harbors in Europe with 1,600 berths for vessels up to 50 m in length. Some might be content merely to stroll the port and admire the yachts. Others might want (need?) to charter one for their own private use (expensive, but memorable). **Forzatre** (Porto Turistico, 18, ☎ 0185.360.205, fax 0185.360.288, forzatre@forzatre.it, www.forzatre.it) has 10 sailing yachts moored in Lavagna that can be chartered for four- or five-day trips along the Ligurian coast, or two-week charters to Capo Corse via the Isle of Elba and the Gulf of La Spezia.

Sestri Levante

Hans Christian-Anderson in 1869

Hans Christian-Anderson visited Sestri Levante in 1833 and gave its two bays the names by which we still know them today – the Baia delle Favole (Bay of Fables) and Baia del Silenzio (Bay of Silence). Perhaps he was inspired by the locale to write his famous story *The Little Mermaid*. Legend maintains that the isthmus connecting headland to shore was formed when lovelorn Tigullio attempted to abduct Segesta, most lovely of the Sirens, and was turned to stone by her father Neptune.

The setting is indeed like something from a fairytale, the geography entirely unique. It attracted the ancient Tigulli, and then the Romans. It was in turn conquered by the Byzantines, the Longobards, and the Obertenghi. Like many towns in the area, it was a pawn in the power struggle between Genoa and the powerful Fieschi, who held it as a fiefdom during the 11th century, lost it to Genoa early in the 12th, regained it again soon after, and lost it for good in the 13th century. Uniquely visible along the coast – it beckons like a finger to passing ships – Sestri Levante was beset by pirate attacks until the early 17th century.

Despite all this turmoil, the fishing village prospered. The nobility of Genoa found the town attractive and constructed numerous villas here. Today they have been converted to hotels or private residences, testimony to the town's charm – it is a favorite destination with Italians on their own holidays.

Getting There

By Train: The **FS** station is at the top of Via Roma, near the Piazza San Antonio (north side of town, facing Bay of Fables).

By Car: The Via Aurelia runs through the town. Sestri Levante has an exit from the A12 autostrada.

By Boat: During the Easter holiday and the summer months, Sestri Levante is serviced by the ferries of **Servizio Marittimo**

del Tigullio, connected to the neighboring towns on the Tigullio and to Cinque Terre and Portovenere farther east.

Resources

- www.apttigullio.liguria.it
- www.comune.sestri-levante.ge.it
- **Tourist Office:** Piazza San Antonio, 10, ☎ 0185.457.011.

Being There

The **Baia dell Favole** (Bay of Fables) is the larger of the two bays, facing north. Along its shore are a promenade and several beach resorts. The smaller **Baia di Silenzio** faces south and has a beach where fishermen pull their boats up onto the sand. The **Via XXV Aprile** – nicknamed *budello* – runs up the

Sestri Levante

Ligurian Sea

Bay of Fávole

Bay of Silence

N

300 M
1000 FT

© 2006 HUNTER PUBLISHING, INC.

1. Piazza Matteotti; Palazzo Durazzo Pallavicini (Town Hall); Basilica of Santa Maria di Nazareth
2. Ruins of Oratory of Santa Caterina
3. Church of San Nicolò dell'Isola
4. Castelli Park, Marconi Tower
5. Vico Macelli; church of San Pietro in Vincoli; Galleria Rizzi
6. Piazza A. Moro
7. Piazza San Antonio
8. Train Station

middle of the isthmus, terminating at the Piazza Matteotti in the heart of the old town. The streets here are narrow and shady, which heightens the effect of sunlight when you leave the caruggi onto the waterfront. The headland is largely taken up by the **Parco dei Castelli**, now the private domain of the exclusive Grand Hotel dei Castelli.

Basilica Santa Maria di Nazareth

This 17th-century church with a 19th-century façade stands on the Piazza Matteotti, heart of the old town. The interior is Baroque and has several artistic treasures, including *Pentecost* by Domenico Fiasella and *Madonna del Crmine with St. Lawrence and St. John the Baptist* by Lazzro Tavarone. The 12th-century crucifix is a relic of shipwreck. The founding of the church is celebrated every September 15. Near the church is the Villa Durazo-Pallavicini, a family palace now used as the town hall.

Church of San Nicolo dell'Isola

The pale, striped church forms a picturesque backdrop to the

Bay of Silence. Built in 1151, it was the first parish church of Sestri Levante between the 12th and 17th centuries (when the basilica was constructed). Recent renovations have revealed its Romanesque structure, with a semicircular apse and bell tower with spire and mullioned windows. The façade is 15th-century.

Rizzi Gallery

The palace and collection were bequeathed to the city by Marcello Rizzi upon his death in 1960. The first floor preserves the furnishings and decorations of a rich bourgeois home, while the second and third floors display paintings and sculptures – collected by Rizzi and his father – in chronological order from the 15th through 18th centuries. The works are primarily from the Italian and Flemish schools, and include paintings by Rubens, Rafello, and Tiepolo. (Via Cappuccini,

☎ 0185.413.00; open April-October on Sundays from 10 am-1 pm; May-September on Wednesdays from 4-7 pm; 20 June 20-September 6 on Fridays and Saturdays 9:30-11:30 pm; entrance fee €3)

Ruins of the Oratory of Santa Caterina

Off the Via Penisola di Levante on the promontory, the oratory was destroyed during WWII air raids and was never rebuilt. Instead, in 1994 a statue of St. Catherine and a plaque were placed here. The paintings and furnishings of the church were removed to the church of San Pietro in Vincoli, where you'll also find a wooden group dedicated to the martyrdom of Santa Caterina by Anton Maria Maragliano.

Only in Sestri Levante

Punta Manara

The promontory of Punta Manara, to the east of Sestri Levante, is a wilderness of Mediterranean scrub and olive groves that is crossed by several well-marked hiking trails. Trail n°1 departs from Sestri Levante near Via XXV Aprile and Vico del Bottone and ascends the Cresta di Punta Manara. Near Mandrella it meets up with trail n°2 that goes to Mount Castello and loops back toward Sestri Levante. In Mandrella you can also pick up trail n°3 that actually starts at the cemetery off Via Val di Canepa, passes through Mandrella, loops near the Mount Castello, and rejoins Sestri Levante at the Via del Chiusa. Get a trail map at the tourist office. If you'd like a guide, **Barbara Biasotti** leads nature walks in the area and can be reached at barbara_biasotti@libero.it.

Val di Vara

Heading inland from Sestri Levante on State Route 523 you enter the Val di Vara, a lush area bordering the River Vara that is popular in summer with vacationers seeking quiet, solitude, and the chance for such activities as fishing, hunting, canoeing, and mountain biking. The town of Varese Ligure – itself lovely and known for the circular old town called the *Borgo Rotondo* – is the put-in spot for canoe trips down the Vara and its tributary, the Magra River (which passes through the Montemarcello-Magra Regional Park, entering the sea near the border with Tuscany). Brugnato is another standout, with a Bishop's Palace and peaceful Benedictine Abbey.

For Active Travelers

Horseback Riding

There are horseback riding trails through the maquis and 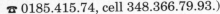 wooded areas up the hills surrounding Sestri Levante. **Rancho Grande** leads guided excursions with advance booking. (in San Vittoria, ☎ 0185.415.74, cell 348.366.79.93.)

Boating

Motonautica Bimare rents powerboats (with skipper) for the day, week, or weekend, and also takes passengers on boating excursions to nearby locations. (☎ 0185.463.90, fax 0185.469.699, www.motonauticabimare.com, info@motonautica-bimare.com) In the suburb of Riva Trigosa (other side of Punta Manara), **VelaRT** rents pedal boats, kayaks, windsurfers, and sailboats (with skipper) by the hour or for half- or full days. (Via Caboto, 35, cell 347.269.03.85.)

Mountain Biking

Explore Punta Manara's trails by mountain bike. **Cicli** **Enrico** rents both mountain bikes and regular bikes and is open Monday-Saturday in the mornings (9:30 am-12:30 pm) and late afternoon (3:30-7:30 pm). (Via Nazionale, 415, ☎ 0185.44.725.)

Tennis

There are several public courts in Sestri Levante. **Centro Sportivo le Mimose** is open every day from 8 am and has two synthetic grass courts, one hard surface court, three calcetto courts, and a squash court. (Via Lombardia, 26, ☎ 0185.482.937.) **Circolo Tennis Pilade Queirolo** is also open every day from 8 am and has five outdoor courts. (Via Fabbrica Valle, ☎ 0185.432.35). There are two indoor courts and one outdoor court at **Circolo Tennis La Fattoria**, open daily from 8 am (Via La Fattoria, ☎ 0185.426.77).

Canoeing

Along the Vare River are landing points with dressing rooms and information boards, and you'll find rental shops in the towns lining the river.

Moneglia

At the close of the 13th century, the men of Moneglia put themselves and their boats at the service of Genoa, fighting in the all-important Battle of Meloria that ended Pisa's aspirations on the Mediterranean. The tiny fishing village – which sits nestled between Punta Moneglia and Punta Rospo – first appears on the records as a staging post on the Roman road, and spent much of the 13th to 15th centuries entangled in power struggles between the Guelphs and Ghibellines (on the side of the Guelphs), and between the Fieschi and Genoa (it had been a Fieschi fief). It was eventually dominated by Genoa.

The castles of **Villafranca** and **Monleone** bookend the town, which is decidedly compact, wedged between the sea and surrounding groves of olive trees. Fronted by a beach protected by two breakwaters, Moneglia is a popular, but very calm, destination for sun worshippers and divers, who explore the sea beds surrounding the promontories.

Getting There

By Train: Moneglia's **FS** station is on the western outskirts of town, a short walk from the town center. For schedules, see www.trenitalia.it.

By Car: From the A12 autostrada exit at Sestri Levante or Deiva Marina. You must then take the Via Aurelia toward Moneglia. Both routes pass through tunnels on an alternating, traffic light controlled one-way system that can mean long delays (up to an hour). Coming on the Via Aurelia from Sestri Levante it's possible to detour to minor road n° 68 and reach Moneglia Via Casale, Camposoprano, and Facciu. Or, n° 35 detours through Tessi and San Saturnino.

Resources

- www.moneglia.com
- www.apttigullio.liguria.it
- **Tourist Office:** Corso Longhi, 32, ☎ 0185.490.576.

Being There

Moneglia is on a decidedly smaller scale than some of the surrounding villages, but does not lack for amenities. The coastline is one long stretch of beach clubs, and the shore is protected by two breakwaters. Just outside the town are olive orchards and greenery, and there are a few sites in the village.

Church of Santa Croce

Fronted by a cobbled *parvis* (courtyard), this church takes its name from its Byzantine crucifix (fourth altar on the left), which is a relic from a shipwreck. Luca Cambiaso (born in Moneglia in the 16th century) painted the *Last Supper* in the sacristy. Elsewhere in the church, a marble slab dated 1290 preserves two chain links from the port of Pisa, reminders of the role played by the men of Moneglia in the Battle of Meloria.

Oratory of the Disciplinati

The interior of this church, founded in the 10th century, is entirely covered in frescoes executed between the 13th and 18th centuries.

Only in Moneglia

Olive Oil Tasting

The groves surrounding Moneglia produce a typically light olive oil that has a slightly citrus flavor and pairs well with seafood. At the *Consorzio Olivicoltori Facciu' di Monegli*, up the hill in the suburb of Facciu, you can taste and purchase their extra virgin oil. (Localita Facciu, 22, ☎ 0185.490.435.)

For Active Travelers

Beaches

La Secca beach, just east of town, has earned a Blue Flag (☎ 0185.492.69). The beach club at **Punta Rospo** rents kayaks and pedal boats (cell 335.624.52.38).

Levanto

Considered the "Gateway to the Cinque Terre," Levanto is an isolated town that nonetheless saw great development in the 1950s and 60s, accounting for the "new town" that sprawls eastward away from the original fishing hamlet. The town's origins are pre-Roman, and it was a fief of the Malaspina, then of the Da Passano family, before falling to Genoa in the early years of the 13th century. In 1637 the town was named a *Capitanato* with jurisdiction over the magistrate seats of the area.

The town sits on a wide, protected bay and has one of the largest sandy beaches in the area. This brought gentrified tourism in the 19th century and several villas remain along the ramparts of the seafront, watched over by the Malaspina castle (now a private residence).

Getting There

By Train: Levanto's **FS** station is behind the town, straddling the Ghiraro riverbed. The town is only serviced by intercity and regional trains. For schedules, see www.trenitalia.it. If you've purchased a Cinque Terre card with rail service you have one-day's worth of unlimited passage between Levanto and La Spezia.

By Car: A winding 13-km/eight-mile road from the A12 autostrada leads to Levanto. Bring Dramamine.

By Boat: Navigazione Golfo dei Poeti has ferries running between Levanto, the villages of the Cinque Terre, and Portovenere (www.navigazionegolfodeipoeti.it, ☎ 0187.732.987).

Resources

■ www.levanto.com

■ www.aptcinqueterre.sp.it

■ **Tourist Office:** Piazza Mazzini, 12, ☎ 0187.808.125.

Being There

The new town was constructed, largely since the 1950s, on the broad, level valley floor at the east side of Levanto. The old hamlet is clustered on a hillside on the west side. The Piazza del Popolo is roughly at its center, where the large loggia was formerly used for public meetings of the magistrates. Once the site of gentrified tourism during the 19th century, today Levanto calls itself the "Gateway to the Cinque Terre," and draws tourists who are headed to the five villages. Situated within the Parco Nazionale di Cinque Terre, it is ideally situated for hiking, but Levanto is also known as a surf town with the biggest surf in mainland Italy.

Church of Sant'Andrea

The 13th-century church, accessed from the Via Don Emanuele Toso off the Piazza del Popolo, has a striped façade of white Carrara marble and local serpentine stone. Inside are two works by Baccesco, dating to 1493, and a crucifix known as the "black cross" (recently restored and no longer quite the same color). To the right of the entrance is a 15th-century tombstone. The **Via Emanuele Toso** (named for a local priest executed during WWII) was also the medieval road connecting the parish church to the town square.

Town Walls

North of the Piazza del Popolo, Via Cantarana leads to the well-preserved medieval town walls and the **Tore dell'Orologio**, a clock tower dating from 1265.

Only in Levanto

Bonassola

This small coastal village to the northeast of Levanto has elegant villas and a walk along the seafront leading to the **Madonna della Punta chapel**, built on a cliff overlooking the sea.

For Active Travelers

Surfing

 Considered the surf spot with the biggest waves in mainland Italy, Levanto has a few surf shops but no rentals so bring a board. The best surf is in October and November, when short, beach-break swells might be as high as 12 feet. (check out the website www.wannasurf.com/spot/Europe/Italy/Mainland/levanto.)

■ The Cinque Terre

The Cinque Terre is arguably the most famous region of Liguria, and the crowds of (mostly American) tourists hiking the trails and sunning themselves on rocky jetties come summer seems testimony that the formerly secret spot is now practically a household name. The onslaught of tourism has put the villages, which are deeply and traditionally tied to their surrounding environment, in the classic predicament of supply and demand. They must determine how many concessions – environmental, societal, cultural, and otherwise – they will make to accommodate the market's hunger for a Cinque Terre experience.

That experience generally involves hiking the trails, formed over centuries, that connect the five villages of Monterosso, Vernazza, Corniglia, Manarola, and Riomaggiore. They cross through olive groves and gardens and areas of natural Mediterranean maquis, offering a vantage to observe the terraced landscape of dry stone walls that enabled habitation of this otherwise inaccessible spot. Once these were the only routes of communication and transport between the hamlets. Then came the railway and just decades ago, road access. Driving is a tortuous experience as cars careen down impossibly narrow and curvy streets from high up the mountainside. And then there's the problem of parking....

All this exposure has had positive and negative impacts on the Cinque Terre, and various institutions are now in place to protect the landscape that's been declared a UNESCO World Heritage Site. The terrain and the sea surrounding it is a national park, and is being carefully stewarded by overseers who hope to turn the Cinque Terre into a model of harmonious integration between humans and their environment. Plans include the opening of natural health centers, where visitors learn traditional earth-based remedies for common ailments, and how holistic living promotes greater individual and planetary peace. In this way the Five Lands intend to transform the Cinque Terre experience into something longer lasting – and more deeply beneficial – than just a tan or some riveting photographs.

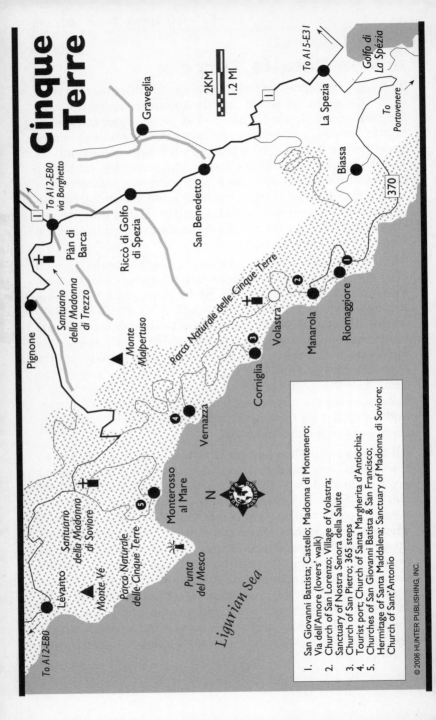

Cinque Terre

To AI2-E80

To AI2-E80 via Borghetto

Pignone

Santuario della Madonna di Trezzo

Piàn di Barca

Riccò di Golfo di Spezia

San Benedetto

Graveglia

2KM
1.2 MI

To AI5-E31

La Spezia

Golfo di La Spézia

To Portovenere

Biassa

370

Monte Malpertuso

Parca Naturalè delle Cinque Terre

Volastra

Manarola

Riomaggiore

2

1

3

Corniglia

Vernazza

4

Monterosso al Mare

Santuario della Madonna di Soviore

Lévanto

Monte Vé

Parco Naturale delle Cinque Terre

5

Punta del Mesco

N

Ligurian Sea

1. San Giovanni Battista; Castello; Madonna di Montenero;
   Via dell'Amore (lovers' walk)
2. Church of San Lorenzo; Village of Volastra;
   Sanctuary of Nostra Senora della Salute
3. Church of San Pietro; 365 steps
4. Tourist port; Church of Santa Margherita d'Antiochia;
   Churches of San Giovanni Batista & San Francisco;
5. Hermitage of Santa Maddalena; Sanctuary of Madonna di Soviore;
   Church of Sant'Antonio

Getting There

By Train: Although each town has its own train station, only local access trains stop at the Cinque Terre villages. Levanto to the north and La Spezia to the south are the connection sites for *Regionale* trains heading to the towns. Between the villages its handy to use the *R* trains, but be certain you consult the timetable (posted at the station) to determine if there are any special exceptions for train traffic on that day (holidays, weekends, etc., may have different schedules). A Cinque Terre Card, purchased in daily increments, gives you unlimited train travel between La Spezia and Levanto. For schedules, see www.trenitalia.it.

By Car: If you're determined to drive, plan on parking far from your destination and lugging your luggage back and forth. Take the A12 autostrada and exit Carrodano-Levanto. Follow the signs to Monterosso (15 km/nine miles), or onward to Vernazza, Corniglia, Manarola, or Riomaggiore.

By Boat: During the Easter holidays and summer season, there is regular ferry service between the villages of the Cinque Terre and the towns on the gulf of La Spezia, provided by the **Consorzio Navigazione-Golfo dei Poeti**. For schedules, see www.navigazionegolfodeipoeti.it. You can purchase a Cinque Terre Card with optional inclusion of unlimited ferry service.

Resources

- www.aptcinqueterre.sp.it

For Active Travelers

The Trails

Most travelers know about the famed hiking trails connecting the five villages of the Cinque Terre. Less well-known are the trails connecting the villages to their respective sanctuaries, and the high-ridge trail connecting Levanto in the west to Portovenere in the east. These are described in detail in *Parks*

of the Cinque Terre, page 204. This chapter also provides information on mountain biking and horseback riding in the Cinque Terre.

Diving

5Terre Diving Center (☎ 0187.920.011, www.5terrediving.com) in Riomaggiore is the dive shop for the Cinque Terre, leading dives to some of the most picturesque spots in the protected marine area, including the Via dell'Amore, the Panettone, and the Landslide of Corniglia. Full equipment rental and certification courses are available. The shop also leads guided snorkel trips to the Via dell'Amore and day trips to some of the exotic coves and beaches of the Cinque Terre. The shop is located in the passageway (Via S. Giacomo) leading to the waterfront in Riomaggiore.

Kayaking/Canoeing

Riomaggiore's **5Terre Diving Center** (☎ 0187.920.011, www.5terrrediving.com) also handles rentals of kayaks and canoes for exploring the coast of the Cinque Terre.

Monterosso

Some relics found here indicate that the Romans colonized Monterosso after the defeat of the Lunigiana, but reliable accounts of the town don't appear before 1056, when a land donation on behalf of the Marquis Guido of the Obertenghi was recorded. The town was contended between the Fieschi and the Malaspina in the 13th century, and passed to Pisa, but in 1276 Monterosso and the rest of the Cinque Terre were incorporated into the Republic of Genoa. (During the failed Fieschi conspiracy against Andrea Doria, however, Monterosso secretly colluded with the Fieschi.) As with other coastal villages, Monterosso endured its share of piracy and built defensive structures to protect its citizens against attack. Its relationship with Genoa not only helped with security, but also helped grow the local economy, based on fishing, the cultivation of lemons and chestnuts, and wine production.

Monterosso is the most developed of the five towns, with a distinct boundary between new and old town roughly demarcated by the Aurora Tower (one of a ring of 13 that once encircled the medieval stronghold). Inside the old town, built upon the hill of San Cristoforo, buildings and residences are much as you'll find them in the other Cinque Terre villages — typically tall, colorful, and narrow and connected by carrugi (alleys) that twine through them. The new town is fronted by Cinque Terre's only true sandy beach.

Being There

In general, Monterosso is not as charming as the neighboring villages, classifying as the only real resort town. Because of development, this is where you'll find the majority of Cinque Terre's hotel rooms but, thanks to the rail lines, ferries, and hiking trails, you can make your home base in Monterosso and still enjoy the relative isolation of the other hamlets.

Tourist Office: Railway Station Monterosso (1st floor), ☎ 0187.817.059, fax 0187.817.151.

Gigante

Monterosso's Gigante is hard to miss, standing as it does at the end of the beach at the entrance to the port. It's a 14-m/eight-foot statue in reinforced steel representing Neptune, and it also bears witness to the history of Monterosso over the last hundred years. Early in the 20th century the town was prosperous, thanks to the fishing industry. Built in 1910 by A. Minerbi and the engineer Levacher, the Gigante once presided over a palatial villa

where revelers danced late into the night on the dance floor of a shell-shaped veranda. The party ended during WWII, when the villa was destroyed by bombings. In 1966, a turbulent storm tore at the coastline and the Gigante was pummeled. It languished for many years until the tourism industry began pumping funds into the local economy. It has since been partially restored, but not reconstructed, perhaps to remind visitors of the fragility of the seaside playground.

Church of San Francesco

The church and its adjoining Capuchin convent were built in the 17th century. Its humble appearance belies the importance of its artistic works, including a *Crucifixion* attributed – albeit controversially – to Van Dyck, and a *Madonna of the Angels* attributed to Oldoino Multedo. Other works include *Veronica* by Bernardo Strozzi and *Derided Christ* by Bernardo Castello.

Church of San Giovanni Battista

Found on the main square of the old town, the church dates to 1244. The façade alternates stripes of white marble and green serpentine and has a rose window attributed to the Masters Matteo and Pietro da Campiglio. Under the window is a pointed arch and lunette featuring a fresco of Christ being baptized by the church's namesake, Saint John the Baptist. Inside, the wooden roof has been restored and ornamentations added over the centuries removed to reveal the stark and elegant original structure. The Baroque altar was added in 1744 to commemorate the church's 500th anniversary. San Giovanni Battista shares the piazza with the *Oratory of the Confraternita dei Neri Mortis et Orationis* and the *Oratory of the Confraternita dei Bianchi of Santa Croce*. Within the former there are frescoes dedicated to the theme of death, and in the latter an organ from the 19th century.

Castle

The castle – built by the Obertenghi family before the village's incorporation into the Republic of Genoa – is today in ruins, standing high atop the hill of San Cristoforo. You can walk the remains of the city wall that once encircled the town, and find watchtowers, including the Aurora Tower, that provided a vantage from which to spot invaders arriving over the sea.

Aurora Tower

Only in Monterosso

Lemon Festival

Held annually on the Saturday proceeding Ascension Sunday (six weeks after Easter Sunday), the Lemon Festival celebrates the citrus that has been so important to the local economy for centuries. The air is perfumed with the scent of lemons and flowers, and the fruits decorate storefronts, windowsills, archways, and residents (small children may be dressed in lemon costumes). Local businesses set out tables with typical lemon products, including *Limoncello* and lemon cakes. A prize is awarded to the biggest lemon grown in Monterosso.

Anchovy Feast

On the second Tuesday of September, the Anchovy Feast is celebrated with free samples of the small, salted fish (caught by local fishermen on the bay of Monterosso), local Cinque Terre wine, music, and dancing on the square until midnight.

Vernazza

Vernazza's splendid and intact medieval architecture is a remnant of the town's profitable relationship with Genoa. Ironically, Vernazza – which was probably a small settlement

in Roman times, but without a large or permanent population because of the frequency of Saracen attacks – had previously incurred the Republic's wrath, because of the raids its sailors carried out against neighboring communities and the maritime traffic of Genoa and Pisa. But when the Fieschi relinquished control of the region in 1276, at which point all the Cinque Terre villages came under Genoa's domain, the cunning and skill of Vernazza's sailors was recognized as an asset and the town was granted lucrative shipping privileges within the Republic.

The town grew prosperous, funding the construction of a magnificent waterfront parish church and a warren of alleyways from which the tall, colorful houses rise, connected by steep stairways that make for intriguing exploring. Genoa also financed the construction of a shipyard (no longer in existence, though the town does have the only "port" in the Cinque Terre) and extensive fortifications inland and along the coast. The Doria castle and its two watchtowers are nearly symbolic of Vernazza, probably the most picturesque of the Five Lands.

Being There

Vernazza's beauty is otherworldly, but that's why everyone's there. In the summer, dining on the piazza, which fronts the tiny beach, is like being at one big party. The residents of Vernazza seem to have taken their popularity – and the crowds – in stride. Maybe that's because in the off-season even Cinque Terre takes a breather, making it a peaceful time to visit. Vernazza is at its most lovely early in the morning, when the fishermen are bringing in the catch and merchants are taking deliveries in the street. It's a good time for a stand-up espresso at the bar while the locals reclaim their turf.

Tourist Office: Railway Station Vernazza, ☎ 0187.812.533, fax 0187.812.546.

Santa Margherita d'Antiochia

Vernazza's parish church is a three-naved 14th-century master-piece. Unusual in Cinque Terre – where churches generally dominate the high regions of the village plan – Santa Margherita is built on the waterfront and waves crash against the side of the building in turbulent weather. Subsequently, the exterior has been renovated several times over the intervening centuries since its construction in 1318. Yet the interior remains intact and virtually unchanged. The entrance is at the apse, rather than the façade, and located near the stairs that were built to accommodate the change in level between the piazza and the church. The front is crowned by an octagonal-shaped bell tower that rises from the space normally reserved for a cupola. The festival of Santa Margherita is celebrated on July 20 with a candlelight procession that departs from the piazza and makes its way uphill, to where the village disappears into vineyards.

Defensive Fortifications

The most strategically important of Vernazza's medieval fortifications was the Belforte, the cylindrical tower rising from the Doria Castle (originally constructed in the 11th century) on the town's rocky spur. From this vantage one could survey the entire coastline and communicate news of any impending attack. Today the tower and castle are among the most photographed sites of the Cinque Terre. The only other fortifications remaining are the squat, square watchtower seaside (now crowned with a restaurant), plus a bit of a tower and town walls reaching out from the garden of a religious site not far from the town center.

Only in Vernazza

Maimuna Grotto

Located between Vernazza and Monterosso, the Maimuna Grotto is a natural aperture extending some 50 feet into the cliff. It's a popular destination for boaters, who drift into the cave and search for signs of the grotto's namesake. Maimuna, a French circus gorilla, supposedly took refuge here after a shipwreck, adapting and surviving for decades on fish.

Holy Feasts

Celebrated on July 20th, the **festival of Santa Margherita** honors Vernazza's patron saint with a candlelight procession from the square to the beginning of the village, followed by fireworks. On the first Sunday of August, pilgrims converge upon Vernazza's sanctuary to venerate the **Madonna of Reggio**, called *Africana* because of her black color.

Corniglia

Corniglia's Roman origins are confirmed both by records that name the land's prosperous farmer, Cornelius (the same records name his mother, Cornelia), and by amphorae found at Pompeii inscribed to indicate they contained the town's famously sweet wine. Though Corniglia shares a common historical theme with its neighbors – it was held by the Fieschi until ceded to Genoa in the 13th century – it developed differently, tied to agriculture rather than fishing and other maritime activities. Perched high above the sea, Corniglia is indeed surrounded by vineyards and it's the home of *sciacchetrà*, Cinque Terre's most famous vintage (made from sun-dried grapes that are squeezed to extract a very concentrated, sugary juice). The village has naturally been moving steadily inland for centuries, as landslides sparked by coastal erosion pulled segments of the southern reach of the village into the water below.

Being There

Corniglia's buildings are lower-slung than their counterparts elsewhere in Cinque Terre (or indeed along the Ligurian coast), more reminiscent of typical inland dwellings. They are organized around the Via Fieschi, named for the town's ancient feudal family. To reach the sea you must take the *Lardarina*, a set of 337 stairs that switchback downhill until they reach the level of the railway station. Then it's an additional hike before you reach Corniglia's famous Guvano beach.

Tourist Office: Railway Station Corniglia, ☎ 0187.812.25.23, fax 0187.812.900.

San Pietro

Built between 1330-1334 in the Baroque style, the exterior wall of the church of St. Peter incorporates portions of a wall from an even older building, built sometime before the 11th century. Construction of the new church was funded by the Fieschi family (even though possession of Corniglia had passed to Genoa a century before). Within the rose window, a 14th-century work attributed to the masters of Pistoia, Matteo, and Piero da Campiglio, is a depiction of a deer, symbol of the village. There is also a 12th-century baptismal fount and a polyptych showing the masters of the church, found at the end of the right aisle. Under the church square is a building with black-stone Gothic arcades, believed to be an old post building of the Fieschi family seat. The church maintains yet another tie to its benefactors. Each June 29th it is the site of the *Torta dei Fieschi*, similar to the celebration in Lavagna in which a cake is shared among the gathered celebrants.

Oratory of Santa Caterina

Saint Catherine Fieschi-Adorno is honored by the Oratory of the Disciplinati, dating to the 18th century and located to one side of the *Largo Taragio* (the town square). The terrace has a magnificent view of the Cinque Terre.

Only in Corniglia

Guvano Beach

In Europe the correct term for a nude beach is "naturalist," and Guvano is just that, taking advantage of its seclusion and aura of secrecy. Finding the beach is a little like finding an exclusive club. To get there, take the stairs down from the village to the level of the train station. At the base you'll see a hand-painted marker reading "Guvano" and pointing down a ramp, away from the path to the train station. Walk  down the ramp past some buildings to reach a gated disused train tunnel. Ring the bell and the gate will slide open, revealing a dimly lit passage through which you'll walk for about 10 minutes before reaching the beach, where an entrance fee (around €5) is collected.

Manarola

The birthplace of Linibaldo Fieschi, who would become Pope Innocenzo IV and orchestrate a power play between the Fieschi and Genoa in the 13th century that resulted in the loss of the region to the Republic. Manarola started life under the Romans. Then, it was likely the land of a family who had a temple here (*Manium Arula*) dedicated to the souls of the departed (*Manes*). It was populated in the 12th century by settlers from Volastra, the town up the hill that was a post station on the Roman road. A castle that once stood here was destroyed in 1273, during the showdown between Genoa and the Fieschi clan, and the remains incorporated into the town visitors see today.

Being There

One of Manarola's most striking features is the seafront, where a massive tunnel channels the waters that once ran down the hillside and empties them into the sea. Over the tunnel is a walkway, which forms part of the town's small lower piazza. Here you can lean over the railing and watch the stream torrent or trickle – depending on the season – and mingle with the waves crashing on the massive rocks that tumble into the sea. The village clusters on the eastern slope of the hillside, with the western slope a vista of vineyards terraced with characteristic dry-stone walls. Up the hill is the town's main piazza, surrounded by the church, oratory, bell tower, and a strange white-painted pyramid that serves as a visual reference for fishermen out working the water.

Tourist Office: Railway Station Manorial, ☎ 0187.760.511.

San Lorenzo

Manarola's parish church is dedicated to the Nativity of the Virgin Mary but known as the church of San Lorenzo. It's a hub of activity every August 10th when the village celebrates the feast day of its patron saint, with parishioners carrying candles down the winding streets and paths that connect the tiers of yellow, pink, and orange buildings to the sea. The church was built in 1338 by the Masters Antelami, and is similar in style to the church built by the same builders at Riomaggiore. Gracing its Gothic façade is a rose window of white carrera marble. Notable works of art in the church are a 14th-century triptych credited to the Master of the Cinque Terre depicting the Madonna and Child flanked by Saint Lawrence and Saint Catherine Adorno-Fieschi, and a second gold-backgrounded triptych with Saint Lawrence, Saint Dominick, and John the Baptist. Also on the piazza are

the square-planned bell tower, the Oratory of the Disciplinati degli Azzurri, and the building of the Lazaret of San Rocco.

Only in Manarola

Hillside Nativity

Each December, Manarola resident Mario Andreoli transforms the hillside opposite the village into a luminous nativity. The figures, entwined with thousands of glowing lights, are made by hand of recycled materials, and new statues are added each year. The scene commences on December 8, and is lit through the Feast of the Epiphany in January.

Riomaggiore

The easternmost of Cinque Terre's villages – the name of which derives from *Rivus Major*, the river (now paved over) running through the middle of town – was founded in the seventh century by Greek refugees escaping religious persecution. Some 500 years later the village became a fief of Marquis Turcotti, Lord of Ripalta (near Brugnato), who built the castle that perches above the town on the hill of Cerrico. Riomaggiore then passed to Nicolo Fieschi, and eventually to the Bishop of Luni, Antonio Fieschi. The family's domination of the region ended in 1276 when the Cinque Terre passed to the Republic of Genoa. The citizens of Riomaggiore, who populated the coast from the inland villages in the 14th century, pursued fishing and transported marble.

Being There

The easternmost of Cinque Terre's five villages is, like Monterosso on the western extreme, larger than the middle three. It's the seat of the national park, with an excellent visitors center located in the train station outside town to the east. From there, it's a short walk through a blue-domed tunnel with mosaic-tiled walls to reach the town. Riomaggiore has plenty of rental services and one of the Cinque Terre's only dive shops, making it a convenient place to organize your water sports itinerary.

Tourist Office: Railway Station Riomaggiore (ground floor), ☎ 0187.920.633, fax 0187.760.092.

San Giovanni Battista

Set high on the western slope of a hill overlooking the village, the church of San St. John the Baptist was built in 1340 under the leadership of the Bishop of Luni. The church is in the Romanesque style and attributed to the Masters Antelami from Genoa, with three naves supported by arches and columns of alternating black and white stones. Notable works of art in the church include the altar crucifix attributed to Anton Maria Maragliano (1664-1739) and Domenico Fiasella's (1589-1669) painting of the sermon of St. John the Baptist. The church façade was made over in the Gothic style in 1870, replacing the crumbling original.

Castle

Behind the village on the hill of Cerrico are the ruins of the 13th-century castle that today serves as a community center for cultural events. The castle fortifications were part of the town's defense system, providing a panoramic lookout over the Ligurian sea. Next to the castle is a small chapel dedicated to St. Rocco and St. Sebastian, commemorating an epidemic that hit the village in 1480 and that, over the course of seven short months, killed 1,500 of the 2,000 villagers. Inside, find a tempera triptych with a gold background attributed to the Tuscan Genoese School portraying the Virgin with Child and two saints.

Only in Riomaggiore

Via dell'Amore

The most famous of the Cinque Terre's trails connects Riomaggiore with its nearby neighbor, Manarola. Though it hails from a decisively unromantic past – it was originally constructed as a route to a powder magazine – on a warm spring or summer day it can become crowded with visitors who take in the sumptuous views and enchanting atmosphere.

Torre Guardiola

To the left of Riomaggiore's marina is **Fossola beach** (really a bunch of rocks), from which a nature trail leads to the **Torre Guardiola**. The former lookout tower is now a center for environmental education, and a rendezvous point for birdwatchers who trek through the Mediterranean maquis observing native species. The tower sponsors a writing program, encouraging visitors to chronicle their experiences with nature in the Cinque Terre.

■ The Bay of La Spezia

The area around the Bay of La Spezia was immortalized in the 19th century by Byron and Shelley, the two poets of the Romantic era who lived, worked, loved, and – in the case of Shelley – died on the bay. It was under their influence that the bay derived its lyrical alias, *Golfo dei Poeti* or "Gulf of Poets." They were drawn to the pristine natural environment. Probably, its very inaccessibility was what made the

Percy Byshe Shelley

towns an elusive goal and the coast a wilderness.

This same inaccessibility kept the area fragmented for much of its history. Individual towns achieved prominence – the now deserted village of **Luni** was an important Roman and medieval port; today its ruins are a fascinating daytrip – but a distinct and interdependent region never emerged.

Even today, the communities retain very separate identities. **La Spezia** is the big city of the gulf, though for much of its history it was in the shadow of the port at Luni or the thriving inland town of Sarzana. The arrival of Napoleon in the first years of the 19th century, and the declaration of La Spezia as

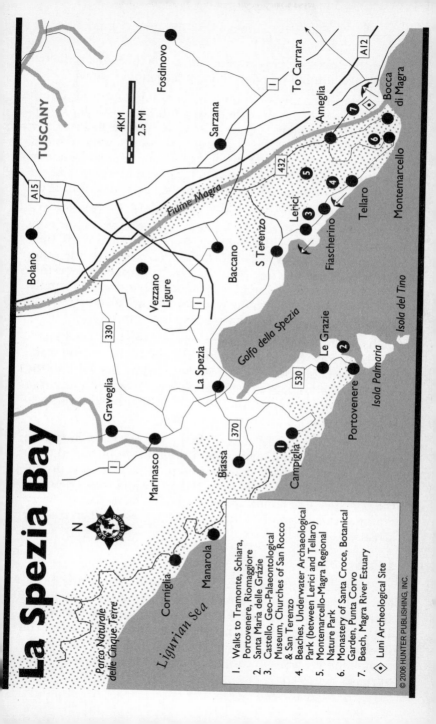

a military prefecture, changed the city's fate (but unfortunately also altered its more charming original layout).

Portovenere guards the mouth of the bay and is arguably the most cosmopolitan little fishing village most people will ever visit. Its beauty has always evoked a passionate response. In 1338 Petrarch wrote "to those who arrive by sea it appears on the shore of the port of Venus and here – among the olive-cloaked hills – it is said that even Minerva was led by so much sweetness to forget Athens, her homeland…."

On the other side of La Spezia, almost exactly opposite Portovenere, is **Lerici**. An ancient village that may or may not have been founded by refugees from the Trojan Wars, thus deriving its former name of *Portus Iliycis* (possibly a variation of *Ilium*, Greek for Trojan), Lerici's early fortunes were established as pilgrims bound for Rome came and went from its port. Today, it's a maze of piazzi and carrugi (alleyways), and walks lead into the hills to evocative hamlets.

High on a hill at the far eastern reach of the bay – and just a stone's throw from the end of Liguria at the border with Tuscany – is Montemarcello. Surrounded by the wilds of the Montemarcello-Magra Regional Nature Park, it's a haunt of intellectuals from Milan and nature lovers who come to explore the park's extensive wetlands.

Traveling inland up the Magra River you arrive at **Sarzana**, capital of the inland territory of Lunigina – a medieval town of fortresses, castles, churches and palazzi. It gained prominence after the fall of the Luni bishopric, and was a point on the pilgrimage to Rome. Today it's most famous for numerous crafts workshops and an annual antique fair held on the city streets.

La Spezia

La Spezia's early history has been eclipsed – especially physically – by its role as the first military port of the Kingdom of Italy. The traveler's experience today is a byproduct of the 19th century, with poignant reminders (as in the case of the Castle of St. George) of what it was like before it was largely demolished, reconfigured, and reconstructed to serve that purpose.

La Spezia

1. Cathedral; Piazza Europa
2. Waterfront promenade
3. Bay of Spezia; Ferries to Lerici, Portovenere, Cinqueterre
4. Museo Tecnico Navale; P'za Chioda
5. Arsenale
6. Santa Maria Assunta; P'za Beverini
7. Castello San Giorgio
8. MAL (Museo A. Lia)
9. Museo Civici; Palazzo Crozza (municipal library)
10. Sports Complex (tennis, pool)
11. Parco del Colombaio
12. Church of Nostra Signora della Salute; Piazza Brin
13. RR Station (*ferrovie*); Piazza St. Boniface
14. Parco di Gaggiola; Parco della Rimembranza
15. Porta Castellazzo; Observatory
16. City Walls
17. To RR Station (Migliarina); Corso Nazionale; Parco Della Maggiolina
18. Piazza Matteotti

Earlier in its existence, La Spezia was a part of Niccolo Fieschi's feudal estate, and because of that affiliation with one of the region's most contentious (in the eyes of Genoa) families, found itself embroiled in conflict between the two powers. But it did eventually come under Genoa's domination as part of the coastal defense system. In the early 17th century, the Castle of St. George – originally constructed in the 13th century – was altered and given the form we see today to fulfill its role in the gulf's protection.

The 19th-century remodeling of the town began in the first years of that century, when Liguria accepted annexation by the French Empire. Napoleon himself called the bay "the most beautiful gulf in the world," and proclaimed La Spezia a military prefecture. Plans were drafted to create a fortified defense system in front of an envisioned town of Napoleonia, to the west towards Portovenere. But the Empire was short-lived and these plans never materialized. The brief reign, however, did bring a building boom as troops, merchants, and others drawn to the economic promise of the prefecture began to populate the town. The medieval walls were literally, and figuratively, broken down as the town moved toward its current incarnation.

The minister Cavour again took up the military significance of the port at La Spezia after the pronouncement of the Kingdom of Italy in 1861. Gigantic building operations were directed by Domenico Chiodo, lasting eight years, with the military shipyard (known as the Arsenal) inaugurated on August 28, 1869.

The populous and prosperous town of the 19th century acquired spaces suitable for the functions of a lively social life. The extensive Public Gardens were orchestrated and villas and hotels were built (or rebuilt) to accommodate wealthy residents and the tourists that were beginning to discover the warm weathered coastal towns of Liguria.

La Spezia continued to grow through the 20th and into the 21st centuries. Buildings from the 1920s are concentrated around the Piazza Verdi and are representative of the artistic movements of that time. Embellishments from later in the century are less harmonious and mostly evident in the eastern sprawl of suburbs. In recent years a series of extensive renovations have sought to reclaim the finer parts of the city's heart, and La Spezia may soon enough become more than a way-station while in transit to the more archetypal towns of the Bay of Poets and the Cinque Terre.

Getting There

 By Train: La Spezia's **FS** station is located just off the city center at Via Fiume. For train information see www.trenitalia.it.

 By Car: From Genoa, La Spezia is off the A12 autostrada. From the east it's on the A15 (La Spezia-Parma) autostrada.

 By Boat: Ferry service between the towns of the gulf and the Cinque Terre is provided by the **Consorio Marittimo Turistico 5 Terre-Golfo dei Poeti** (☎ 0187.732.987, fax 0187.730.336). La Spezia is also a popular launching point for boat travel to (or from) Corsica and Sardinia.

Resources

- www.aptcinqueterre.sp.it
- www.comune.sp.it
- **Tourist Office:** Viale Mazzini, 47, ☎ 0187.254.311, fax.0187.770.908; Piazza Stazione, 1, ☎ 0187.254.311; Viale Mazzini, 45 , ☎ 0187.770.900.

Being There

Though most arrive there by car or train, La Spezia is best appreciated from the sea. Then you see it the way millions of sailors have seen it over the centuries. The main sites cluster to the west backdropped by the imposing Castle of St. George, the streets laid out in an orderly grid. The waterfront is given over to port and shipbuilding activities with the Arsenale – now in part a historical museum complex – occupying pride of place. There's a seafront promenade running parallel to the Viale Italia adjacent to where ships board for passage to Lerici, Portovenere, and the Cinque Terre. Backed by the grounds of the Public Gardens, it's an important socializing spot for town residents.

Castello di San Giorgio

Standing on the Poggio hill is the Castle of St. George, originally built in the 13th century (and entirely rebuilt before that century's close), and subjected to several modifications over the hundreds of intervening years. It acquired the form we see today in the first years of the 17th century when it was remodeled to better suit its role within Genoa's coastal defense system.

After a recent renovation, it is reopened and houses the **Civic Archeological Museum**. Many of its relics were unearthed during construction of the Arsenale in the mid-19th century. These include relics of the Lunigiana culture, including a notable collection of Bronze Age statue-stelae – fascinating anthropomorphic sandstone slabs that were markers throughout the territory. There are also Roman antiquities, many salvaged from the ruins at Luni. (☎ 0187.751.142, fax 0187.754.280, www.castagna.it/sangiorgio, sangiorgio@castagna.it; open Wednesday-Monday, summer 9:30 am-12:30 pm and 5-8 pm; winter 9:30 am-12:30 pm and 2-5 pm; entrance fee €5 adults, €4 students 14-17, €3 children six-13, under six free. €8 combined admission with Museum of Seals and the Museo Amadeo Lia.)

Arsenale

The construction of the Arsenale permanently altered the face and fate of La Spezia. The military/industrial complex spreads over 462 acres, including docks, roads, and mooring basins. Previously only open on holidays and feast days, today there are guided tours of the industrial areas on the weekends.

Along the eastern border of the Arsenale, at the Piazza di Chiodo (named for the architect who brought the complex into being), is the **Museo Tecnico Navale della Spezia**, housing an eclectic collection of memorabilia and artifacts related to the sea and navigation. Most impressive are the collection of ship figureheads. (www.museotecniconavale.it; open Monday-Saturday 8 am-6:45 pm; Sunday 8 am-1 pm; closed March 27-28; August 15; November 1; and December 8, 24-26, and 31; entrance fee €1,55.)

Museo Civico d'Arte Antica, Medievale e Moderna Amedeo Lia

Its present incarnation as a museum is just one of many roles this building has played. Originally a 17th-century Paolotti convent, it was strategically located where the road to Genoa passed through La Spezia's surrounding walls. Via del Prione is one of the few ancient streets remaining in La Spezia. Its name derives from the term for a stone where town criers used to read proclamations to the citizens.

In the last years of the 18th century the building was secularized following suppression of an attempted Jacobin revolution, becoming first a military and then a civic hospital. During its tenure as a hospital the physical form was dramatically changed, with a series of pilasters added inside the church to create spaces to serve as hospital wards. Further changes were made in the 19th and 20th centuries as the building was adapted, becoming a barracks, a residence, and then municipal offices.

The restorations made for the purpose of housing the works donated to the city by Amadeo Lia have created a worthy backdrop for a collection that's been called one of the most important in Europe. Arranged chronologically, the visit passes through rooms of liturgical objects, miniatures, and archaeological relics from the Mediterranean before reaching the paintings. The 13th-18th centuries are represented, with works by some of the most important artists of their genres. Included are Giovanni Bellini's *Nativity*, the *Portrait of a Gentleman* by Titian (largely considered one of his best works of portraiture), and a *St. Martin and the Pauper* attributed to Raphael. The tempura *Self Portrait* on terracotta by Pontormo has become the museum's symbol. There are also bronze and marble sculptures and glass, terracotta, and

The Bay of La Spezia

majolica objects, including an incredibly rare gold-banded bottle dated to the mid-first century BC. (☎ 0187.731.100, fax 0187.731.408, www.castagna.it/mal, segreteria.museolia@comune.sp.it; open Tuesday-Sunday 10 am-6 pm; entrance fee €6 adults, €4 students 14-18, €3 children six-13, under six free.)

Museum of Modern & Contemporary Art

Located on the Piazza Cesare Battisti near the Arsenale and the Public Gardens, the recently opened *Centro Arte Moderna e Contemporanea della Spezia* houses both the civic collection and about 900 works of the Cozzani collection. The civic selection includes works by late 19th-century view-painters Fossati, Valle, and Pontemoli, who were interested in the historical development of the town and its surroundings. It's an intriguing examination of La Spezia's reorganization with the arrival of the Arsenale. Also on offer are works deriving from the Premio del Golfo competition, begun in 1933 and re-instituted between 1949 and 1965, representing the artistic argument over abstract and figurative art that characterized the post-war period.

The Cozzani collection has paintings and drawings from the Expressionist and historical avant-garde movements and proceeds through contemporary works augmented by frequent exhibitions of the works recently contributed by art critic Ferruccio Battolini. (☎ 0187.734.593, fax 0187.256.773.)

Only in La Spezia

Palio del Golfo

On the first Sunday in August this colorful festival transforms the waters just off the promenade. La Spezia's 13 districts compete in a rowing contest for the Palio Prize, a banner representing Saint Venerio, patron saint of lighthouse men and the Gulf of La Spezia. There are also floats, medieval costumes, bands, a feast and folk show, and fireworks on the sea.

Festival of San Giuseppe

La Spezia's patron saint is honored with a three-day party on March 19 (and the days immediately following). Begun in the 16th century, the fair features more than 600 stalls vending various crafts and Ligurian specialties, set up along Viale Mazzini, Via Don Minzoni, Viale Italia, Piazza Europa, and the Morin promenade on the waterfront. On the Sunday preceding, visitors are allowed to visit the Arsenale and to board some of the ships.

Corsica

It's not impossible that Napoleon favored La Spezia because of his Corsican roots – the city and the French island remain in close contact today with ferries departing from the Molo Italia, at the eastern extreme of the Morin promenade, and Molo Garibaldi, off Viale San Bartolomeo. On the other hand, it's entirely probable that Napo-leon regarded La Spezia favorably because his family originally hailed from inland Sarzana.

You can also cruise from La Spezia to Sardinia and Tunisia. Operators include **Happy Lines** (www.happylines.it) to Bastia in Corsica, **Tirennia** (www.tirrenia.it) to Palau in Sardinia and Porto Vecchio in Corsica, and **Medmar** (www.medmargroup.it) to Porto Vecchio and Tunisia.

Cooking Lessons

The La Francesca Holiday Village in Bonassola is a retreat set on 42 acres of parkland. Students sign on for five days of three-hour lessons under the direction of chef Valerio Ellero who teaches the techniques of fresh pasta making and guides students in the preparation of fresh fish dishes (including how to buy and clean whole fish), in addition to other skills and Ligurian cooking recipes. (☎ 0187.813.911, www.villaggilafrancesca.it.)

For Active Travelers

Hiking

La Spezia is the ideal spot for launching hiking trips along the gorgeous trails of the Cinque Terre: There is regular train and ferry service between La Spezia and the five villages. For detailed information on the hiking trails – plus mountain biking and horseback riding in the Cinque Terre – see *Parks of the Cinque Terre*, page 204.

Boating

There are numerous operators in La Spezia renting sailboats and catamarans for sailing on the Gulf of the Poets. Try the **Centro Catamarani Italia** (Via da Passano, 2, ☎ 0187.751.501, www.centrocatamaranitalia.it, info@centrocatamaranitalia.it), which has a sailing school and has been in business in the town for more than a decade.

Portovenere

The name Portovenere derives from Portus Veneris, the town's ancient name that honored a temple to Venus on the site of the current-day Church of San Pietro. In 1113 the village was gifted to the Maritime Republic of Genoa by the Lords of Vezzano, and became Genoa's bastion on the Tyrrhenian sea. The fortified village was built by the Genoese, who erected the fortified walls and castle in 1160. The alleyways that lead from the Calata Doria (the waterfront promenade), called *capitoli*, were strategically narrow, designed with a system of trapdoors and wall slits for defensive purposes. Defense was important, as Portovenere was attacked repeatedly; during the wars between Genoa and Pisa (1119-1290), with the French (1396), with Aragon (1494), and by the Saracen pirates that terrorized the Riviera coastline.

An archway in the loggia leads to Grotto Byron, named for the English poet. In 1816, the writer who would inspire the cult of the defiant, melancholy "Byronic Hero," left England and set-

Above: Chiavari (Casey Finley)
Below: Building in Chiavari (Casey Finley)

Above: On the trail, Cinque Terre (Casey Finley)

Below: Pointing the way to the trails, Cinque Terre

Above: Hilltop Corniglia, Cinque Terre

Below: Vernazza, with the Belforte at the end of the point

Above: The harbor at Vernazza
Below: Vernazza's beach and piazza

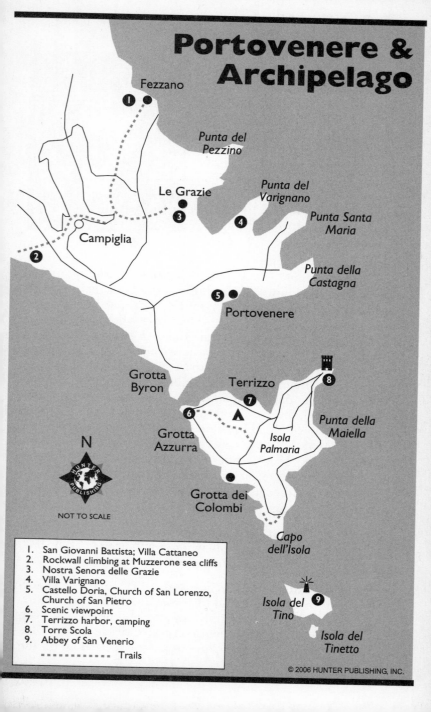

Portovenere & Archipelago

Fezzano

Punta del Pezzino

Le Grazie

Punta del Varignano

Punta Santa Maria

Campiglia

Punta della Castagna

Portovenere

Grotta Byron

Terrizzo

Grotta Azzurra

Isola Palmaria

Punta della Maiella

Grotta dei Colombi

Capo dell'Isola

Isola del Tino

Isola del Tinetto

N

NOT TO SCALE

1. San Giovanni Battista; Villa Cattaneo
2. Rockwall climbing at Muzzerone sea cliffs
3. Nostra Senora delle Grazie
4. Villa Varignano
5. Castello Doria, Church of San Lorenzo, Church of San Pietro
6. Scenic viewpoint
7. Terrizzo harbor, camping
8. Torre Scola
9. Abbey of San Venerio
- - - - - - - - - Trails

© 2006 HUNTER PUBLISHING, INC.

tled in Geneva with Mary and
Percy Shelley. The trio eventually relocated to Italy and in 1822
were living on the Bay of Poets.
Byron is said to have repeatedly
swum between Portovenere and
Lerici – on the interior of the bay,
a distance of some 50 km/30
miles – visiting the Shelleys. The
Grotto is mythologized as the
spot where he would lie in the
sun, resting and composing
poetry after these prodigious
swims.

Lord Byron

Today, Portovenere is a stylish resort town. Strolling up the
Via Capellini – known colloquially as the *Carruggio* – you'll
notice, in addition to shops peddling standard postcards,
t-shirts and other tourist fare – boutiques where artisan versions of everything from leather shoes to pesto are on offer.
Unlike nearby Cinque Terre – where during the summer the
language of the street seems to be English, thanks to the
hordes of American tourists – the vibe is cosmopolitan Italian.
Older women in dark sunglasses and good shoes carry shopping bags on their arms, and tan children in sandals run up
and down the cobblestone streets while their parents and
often grandparents sit in cafés or stroll leisurely, deep in con-
versation. This is a holiday destination for Italians who
appreciate, among other things, the numerous restaurants
serving good, authentic regional cuisine.

Getting There

By Train: The nearest train station to Portovenere
is at La Spezia, from where you'll need to drive, bus,
or boat. For schedules, see www.trenitalia.it.

By Bus: From La Spezia, the **ATC** line has bus service on lines P and 11. From July-August and during weekends from Easter to September buses run
from 10 am-8 pm with on-board ticket service. Bus
stops are Portovenere and Campiglia (see section on hiking

from Portovenere to Campiglia, below). For information, see www.atclaspezia.it or ☎ 0187.522.511.

By Car: A12 motorway from Genoa-Livorno, or A15 motorway from La Spezia-Parma. Exit at the tollbooths for Las Spezia. Take SS 330 to Portovenere.

By Boat: Numerous big and small companies and operators run boats between La Spezia, Portovenere, and the villages of the Cinque Terre. You'll find their docks and ticket offices harborside during the summer months. The largest and most reliable operator is **Navigazione Golfo dei Poeti** (www.navigazionegolfodeipoeti.it, ☎ 0187.39.732.987), which is part of the Consorzio Marittimo Turistico 5 Terre. In addition to discovery excursions around the bay and to the islands of the archipelago, they run ferry service to the Cinque Terre.

Resources

- www.portovenere.it
- www.golfodeipoeti.com
- **Tourist Office:** Piazza Bastreri, 7, 19025 Portovenere, ☎ 0187.790.691, fax 39.0187.790.215.

Being There

You can reach Portovenere by land, coming via car or train, but approaching from the sea is one of the pleasures of traveling in this region of Liguria. Sheer granite cliffs plunge into the sea between the

town and Riomaggiore, the last town of the Cinque Terre. The contrast in colors – the turquoise of the sea, the white-burned grey of stone, the chartreuse and mustard yellow of clinging

The Bay of La Spezia

Portovenere

Mare Ligure (Ligurian Sea)

Strada com. Crocetta

Salita al Castello

Via Tre Tori
Via Colonna
Via Capellini

Via della Chiesa

Via Capellini

Piazza Spallanzani

Via Martina

Via Garibaldi

Via dell'Olivo

Harbor

1. City Gate, chapter tower
2. Piazza Bastreri; Tourist office
3. Town hall, bank, local police
4. Church of San Lorenzo
5. Castillo Doria
6. Cemetery
7. St. Ambrose's Fort (Lambrescia)
8. Arpaia Bay; Byron's Grotto
9. Church of San Pietro; carabinieri
10. "Le Bocce"
11. Calata Doria (quay)
12. Molo Dondero
13. Pontile (dock); ship harbor
14. Passeggiata Aldo Moro

sea scrub – is remarkable, and then emotionally punctuated by the appearance of castle ruins that seem hewn from the cliffs themselves. Byron's Grotto opens, as wildly romantic as one would assume, just before the harbor's entrance, which is heralded by the unlikely Church of San Pietro at the extreme end of the promontory. Passing through the gap between the promontory and Palmaria Island, the entrance to the Bay of La Spezia, the town becomes visible in all its colorful glory.

Via Capellini

The village's main street runs uphill parallel to the waterfront, ending at the open space before the church of San Pietro, once the center of the *castrum vetus* and today named for the 18th century biologist and naturalist Spallanzani. At the down slope of Via Capellini, on the small square that fronts the harbor, you'll find the medieval door of the village, where the inscription *Colonia Januensis 1113* and three marble grain-measuring basins from 1606 can still be seen. In 1896, in a niche above the inside of the gateway, a fresco of the Madonna Bianca dated to 1494 was discovered.

Church of San Lorenzo

Built in 1116 and consecrated by Pope Innocent VI in 1130, the church sits above the village off the Via Capellini, accessible via a flight of stairs beginning midway up the "mount to the castle." A 15th-century altarpiece contains a 14th-century parchment painting that is the subject of local legend. The *Madonna Bianca*, or White Madonna, patron saint of the village, was believed brought to Portovenere by the sea in 1204, and miraculously transformed into its current form on August 17, 1399. This is celebrated each year on that date with a torchlight procession and the lighting of some 1,500 oil lamps that are placed all over the promontory of San Pietro. Other treasures found within the church include a trunk of Lebanese cedar, believed to have transported the Madonna's image, and several Byzantine and Syriac ivory coffers dating to the 10th-11th centuries. The campanile (bell tower) of the Church of San Lorenzo was destroyed in 1494 during the battle with the Aragonese, and immediately rebuilt in its current form.

Church of San Pietro

Built in 1277 on the foundation of the Roman temple to Venus, today it is the postcard symbol of Portovenere. It rises dramatically over the sea on the very edge of the promontory that guards the harbor. An early sixth-century Christian building of black Palmaria marble was extended, featuring typically Genoese bands of black and white stone. The Romanesque *loggetta* (loggia) was added later.

Castello Doria

High above Portovenere, on the slope of the hill, is the castle built under Genoese rule in 1160 and augmented in the late 15th and early 16th centuries. The massive structure is largely intact and has astonishing views. Notable among the many great halls, fortresses, and ramparts is the large "hypostyle" room, so named for the great columns supporting a flat roof. Under Emperor Napoleon's rule, beginning in 1797, the castle was used as a political prison. The hypostyle room was divided into cells, and today deep scratches in the stone testify to the bars that created cages for unlucky captives. (Open Saturdays and Sundays 10 am-1 pm and 2-5 pm; entrance fee €2.10, free to children under seven.)

Only in Portovenere

Saying 'I Do'

If you'd like to celebrate your nuptials in Portovenere, the Castle is available to overseas visitors for civil wedding services. Ceremonies can be held in one of the halls, on the panoramic terrace, or in the amphitheater. The cost is nominal (around €550), and more information is available at the tourist office or at www.portovenere.it.

Le Grazie

Picturesque Le Grazie lies on an inlet of the bay between Portovenere and La Spezia. It's a quiet hamlet, built around the Church of Our Lady of Le Grazie, built in the 14th century. In the church you'll find a wooden choir stall credited to Fra Paolo di Recco, a refectory frescoed by Nicolo Corso, and several paintings including the Madonna delle Grazie attributed to Andrea de Aste.

The church was a part of the larger monastery complex owned by the Olivetani monks, who were entrusted with the Abbey of Tino by Pope Eugenio IV in 1432. Today, much of the monastery has been converted into private homes.

A road from Le Grazie leads to an important Roman archaeological site at Varignano. The villa ruins were unearthed between 1965 and 1986, and include a residential area for the *dominus* (owner) and another for the *villicus* (farmer). Visitors can investigate a thermal plant, cistern, oil mill, ceramic remains, containers, and statues. A small museum is underway.

Those who choose to stop in Le Grazie will appreciate the tranquility to be found under the palms during a stroll along the picturesque waterfront promenade, which runs the entire length of the bay from the point of Varignano to Pezzino point.

Exploring the Archipelago

A notable geographic feature of Portovenere is the nearby archipelago, composed of the islands of Palmaria and Tino and the islet of Tinetto. Palmaria is the largest of the three, located on the other side of *Le Bocche*, the strait separating the island from the mainland. Its beaches are popular with residents of La Spezia, who come for the weekends in summer. The islands are accessible by ferry from La Spezia.

Most casual visitors take a sea trip around the three islands. It's a good way to admire their dramatic polychrome cliffs. Combinations of several different types of rock – grey, pink, and red limestone; white, pink, and gold-spotted dolomite; greenish marl; red-purple jasper; grey and purple flint – create layers of color that plunge into the blue sea.

The Bay of La Spezia

Sea trips depart from the harbor at Portovenere, generally heading into the bay to circumnavigate Palmaria and Tino, rounding Tinetto back into the Ligurian Sea, and re-entering the Bay to dock. As you leave Portovenere, look back toward the land on the interior of the bay, away from the village center. You might notice supports and buoys marking the mussel farms of the Seno dell'Olivo. More of these are visible off Palmaria, inside the little cove of Seno del Terizzo, past the docks at Terizzo (where most of the island's buildings are clustered).

● **Palmaria**

If you've opted, rather than a trip around the three islands, for a trip exclusively to Palmaria, you'll dock at Terizzo. Exploring by foot, the trail is marked by the letter "a" bracketed by two red rectangles. You'll head eastward along Via Schenello, walking toward the Forte Umberto I and a view of the Scola Tower that rises out of the sea off the coast, today used as a lighthouse. The fort was built in the 19th century, but the Tower dates from 1606-1608. It has 12-foot-thick walls, built to resist artillery bombardment, and was intended to guard the Seno del Terizzo from attack.

A dirt road leads away from the fort toward Punta Mariella, and then onward toward Cala del Pozzale, where there are resorts used exclusively by the Italian Air Force. It then continues toward Punta Ziguella, from which there is a view of the island of Tino. Near here the footpath runs above the **Grotta dei Colombi** (Cave of the Pigeons), which is accessible but dangerous to reach, requiring the assistance of a rope hanging for that purpose. The famed **Grotta Azzurra** (Blue Cave) is also on the western cliffs, but accessible only by sea. It is generally featured on the itinerary of sea trips around Palmaria, or around the three islands as a group.

The northwestern tip of the island is reached by a dirt road that departs from the paved path between Forte Cavour and Batteria Semaforo. It goes steeply downhill through pine trees, then turns along the northern coast, passing the Villa San Giovanni – which may have been the site of an ancient convent – then arrive back at Terrizzo.

By sea, after passing the wharf at Pozzale, the boats head south toward Tino, which is today a military zone. Access by foot to the island is limited to the festival of Saint Venerio, annually on September 13th, when his feast is celebrated with a candlelit procession to the 11th century monastery remains. Venerio, born on Palmaria in 560, was charged with reforming the wayward monks of the monastery at Portovenere, precursor of the church of San Pietro. He became beloved of his followers, retired to Tino, and died in 630. He is the saint of the Gulf of La Spezia and protector of its lighthouse keepers. Visitors to Tino might also be lucky enough to see the leaf-fingered gecko, a rare and protected species found in Liguria only on Tino, Tinetto, and in Torre Quezi near Genoa.

It is then on toward **Tinetto**, which is little more than a rock surrounded by dangerous shoals. After rounding the island, boats proceed up the western coast of Tino, and the **Grotta del Lupo** (Cave of the Wolf) can be seen. It is so named for the sound the waves make as they enter and exit the grotto.

For Active Travelers

Hiking to Campiglia –
Rock Climbing at Monte Muzzeronek

A hiking path, marked as "1" and "1a," leads from the square on the waterfront, directly in front of the medieval door at the foot of the Via Capellini. It travels toward Campiglia, a small coastal village that is the crossroads for many other hiking paths and terminal for buses to La Spezia. It is possible to hike to Campiglia, then take a bus back to Portovenere.

At first, the path climbs steeply uphill, skirting the castle walls. It then enters abandoned olive groves overgrown with Mediterranean maquis. If you fork to the left, the trail descends toward the church of San Pietro. This part of the trail, the *Sentiero dell'Infinito* (the Infinite Path), passes the cemetery and botanical gardens.

To the right, the trail joins the road to Monte Muzzerone, from which trail 1a branches off uphill to the 19th-century Forte Muzzerone. Around the fort there are several rocky mountainsides suitable for rock climbing. There are more than 400 itineraries of different difficulties, used by the **Free Climbing School of the Club Alpino Italiano** (C.A.I.) of La Spezia (www.cai.it).

The main path goes on and off the paved road heading toward Pitone, where there is a lookout with a panoramic view of Portovenere and Palmaria island. A narrow path from here leads to a castle-shaped private building. The main trail then goes over the Valle d'Albana, meeting the paved road that leads to La Spezia. It leaves the pavement again after a short bit, heading through pine trees. Trail 11a branches from here, leading to the bottom of the Valle d'Albana. The main footpath passes an old windmill once used to grind chestnuts, passes the church of Santa Caterina, and then ends at the square of Campiglia.

Along these paths, one notices abundant flora and fauna. There are sword lilies and wild orchids, oleasters, holm oak and Aleppo pine trees. The cliffs and the verdure attract red-legged partridges, ravens, blue rock thrushes, red-rumped swallows, and peregrine falcons. Perhaps even more spectacular, however, are the sweeping views over the sea and Gulf of La Spezia.

Beaches

 Two beaches – **Arenella** and **Sporting Beach** – are located away from the city center on Via dell'Olivio. Per the Ligurian norm, beaches are characterized by bright umbrellas, pebbly sand, bars where you can buy drinks and ice cream bars for refreshment. There is a fee for entrance. For more information, contact Arenella at ☎ 0187.790.380 or Sporting Beach at ☎ 0187.790.666.

On Palmeria, **Il Gabbiano** beach is located at Terizzo, with a view across La Bocche to Portovenere. For more information, ☎ 0187.792.710, or spiaggiagabbiano@tiscalinet.it.

Lerici

Lerici is a town that has for millennia made its fortune from the coming and going of others. Early in its history Lerici – then closely tied to the town of Luni – was a landing harbor for Greek and Phoenician traders (and possibly refugees from the Trojan War). An important port, it was conquered by the Romans, who used it for both military and commercial purposes.

In the middle ages Lerici was an important waystation for pilgrims. Bound for St. Jacopo di Campostela or Rome, they passed through Lerici on their way to Sarzana, a point on the Francigena Road (named for its French origin) that was a medieval thoroughfare for the faithful.

In the 13th century the port was disputed between and Genoa and Pisa, who occupied the town until 1256, building both the castle and the walled hamlet. Modifications to the castle were made after the town was conquered by Genoa, and it became a popular destination for the wealthy Genoese, including the Doria. It is said that in 1528 Andrea Doria took refuge in a Lerici palace while deliberating the decision to change allegiance from France to Spain and Charles V – a portentous decision for the Republic.

During the Risorgimento the town distinguished itself, winning praise from Garibaldi who called its population "the strongest and most energetic of Italy." Giuseppe Petriccioli, a native of Lerici, was atop the Duomo of Milan raising the tri-colored Italian flag after fighting on the barricades during the famous "Five Days" battle.

Getting There

By Train: The nearest **FS** stations are at La Spezia or Sarzana. From there you can take an ATC bus from the train station. For schedules see www.trenitalia.it.

By Car: Exit at La Spezia from both the A12 and A15 autostrada.

By Boat: Numerous ferries call at Lerici. For service around the gulf or to the Cinque Terre, look for the **Navigazione Golfo dei Poeti** boats (www.navigazionegolfodeipoeti.it, ☎ 0187.39.732.987).

 By Bus: Bus service around the gulf is provided by **ATC** (www.atclaspezia.it).

Resources

- www.aptcinqueterre.sp.it
- www.comune.lerici.sp.it
- **Tourist Office:** Via Biaggini, 6, ☎ 0187.967.346.

Being There

Popularized with travelers during the Romantic period, when Byron and Percy and Mary Shelley were frequently found here, Lerici is still a favorite destination, but isn't as picturesque as others on the gulf due to new construction. The castle sits on a promontory overlooking the gulf and a tangle of narrow streets and stairs flow down the hill toward the waterfront. Near the castle are the remains of 16th-century Jewish quarter, marked by an archway (at the intersection of Piazza Mottino and Via del Ghetto) where once a gate enclosed the population at night.

Castle

 Built by the Pisans in the 13th century – when the town was disputed between the Tuscan town and Genoa – the castle is one of the best-preserved military complexes in Liguria. It was the Genoese who added additional fortifications in the 16th and 17th centuries, including the pentagonal tower and the

outer walls. Inside, there is a lovely 13th-century Chapel of Sant'Anastasia. The castle is also home to the **Geo-Palaeontological Museum**, dedicated to the age of the dinosaurs. (☎ 0187.969.042; open November-March, Tuesday-Saturday 9 am-1 pm and 2:30-5:30 pm, Sunday and holidays 9 am-6 pm; September, October, and April-June, Tuesday-Saturday 9 am-1 pm and 3-7 pm, Sundays and holidays 9 am-7 pm; July and August, 10 am-1 pm and 5-midnight.)

Oratory of San Rocco

This 14th-century church was originally dedicated to Saints Martino and Cristoforo. There's a tablet testifying to this fact on the front of the bell tower, originally constructed as a lookout point. It was consecrated to Saint Rocco, patron of the plague-stricken, in 1523 after the town endured several pestilences. The artistic works mostly date from that period, including a *Madonna della Salute* executed on slate. The high altar has a painting of *St. Bishop Martin, St. Christopher, St. Sebastian and St. Roch* on wood.

Church of San Francesco

The oratory here is dedicated to San Bernardino, popularly believed to have delivered a sermon from the slate pulpit here in the 16th century. The church itself, rebuilt in the 17th century, has altarpieces from the Genoese school.

Only in Lerici

San Terenzo

A stone's throw from Lerici, heading toward La Spezia, is the seaside town of San Terenzo. It was here, in the waterfront **Villa Magni**, that Lord Byron and Percy Bysshe and Mary Shelley  were staying at the time of Shelley's drowning. Ten days after his death he was cremated on a funeral pyre on the beach. A museum in the castle (originally completed in the 15th century and modified in the 16th) is now dedicated to the lives of the

Shelleys. The **Villa Marigola** facing the San Terenzo Bay is now a conference center surrounded by lush gardens.

Tellaro

Take a boat or hike to the small coastal hamlet of Tellaro, between Lerici and Montemarcello. The small fishing village is as picturesque as any of the Cinque Terre but is less over-run with American tourists than the famed five. Legend maintains that an octopus once crept ashore and rang the church bells, warning the inhabitants of an impending pirate attack and saving Tellaro. Between Lerici and Tellaro is the Caletta Bay, where the remains of a Roman ship are sunk at a depth accessible to skin divers. There's a path to the public beach on the site.

For Active Travelers

Hiking

Several walks into the hills (part of the Parco Regionale di Montemarcello-Magra) depart from Lerici. In one hour you can reach the hamlet of **Barbazzano** situated in an olive grove. From Piazza Garibaldi go up Via Andrea Doria and then the provincial road for Tellaro; the trail splits off in front of nº3 and leads to Barbazzano; return by the same route. In two hours you can reach **La Serra** with a view of the eastern gulf. Take Via Andrea Doria to the provincial road for Tellaro; cross the road and take the mule-track to La Serra. Return by the provincial road to Barcola and then Via Canata to reach the waterfront promenade near the gardens. Around La Serra there is evidence of a megalithic civilization, with dry-stone dwellings that may have been used in funeral rites.

Diving

Try **Tropicana Diving** for guided trips to spots in the gulf. They're on the Marina del Muggiano. (☎ 335.532.77.35, fax 0187.562.356, info@tropicanadiving.com.)

Montemarcello

Of very ancient origins, Montemarcello is a hilltop village probably named for the Roman consul Claudio Marcello, who

vanquished the Liguri Apuani in 155 BC. The area was strategically important. Just west of the Magra river was the
prosperous town of Luni and the Carrara quarries, famed
source of lovely white marble. The river itself forms a fertile
plain stretching inland. From the town's hilltop vantage you
can survey the gulf to one side, and the mouth of the Magra,
the stretch of the plains, and the Apuane Alps on the other.
Reflecting its history, the streets are laid out in the Roman
"castrum" fashion with narrow, perpendicular alleys.

After the fall of Rome there were tumultuous years before the
ascendance of the Luni bishopric, which dominated the town
until the 13th century. It then became the property of
Castruccio Castracani, lord of Lucca, who established a
podestà (a local administrator appointed by the Republic)
inland at Ameglia governing Montemarcello, Ameglia, and
Barbazzano.

Eventually – as with most of Liguria – the town came under
the domination of Genoa, an event preceded by the brief
15th-century Montemarcello independence. This was
declared after the residents refused to be recruited for labor to
build Ameglia's castle walls. They instead petitioned Genoa
to build their own. A door in the castle walls faces in the direction of Ameglia.

In the 20th century, Montemarcello was a German WWII
stronghold with batteries placed against the advancing
"Gothic Line." The Allies vigorously bombed the town. The
main evidence of this today is the Piazza November, formed of
five ruined homes lost in the attack. After the war
Montemarcello slipped into obscurity until it was "discovered" near the end of the 1950s by intellectuals from Milan.
Today its incorporation into the Montemarcello-Magra Regional
Park protects it from any development, encapsulating its
ancient atmosphere and magnificent natural environment.

Getting There

 By Train: The nearest train stations are at La
Spezia or Sarzana. From the station take an ATC
bus to Montemarcello.

The Bay of La Spezia

By Car: From the A12 or A15 autostradas, exit Sarzana. Accessible from the Via Aurelia.

 By Bus: You can reach Montemarcello by **ATC** bus from La Spezia or any of the towns along the gulf. See www.atclaspezia.it.

Resources

■ www.parks.it/parco.montemarcello.magra

■ www.parcomagra.it

Being There

Montemarcello is small, calm, and quiet; more profoundly influenced by its proximity to the rich regional park than tourism. There are few sites but plenty of natural beauty and visitors are drawn to its rustic, sleepy ambiance. From the hilltop, hiking paths lead through the maquis to the beach at Punto Corvo. The area beaches are only accessible by foot or boat, lending them an air of seclusion. Paths lead to neighboring hilltop towns (like Ameglia), and to the rich fluvial plain bordering the Magra River. The botanical garden is a standout for nature lovers.

Monastery of Santa Croce

The apse and part of the presbytery are all that remain of the original church upon which Benedictine monks raised the monastery in 1176. The first structure is the subject of legend. It commemorated a boat that arrived on the shore without sailors, transporting the crucifix of San Nicodemo and relic of the saint's blood. Dante visited the monastery, which sits near the hilltop of Punta Bianca at the southern tip of the promontory, during his trip to negotiate a peace between the Prince-Bishop of Luni and the Marquis of Malaspina. In the early 19th century the monastery was seized and sold to a businessman who built the castle. Today it is home to the House for Spiritual Exercises of the order of Barefoot Carmelites.

Botanic Garden

The splendid Montemarcello-Magra Botanical Gardens sprawl over several acres of the summit of Mt. Murlo, a peak north of the city (accessible by the provincial road between Montemarcello and La Serra or the hiking trail n°1 from Montemarcello). Local flora are clustered and presented in zones representing the types of typical vegetation environments – Mediterranean maquis, Aleppo pine woods, deciduous oak forest, and herbs and flowers. There are also protected species, including cream narcissus and wild orchids, and medicinal plants. The park has a welcome point, rest areas, and offers guided tours. (☎ 0187.691.071, info@parcomagra.it.)

Only in Montemarcello

Parco Naturale Regionale di Montemarcello-Magra

Established in 1995, Montemarcello's regional park covers 7,533 acres stretching across the Caprione promontory and up the fluvial plain of the Magra river, reaching its junction with the Vara River. There are several distinctly different environments captured within the park's boundaries and neatly encapsulated in the Botanic Garden at Mt. Murlo. The wetlands along the riverbanks are lush with willows and alders and other aquatic plants, home to a startling variety of birdlife. The terrain climbing toward the promontory peaks is wooded with maritime pines and groves of deciduous trees, changing to Mediterranean maquis and Aleppo pine woods along the rocky coast. While hiking the trails you might come across wild boar, hedgehogs, weasels, or badgers.

Year-round the park organizes Sunday morning guided walks in the Montemarcello promontory and along the river (some on bikes). Through a program called *Il Parco in Battello* they also host boat trips from Fiumaretta at the river's mouth to Tellaro up the coast, led by a naturalist guide. For more information on any of these programs, contact the park offices in Sarzana. (☎ 0187.691.071, fax 0187.606.738.) There's also a welcome center in the village of Montemarcello, but it is open only sporadically.

Punta Corvo

The peaceful beach of Punto Corvo is nicknamed *spiggione*, or "big beach," which is a relative term in this area, where beaches are the product of landslides. Reached by trail n°3d from Montemarcello, it has dark grey sand and crystal clear water over a rocky sea bottom.

Luni

Accessible from the Via Aurelia on the other side of the Magra, the excavations at Luni are a powerful reminder of the impermanence of human fortune (or, at least Petrarch thought so). Founded in 177 BC, it was a thriving Roman city

Roman amphithater at Luni

– the amphitheater could seat 5,000 – built next to the ancient coastline, which began to silt up several hundred years later. At first the inhabitants stayed on, but after malaria outbreaks in the 11th and 12th centuries the site was abandoned and its people moved inland, swelling the population of towns like Sarzana. The **Museo Archeologico Nazionale** is on the excavated site, exhibiting Roman and other artifacts. (☎ 0187.668.11; closed Mondays, January 1, May, and December 25; open 9 am-7 pm.)

Cooking Lessons

The **Locanda dell'Angelo** in Ameglia has week-long cooking lessons for enthusiastic gourmets with chef/owner Angelo Paracucci and other Michelin-starred chefs as teachers. Ligurian cuisine is emphasized, but you'll also find courses dedicated to the use of chocolate in dessert making. Seminars including lessons, meals, lodging at the hotel, and excursions to neighboring areas (Cinque Terre, Luni, Lerici, etc.). (☎ 0187.643.91.2, fax 0187.643.93, info@paracucchi-locanda.it, www.paracuccilocanda.it.)

For Active Travelers

Hiking

 The best way to explore the Montemarcello-Magra regional park is on foot, and it is crisscrossed by a network of well-maintained trails (some of which are also open to mountainbikers) that pass through some of the promontory's small villages. The paths are signaled by a red and white marker.

From Montemarcello:

- Trail n°1 leads to **Mt. Murlo** (site of the Botanic Gardens), then onward to **Zanego** from which n°3 and then n°3h lead to **Tellaro**, a fishing village on the coast.

- Taking trail n°3 east toward the river brings you to **Bocca di Magra** (a popular yachting town).

- Splitting from trail n°3 before Bocca di Magra is trail n°3a, leading to the cliffs of **Punta Bianca** and the **Santa Croce monastery**.

- Trail n°3d is the path to the beach at **Punta Corvo**.

- Hiking trail n°1 a brief stretch and then trail n°2 you can reach the town of **Ameglia**.

Diving

 There are dive shops in the nearby towns of Bocca di Magra and Fiumaretta, on the right and left banks of the Magra River respectively (where the river empties into the sea). **Osso di Seppia** (☎ 0187.609.042, ossodiseppiadiving.com, diving@ossodi-seppiadiving.it) is a full-service center leading dives to some of the underwater caves and grottos in the area. **Lorenzo Sub** (☎ 0187.640.11, www.lorenzosub.com, lorenzo-sub@lorenzosub.com) does full- and half-day dives around the gulf and to sites along the Cinque Terre. Both shops will provide transport from the Sarzana train station if you're arriving by rail.

Sarzana

The inland town of Sarzana, sitting on the eastern banks of the Magra river, is mentioned for the first time on a document

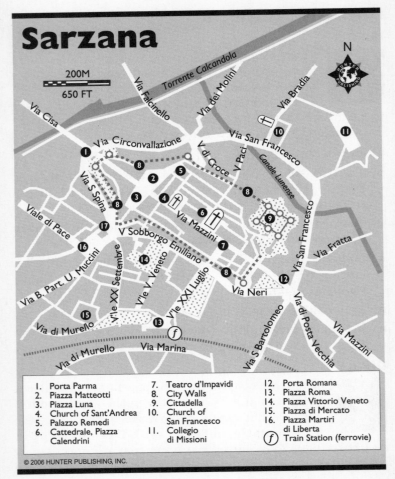

Sarzana

200M
650 FT

N

1. Porta Parma
2. Piazza Matteotti
3. Piazza Luna
4. Church of Sant'Andrea
5. Palazzo Remedi
6. Cattedrale, Piazza Calendrini
7. Teatro d'Impavidi
8. City Walls
9. Cittadella
10. Church of San Francesco
11. Collegio di Missioni
12. Porta Romana
13. Piazza Roma
14. Piazza Vittorio Veneto
15. Piazza di Mercato
16. Piazza Martiri di Liberta
(f) Train Station (ferrovie)

dated 963. A few hundred years later the population would swell, thanks to the arrival of refugees from Luni, the once thriving coastal town, who departed after the harbor silted-up and the resulting bogs and marshes spawned devastating outbreaks of malaria. The powerful bishopric of Luni was also transferred early in the 13th century, and for a short time Sarzana was a powerful, independent commune.

But its strategic position on the valley floor – it effectively controlled all roads passing through from the gulf to the inland reaches beyond, including the Francigena road carrying pilgrims to St. Jacopo di Campostela or Rome – made it too tempting a prize. Recognizing its vulnerability, Sarzana constructed its first city walls. But this did not ward off attack. Castruccio Castracani, Master of Lucca (who also held nearby Montemarcello) dominated the town from 1314 to 1328. Soon the Pisans conquered, then the Visconti, and at the height of Medici rule in Florence under Lorenzo the Magnificent, Sarzana fell to the Florentines. Genoa seized control in the 16th century (first under the auspices of the Bank of St. George) and in 1562 the town became an official commune of the Republic of Genoa. It was during this time that Francesco Buonaparte, ancestor of Napoleon, left Sarzana for Corsica. The family's tower-residence was near Via dei Fondachi.

The ancient core of Sarzana remains largely intact and encircled by its medieval walls, with a large *cittadella* complex at its western end and, closer to the river, the Piazza Matteotti, around which are clustered several palaces. The course of the Francigena road is still represented by Via Bertoloni and Via Mazzini, which enters the old town at the Porta Parma and exits at Porta Romana, near the fortress.

Getting There

 By Train: The **FS** station is at Piazza Roma outside the old town off Via XXI Luglio. For schedules see www.trenitalia.it.

 By Car: Exit the A12 or A15 autostradas at Sarzana. The Via Aurelia also passes through the town.

Resources

- www.comune.sarzana.org
- www.valdimagra.com
- **Tourist Office:** Piazza San Giorgio, ☎ 0187.620.419, iatsarzana@libero.it.
- **Montemarcello-Magra Regional Park:** Via Paci, 2, ☎ 0187.691.071.

Being There

Sarzana has an entirely different ambiance than the coastal villages, in part established by its Tuscan architecture, a remnant of the rule of the Medicis during the 15th century. Because it was built on a relatively flat plain it is larger than the seaside hamlets, and has a grid layout with wide streets. Trapezoidal **Piazza Matteotti** – adjacent to the main trade corridor (Via Mazzini) – became the heart of the town in the 15th and 16th centuries, and several palaces were built around its perimeter. In August the streets of the old town are enlivened when the **Soffita della Strada** (Attic on the Street) is held. Sarzana is a great departure point for exploring the castle-filled **Val di Magra**.

Cattedrale S. Maria Assunta

Sarzana's cathedral stands on a square dedicated to Pope Niccolo V, born in the town in the 14th century. An 18th-century statue of the Pope – flanked by others of St. Eutichiano and Sergio VI – crowns the white marble façade. A mishmash of artistic styles representing several renovations over the intervening centuries, the cathedral was constructed on the remains of the church of San Basilio in the 13th century. All that remains of the former structure is the church tower. Inside, in the Chapel of the Crucifixion, is a precious crucifix known as  the *Cross of Maestro Guglielmo* from the 12th century. Other treasures include several paintings (*The Visitation of Mary to St. Elizabeth, Massacre of the Innocents*, and the *Martyrdom of St. Andrew*). The latter has a supposed self-portrait by Domenico Fiasella, a 16th-century artist hailing from the town and known as *Il Sarzana*.

Pieve di S. Andrea

One of Sarzana's most ancient structures, the Romanesque church of Sant'Andrea was built late in the 10th century, though recent renovations suggest an even older building was on the site first. Remodeled in the 15th and 16th centuries, it has an unusual door that probably originally graced a secular residence. Another Fiasella work (*The Vocation of Saints James and John*) is found here, along with other paintings from the 14th through 16th centuries.

Cittadella

When the Florentines conquered the town in the mid-15th century, the first thing to go was the castle erected by the Pisans in 1429. Under the direction of the architects Franceso di Giovanni and Domenico di Francesco the *Firmafede* fortress arose, dominating the eastern part of the old town. Under the Genoese the defensive structure, including its encircling moats, was enlarged. In the 19th century the cittadella was modified to serve as a prison.

Only in Sarzana

Soffita nella Strada

An August tradition since 1965, the "Attic in the Street" brings antique dealers and other peddlers to the streets of the historic center. Vendors come from all over Europe and the market is considered one of the best in Italy, with jewelry, period furniture, vintage clothing, rugs and carpets, oddities and collectibles, and art representing almost every period imaginable. (For more information, contact the town hall, ☎ 0187.61.41, the tourist office, ☎ 0187.620.419, or iatsarzana@libero.it.)

Val di Magra

The Val di Magra has been called the "land of 100 castles," for the fortresses and defensive towers built throughout the territory. These arose as the area was an important trade route, and control over the valley was fiercely disputed between

The Day of La Spezia

rival powers (and powerful families). Today the valley is split between Liguria and Tuscany. A tour of the most beautiful castles of the lower valley begins with the **Fortressa di Sarzanello** just outside Sarzana (leaving the town by the Porta Romana). At Castlenuovo Magra (southeast of Sarzana) is the **Vescovi Castle**, built in the 12th century by a powerful bishop seeking to control the segment of the Francigena road that passed through here. The

Malaspina Castle

Malaspina Castle in Fosdinova (technically no longer in Liguria, but over the border in Tuscany north east of Sarzana) is a wonderfully preserved marvel that is open to the public. Its most famous room is the so-called "Dante's Room," where the poet/ambassador reportedly stayed while negotiating a peace between the Malaspina and the Bishop of Luni.

For Active Travelers

Trails

There are beautiful routes along the Magra River. Departing from Battifola (on the road between Sarzana and Romito heading due west), trail nº5 is open to hikers, mountain bikers, and riders on horseback and crosses a series of streams and waterways as it jogs along the river. It's amazingly scenic but unfortunately the trail – though maintained – is unmarked. Inquire at the park seat (Via Paci, 2, ☎ 0187.691.071) for a guide.

■ Parks of the Portofino Promontory

Lush with Mediterranean maquis, groves of citrus, and woods of chestnut and olives, and dotted with ancient coastal villages maintaining traditional crafts and activities, the Portofino Promontory is one of Liguria's natural and cultural treasures. In 1935 the Italian government established the Parco Naturale Regional di Portofino, protecting the land mass and its wealth of flora and fauna from development and exploitation. In 1999, the Area Marina Protetta Portofino was declared, forming a marine sanctuary that wraps around the promontory. Together they establish a unique regional park environment, where people are encouraged to explore and deepen their respect for the natural world.

Parco Naturale Regional di Portofino

The regional natural park covers 10,000 acres, including the protected area and its surrounding "frame area." The inland northern section is thickly wooded while the southern slope is covered by pines, oaks, grasses, and Mediterranean maquis composed of heather, strawberry trees, and myrtle. The eastern section of the park is characterized by terraced olive groves, once important to the feudal economy under the agricultural system imposed by the monks of San Fruttuoso. This fragrant environment with its drop-dead gorgeous views is thickly crisscrossed by trails leading to rural settlements and the "urban" coastal villages. It's a hiker's paradise best explored on foot (though mountain bikes and horses are also allowed), with the most popular trail (marked and detailed below) joining the villages of Camogli and Portofino via the isolated seaside abbey of San Fruttuoso.

The paths are well-marked and maintained, sometimes with wire barriers along the hairiest cliff sections. Be sure to wear appropriate footwear and bring sunscreen and plenty of water. A cell phone can come in handy in case of emergency. Regardless of how they're listed here, the starting and ending points of the trails can be reversed, of course. A trail map is recommended – pick one up at the local tourist office (Camogli, Portofino, Santa Margherita Ligure) or at the Park Authority in Santa Margherita Ligure (see below).

Useful Information

Portofino Park Authority: Viale Rainusso, 1, Santa Margherita Ligure, ☎ 0185.289.479, fax 0185.285.706 (sells trail maps, books, and other materials).

www.parks.it/parco.portofino (English and Italian)

www.parcoportofino.it (Italian only)

The park hosts guided walks along the trails of the promontory. A list of the walks scheduled for the year (with fees, recommended equipment, and difficulty levels) is on the Web at www.parks.it/parco.portofino/Eman.html.

In Case of Emergency: Dial 112 (summons the *soccorso alpino*, CAI rescue corps).

In Case of Medical Emergency: Dial 118.

Hiking Trails

 The most popular route on the promontory connects the seaside villages of Camogli and Portofino via the isolated seaside abbey of San Fruttuoso. It hugs the coastline high above the sea and has expansive views over the Golfo Paradiso. Other hikes on the promontory pass through rural settlements and lead to the summit at Monte di Portofino. Only the hike between Camogli and Portofino is detailed here. Markers, start and end points, and travel times are listed for other interesting routes, with notes where there are spots of particular significance. Purchase a trail map for more detailed information on these hikes.

Camogli – S. Rocco – S. Fruttuoso – Portofino

- Marker: Two solid red circles
- Starting Point: Beside the Civico Museo Marinaro (Town Maritime Museum) in Camogli
- Ending Point: Near Castello Brown in Portofino
- Approximate Travel Time: five hours

A half-hour's hike (sometimes steeply uphill) from Camogli ends at San Rocco. The original village church here was built sometime before the 15th century, but destroyed in 1863 to make room for the bigger building you see today. Inside a marble statue representing the glory of the angels dominates the high altar. The Panificio Maccarini sells *galletta del marinaio* (sailor's flatbread) in addition to other local specialties, which makes for nice munching and refueling while taking in the view from the terrace in front of the church.

The trail splits at San Rocco. The trail marked with a red "O" leads to Pietre Strette then on to Santa Fruttuoso, an alternate trail to the abbey. From San Rocco to San Fruttuoso is about two hours. The trail marked with two solid red circles continues south and eventually passes by the Romanesque church of San Nicolò, built between 1100 and 1440 by the brotherhood of San Rufo. A double staircase leads to the entrance door over which there is a rose window and two suspended arches. Inside, the marble high altar probably dates to the 12th century. There's another junction at Fornelli, where the trail marked by two open red triangles veers away inland. If you choose to take this path, which avoids some exposed sections, continue on the open red triangle trail to Toca, then take the trail marked by three triangles forming a pyramid to Pietre Strette. From there, follow the open red O to San Fruttuoso.

Continuing on the trail marked by two solid red circles, you can make a steep descent to Porto Pidocchio. One of the last *tonnare* (an ancient method for netting bluefin tuna as they migrate from the cold North Atlantic to the warm waters of the Mediterranean) is enacted here from March to September by six-man crews working from small boats known as "armchairs." (The **Cooperativa Pescatori Camogli** arranges guided visits; ☎ 0185.772091 for more information.) Past the harbor lies Punta Chiappa. If you're here the first Sunday in August, the Stella Maris festival is celebrated with a mass and 10,000 flickering candles set afloat on the sea.

The two solid red circles trail has several long ascents and steep descents before it reaches San Fruttuoso, an isolated village on a protected cove. You can visit the abbey or relax on the pebbled beach here and, if you're too weary to trudge on, take the ferry back to Camogli or on to Portofino. **Trasporti Marittimi Turistici Golfo Paradiso** (www.golfopardiso.it, ☎ 0185.772.091) runs boats back to Camogli. **Servizio**

Parks of Portofino

Marittimo del Tigullio (www.traghettiportofino.it, ☎ 0185.284.670) provides service to Portofino and other points east.

It's a zigzag climb uphill from the abbey on the two red circles trail, then a walk along the cliffs to Portofino, passing through dense Mediterranean maquis. The former fishing village, now synonymous with *la dolce vita*, has several waterfront cafés and restaurants as well as posh shopping. You might change out of your grubby hiking clothes before hitting the boutiques, though.

Camogli – S. Rocco – Pietre Strette – San Fruttuoso

- Marker: An open red circle
- Starting Point: Beside the Civico Museo Marinaro (Town Maritime Museum) in Camogli
- Ending Point: The abbey at San Fruttuoso
- Approximate Travel Time: 2½ hours
- Of Interest: The trail passes through Portofino Vetta, home of the Portofino Kulm Hotel. Opened in 1906, the Art Nouveau hotel with its panoramic view became a favorite with artists, royalty and nobility.

Ruta – Pietre Strette – Olmi – Portofino

- Marker: A solid red square
- Starting Point: The village of Ruta, east and uphill of Camogli off the SS1 (Via Aurelia, the coastal highway)
- Ending Point: Near the Castello Brown in Portofino
- Approximate Travel Time: 2½ hours
- Of Interest: The panoramic village of Ruta is home to the Our Lady of the Boschetto Sanctuary. The Virgin Mary appeared to a 12-year-old shepherdess here in 1512 and requested the construction of a chapel. That building has long since disappeared beneath 17th, 18th, and 19th century renovations, but the miracle is represented on the chapel vault in a 17th-century fresco by Paganelli, and to the side of the high altar in a 19th-century painting by Paolo de Servi from Lucca. The silver frame around the

portrait of the Madonna and Child on the high altar was a gift from the citizens of Camogli in 1887.

Santa Margherita - Nozarego - Olmi - San Sebastiano - Portofino

- Marker: A red cross to Olmi, then two solid red circles through San Sebastiano to Portofino
- Starting Point: Santa Margherita Ligure
- Ending Point: Near Castello Brown in Portofino
- Approximate Travel Time: 2.15 hours
- Of Interest: After passing through Nozarego, the trail enters the Vallone dell'Acqua Viva, an important wetlands that fed the mountain agricultural system through a network of channels and basins that powered more than 35 working mills in the 18th century (in ruins today). From Olmi to San Sebastiano the path crosses olive groves planted centuries ago under the monks of San Fruttuoso. Olive oil production was an important part of the local economy.

Area Marina Protetta Portofino

The Area Marina Protetta (AMP) Portofino, established in 1999, wraps around the Portofino promontory and protects a wealth of microenvironments rich with animal and plant species. Through strict regulation the AMP promotes environmental knowledge and encourages environmentally friendly activities that also buffer the traditional economic activities of the local towns and villages.

Useful Information

Office of the Area Marina Protetta (AMP) Portofino, Via Rainusso, 14, Santa Margherita Ligure, ☎ 0185.289.649, fax 0185.293.002, amp.portofino@parks.it, www.riserva-portofino.it.

The southern slope of the promontory dips into the ocean forming submerged cliffs rich in ravines, caves, and fissures that are home to red coral, a rare species in the rest of the Ligurian sea. Around the southern and eastern sides of the outcrop are beds of seagrass that form perfect marine nurseries for a seemingly endless variety of small fish. Some standout species found in the waters around the promontory include grouper, seabream, medusa jellyfish, spiny and European lobsters, moray eels, and scorpion fish. For divers, visibility is generally very good, as east-west moving sea currents prevent the formation of polluted backwater near the coast. (The Genoa aquarium does an excellent job of explaining and presenting the life of this complex and integral ecosystem.)

Divers are also drawn to San Fruttuoso Bay, where the submerged Cristo degli Abissi, a massive bronze statue, beckons at a depth of 56 feet.

Diving & Boating

The AMP is divided into three zones – a, b, and c. Diving and boating are regulated within these areas. The following information, provided by the AMP, explains the regulations.

Zone A – No entry zone
- The inlet at Cala dell'Oro, between Punta del Buco and Punta Forreta (just west of San Fruttuoso).
- Rescue and scientific activities only.

Zone B – Generally protected zone.
- Along the southern slope of the promontory, between Punta Chiappa and Punta del Faro (excludes the inlet at Cala dell'Oro).
- Swimming and free diving permitted.
- Sailboats and rowboats permitted (maximum length 10 m/28 feet) with maximum speed five knots.
- Motor boats permitted (maximum length 24 m/68 feet) with maximum speed five knots only to reach orange-buoyed mooring points at west side of San Fruttuoso.
- Small boat mooring on white buoys at Cala Inglesi, Punta Chiappa, and east side of San Fruttuoso.
- Fishing only allowed by residents of Camogli, Santa Margherita, or Portofino.

- Day scuba diving at 20 sites, through AMP-authorized dive centers, or by individuals who have applied for a daily scuba diving permit from the AMP.

- Night scuba diving permitted only through AMP-authorized dive centers.

- Anchoring and spear fishing not permitted.

Zone C – Partially protected zone.

- Along the western slope from Punta Chiappa to Punta Cannette (south of Camogli).

- Along the eastern slope from Punta del Faro to Punta Pedale (south of Santa Margherita Ligure).

- Swimming and free diving permitted.

- Sailboats and rowboats permitted (maximum length 10 m) with maximum speed five knots.

- Motor boats permitted (maximum length 24 m) with maximum speed five knots exclusively in a route perpendicular to the coast to reach mooring points.

- Fishing with permit from AMP.

- Day scuba diving allowed with signal buoy or support boat.

- Night scuba diving permitted only through AMP-authorized dive centers.

- Anchoring may be permitted – look for green local area signs with an anchor.

- Spear fishing not permitted.

For a selection of AMP-authorized dive centers, see the *For Active Travelers* entries under Camogli, Portofino, and Santa Margherita Ligure.

Cetacean Sanctuary

 In 1999, France, Italy, and Monaco signed an agreement creating a Cetacean Sanctuary in the Corso-Ligurian Basin, the area of the Mediterranean with the highest sighting frequency of whales and dolphins and a principal feeding ground for fin whales in the region. Bounded by Toulon on the French Riviera, Capo Falcone in western Sardinia, Capo Ferro in eastern

Sardinia, and Fosso Chiarone in the region of Tuscany, the sanctuary is approximately 3,900 square miles and encompasses the whole of the coastline of Liguria. Among other things, the creation of the sanctuary regulates fishing techniques within its domain (drift nets are banned) and phases out the discharge of toxic waste into the waters. The agreement was heralded as an important example of international environmental cooperation in Europe. Other multinational sanctuaries are envisioned in the future.

A rich variety of cetaceans are found in the Corso-Ligurian sanctuary: bottlenose dolphins, pilot whales, Risso's dolphins (sometimes called cowfish), sperm and fin whales, even orcas (killer whales). The public plays an important role in monitoring their movements. The "Onde del Mare" project collects sighting information. If you happen to spot a whale while on a boat trip (dolphin sightings are more common), go to the web at www.acquario.ge.it, www.tethys.org, or www.agora.stm.it/eco to download and fill out a sighting form.

Servizio Marittimo del Tigullio charters boat trips to the sanctuary in July and August, with morning departures from Santa Margherita Ligure, Rapallo, Sestri Levante, Lavagna, and Chiavari. An all-day excursion, the trip features a biologist on board teaching the identifying characteristics of various species and helping classify them on sighting. For more information, see www.traghettiportofino.it or contact infortraghetti@traghettiportofino.it. Reservations (up to 160 passengers per boat) are required by calling ☎ 0185.284670 or faxing 0185.281.598.

Alimar charters boat trips to the sanctuary in June, July, August, and September, with morning and early afternoon departures from Alassio, Savona, and Genoa. It's an all-day trip and participants are advised to bring binoculars and cameras. For more information, see www.alimar.ge.it or contact alimarsrl@tin.it. Reservations can be made by calling ☎ 010.256.775, 010.255.975 or faxing 010.252.966.

■ Parks of the Cinque Terre

 In a region of so much beauty, the Cinque Terre stands apart as uniquely scenic and memorable. It's a comprehensive loveliness, born of the harmonious relationship between people and nature.

Thousands of miles of dry-stone walls enclose terraces of vineyards and gardens, creating groves for the cultivation of olives. The remade landscape supports a traditional way of life that sustains the community, including proceeds from eco-tourism, which is flourishing. There are bays and small beaches and fishing remains an important part of the local economy. Recognizing this, the area was declared a UNESCO world heritage site in 1997, and a national park and protected marine environment two years later. Today the Cinque Terre is probably the most heralded natural site in Liguria.

Parco Nazionale delle Cinque Terre

The national park consists of nearly 10,900 acres of land marked by steep slopes and the lack of any level stretches. The Cinque Terre villages are therefore small, tucked into crannies, and characterised by their sloping streets. Not naturally hospitable, the coast is high and jagged with a few inlets and promontories, and pocked by sea caves. The few sandy and pebbly beaches are the result of streams and rivulets, landslides, or the accumulated materials left by man as the area was populated, terraced, and cultivated over a thousand years.

What draws many travelers to the Cinque Terre are the trails. The first stories they've heard of these villages are inevitably about hiking through stone-terraced vineyards and orchards overlooking the turquoise sea. It sounds almost too romantic to be true, until you arrive and realize that the trails are exactly that enchanting. For anyone who's ever wanted to turn back time and experience what life was like before cars, roads, and rapid transit – when friends living a village apart took a stroll through the wilds to call on one another – Cinque Terre is a dream come true.

The paths are for the most part the product of millennia of use, worn into the ground by countless foot and hoof steps. Today, most all the trails around Cinque Terre are a part of the Italian Alpine Centre (C.A.I.) of La Spezia, and they are numbered and maintained within that system. They vary in steepness, length, challenge, and character. Every hiker is sure to find a favorite. The most popular – covered in detail below – is trail #2, known as *Sentiero Azzuro* or Blue Path. The park's border towns are Levanto in the northwest and Portovenere in the southeast, and there is a hiking trail (#1) high along the ridgeline linking these two extremities.

Useful Information

Visitor Centers

Railway Station **Riomaggiore** (ground floor), ☎ 0187.920.633, fax 0187.760.092.

Railway Station **Manarola**, ☎ 0187.760.511.

Railway Station **Corniglia** (above the railway), ☎ 0187.812.25.23, fax 0187.812.900.

Railway Station **Vernazza**, ☎ 0187.812.533, fax 0187.812.546.

■ Railway Station **Monterosso** (1st floor), ☎ 0187.817.059, fax 0187.817.151.

■ Railway Station **La Spezia** "Central," ☎ 0187.743.500, fax 0187.709.743.

You must purchase a trail pass from the visitor center and stamp it at each of the kiosks along the trail.

The visitor center also sells trail maps and the Cinque Terre Card, which for a combined fee gives you access to the trails and unlimited train travel (for one day) between Levanto and La Spezia.

The park's "Torre Guardiola" Nature Observation Center in Riomaggiore organizes trail walks focusing on recognizing wildlife native to the Mediterranean maquis, and birdwatching trips.

■ www.parks.it/parco.nazionale.cinque.terre (English and Italian)

■ www.parconazionale5terre.it (Italian only); accoglienza-riomaggiore@parconazionale5terre.it

■ **In Case of Emergency:** Dial 112 (summons the *soccorso alpino*, CAI rescue corps).

■ **In Case of Medical Emergency:** Dial 118.

Hiking Trails

 The most popular trail of the Cinque Terre is the **Sentiero Azzuro** or Blue Path, a coastal route that links the five villages passing through Mediterranean maquis, olive groves, and the terraced vineyards and gardens that are iconic of the area. Other hikes in the area include the **Via dei Sanctuari** (a network of trails that connect each village to its hilltop sanctuary) and various paths through the hinterland of the national park between Levanto and Portovenere (including trail #1, which goes along the ridge line between the two extremities). Only the Sentiero Azzuro is detailed here, broken down by segments from village to village. Markers, start and end points, and travel times are listed for other interesting routes, with notes where there are spots of particular significance. Purchase a trail map for more detailed information on these hikes. The trail numbers below are bracketed by two red rectangles. Along the way, trail directions are indicated by a red and white marker.

The Sentiero Azzuro

Monterosso – Vernazza – Corniglia – Manarola – Riomaggiore

- Trail: Number 2.
- Starting Point: Next to the Palazzo Comunale in Monterosso (an alternate trailhead is on the walkway going up towards the Porto Roca Hotel). The paths eventually converge).
- Ending Point: Near the Riomaggiore train station.
- Approximate Travel Time: Five hours.

I've presented the hike here in stages, because few will want to complete the entire circuit – nearly seven miles – in one go. It's not that it would be too difficult (though there are challenging sections), just too difficult to pass up a break for gelato, or a bit of olive oil-slicked focaccia, or a dip off the rocks in one of the turquoise coves.

● Monterosso - Vernazza

- Starting Point: Next to the Palazzo Comunale in Monterosso. An alternate trailhead is on the walkway going up towards the Porto Roca Hotel – the paths eventually converge.

- Ending Point: Above the seafront piazza in Vernazza.
- Length in Distance: 2.36 miles.
- Approximate Travel Time: Two hours.
- Characterized By: Steepness, stone walls, gardens.
- Be on the Lookout for: Garden doors that seem to open into nowhere.
- Natural Wonders: Mediterranean scrub, heather, juniper, lush varied greenery in the garden section.

This is the most beautiful of the trails in the Cinque Terre – the one to do if you only have time for one hike – and one of the longest and most strenuous. It begins with a climb up more than 500 stairs. The path then snakes through gardens and groves, past stone walls, and along cliffs with a view over the sea. Eventually the harbor at Vernazza comes into view, protected by its hilltop castle, before the steep descent down stairs and cobbles past the church of St. Mary of Antioch, arriving at the seafront piazza.

● Vernazza – Corniglia

- Starting Point : Just above the village of Vernazza.
- Ending Point: Eastern edge of Corniglia, near the road.
- Length in Distance: 2.11 miles.
- Approximate Travel Time: 1½ hours.
- Characterized By: Vineyards, olive groves.
- Be on the Lookout for: Path 2b that meanders through an olive grove before rejoining the main trail.
- Natural Wonders: Groppo stream, olive trees, anemones, orchids, Mediterranean scrub, yellow snapdragon.

Leaving Vernazza you can look back for a glimpse of the Belforte standing proud on its peninsula, guarding the ruins of the Castle Doria. This is probably the most verdant of the trails, with long sections winding through vineyards, meadows and olive groves. In addition to the grapes planted in the terraced vineyards, notice the vegetable plots where residents grow cardoons, artichokes, and varieties of squash and tomato. From several points on the trail, paths break away and lead uphill toward San Bernadino, a stop on the path of the sanctuaries.

● **Corniglia - Manarola**

■ Starting Point: Train station down the stairs from Corniglia.

■ Ending Point: Marina in Manarola.

■ Length in Distance: 1.74 miles.

■ Approximate Travel Time: 45 minutes.

■ Characterized By: Switchback trails.

■ Be on the Lookout for: A small chapel dedicated to the Madonna.

■ Natural Wonders: Mediterranean scrub, tropical plants, pines.

Follow the trail markers (or other hikers) from the train station. You'll pass through a tunnel to reach the path that goes alongside some old beach cottages before the trail breaks into the open. It's a mostly level climb through scrub with wonderful views. Outside Manarola there's a series of stairs and terraces leading down to a rocky cove popular with sunbathers and snorkelers. There are picnic benches here and it's a nice spot for a picnic.

● **Manarola - Riomaggiore: Via dell'Amore**

■ Starting Point : Just above the Manarola train station.

■ Ending Point: Near the Riomaggiore train station.

■ Length in Distance: .62 miles.

■ Approximate Travel Time: 20 minutes.

■ Characterized By: Its romantic ambiance.

■ Be on the Lookout for: Fresco paintings dedicated to the Cinque Terre.

■ Natural Wonders: Mediterranean scrub, pine trees, agaves, mock orange trees, prickly pears, fig trees, tropical plants, wildflowers.

The Via dell'Amore, or Lover's Lane, ironically began life associated with war, not love. In the 1930s it was used to access a powder magazine that was part of a munitions operation. The lore surrounding it, however, maintains that even before this turn of events a seafront path had been popular with lovers who came here, away from prying eyes, to confess the deepest secrets of their hearts. The legend partly explains its popularity, but the rest is surely a factor of ease (it is the shortest and easiest trail of the four) and natural beauty (the trail is etched into the cliffside overlooking the crashing waves below).

Other Hikes in the Parco Cinque Terre

Via dei Santuari

- Monterosso – Santuario Madonna di Soviore.
- Trail: Number 9.
- Starting Point: Via Roma in Monterosso.
- Ending Point: The Sanctuary.
- Approximate Travel Time: 1¼ hours.
- Of Interest: This is the oldest sanctuary dedicated to the Virgin Mary in Liguria, and the wooden statue of the Madonna and Child dates to the year 600. Lost for nearly 150 years, it was miraculously rediscovered in 740 by a priest who was led to it by a dove. Every 25 years it is the object of a jubilee procession through the streets of Monterosso.

● Vernazza – Santuario Madonna di Reggio

- Trail: Number 8.
- Starting Point: North of Vernazza, near the graveyard.
- Ending Point: The Sanctuary.
- Approximate Travel Time: 45 minutes.
- Of Interest: Built in the shape of a Latin cross, the Sanctuary of Our Lady of Reggio sits on a shady piazza surrounded by olive trees. The effigy of the Madonna is known as *L'Africana* (or Black Madonna) and is said to have been brought back by Crusaders returning from the Holy Land. On the first Sunday of August, the feast of Our Lady of Reggio is celebrated and devotees and pilgrims come to the Sanctuary to pay homage.

● Corniglia – Santuario Madonna delle Grazie

- Trail: Number 7a to Prato del Monte, a brief jog on Number 1 to La Cigoletta, then Number 7 to San Bernardino.

- Starting Point: Road toward Vernazza from the town square.
- Ending Point: The Sanctuary.
- Approximate Travel Time: One hour.
- Of Interest: The 15th century church is located in the hamlet of San Bernardino. The name *Madonna delle Grazie* (Our Lady of Grace) refers to a painting depicting Mary with St. Catherine of Siena.

● **Manarola – Santuario Madonna della Salute**

- Trail: 6.
- Starting Point: Car park uphill from Manarola.
- Ending Point: The Sanctuary.
- Approximate Travel Time: 40 minutes.
- Of Interest: The Sanctuary of Our Lady of Health is located in the town of Volastra above Manarola. Volastra was founded under Roman rule and was a post station where horses were changed. It is also known as "the town of olives," and you'll certainly notice the groves of hearty trees. The Sanctuary is Volastra's parish church and dates to the 10th century.

● **Riomaggiore – Santuario Madonna di Montenero**

- Trail: 3.
- Starting Point: Carpark at Riomaggiore
- Ending Point: The Sanctuary.
- Approximate Travel Time: 45 minutes.
- Of Interest: Legend holds that Greek refugees founded the Sanctuary to Our Lady of Montenero in the eighth century. The current building dates to the 14th century. There's also a hiking center and refreshment stand on the grounds of the sanctuary.
- Alternate Destination: From the sanctuary at Telegrafo you can pick up trail 1 and hike on to Portovenere, approximately 3½ hours away. Before you reach Portovenere there is a wonderful view of the Bay of Poets and the islands of Palmaria and Tino.

Cinque Terre Alta Via

● **Portovenere - Levanto**

■ Trail: 1.

■ Starting Point: Portovenere.

■ Ending Point: Levanto.

■ Approximate Travel Time: 12 hours.

Note: It is suggested that you break the hike down into segments as follows:

Portovenere – Campiglia (two hours).

Campiglia – Telegrafo (one hour).

Telegrafo – Sella la Croce (one hour).

Stella la Croce – La Cigoletta (one hour 40 minutes).

La Cigoletta – Drignana (two hours).

Drignana – Soviore (one hour).

Soviore – San Antonio – Levanto (two hours 30 minutes).

The Trails by Mountain Bike

 The park has recently opened several mountain bike trails through the inland area of Cinque Terre, starting from the Madonna di Montenero sanctuary on the hill above Riomaggiore. Here you'll find also find a hiking center, refreshment stand, some spartan lodgings, and a place for mountain bike rental (*noleggio*). Rentals are also available at various points along the asphalt road connecting the sanctuaries, including at San Bernardino, Volastra, and Telegrafo.)

The paths are all circular (same start and end point) and mostly make use of the existing hiking trails with a few segways. They represent a range of difficulty and terrain, accommodating amateur and expert cyclists. Notes are provided below regarding difficulty as well as any other pertinent details.

MTB Trail °1

■ Starting Point: Montenero Shrine (up the hill from Riomaggiore).

- Approximate Travel Time: Three hours.
- Description: From the shrine, bikes must be carried 300 yards up to the beginning of the hiking trail to Telegrafo (marked 1). Then there is an asphalt road going uphill (medium difficulty) merging with MTB Trail º1. It continues along until just above Corniglia, then jogs down to catch the road for Volastra. From there, a dirt track brings you back to the starting point.

MTB Trail º2

- Starting Point: Montenero Shrine (up the hill from Riomaggiore).
- Approximate Travel Time: All day (with breaks).
- Description: The longest and most demanding of the trails, with uphill slopes, technical downhills, and small jumps. The path mimics MTB Trail º1 (and mirrors hiking trail 1), but passes the turnoff (above Corniglia) for the road to Volastra, continuing on to the Soviore Shrine. Coming back it takes the asphalt road past the sanctuaries to Volastra, and ends with the dirt track that returns to the starting point.

MTB Trail º3

- Starting Point: Montenero Shrine (up the hill from Riomaggiore).
- Approximate Travel Time: Three hours.
- Description: The shortest trail, but the most difficult (for experts only). The path begins the same as MTB Trail º1, continuing on to Stella La Croce path º01, heading in the direction of Carpena. This is a fast downhill with difficult technical stretches. From Carpena it takes a road that rejoins MTB Trail º1. An alternative trail leads back to Montenero Shrine and includes a difficult uphill slope and a few sections where you'll need to carry the bike over rocks.

MTB Trail º4

- Starting Point: Fornacchi (inland between Corniglia and Vernazza).
- Approximate Travel Time: Three hours.

■ Description: The trail goes along to the road to the San Bernardino sanctuary and then in the direction of Portovenere until it intersects with hiking trail 7 to return to the starting point.

The Trails on Horseback

 You can also see the trails of the Cinque Terre by horseback or on a carriage ride. Excursions are organized by the Equestrian Tourism Center of the Cinque Terre National Park. The information provided below is subject to change. For current information, contact the **Cinque Terre Visitor Centers** in Monterosso (☎ 0187.817.059), Vernazza (☎ 0187.812.533), Corniglia (☎ 0187.812,523), Manarola (☎ 0187.760.511), or Riomaggiore (☎ 0187.920.633).

Paths on Horseback

● **Excursion 1: Pianca – Fornacchi – Cigoletta – Pianca**

■ Two hours.

■ Minimum two, maximum four people.

■ Fee €27 per person (€25 with Cinque Terre Card).

■ For booking contact **Equestrian Center/Alessandro Crovara** (☎ 349.751.44.46 or 320.439.11.06) or a Cinque Terre visitor center.

● **Excursion 2: Pianca – Menhir di Monte Capri – Strada dei Santuari – Volastra – Pianca**

■ Four hours.

■ Minimum two, maximum four people.

■ Fee €50 per person (€45 with Cinque Terre Card).

■ For booking contact Equestrian Center/Alessandro Crovara (☎ 349.751.44.46 or 320.439.11.06) or a Cinque Terre visitor center.

● **Excursion 3: Pianca – Menhir di Monte Capri – Telegrafo – break at Montenero – Strada dei Santuari – Volastra – Pianca**

■ Six-eight hours.

■ Minimum two, maximum four people.

■ Fee €70 per person (€65 with Cinque Terre Card).

- Possibility of lunch at the Shrine with fixed-price menu (€15) or à la carte selections.

- For booking contact Equestrian Center/Alessandro Crovara (☎ 349.751.44.46 or 320.439.11.06) or a Cinque Terre visitor center.

● **Excursion 4: Weekend Trip. Pianca – Volastra – break at Montenero – Telegrafo – Campiglia – Telegrafo – Menhir di Monte Capri – Pianca**

- Two days.

- Minimum four, maximum eight people.

- Fee: €150 per person with own horse (includes guide, stable space, feed); or €160 per person (maximum four people) with horse provided by Center (includes guide and horse).

- Dinner, overnight accommodations, and breakfast at the Shrine for €40 per person.

- For booking contact Equestrian Center/Alessandro Crovara (☎ 349.751.44.46 or 320.439.11.06) or a Cinque Terre visitor center at least a week in advance.

Paths by Carriage
Excursion A

- One hour.
- Fees: Two people €50; four people €80; six people €100; family €50 + €10 for each child.

- For booking contact Equestrian Center/Alessandro Crovara (☎ 349.751.44.46 or 320.439.11.06) or a Cinque Terre visitor center.

Excursion B

- 1½ hours.

- Fee: Two people €70; four people €100; six people €130; family €70 + €15 for each child.

- For booking contact Equestrian Center/Alessandro Crovara (☎ 349.751.44.46 or 320.439.11.06) or a Cinque Terre visitor center.

Excursion C

- Three hours.
- Fee: Two people €90; four people €120; six people €160; family €90 + €30 for each child.
- For booking contact Equestrian Center/Alessandro Crovara (☎ 349.751.44.46 or 320.439.11.06) or a Cinque Terre visitor center.

Area Marina Protetta Cinque Terre

 The marine park of the Cinque Terre stretches between Punta Mesco – the headland just west of Monterosso – and Punte Montenegro, site of the town of Riomaggiore. Established at the same time as the national park in 1999, the protected environment safeguards a rich diversity of plant and animal life. Near the headlands the seabeds slope steeply and are characterized by a rocky bottom. Elsewhere, the clear water is darkened by the presence of large posidonia (sea grass) meadows on the otherwise sandy bottom.

The diversity of environments makes the area popular with divers, and the activity is strictly regulated through the authorization of dive centers, though there are sites where you can dive without an authorized guide. Boating activities are likewise regulated within the most vulnerable areas of the park, but it's obvious that boating remains one of the most popular pastimes along the coast. And with good reason – there's an extensive amount of territory only accessible by sea.

Useful Information

Area Marina Protetta Cinque Terre, Via T. Signorini, Riomaggiore, ☎ 0187.760.000, fax 187.760.061, parconazionale5terre@libero.it, www.parconazionale5terre.it, www.parks.it/parco.nazionale.cinque.terre.

Diving & Boating

 The marine park is divided into three zones – A, B, and C – and diving and boating are regulated within these areas. The following information, provided by the Area Marine Protetta Cinque Terre, explains the regulations.

Zone A

■ Bordered by marker buoys, around the headland of Punta Mesco. (The area of the rocky seabed where colonies of delicate sea fans are found, and where certain species are being re-established.)

■ Diving forbidden unless with authorized guide.

■ Mooring and anchoring forbidden.

■ Access forbidden to motor-driven craft.

■ Professional and sport fishing forbidden.

■ Swimming is allowed.

Zone B

■ Bordered by marker buoys wrapping around Zone A and extending to include a posidoni meadow to the west of Monterosso, the most important along the Cinque Terre coast. Also surrounding the Punta Montenegro.

■ Mooring is generally forbidden, but there are specifically authorized places where mooring is allowed (posted).

■ Professional fishing is forbidden.

■ Underwater spear fishing is forbidden.

■ Motorboats may pass at speeds below eight knots.

■ Diving is permitted, even without an authorized guide (must abide by protection policies).

■ Sport fishing is permitted with lines and fixed rods.

Zone C

■ Includes the two terminal headlands and the marine environment linking them.

■ No specific restrictions, but activities must be compatible with the park's protection policy.

■ For dive centers, see the *For Active Travelers* entries under Cinque Terre, Portovenere, and La Spezia.

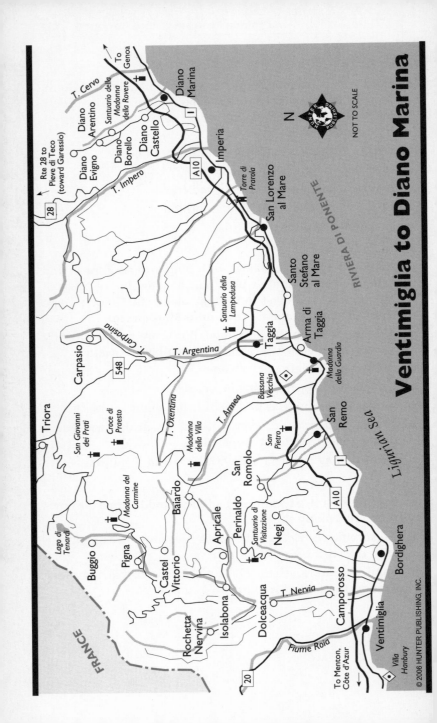

Ventimiglia to Diano Marina

© 2006 HUNTER PUBLISHING, INC.

Riviera di Ponente

■ Ventimiglia – Bussana Vecchia

Liguria's westernmost region bears an international stamp, which is hardly surprising as it's just a stone's throw from France. Traveling on the A10 autostrada, the signs near Ventimiglia are in French and in English, and the seaside towns close to the border have always seen a lot of international traffic.

Ventimiglia is an ancient city, with distinct Roman, medieval, and modern sections. In its early history it was the administrative center for a large district of coastal and inland towns, many of which (in the hinterland) are now beyond the French border (an artifact of redrawn borders following WWII). Just outside the town proper are the **Giardini Botanici Hanbury**, created in the 19th century by a wealthy Englishman in collaboration with a crew of foreign botanists, agronomists, and landscape architects. The gardens (which surround a hilltop villa) are so prized they were designated a protected regional park in 2000.

Flowers are a hallmark of this part of Liguria, giving rise to its alias *Riviera dei Fiori*, or Riviera of the Flowers. The temperate area with its good soil is largely south-facing and gets the most hours of sun each year. Almost everything grows well here, which might be one reason why the British – with their stereotypical zeal for gardening – were so taken with **Bordighera** in the 19th century. English tourism to the Italian Riviera officially launched in the town. The wealthiest constructed private villas and parks and spent most of the year living seaside. Others stayed in one of Bordighera's many Art Nouveau hotels. The tourists eventually spilled over into next-door **Ospedaletti**, a former fishing village originally founded by the Knights of Rhodes in the 14th century, said to be *the* town with the best weather in all of Liguria.

It was then on to **San Remo**, the charming old town of which (La Pigna) still clusters on a hill overlooking the former fishing village, now transformed into a district of mansions, private villas, hotels, and gardens. In the 19th and early 20th centuries San Remo was the height of chic, but today it's lost some of its luster. This doesn't stop yachts from dropping anchor in the marina, however, while their owners come ashore for a night of gambling in the casino.

A perfect antidote for San Remo's timeworn glam is found at **Bussana Vecchia**, located eastward on the Via Aurelia, inland from the modern town of Bussana. The medieval hilltop hamlet was almost completely destroyed by an earthquake in 1887 and its residents moved to the coast, founding the new town. In the 1960s the ruins were appropriated by an international mix of artists, who in the nearly half-century since have transformed the tumbledown village into a bohemian haven of workshops and showrooms, with a sprinkling of organic restaurants and minimal intrusion of modern technology.

Ventimiglia

Ventimiglia's Roman ruins are found on the eastern edge of the city, and testify to a time when the town was the prosperous administrative center of a district stretching along the coast and up into the hinterland. Artifacts from this period are found in the city's **Museo Archeologico Gerolamo Rossi**.

After the fall of the empire, the population center moved to a more secure position at the top of the Cavo hill, dominating the right bank of the River Roia. In keeping with the political turbulence of the era, the medieval town – controlled by the Lords of Ventimiglia, from whom the town takes its name –

Terraced hillsides in the Cinque Terre

Above: A popular swimming cove off the trail
before Manarola (Amy Finley)
Below: Calata Doria, Portovenere

was fortified with walls and defensive towers. In the 12th century, when the Ventimiglia controlled much of the territory (coastal and inland) between the town and Imperia, facing a bloody showdown with Genoa over territorial hegemony, Guido Guerra, Lord of Ventimiglia, swore allegiance to the Republic and ceded portions of the family's feudal land.

However, in the 13th century the city capitulated outright and was annexed to Genoa, which added additional fortifications. Under Genoese domination several impressive buildings were constructed along what is today Via Garibaldi, including palatial residences with hanging gardens at the level of the *piani nobili*. The castle of the Ventimiglia was razed in the 16th century, becoming the base for the convent of Lateran Canonesses.

The Free Commune of Ventimiglia was briefly revived in the late 18th century, when the Republic of Liguria was proclaimed, prior to the annexation of the whole region by Napoleon. The city's fate then followed the trajectory of the Italian state, becoming part of the Kingdom of Italy under Piedmont-Sardinia, and finally a frontier town in the modern country of Italy. Prior to the establishment of the euro under the European Union, Ventimiglia's fortunes were buffered by the sale of cheap cigarettes and alcohol to visitors who crossed over from France and Monaco. It is now feeling its way to a new tourism-driven economy, but so far with less success than other towns in the area.

Getting There

By Train: Ventimiglia is easily reached by both French and Italian trains. For a schedule of trains originating in France (and traveling to Ventimiglia by way of Nice), see www.sncf.com. For Italian trains, see www.trenitalia.it. The **FS** station is in the center of the modern side of town.

By Car: Ventimiglia's exit is just beyond the French border on the A10 autostrada. The Via Aurelia coastal route begins in Ventimiglia.

Resources

■ www.rivieradeifiori.org

■ www.comune.ventimiglia.it

■ **Tourist Office:** Via Cavour, 61, ☎ 0184.351.183.

Being There

The most intriguing part of Ventimiglia is the medieval town, on the Cavo hill across the river from the modern city (which holds the dubious distinction of having the highest concentration of liquor stores in Italy). Here are the remains of Ventimiglia's illustrious past, surrounded by fortifying walls erected by Genoa in the 16th century. On the western edge of the walls, the 13th-century **Porta Canarda** (with a bas-relief depicting the arms of the Banco di San Giorgio, a remnant of Genoese domination) once guarded the route to Provence. New Ventimiglia has a seafront promenade lined with palm trees, and is the site for the city's raucous street market held every Friday.

Cattedrale dell'Assunta

Ventimiglia's cathedral was built in the 11th century on the site of an eighth-century church, the remains of which are evident in the crypt. An inscription there to Juno, wife of Jupiter, is the foundation of theories that the first church was constructed over a pagan temple. Altered and enlarged several times over the intervening centuries, the cathedral has a Romanesque façade and a Baroque bell tower, with other elements deriving from the 13th, 16th, and 19th centuries. The baptistery behind the church is from the 11th century, with a 16th-century ceiling, and the baptismal pool has an inscription dated 1100.

Museo Archeologico Gerolamo Rossi

The *Forte dell'Annunziata* to the west of the medieval town (toward the French border) was a 16th-century convent, converted for military use in the 19th century to fortify the French border after the fall of the Napoleonic empire. In 1984 the site was selected to house Ventimiglia's archeological museum, which opened in 1990. The collection includes items excavated from the city's Roman ruins – displayed through six rooms of the building – and features sculptures and carved inscriptions, funerary items, and ancient glassware. (☎ 0184.35.11.81, info@fortedellannunziata.it; open Tuesday-Saturday 9 am-12 pm and 3-5 pm, Sunday 10 am-12:30 pm.)

Church of San Michele

Some cite this 10th-century church – once belonging to the Benedictine Monks of the Isle of Lerin – as a possible repository site of the Holy Grail. This stemmed from the monks' relationship to the nearby

principality of Seborga, from whence the Knights Templar originated. Found on the northern extreme of the old town, the church retains an ancient structure. Two columns of the crypt are said to come from a pagan temple to Castor and Pollux, while another is a Roman millstone.

Only in Ventimiglia

Hanbury Gardens

There are 5,800 species of plants represented in these spectacular gardens, declared a regional reserve in 2000. Laid out by the brothers Thomas and Daniel Hanbury in 1867, the grounds surround a villa and are organized into themed groupings – an Australian Forest (with eucalyptus and acacia), succulents, the Garden of the Fragrances, the Giardinetti (with ancient varieties of peonies and roses), the Exotic Orchard (home to passion flowers), and the Citrus Grove. Various itineraries lead visitors over the grounds, discovering fountains and other water features, statuary, the ancient Roman road (*Via Julia Augusta*, which passes through), and an avenue of olive trees ending at an oil press. Guided tours are available with advance booking. (☎/fax 0184.229.507, www.parks.it/giardini.botanici.hanbury, info@cooperativa-omnia.com; open 9:30 am to 4, 5 or 6 pm, depending on the season.)

Principalities

Seborga (photo Luciano Rosso)

Less than a half-hour's drive in either direction (west or east) can lead to one of Europe's rare principalities. Traveling west over the French border the road leads to **Monaco**, home of high-stakes gambling in the casinos of Monte Carlo. In the opposite direction (east to Bordighera, then inland) is **Seborga**, the principality that history forgot. It owes its existence to poor record keeping during the many treaties defining territory since the 11th century, when Seborga was first recognized by the Holy Roman Empire. Today it has a population of just over 325 residents, who inhabit the hilltop town that is the center of the now 10-sq-mile nation.

Seborga (photo Luciano Rosso)

Bordighera and other nearby towns were once part of the principality. Seborga is distinguished by its history with the Knights Templar, the famous order of warrior monks founded here in the 12th century. Saint Bernard traveled here to join the order and help guard "The Great Secret," which many take to be the whereabouts of the Holy Grail, the Arc of the Covenant, and other important religious relics taken during the knights' excavations under the Temple Mount in Jerusalem. (For more information, see www.seborga.net.)

The Dawn of Man's Time

West of Ventimiglia (by the village of Grimaldi, just before the border) are the Balzi Rossi caves, where evidence of prehistoric man dates to the Upper Paleolithic period 400-850 years ago. The six caves, which were first excavated in the mid-19th century, have yielded several full and fragmentary skeletons, including a hipbone from Homo Erectus found in the Cave of the Prince. The most famous find – the so-called **Triple Grave** found in 1892 in the Barma Grande cave – is now exhibited at the **Museo Preistorico dei Balzi Rossi** and consists of the remains of an adult and two adolescents together with their funeral gifts, dating to the last stage of the Würm Glaciation (16,000-29,000 years ago). The museum also has fertility figurines, tools, and fossils of warm and cold climate animals (elephants, hippos, rhinoceros, marmots, reindeer) that lived during the period, providing evidence of great climactic change. There's a walkway connecting to the caves (guided tours depart every 45 minutes), where visitors can see Upper Paleolithic rock carvings, the only ones of their kind ever found in northern Italy. (☎ 0184.381.13; open Tuesday-Sunday 9 am-7 pm.)

For Active Travelers

Surfing

An anomaly in an area of pebble beaches, **Le Calandre** is a laid-back, sandy beach (past the headland on the west side of the river) that is popular with surfers. Reach it by walking west along Ventimiglia's seafront, then picking up the trail heading past some ruins (about a 10-minute walk). There's a beach bar.

Skiing

From December to April there is (sometimes) decent snow skiing at the Riserva Bianca resort, a 45-minute drive from Ventimiglia in Limone Piemonte (also accessible by train from Ventimiglia, on the Torino-Cuneo-Ventimiglia line). For more information, see www.riservabianca.it.

Bordighera

When the first British tourists began to arrive – hot on
the heels of the publication
of Giovanni Ruffini's 1855
novel *Doctor Antonio* (set in
Bordighera) – they found a
small hamlet atop the
Sant'Ampelio promontory
and a fishing village down
below. These were the nuclei

from which Bordighera grew, with much of that growth coming after the advent of tourism and then the opening of the
railway in 1872. Prior to that time, the villages were part of
the *Magnifica Comunita degli Otto Luoghi*, a community of
eight towns that broke from the Free Commune of
Ventimiglia in the 17th century.

Bordighera's 19th-century history defines the town. The first
English to arrive came by way of Provence, already a popular
winter destination for escapees from Britain's cold and wet
season. Lured by the promise of year-round sun and stunning
scenery (the palms growing amidst the Mediterranean
maquis are thought to have been seeded by St. Ampelio, who
arrived here in the sixth century and lived in a seaside cave),
they stayed, built villas, established a community that sometimes outnumbered the Italian residents, and set up cultural
institutions reminiscent of those they'd left behind.

Among those was the first tennis club in Italy, opened in 1878.
A year later, Clarence Bicknell founded a museum of paleontology (the surrounding areas are rich in ethnographic finds),
and soon after the international library. As Bordighera grew
in popularity, celebrities began to take notice. Claude Monet
painted here (*View of Bordighera*, above, hangs in the Art

Institute of Chicago) and is honored with a garden bearing his name. The Frenchman Charles Garnier, architect of the Paris Opera, built a seaside villa and was entrusted with the town's urban development in 1870. Queen Margaret of Savoy was a longtime resident at a villa on Via Romana and died in the town in 1926.

Today, tourism in Bordighera remains genteel, if slightly less urbane than at Portofino or Santa Margherita Ligure on the opposite coast of the Riviera. The marina welcomes sailing enthusiasts, and the town is a good base while discovering the nearby valleys.

Getting There

By Train: Bordighera's train station is located seaside off the Lungomare Argentina. For schedules, see www.trenitalia.it.

By Car: Exit the A10 autostrada at Bordighera. The Via Aurelia runs through town.

By Bus: Bus service in the area is provided by **Riviera Trasporti**. For fares, schedules and information, see www.rivieratrasporti.it.

Resources

- www.rivieradeifiori.org
- www.bordighera.it
- **Tourist Office:** Via Vittorio Emanuele II, 172-174, ☎ 0184.262.322.

Being There

Modern Bordighera stretches along the Lungomare Argentina, a pedestrian promenade to the west of the Capo Sant'Ampelio. The town's characteristic villas and parks are found between Via Vittorio Emanuele II (just off the waterfront) and Via Romana, both of them running up the hill. At the tip of the cape, at the end of the Lungomare, are public gardens and the Piazza des Amicis. From there you can reach the esplanade of the **Spianata del Capo**, which has lovely panoramic views, and the medieval town.

Church of Santa Maria Maddalena

The 17th-century church on the Piazza del Popolo has Rococo stuccos and a 17th-century bell tower that was probably built as a lookout. The statue of the *Magiarge* in front of the town hall honors a victim of a Saracen attack. Inside, on the high altar, is the marble statue *Maddalena in Gloria*, attributed to Bernini's pupil, Filippo Parodi. Others contend it's by Filippo's son, Domenico.

Church of Sant'Ampelio

On the cliff adjacent the *Spianata*, this Romanesque church honors the town's patron saint. St. Ampelio is thought to have traveled here from Egypt in the fourth century, bringing with him the palm seeds that started the plantings that now characterize the Riviera landscape. A hermit, he is thought to have lived in a cave, atop which the church was raised in the 12th century. His relics are kept in the crypt.

Clarence Bicknell Museum and Library

The museum, founded by British scholar and philanthropist Clarence Bicknell in 1878, has moldings of the rock carvings, dating from the late Neolithic to the Iron Age, found in the Vallée des Merveilles in France. Co-located with the museum is the *Mostra Permanente Pompeo Mariani*, displaying works by and dedicated to the artist whose villa is outside town, reached by the winding Via dei Colli. (☎ 0184.263.694; open Monday-Friday 9:30 am-1 pm and 1:30-4:45 pm.)

Only in Bordighera

Palm Sunday

If you happen to attend mass in Bordighera on Palm Sunday (the Sunday before Easter), you'll receive some of the same palm fronds distributed at the Vatican. Fitting for the town where the palm was introduced to Europe, Bordighera has been providing the fronds to the Holy City for more than 100 years.

Ospedaletti

Founded by the Knights of Rhodes in the 14th century, Ospedaletti sits between Bordighera and San Remo and gets a little over-flow tourism from each, though it's markedly calmer and quieter than either of its neighbors. Ospedaletti is said to have the best weather in all of Liguria, and has pebbled beaches on which to enjoy the sun. The old town and its twisting alleyways is particularly charming.

For Active Travelers

Water Sports

Sportshore (☎ 348.518.38.58, sportshore@virgilio.it) rents boats with or without skipper, canoes, kayaks, water bikes, and jet skis, and takes the adventurous parasailing on the sea surrounding Bordighera.

Fishing

The skippers of *PerMare* charter fishing trips for swordfish, tuna, and other big game fish of the Ligurian sea (the catch depends on the season), departing from the tourist port at Bordighera. (For more information, contact **nuccio@permareonline.it**.)

San Remo

The ancient Ligurians had hilltop settlements in the vicinity of San Remo before the arrival of the Romans, who founded the town of *Villa Matutiana* in the second century BC. Nearly 1,000 years later, the Genoese Bishop Romolo converted the town to Christianity and it took the name San Römu, which eventually morphed into San Remo.

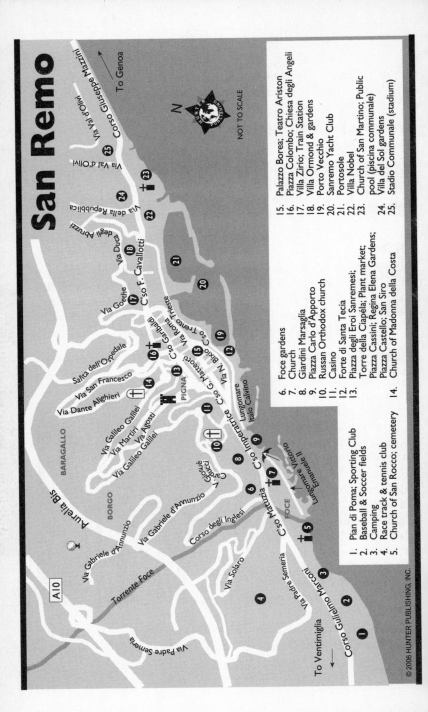

San Remo

NOT TO SCALE

1. Pian di Poma; Sporting Club
2. Baseball & Soccer fields
3. Camping
4. Race track & tennis club
5. Church of San Rocco; cemetery
6. Foce gardens
7. Church
8. Giardini Marsaglia
9. Piazza Carlo d'Apporto
10. Russan Orthodox church
11. Casino
12. Forte di Santa Tecia
13. Piazza degli Eroi Sanremesi;
    Torre della Ciapèla; Plant market;
    Piazza Cassini; Regina Elena Gardens;
    Piazza Castello; San Siro
14. Church of Madonna della Costa
15. Palazzo Borea; Teatro Ariston
16. Piazza Colombo; Chiesa degli Angeli
17. Villa Zirio; Train Station
18. Villa Ormond & gardens
19. Porto Vecchio
20. Sanremo Yacht Club
21. Portosole
22. Villa Nobel
23. Church of San Martino; Public
    pool (piscina communale)
24. Villa del Sol gardens
25. Stadio Communale (stadium)

The oldest part of the town – **La Pigna** – encircles its hilltop in concentric rings like the quills of its namesake pinecone. A statue of a *pigna* still stands outside the **Porta San Giuseppe**, which dates to the 17th century. The old town was continuously enlarged and fortifications were added between the 11th and 18th centuries, resulting in a warren of alleys connected by stairs and tunnels. In theory, the confusing labyrinth was meant to thwart an invasion. However, in 1543 (just five years after Pope Paul III sojourned in San Remo on his way to Nice) the town was destroyed in an attack by the pirate Barbarosso.

A free government for a time during the Middle Ages, then a Doria fief (some say the *Santuario Madonna della Costa* was built to commemorate San Remo's 14th-century liberation from the family's rule) the town was a noncompliant dominion of Genoa by the 18th century. The Republic – wary of the potential power of San Remo's port – first built a fort on the waterfront to keep watch over its activities, then silted up the harbor, decimating maritime trade.

The arrival of the railroad in the mid-19th century was the nail in the coffin of the town's commercial port, but opened up opportunities for tourism, which completely redefined San Remo. An entire British quarter was established, and a Russian colony, representing the crème de la crème of society and including members of the nobility, aristocracy, and royalty, in addition to celebrities from the arts. At first, guests were accommodated in a private villa belonging to Countess Adele Roverizio di Roccasterone, but their intentions to linger throughout the seasons soon gave rise to a rash of building during which private villas, some 200 by the turn of the century, and Art Nouveau hotels were constructed around town. The wealthy foreigners also built their own churches, such as the Russian Orthodox San Basilio, with its characteristic onion domes, and provided amply for their amusement. The Casino Municipale was designed by the French architect Eugene Ferret and built between 1904 and 1906.

San Remo is still a cosmopolitan destination, these days favored by the wealthy Russians that can be found around the roulette tables in the casino. Yachts still drop anchor in the harbor and the San Remo Rally – the Italian leg for the world championship auto racing title – draws a surprisingly sophisticated crowd. The bloom is off the rose, but San Remo retains

Ventimiglia – Bussana Vecchia

an aura of excitement, especially in the height of the summer season, that is reminiscent of its glamorous past.

Getting There

By Train: San Remo's train station is close to the casino on the waterfront at the western edge of town. For schedules, see www.trenitalia.it.

By Car: Take the San Remo exit from the A10 autostrada and follow the signs downhill. The Via Aurelia runs through the town and is the road for neighboring towns Ospedaletti and Bordighera.

By Bus: Bus service in the area is provided by **Riviera Trasporti**. For fares, schedules and information, see www.rivieratrasporti.it.

Resources

- www.rivieradeifiori.org
- www.sanremoguide.com
- **Tourist Office:** Largo Nuvoloni, 1, ☎ 0184.571.571 or 0184.590.59.

Being There

There's a lot of exploring to be done in San Remo, which is one of the largest towns on this side of the Riviera. The old district of *La Pigna* overlooks the heart of San Remo. Though fascinating and loaded with sites, it should be visited during the day. It's a bit derelict and neglected. The casino is at the western edge of town, before the Parco Marsaglia. Behind the park is the **Corso degli Inglesi**, a winding street lined with beautiful villas and their gardens. **Corso Matteotti**, a cosmopolitan cobbled street lined with shops and cafes, starts in front of the casino and works its way toward the **Piazza Colombo**. The **Corso Garibaldi** picks up here, thronged with scooters at night when the *stroll* (an Italian ritual) is on. There are two harbors – the **Porto Vecchio** (old port) closer to the middle of town around which there are numerous restaurants and cafés, and the **Porto Sole**, the tourist port and marina.

La Pigna

A walk through the old city begins at the 14th-century **Porto San Stefano** near the church of San Siro. La Pigna is a labyrinth of narrow, twisting, often covered alleys connected by stairs and archways. **Via Palme** is the main street, and at n°21 is the house, home of the Manara family, where Pope Paul III stayed on his way to Nice in the 16th century. A brief sidestep onto Via Montà takes you to n°18, the palace of **Count Sapia Rossi**, where another illustrious guest, Napoleon, stayed in 1794. Farther uphill on Via Palme is the **Piazza San Giuseppe** and the ancient door and 19th-century church named for the same saint. It boasts two distinctive altars. The high altar designed by Soli (the engineer who also designed the Villa Nobel), and a presbytery altar that started life as a drinking trough for mules and horses. At the very top of the hill is the **Santuario della Madonna della Costa**, fronted by the Regina Elena gardens. The church has several notable works of art, including an 18th-century frescoed dome by Giacomo Antonio Boni and the *Madonna col Bambino* ascribed to Niccolò da Voltri.

San Siro

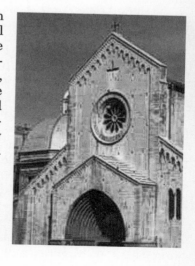

At the base of La Pigna, San Remo's 13th century cathedral has a façade of yellow limestone quarried at Verezzo. It's attributed to the Comacini Masters, who designed a Romanesque building that was later covered with Baroque additions (painstakingly removed in the early 20th century). Inside, a 16th-century painting of *St. Siro between St. Peter, St. Paul, John the Baptist, and Romulus* is by Raffaele de Rossi. The pulpit and holy water font are modern, sculpted in 1950 by Dante Ruffini.

Palazzo Borea d'Olmo

In the 15th century San Remo acquired its own Strada Nuova (the name of the illustrious street of mansions in Genoa, known today as Via Garibaldi). Today it is known as Via Matteotti, a popular walking street lined with shops, restaurants, and cafes. At n°143 is the palace of the aristocratic Borea d'Olmo family. Named the marquises of Olmo by the Savoys, the family was conferred the title of barons during the Napoleonic Empire, and then of dukes during the Kingdom of Italy (Duke Borea d'Olmo served as grand master of ceremonies to the House of Savoy for more than 75 years). The palace (constructed in the 15th century) has Baroque stuccos on the façade and 16th-century statue-decorated portals.

The *piano nobile* – which has frescoes by Giovanni Battista Merano – is now home to the **Civic Archeological Museum**. Three distinct sections are devoted to archeology (with prehistoric and Roman remains from the San Remo area), the paintings and engravings left to the museum by the poet Laurano, and Risorgimento memorabilia.

Orthodox Russian Church

The onion-domed church near the casino at the base of Via Matteoti was inspired by Russian Empress Maria Alexandrovna, who wintered in San Remo in 1874. It was consecrated to Christ the Redeemer and St. Catherine in 1913.

Casino Municipale

Designed in the Liberty or Art Deco style by the French architect Eugenio Ferret, San Remo's casino opened to great applause in 1905. By the 1930s its reputation was firmly established among genteel gamblers. Erika and Klaus Mann (the children of Nobel prize-winning author Thomas Mann) said of it, "…if you lose in San Remo, you lose it elegantly, in a respectable way." The casino's clientele is arguably less elegant today, and the noisy slot-machines and other modern casino staples detract from a cultivated vibe, but there are high-rollers around the blackjack and roulette tables (where the minimum bet ranges from €5 to €20 and is often much more). Bring your passport if you want to visit upstairs – you'll need it when you sign-in at the concierge desk. There's no smoking, no cameras, and no cell phones allowed.

Only in San Remo
Racing

The 1,389-km/833-mile San Remo Car Rally Race is held the first two weeks of October. The first and third laps pass through the hinterland behind San Remo, with the second held in the hills of High Monferrato in Piedmont. The event is one of the last of the World Championship series, followed by rallies in Australia and Great Britain. In April, the town hosts the San Remo Historical Car Rally, first organized in 1928 and open to vintage automobiles manufactured between 1919 and 1971 (the cars race in five separate categories). Another spring event is the Milano-San Remo Cycling Race, which unfolds along the foggy plains of Milan and reaches the sea at San Remo.

Song Festival

Before there was *American Idol*, there was the San Remo Song Festival, first held in 1951 and now an institution in the Riviera town and an important cultural event for the whole country. Held the last week in February, the festival features some of Italy's biggest names in (mostly pop) music, competing for honors before a voting audience and a jury of moguls from the recording industry. Broadcast from the Ariston Theater, the event is accompanied by parties and paparazzi (and usually a scandal or two) as Italian celebrities converge on San Remo.

For Active Travelers
Golf

Italy's first golf country club was built in San Remo in the 1930s. **Degli Ulvi** has 18 holes set among groves of olive trees overlooking the sea. Advanced reservations are required, and golfers must bring proof of handicap. Shuttle service is provided from some of the city's upscale hotels; inquire upon booking. (☎ 0184.557.093, fax 0184.557.388.)

Ventimiglia - Bussana Vecchia

Tennis

The **Sporting Club Solaro** has six clay and six hard courts for singles or doubles play, and is a training ground for the Italian Davis Cup team. The club is located on the west side of town on Via Solaro. Call in advance for reservations. (☎ 0184.665.155, fax 0184.666.202, solaro@freemail.it.)

Boating

The **Yacht Club San Remo** hosts regattas, teaches classes, and rents sailboats, motorboats, kayaks, and windsurfs. They're located at the new marina, **Portosole**, on the east side of town. (☎ 0184.503.760, fax 0184.546.038, ycs@libero.it.)

Diving

There are two diving centers in San Remo, both of which lead dives to the seabeds off Ventimiglia, considered some of the finest in the area. **San Remo Sub** is at ☎ 0184.535.335 or 0184.531.631, and the **Centro Immersioni Aton** is at ☎ 0184.510.643.

Bussana Vecchia

Today a bohemian village of international artists, Bussana Vecchia was founded in Roman times and named *Bissana*, meaning "twice blessed," because of the fresh mountain and sea air that wafted through the hilltop village, set inland but in sight of the water. In the 12th century, the tiny town was under the dominion of the counts of Ventimiglia, and in the 13th passed to the Republic of Genoa. The 15th and 16th centuries were a period of development, when the town expanded both outward and upward (some of the buildings reached a height of four stories, with the ground floor used as a workshop).

In the mid-19th century a series of minor earthquakes rattled the town, and precautionary measures were taken to reinforce the vaulted alleyways and tallest buildings. But disaster struck on February 23, 1887, when a major earthquake rocked Bussana, collapsing buildings and burying inhabitants beneath the rubble. The town was declared uninhabitable, and a new site for the village was chosen seaside on the

Capo Marine plateau. Singing a hymn about the exile of the Israelites in Egypt, the population left the newly named Bussana Vecchia (the *vecchia* added to designate it as the old village) on Palm Sunday 1894, the seventh anniversary of the quake.

Bussana Vecchia sat abandoned and decaying for more than half a century, until Clizia, a potter and artist from Torino "discovered" the town and conceived the idea of an international artists' village, which he founded in 1961 with artist Vanni Giuffré and poet Giovanni Fronte (Clizia left in 1963, perhaps because of schisms over how communal the town and its limited resources should be). Though faced with eviction in 1968, the village continued to grow, with artists refashioning the least-damaged buildings into studios, workshops, and display spaces.

Electricity arrived in the late 1970s, and ownership of various properties organized within a legal framework (though this issue was highly contested, both between artists in the village, and descendents of residents of the pre-earthquake Bussana). Further legal issues were raised through the 1980s and 90s as the artists fought the State for the right to determine the architectural and cultural direction of their hand-crafted village.

Getting There

By Train: The nearest **FS** station is at Bussana. For schedules, see www.trenitalia.it.

By Car: Follow the signs from Bussana, located off the Via Aurelia (take the A10 autostrada and exit at San Remo, then take the coastal highway to Bussana). It's a very narrow road, and parking is limited and only available outside the village.

Being There

Visitors inevitably arrive at the village on foot, since there's no parking and no automobile traffic inside Bussana Vecchia (leave your car along the road before reaching the turn-about point). This lends a peaceful air to the ramshackle town, which has been transformed over the years with gardens and colorful wall murals. Despite the presence of artists and travelers Bussana Vecchia still maintains the sense of a ghost town, especially early in the morning when the streets are mostly deserted and the village cats have their run of the ruins. With no sights to see – just loads of workshops and galleries to amble through – the only thing to do is be present and allow your own experience to unfold.

Il Giordino tra i Ruderi

This peaceful garden near the summit of the town (in the neighborhood of Le Rocche, which was hardest hit by the earthquake) has several paths that snake through grottos and up and over ruins, and several vantage points from which to see the coast, the village, and the bell tower of the church of Sacro Cuore. The plants – which grow in wild groupings – are marked with their botanical names and there are several benches where (if you can chase away the slumbering cat) you can while away some time in contemplation. Near the end a small museum presents the history of the artists' village. (Closed November, December; entrance fee €2.)

■ Val Nervia

Leaving the sea behind at Ventimiglia you enter the Val Nervia, which stretches for 20 km/12 miles up toward the Maritime Alps. The River Nervia winds through the bottom with many of the valley's towns dotted along its banks. The first is **Camporosso** – now a bedroom community for the coastal resort towns. It was once part of the *Magnifica Comunità degli Otto Luoghi*. The road then leads to **Dolceacqua**, divided in two by the river. The old town, *Terra*, dominated by the Doria castle, is attached to the new town, *Borgo*, by a medieval bridge that Claude Monet (who painted it several times) called "a jewel of lightness." Traveling farther, you arrive at **Pigna**, a hillside village whose churches house several precious works of art. From the town you can spot **Castel Vittorio**, Pigna's ancient archrival, high atop a hill overlooking the valley. Time seems to stand still while walking its cobbled streets. Doubling back and then detouring to a side road at the junction town of Isolabona, you arrive at **Apricale**, known as the "village of the artists" for its many craft workshops and the murals that adorn its inner sanctums. Then it's on to **Perinaldo**, birthplace of the astronomer Cassini, who is honored in his hometown with an observatory.

Considering the short distance one travels to get there, the inland towns have little in common with the coastal resorts. Ancient architecture reigns supreme, and the surrounding hillsides – covered with Mediterranean maquis to nearly 1,000 feet of altitude, then giving way to pines – are quiet and bare of development. Some of the towns themselves seem scarcely populated. More and more residents have shuttered their homes and moved in search of employment on the coast.

At the lower altitudes around Camporosso and Dolceacqua, flower cultivation for the market at San Remo is a mainstay of the economy, but higher up the more traditional activities of winemaking and olive growing are pursued. The famed wine of the valley is *Rossese di Dolceacqua*, though the vines are cultivated throughout the Val Nervia, and there are ample opportunities to taste it at quaint *osterie* throughout the area. Olive oil (especially that from Castel Vittorio and Apricale) dresses simple dishes at such places. Perhaps the best way to work up an appetite is to hike the beginning of the *Alta Via dei Monti Liguri*, the High Ligurian Trail that starts at the mouth of the Nervi and ends at the Tuscan border.

Getting to the Val Nervia

 By Train: The nearest **FS** station is at Ventimiglia. From there you'll need to proceed by car, foot, bike, or bus. For schedules, see www.trenitalia.it.

 By Car: Exit the A10 autostrada at Ventimiglia, then take the SS64 that leads to Camporosso, Dolceacqua, Pigna, and Castel Vittorio, minding the road signs. For Perinaldo and Apricale, return to Isolabona (between Dolceacqua and Pigna) and follow the signs.

 By Bus: Bus service in the area is provided by **Riviera Trasporti**. For fares, schedules and information see www.rivieratrasporti.it.

Val Nervia

Resources

■ www.rivieradeifiori.org

For Active Travelers

Hiking the Alta Via dei Monti Liguri

Trails 1-3 of the High Ligurian Trail pass through this part of the Val Nervia, with link-up trails that lead to Dolceacqua and Pigna. These are fairly demanding, uphill hikes (with sections of downhill), passing through the maquis in the low altitudes (trail n°1 and part of n°2) and through pine forests at higher elevation (rest of n°2 and n°3). For more information, see www.altaviadeimontiliguri.it. The entire Alta Via is described starting on page 212.

Trail n° I

■ Starting Point: Ventimiglia.
■ Ending Point: La Colla.
■ Distance: Roughly 10 km/six miles.
■ Average travel time: 3½ hours.
■ Link-up trail: From La Colla to Dolceacqua, an additional 1½ hours.

Trail n°2

■ Starting Point: La Colla.
■ Ending Point: Colla Sgora.
■ Distance : Roughly nine km/five miles.
■ Average travel time : 2½ hours.

Trail n°3

■ Starting Point: Colla Sgora.
■ Ending Point: Colla Scarassan.
■ Distance : Roughly 12 km/seven miles.
■ Average travel time : 4½ hours.
■ Link-up trail: From Gola di Gouta (near the end) to Pigna, an additional three hours.

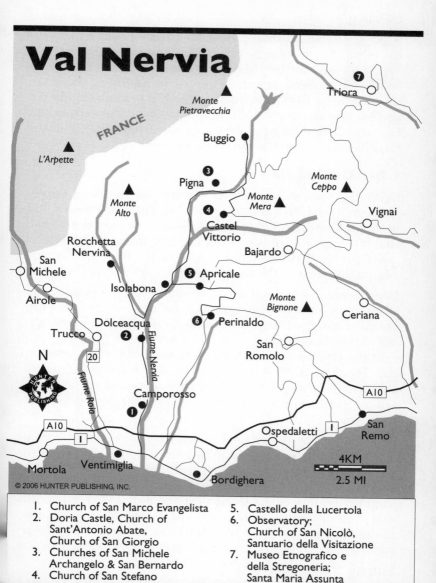

Val Nervia

Monte Pietravecchia

L'Arpette

FRANCE

Buggio

Monte Alto

Pigna ❸

Monte Ceppo

Monte Mera

Vignai

Rocchetta Nervina

❹ Castel Vittorio

Bajardo

San Michele

❺ Apricale

Isolabona

Monte Bignone

Ceriana

Airole

Dolceacqua ❷

❻ Perinaldo

Trucco

San Romolo

20

N

A10

Camporosso

❶

A10

Ospedaletti

San Remo

Mortola

Ventimiglia

Bordighera

4KM
2.5 MI

Triora ❼

Flume Nervia

Flume Roia

© 2006 HUNTER PUBLISHING, INC.

1. Church of San Marco Evangelista
2. Doria Castle, Church of Sant'Antonio Abate, Church of San Giorgio
3. Churches of San Michele Archangelo & San Bernardo
4. Church of San Stefano
5. Castello della Lucertola
6. Observatory; Church of San Nicolò, Santuario della Visitazione
7. Museo Etnografico e della Stregoneria; Santa Maria Assunta

Biking

 Though steep, the state road connecting the villages of the Nervia Valley is popular with cyclists, and the hiking trails of the Alta Via are also accessible to mountain bikers. In addition, there are trails leading away from most of the hill towns, including a particularly noteworthy biking trail between Dolceacqua and Soldano. **Cicli Action** in Ventimiglia (☎ 0184.232.007) at the mouth of the valley has mountain bikes for rent.

Camporosso

Given the town's proximity to Ventimiglia – once an important administrative center on the *Via Julia Augusta* – it is probable that Camporosso was known in Roman times, and that it acquired its name during that era. *Rosso*, which means "red," probably referred to the color of the local soil, or perhaps to the color of the oleanders that were cultivated here.

Considered the "door of the Val Nervia," Camporosso found itself in an uncomfortable position for much of its history. A possession of the Dukes of Ventimiglia, it was also the neighbor of Dolceacqua, ruled by the Doria of Genoa from the 13th century. The Nervia Valley was a setting for conflict between the Republic and Piedmont-Savoy – land-locked a stone's throw to the north. Camporosso represented an outlet to the sea for Savoy, which therefore repeatedly pressed to control the town.

In 1686, with the backing of Genoa (seeking counterbalance against Savoy, which had taken control of Dolceacqua in 1524), Camporosso broke from the Ventimiglia, joining the Genoa-allied *Magnifica Comunità degli Otto Luoghi* (Magnificent Community of the Eight Towns). The Otto Luoghi lasted more than a century, ending with the arrival of Napoleon and the establishment of the brief Republic of Liguria, and then movements to establish the Kingdom of Italy, which it joined.

Being There

Camporosso's fertile soil and flat terrain made it naturally suited for agriculture. The cultivation of grapes and olives (and today, flowers) has been a mainstay of the economy, helping the town grow to become the largest in the valley. Its population has swelled further in recent years as workers from the coastal resorts have moved to Camporosso seeking cheaper housing. The town is therefore in distinct sections, with the medieval center around the Piazza Garibaldi the most interesting to explore.

Tourist Office: Corso Repubblica, ☎ 0184.288.037.

Church of San Marco Evangelista

Camporosso's 15th-century parish church, which was renovated in the 18th century, has a painted tablet of the *Martyrdom of St. Sebastian* by Lodovico Brea. Martyred in 288, Saint Sebastian is the patron saint of the village and his January 20 feast day is celebrated with a procession in which members of the confraternities carry a laurel wreath covered in colored Communion wafers along the streets. The saint, according to tradition, was denied communion before his execution, and an angel appeared from heaven bringing the holy wafer.

Dolceacqua

During the period of Roman domination of Ventimiglia and the lower Nervia valley, the area of villages, pastures, and fields around Dolceacqua was fortified and protected by the Celtic Intemeli Ligurians. Thus the name Dolceacqua – which means "sweet water" – might actually be a corruption of the Celtic *Dus-Aga*, which was the name of the Gaul God of Spells. An alternate theory envisions a Roman country property belonging to *Dulcius*.

By the 12th century Dolceacqua belonged to the Lords of Ventimiglia, who erected the first castle upon the rocky summit of the river's left bank. In the late 13th century, Admiral Oberto Doria bought the castle and territory. It was the begin-

Val Nervia

ning of a period in which the ascendant family sought to consolidate their power through acquisition, following the decisive victory of Genoa over Pisa at the Battle of Meloria, in which Doria had distinguished himself.

The Doria were not popular rulers of Dolceacqua, however, in part because of traditions like the *jus primae noctis*, which granted the lords the right to deflower a bride on her wedding night. The presence of the Doria also made for contentious relations with other neighbouring towns and their powerful families, coming to a head during the battles between Guelphs and Ghibellines in the late Middle Ages. The Grimaldi (allied with the Guelphs on the side of the papacy) were consolidated around present-day Monaco and directly opposed the Doria (allied with the Ghibellines on the side of the Holy Roman Emperor), though there were ties between the two families. In 1523, Luca Doria killed his maternal uncle Luciano Grimaldi in an attempt to seize the principality. One year later, the town appealed for, and was granted, protection by Savoy. It remained a marquisate of Savoy until the formation of the Kingdom of Italy under Piedmont-Sardinia.

Being There

The Doria castle dominates *Terra* on the left bank of the Nervia River. The perfectly preserved old town spills down the hillside in a jumble of covered alleys and tall, narrow houses. The 16th century Doria *palazzo* is found at the base of the hill, by the parish church. Connecting *Terra* to *Borgo* is a late medieval bridge that is a marvel of engineering, spanning 33 m/93 feet in a single arch. The new town clusters around Piazza Garibaldi.

Tourist Office: Via Barberis Colomba, 3, ☎ 0184.206.666.

Doria Castle

The original structure was raised by the Lords of Ventimiglia in the 12th century and restructured several times after its transfer to the Doria in the 13th century. A larger ring of walls was added in the 14th century, after which the castle was transformed into a lavishly decorated fortified residence arranged around a central court. In the 16th century, around

the time that Dolceacqua came under the protection of Savoy, the family moved to a palace on the riverfront near the parish church. In 1744, during the war of Austrian Succession, in which Savoy was called upon to defend Austria's possessions in Italy against Spanish attack, the castle was partially destroyed by a Spanish-French bombardment and was abandoned. It was further damaged in the earthquake of 1887. Though the Doria family retained possession of the castle into the 20th century, it now belongs to Dolceacqua. (Guided tours are possible between 10 am-1 pm and 3:30-6:30 pm by contacting ☎ 0184.229.507 or 0184.351.183.)

Church of Sant'Antonio Abate

Dolceacqua's Baroque parish church was built in the 14th century and has, at the base of its bell tower, a fragment of the ancient town walls. Inside, it is richly decorated and has among its treasures the polyptych of *Santa Devota*, painted in 1515 by Lucovico Brea. From the time of their removal to a palace next to the church, the Doria could enter by means of a secret passageway connecting to their residence.

Church of San Giorgio

The medieval bridge lands on the *Borgo* side near the church of San Giorgio, the oldest parish church of Dolceacqua. Its Romanesque origins are evident in the façade and bell tower. The crypt has the tombs of Stefano and Giulio Doria (1589 and 1608).

Pigna

The hillside village that still maintains the ancient Intemelia dialect has always been distinguished from its neighbours in the Val Nervia. Though arranged in concentric circles like a pinecone, its name derives not from this appearance but from the pine forests that surround it. In fact, its current location (and form) is not original. In the 10th century the town was located closer to the valley floor around the church of San Tommaso (now in ruins). But the position was too vulnerable, and the politics surrounding the town too volatile, so the location farther up the hillside was chosen for a new settlement.

Prior to 1258 Pigna was a possession of the Ventimiglia, but in that year it yielded the town to the Anjou of Provenza (Provence). Soon after, the conflict between Guelphs and Ghibellines was raging in the valley, with Pigna on the side of the Guelphs (owing to its relationship with Provence) against the Doria (Ghibellines) of Dolceacqua. In 1365 an historic peace was signed between the two factions at Pigna's Lago Pigo Bridge, which became the dividing line between the territories of Provenza and the Republic of Genoa.

With the Dedition of Nice in 1388 (a peacefully-negotiated territory transfer, artfully managed by the Grimaldi of Monaco), Pigna passed from Provence's control to that of Savoy, which reignited tensions with the neighboring village of Castel Vittorio (an ally of Genoa). At times, this conflict would bear resemblance to the rivalries between two college frat houses. In 1727 some residents of Pigna stole the bells from Castel Vittorio's bell tower. The town retaliated by stealing the stones from the town square. For a brief period, from 1625 to 1633, Pigna fell to the Genoese, but it was soon back under Savoy's control, and remained so until the establishment of the Kingdom of Italy.

Being There

Pigna is characterized by its *chibi*, the somewhat dark alleyways laid out in concentric circles around the houses. The remains of a medieval castle are evident in the **Loggia della Piazza Vecchia** connected to the church of San Michelle, where units of measurement are carved into the stone. Around town one can find evidence of the ruling families of the past through patterns, designs, and monograms cut into the stone of their former residences. This set of symbols was shorthand for privileges and benefits granted to the families. At the top of the town are the bell tower and the **Piazza Castello**, from where there is a magnificent view of nearby Castel Vittorio. Local tradition is kept alive with the **Festival della Poesia e della Commedia Intemelia**, held the first week in August, where poetry and plays are performed in the local Intemelia dialect.

Tourist Office: Via Isnardi, 50, ☎ 0184.241.016.

Church of St. Michele Arcangelo

The most important monument in Pigna, the parish church was constructed in the 15th century and boasts a rose window depicting *Agnus Dei* surrounded by stained-glass panels with the 12 Apostles. It's an early work by Giovanni Gaggini of Bissone, who went on to earn great fame for similar works in Genoa. Inside is the polyptych of St. Michael, representing the later years of another prolific artist's career – Giovanni Canavesio was active from 1450 to 1500 and the painting dates to 1500.

Church of San Bernardo

Canavesio chose the theme of death and judgment for a cycle of grotesque frescoes executed within the Romanesque cemetery-church of San Bernardo. The cycle, showing the *Passion of Christ* and *Judgment Day*, dates from 1482.

Castel Vittorio

Castle Vittorio's ghost town atmosphere is a byproduct of the 20th century, as many of the town's residents have left to find employment in the big-

Chiesa di San Bernardo

Val Nervia

ger towns of the coast, abandoning the agricultural tradition that was a mainstay of the valley's economy. It's a sharp contrast to the bustle of Castel Vittorio's earlier years, when – as *Castrum Dodi* – it was a military garrison for Genoa. Before that it was a fortressed stronghold of the Counts of Ventimiglia.

The town's medieval walls remain around the town center, which encompasses a small square, the town hall, the parish church, and a lovely old fountain from which the villagers could take their drinking water. Climbing the winding streets – purposefully narrow and twisting to thwart invaders – you reach the bell tower, from which archrival Pigna stole the bells in 1727.

Being There

Visitors will have the village largely to themselves, and may wander the streets of the medieval center without ever encountering another soul. Consequently Castel Vittorio is one of those places that transports visitors back in time, though Castel Vittorio was actually a bustling military town in the past. Taggiasca olives are grown in the surrounding groves, harvested to make a superior olive oil that can now be purchased online (e-commerce being one of the ways the village might save itself, and its agricultural tradition, from obscurity; see www.castelvittoriosrl.it). There's also a small shop and tasting room in the village.

San Stefano

The parish church is at the summit of the town, adjacent the bell tower. Built in Baroque style, its interior is surprisingly ornate after the somber atmosphere of the village. The crucifix is by Maragliano.

Buggio

Returning toward Pigna is the turnoff for the rural town of Buggio, traditionally founded by three French thieves fleeing prosecution. The village, which sees very few tourists and maintains a rustic identity, has the only church dedicated to *San Siagrio* (a bishop from Nice), and fantastic views of the valley.

Apricale

In 2003 Apricale was designated one of the most beautiful villages in Italy (only six other towns in Liguria have received the same honor). Its name means "exposed to the sun," and indeed a warm, honey-toned light pervades the south-facing village. The ubiquitous sunlight has drawn artists who've colonized the steep caruggi with their workshops and galleries, and benefits a robust network of olive oil producers who work the groves of Taggiasca olives surrounding the village.

Apricale was established around 1000 with the construction of the castle by the Counts of Ventimiglia. Soon a ring of houses surrounded the castle, built upon the rocky summit. The Ventimiglia ruled Apricale until 1267, when the town declared itself independent and published its own set of statutes governing civic life in the commune. The prized documents – which punished murderers by burying them alive with their victims and decapitated women for committing adultery – are on display in the town's historical museum, located in the castle. Autonomy was short-lived, however. In

Val Nervia

1276 Apricale became a fief of the Doria of Dolceacqua and remained so for the next five centuries, except for a brief period in the 15th century when it fell to the Grimaldi of Monaco. Much of the village was constructed under Doria rule in the 15th century.

The 18th century was a period of great difficulty, as the town weathered first severe frosts (1709) and then drought (1718) that ravaged local crops and set the stage for plague (1720) and famine (1735). Another famine hit in 1764 and is commemorated by a carving in the stone hinges of one of the three doors surviving from the town's original medieval walls. In 1795, under Napoleonic rule, Apricale – which under its own statutes had once *required* citizens to attend mass on Sundays and all religious holidays – had its church bells confiscated and religious expression suppressed.

Apricale's standing in the world of art was established in the mid-20th century, first with the founding of a ceramic school that went on to produce several important artists in the craft, and then with the arrival of a group of painters from the Côte d'Azure whose ateliers attracted prominent collectors and other artists.

Being There

Apricale's artistic tradition is expressed each year with the **Giornata Annuale dell'Affresco**, or "Day of the Frescoes," (begun in 1984). On this day, the painted murals on the walls of buildings on Via Roma, Via Martyrdoms, and Via Cavour are refreshed and re-imagined by contemporary artists. The town now gives itself over completely to the arts, having

Apricale

1. Porta deu Carugiu ciàn
2. Piazza Vittorio Emanuele II
3. Chiesa parrocchiale di Apricale
4. Campanile della chiesa parrocchiale
5. Castello della Lucertola
   (Castle of the Lizard)
6. Museo della Storia di Apricale
7. Via Martiri (Carugiu ciàn)
8. Oratorio di San Bartolomeo
9. Via Cavour
10. Chiesa di Sant'Antonio abate
11. Via Castello
12. Porta di Cousoutàn
13. Via degli Angeli
14. Chiesa di Santa Maria degli Angeli
15. Piazza Via Veneto

100 METERS

320 FEET

established its tourism economy on its merits as a destination for art lovers, and it doesn't disappoint. There's a packed calendar year-round of events, exhibitions, and productions, in addition to the numerous workshops and galleries. The castle is at the center of many of these activities, and dominates the **Piazza Vittorio Emanuele** at the top, and at the heart of, the town.

Tourist Office: Via Roma, 1, ☎ 0184.208.641, www.apricale.org.

Castello della Lucertola

Apricale's "Lizard Castle" (so-known since soon after its construction in the 11th century, but why is seemingly lost to history) has recently been fully restored. Built by the Counts of Ventimiglia, it passed to the Doria upon their acquisition of the town in the late 13th century. In the 16th century the castle was partially destroyed during the Grimaldi siege and reconstructed. It was sold to the Cassini family in 1806, who added the lovely sculpture-adorned hanging gardens. The castle was recently recovered by the town and – following the renovation – opened for artistic and cultural events. A portion is given over to the town museum, which covers local history, legends and the village's artistic heritage.

Perinaldo

The village of Perinaldo was founded around the year 1000, when Count Rinaldo of Ventimiglia bought the territory and began construction of a castle stronghold on the hill, later to be named Podium Rainaldi. In the 13th century, soon after the defeat of the Pisans at the Battle of Meloria, Admiral Oberto Doria bought the property as part of the family's power consolidation in the Val Nervia.

Though bitter rivals, the Doria and the Grimaldis of Monaco were related both by blood and marriage. In the early 16th century, upon the death of Luca Doria, his wife Lady Francesca Grimaldi, daughter of the Sovereign Lord of Monaco, became regent of the Doria fiefs in the Nervia valley, including Perinaldo. Luca had killed his maternal uncle Luciano Grimaldi in an attempt to seize the principality of Monaco in 1523. Owing to such excesses, Dolceacqua, the

Doria seat, had appealed for, and been granted, protection by Savoy, becoming a marquisate. Upon Luca's death and the transfer of the fiefs to his wife's regency, Perinaldo, too, passed to the Savoy.

In 1622 Perinaldo's most famous son was born in the village. Gian Domenico Cassini began his studies as an astrologer, and in 1644 received an appointment to the Panzano Observatory in Bologna, where he worked developing more accurate tables to give the astrological coordinates of celestial bodies at various times of the year. This work introduced him to the budding field of astronomy, to which he quickly converted. In 1669 Cassini attracted the attention of Louis XIV of France, who'd recently established the Royal Academy of the Sciences and invited the astronomer to set up the Paris Observatory and become the court's astronomer. Among his most important discoveries were the true dimensions of the solar system and the spacing of the rings of Saturn.

Being There

The high hilltop village of Perinaldo has lovely views of the peaks of mounts Bignone, Ceppo, Toraggio, Pietravecchia, and Grai, covered in snow a good part of the year. Napoleon stayed here, in the Castello Maraldi (Cassini's childhood home), during the Italian campaign and introduced the Provençal variety of artichoke (carciofe) to the local cooks. It's now cultivated in nearly every garden, and features prominently on spring menus. Throughout town you'll see signs of homage to Cassini and his nephew Giacomo Filippo Maraldi (the main street is named for him).

Tourist Office: Town Hall, Piazza S. Antonio, 1, ☎ 0184.672.00.

Val Nervia

Observatory

In 1989 the town dedicated an observatory to its most famous resident, Cassini. Housed in the former Franciscan convent of San Sebastiano on the town's eastern outskirts, the observatory is open several evenings during the year and has three telescopes through which visitors can take a guided tour of the night sky, led by observatory astronomers. Next door, in the Town Hall, is a museum dedicated to the life of Cassini and his discoveries. The observatory publishes a schedule of "public openings" – generally two each month, usually on a Saturday evening – during which a guide operates the telescopes and points out objects in the sky. For the schedule, see www.astroperinaldo.it, ☎ 0184.672.095. The museum is open Monday-Saturday, 8:30 am-1:30 pm.

Parish Church of San Nicolò

The prized painting of the *Madonna and the Souls in Purgatory*, attributed to the Guercino school, was donated to Perinaldo's parish church by Gian Domenico Cassini in 1672. Founded in 1489 (note the date carved above the right-hand entrance door), the church was made-over in the Baroque style in the 18th century.

Santuario della Visitiazione

This country church outside the village is better known as the "Sanctuary of the Rock of the Wicked," because it is a traditional destination for penitents seeking atonement. It was constructed in 1695 under the supervision of Cassini, who aligned the church with the Liguria Meridian, or the line of longitude for Liguria. Consequently, on the longest day of the year at the summer solstice (June 21), the church casts no shadow.

■ Valle Argentina - Imperia

Though the coast of this stretch of the western Riviera is dotted with resort towns, some of the most interesting places to visit and explore lie inland. During the period of burgeoning international commerce that began in the Middle Ages, goods traversed the Mediterranean by ship, but eventually required overland routes to reach their markets. Liguria's unique geography – a network of valleys leading to the plains of Northern Italy and Europe, anchored by the port at Genoa – facilitated the movement of foodstuffs (especially salt, wine, and olive oil), cloth, spices, timber, and luxury goods. The Genoese Republic's continual press to dominate the coastal and inland towns of Liguria ensured that the valuable trade routes continued through the valleys unfettered, and that Genoa received little competition from other states.

Though in a somewhat compromised position today, since it sits practically under the A10 autostrada, the town of **Taggia** at the mouth of the Valle Argentina once profited from its geographical position. Originally a small fluvial port closer to the water (where now stands the resort town of Arma di Taggia), Taggia was founded when the population fled inland from the Lombard invasion, seeking refuge around a Benedictine mon-

Triora

astery. The monks introduced the cultivation of the *Taggia* olive (also known as the *Taggiasca*), which now flourishes throughout the Riviera dei Fiori and which fueled Taggia's economy for centuries.

Farther inland, traveling up the Valle Argentine, is **Triora**. From the late 13th century the town was a stronghold of the Genoese, who constructed elaborate city walls with seven gates, not to mention five fortresses and castles, all of which are now in ruins. In the Middle Ages Triora was a bustling, urban center, but today it is scarcely populated (with under 500 residents). Nonetheless, its charming medieval atmosphere, surrounding natural environment, and the lingering notoriety from the witch burnings that took place here in the 16th century still draw visitors.

The westernmost neighborhood of Imperia is **Porto Maurizio**, which has one of the Riviera's most perfectly intact medieval town centers, characterized by narrow alleys and connecting stairways. It was the capital of the Vicariate of Western Liguria under Genoese domination, when construction of the Duomo began (not to be finished until the 19th century). Imperia's other district, **Oneglia**, was a stronghold of the House of Savoy. In recognition of the long years of animosity between the rival neighborhoods, the **Palazzo Municipale** was constructed in 1932 equidistant between the two on the Viale Matteotti.

Finally, heading inland up the Impero Valley and then on through the Arroscia Valley you arrive at the town of **Pieve di Tecco**. Located on the salt route between Liguria and Piedmont, it was at the height of its prosperity in the 14th and 15th centuries, when under Genoese domination. Wealth funded palaces and richly decorated churches, helping the town's residents diversify into other craft activities such as silk weaving and papermaking. It is still an artisan stronghold, with workshops producing prized handmade walking boots, and locally produced cheeses and breads that win acclaim from gourmets.

Taggia

During the Roman ages Taggia was an important town known as the *Tabiae Fluvius*, located at the sandy mouth of the Argentina river. But in the seventh century, the Lombard invasions sent the population inland to the shelter of the Benedictine monastery near what now is the medieval center of the town. The position was more defensible, and led to a change in economic direction for the residents that once depended on trade and fishing for their livelihood.

The monks introduced the planting of the *Taggia* olive — a small, black variety that produces a light, flavorful oil of very low acidity. By the 12th century, when the town fell under the domination of the Marquises of Clavesana, several mills were producing olive oil of exceptional quality and value. The powerful family built a castle from which to control the territory, but in the 13th century the residents of Taggia rose in revolt against their rule and the Clavesana sold the town to Genoa.

Taggia

The village soon felt the burden of their new dominion. During the 13th century Genoa was engaged in near constant battle with Pisa over supremacy of Sardinia, and Taggia, with a wealth earned from the trade of olive oil, was pressed for both men and money in support of the campaigns. Then in 1270 the village was caught between the Guelphs and Ghibellines when Baliano Doria ensconced himself under siege in the Taggia castle. In recognition of the difficulties endured by the town on Genoa's behalf, in 1439 the Palazzo Curlo was erected, commemorating the end of hostilities between the murderous Guelph and Ghibelline factions.

Though the olive groves lay untended for nearly two centuries between the Guelph siege and the construction of a third set of town walls and a defensive tower in the 16th century, cultivation and production of olive oil eventually resumed and remains a mainstay of the town's economy. Taggia's rural ambiance derives in part from the trees that surround the town, though some 600,000 of these were pulled up during WWII and used as firewood for the desperate local populace.

Getting There

By Train: The **FS** station is a short distance away in Arma di Taggia, the town's coastal suburb. For schedules, see www.trenitalia.it.

By Car: Exit the A10 autostrada at Arma di Taggia/San Remo Est.

By Bus: Bus service in the area is provided by **Riviera Trasporti** (www.rivieratrasporti.it). You can take a bus from the train station at Arma di Taggia to Taggia.

Resources

■ www.rivieradeifiori.org

■ www.taggia.it

■ **Tourist Office:** Located in Arma di Taggia, Villa Boselli, ☎ 0184.437.33.

Being There

Taggia lies on the western bank of the Argentina River, practically in the shade of the autostrada. A medieval bridge with 16 arches spans the river, but there is little to see on the eastern side (a trail from here leads to the sea). Visitors to the historic center, considered the largest and most important outside Genoa, generally enter at the **Porta dell'Orso**, or Gate of the Bear, which was part of the 16th-century city walls. There are several small piazzas dotted throughout the medieval town, and flanking these are the former palazzos of the nobility, identified by carved portals made of the black stone of the Valle Argentina. The most attractive **palazzos** are to be found on Via San Dalmazzo, Via Curlo, Via Gastaldi, and Via Soleri, which is an arcaded street. To the south of Taggia is the coastal suburb of **Arma di Taggia**, which has a sandy beach and a seafront promenade extending from the Annunziata grotto and fortress on one side, to the port and wharf on the other. Its about three km/1.8 miles between Taggia and Arma di Taggia.

Convent of San Domenico

Outside the town proper, on the south side toward Arma di Taggia, is the convent of San Domenico, built in 1490 and once an important cultural center. Some of the leading artists of the 15th and 16th centuries were commissioned to work here, and the convent's gallery has works by the Brea brothers, Gregorio de Ferrari, and Orbetto da Verona. Ludovico Brea is the best represented, with polyptychs in the first and third chapels (*Madonna of the Rosary* and *St. Catherine of Siena with Sts. Agatha and Lucy*), the altar to the left of the presbytery (*Baptism of Christ and Saints*) and the high altar (*Madonna of Mercy with Saints*). Of these, *Madonna of the Rosary* is a standout.

Parish Church of Saints Giacomo & Filippo

Built in the 17th century on the remains of a Romanesque temple, the church is based on a plan by the architect and sculptor Bernini. The father and son, Giovanni and Luca Cambiaso, are responsible for two of the church's impressive works. Luca painted *Sts. Anthony Abbot and Paul the Hermit* and assisted his father with the *Resurrection* found in the Chapel of the Body of Christ.

Only in Taggia

Olive Oil Tasting

Frantoio Boeri, located in the old town at Viale Rimembranza, 34 (☎ 0184.475.301), is a family-run business that's been producing olive oil for four generations. The oils are cold-pressed and bottled on the premises, which dedicates a tiny "museum" to ancient presses and other tools of the trade. One of the younger family members is certified by the *Organizzazione Nazionale Assaggiatori Olio di Oliva* and can lead visitors through an informative tasting of the wares on offer at the store, where you can also purchase typical Ligurian food products and olive-oil based cosmetics.

For Active Travelers

Biking

A clever way to travel the short distance between Arma di Taggia and Taggia is by bike, available for rent from **G.S. Grosso Sport** in the coastal town (Via Aurelia Ponente, 145, ☎ 0184.448.830). Take the bike with you to explore the Valle Argentina, which has several trails through fantastic alpine scenery.

Diving

Polo Sub in Arma di Taggia organizes dive trips along the coast of this part of the Riviera dei Fiori (Via Lungomare, ☎ 0184.535.335).

Triora

The once-bustling alpine town of Triora is sur-rounded by cave-pocked mountainsides where artifacts of human habita-tion have been found dat-ing as far back as 3000 BC. Vase fragments, human remains, and ornamental objects testify to a pastoral people that thrived for centuries, until the arrival of the Romans, against whom they fought bitterly in the second century BC, before succumbing to the Impe-rial Age and, eventually, to Christianization.

By the seventh century, when refugees from the coast escap-ing the Lombard invasions swelled the town's population, Triora's ecclesiastical activities were under the domain of the Bishop of Albenga, a situation that continued even as gover-nance of the town passed to the Lords of Ventimiglia in the 12th century. However in 1190 Ventimiglia ceded the town and many of its other holdings in western Liguria to the Republic of Genoa, which placed a podestà (a sort of local administrator appointed by the Republic) at the head of the town council.

Triora grew in prominence and riches, serving as the granary of Genoa. Wealth was reinvested in building projects, creating a medieval center rich in fortressed-houses decorated with slate portals, churches, fountains, cobbled alleyways and stone arches, surrounded by a defense system of walls and gates. But its role as breadbasket made a famine in the summer of 1587 all the more serious, and the town turned to scapegoating. Two hundred women were accused of witchcraft and tried in Genoa. In the end, many of the women were tortured and 15 were burned at the stake. Today a museum in Triora examines the complex circumstances that led to the village's being named "the town of the witches."

In 1625 the town was under siege by Piedmontese troops, but delivered on August 20, the feast day of Saint Bernardo, who was thereafter proclaimed Triora's patron saint and the day a festival of veneration and liberation. However, Triora was besieged again by Piedmontese troops in 1672, and the surrounding lands ravaged. Just over one hundred years later, the Argentine and Nervia valleys were the scene of battles between French and Piedmontese troops, culminating in the brief Ligurian Republic that preceded the establishment of the Kingdom of Italy, which Triora joined in 1804.

Getting There

 By Train: The nearest **FS** station is in Arma di Taggia on the coast. From there you can take a local bus or drive up the SS548 to Triora. For schedules, see www.trenitalia.it.

 By Car: Exit the A10 autostrada at Arma di Taggia/San Remo Est, then take the SS548 up the Argentine Valley to Triora.

 By Bus: Local bus service is provided by **Riviera Trasporti**. Buses from San Remo, Taggia, and Arma di Taggia head to Triora. For fares, schedules and information, see www.rivieratrasporti.it.

Resources

- www.rivieradeifiori.org
- www.comune.triora.im.it
- **Tourist Office:** Corso Italia, 3, ☎ 0184.944.77.

Being There

The picturesque town of Triora boasts gorgeous natural surroundings, where alpine activities, hiking, and climbing are popular, and an intact medieval center composed of cobbled alleyways and stone buildings surrounded by defensive walls. Built on a hilltop, the streets slope steeply, connected to one another by stairways and vaulted stone corridors. There are several evocative ruins within the town, including several castles. The atmosphere is of quiet isolation, especially as many of the town's residents have left to seek employment along the coast. Today there are fewer than 500 full-time residents living in the village.

Museo Etnografico e della Stregoneria

Triora's museum of ethnography and witchcraft is a hodge-podge of objects and artifacts that cumulatively create a narrative of life in the village at its most exciting and mundane through the centuries. Archeological discoveries from some of the surrounding caves document the region's prehistory, while another room is dedicated to wood statues and processional heads from the 15th century as well as a miniature reproduction of Triora in the 18th. A series of rooms is dedicated to everyday objects used in winemaking and dairy production, and another represents a typical kitchen. Finally there are the documents and other displays related to the witch trials in the 16th century. Outside is a lovely garden of aromatic and medicinal plants. (☎ 0184.944.77; summer – open Monday-Friday 3-7 pm; weekends and holidays 10:30 am-12 noon and 3-7 pm; winter – Monday-Friday 2:30-6 pm; weekends and holidays 10:30 am-noon and 2:30-6 pm; entrance fee €2 adults, €1 children.)

Santa Maria Assunta

Inside the collegiate church – which retains its original Romanesque-Gothic portal and bell tower base – is the *Baptism of Jesus*, painted in 1397 by Taddeo di Bartolo. It is thought to be the oldest painted representation of Christ's baptism in western Liguria.

Only in Triora
The Lower Argentine Valley

To reach Triora you'll pass through the lower Argentine Valley, dotted with small hamlets among terraced hillsides where olives are cultivated. As the road climbs higher the vegetation changes, from per-

Badalucco

fumed Mediterranean maquis closer to the coast to dense forests of chestnuts and beech and fir pines. The first town reached is the fortified village of **Badalucco**, exited and entered by medieval humpbacked bridges. In September gourmets flock here for the *Sagra du Stocafissu a Baücôgna*, a festival surrounding a dish of dried cod prepared according to an ancient town recipe. Also of note is the open-air art museum with murals and wood and ceramic works by local artists. The road then winds to **Montalto Ligure**, which, according to legend, was founded by newlyweds fleeing the *jus prima noctis* exercised by the count of Badalucco. Commonly practiced, and protested, in many villages throughout Liguria during the Middle Ages, it gave a feudal lord the rite to deflower a bride on her wedding night. The upper part of the town is a labyrinth of cobblestone alleys and vaulted passageways crowned by a religious complex. Finally, just before Triora is **Molini di Triora**, named for its ancient watermills (in the late Middle Ages there were nearly two dozen). Molini is a gateway to an extensive trail network for trekking. If you're hiking in September, you might work up an appetite for the town's **Snail Festival**. The delicious *lumaca* are prepared by traditional recipes and offered with Ormeasco wine, local bread, and *bruzzo* (a spicy ricotta cheese produced in the hinterland of this part of Liguria).

For Active Travelers

Climbing

Triora is famed as a destination for rock climbing. This dangerous sport is best practiced with a guide (and reliable equipment) by amateurs, and with due caution and reliable equipment by experienced climbers. The best routes are at Loreto just outside town, where the climbs range from class 4a to 7b (UK classification system). The best advice is to hire a guide who is familiar with the terrain. Inquire at the Triora tourist office. Make sure all equipment is well maintained and in good condition. You might want to purchase a copy of *Guida d'Arrampicata*, a climbing guide to the Argentina Valley by Marco Pukli, available at the tourist office. There is also some excellent information online at www.digilander.libero.it/bike-andclimb/freeclimb (route maps and basic info).

Bungee Jumping

Adrenaline-junkies might thrill to plunge headfirst into the Argentina River gorge from the **Loreto Bridge**, built in 1959 and standing 120 m/340 feet high. A number of outfitters work the bridge in the summer season, assisting jumpers. Check credentials before you leap.

Skiing

Only 55 km/33 miles from the sea but at 1,400 m/3,900 feet altitude, the little ski resort of **Monesi di Triora** is on the slopes of Mt. Saccarello (the highest peak in Liguria). There's not always much snow, but when there is it's particularly worthwhile to take the "Plateau" lift to the mountaintop. The same is possible in the summer months, or there's a hiking path to the top. Overlooked by the *Redentore* – a gold cast iron statue of Christ placed at the pinnacle in 1901 – there's a view over the Alps and the Mediterranean all the way to Corsica. In the winter there is no access to Monesi from Triora. Instead, take the A10 exit at Albenga and proceed inland to Pieve di Teco, then take the provincial road to Monesi.

Imperia

The paired villages of Porto Maurizio and Oneglia – merged to create the town of Imperia in 1923 – present a microcosm of the tensions and loyalties that engulfed the western Riviera for centuries.

The oldest quarter of Porto Maurizio, clustered around the Parasio promontory, began to develop around the 11th century, at which time the village was a free commune with ties to the local Benedictine monks. With a small natural harbor, Porto Maurizio developed into an economic and trade center. During this same period Oneglia began to grow on a small flatland around the mouth of the Impero river. Backed and protected by Castelvecchio (now a suburb of Imperia) – the oldest settlement in the Impero valley and defender of the hinterland – Oneglia was a possession of the bishop of nearby Albenga.

In the 13th century both towns entered the orbit of Genoa, but on unequal footing. In 1241 Porto Maurizio was named the Capital of the Vicariate of Western Liguria at the same time that Genoa established the Capitaneria in the village, with surveillance responsibilities (via a well-equipped fleet) from Savona to Ventimiglia. The concentration of authority and political activity in Porto Maurizio strengthened its allegiance to the Republic, a tie that would remain strong for centuries.

Meanwhile, in 1298 Oneglia was sold to the Doria family of Genoa who, ironically (considering that Oneglia today is the main port of the province of Imperia), used the town more as a residential base, constructing the Doria Palace here (where Andrea Doria was born in 1488). Olive cultivation and fishing were the important industries for the local population, compared to the lofty and politically astute maritime activities concentrated at neighboring Porto Maurizio.

In a baffling move, considering the tensions between the two powers, in 1576 the Doria sold the town to the House of Savoy, who hoped to exploit Oneglia as a port and wedge for Piedmontese expansion in Liguria. Thus divided between rival factions, Porto Maurizio and Oneglia stared each other

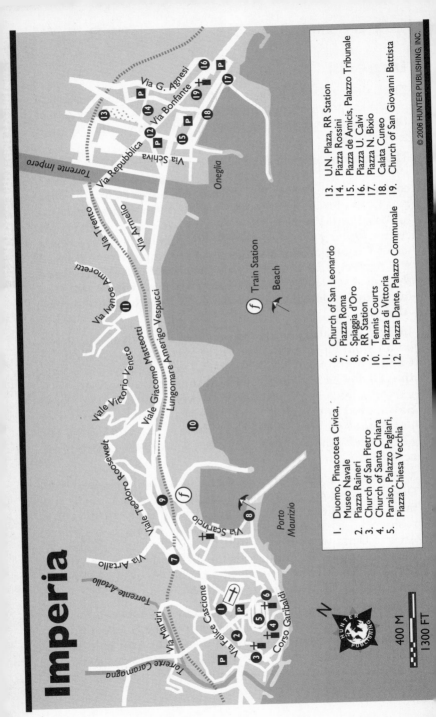

Imperia

1. Duomo, Pinacoteca Civica, Museo Navale
2. Piazza Raineri
3. Church of San Pietro
4. Church of Santa Chiara
5. Paraiso, Palazzo Pagliari, Piazza Chiesa Vecchia
6. Church of San Leonardo
7. Piazza Roma
8. Spiaggia d'Oro
9. RR Station
10. Tennis Courts
11. Piazza di Vittoria
12. Piazza Dante, Palazzo Communale
13. U.N. Plaza, RR Station
14. Piazza Rossini
15. Piazza de Amicis, Palazzo Tribunale
16. Piazza U. Calvi
17. Piazza N. Bixio
18. Calata Cuneo
19. Church of San Giovanni Battista

Church of San Leonardo
Piazza Roma
Spiaggia d'Oro
RR Station
Tennis Courts
Piazza di Vittoria
Piazza Dante, Palazzo Communale

Train Station
Beach

Torrente Impero
Oneglia
Porto Maurizio

Via G. Agnesi
Via Bonfante
Via Schiva
Via Repubblica
Via Trento
Via Armelio
Via Ivanoe
Via Amoretti
Viale Victorio Veneto
Viale Teodoro Roosevelt
Viale Giacomo Matteotti
Lungomare Amerigo Vespucci
Via Scarrico
Via Arrallo
Via Felice Caccione
Via Martiri
Torrente Arrollo
Torrente Carampana
Corso Garibaldi

400 M
1300 FT

© 2006 HUNTER PUBLISHING, INC.

down across a small stretch of sea, remaining hostile to one another even under Italian unification in the 19th century, until they were reconciled administratively by becoming one town in the 20th century. In a great symbolic gesture, the **Palazzo Municipale** was constructed in 1932, equidistant between the two neighborhoods.

Getting There

 By Train: There are **FS** stations in both Porto Maurizio (just off the Viale Giacomo Matteotti, main thoroughfare to Oneglia) and Oneglia (near the Piazza Dante). For schedules, see www.trenitalia.it.

 By Car: For Porto Maurizio, exit the A10 autostrada at Imperi Ouest. For Oneglia, exit at Imperia Est.

 By Bus: Local bus service (including between Porto Maurizio and Oneglia) is provided by **Riviera Trasporti** (www.rivieratrasporti.it).

Resources

- www.rivieradeifiori.org
- www.comune.imperia.it
- **Tourist Office:** Viale Matteotti, 37, ☎ 0183.660.140.

Being There

Viale Matteotti and the **Lungomare Amerigo Vespucci** string together Porto Maurizio (to the west) and Oneglia (to the east), but the two neighborhoods and former rivals are still distinct entities. Porto Maurizio is characterized by the nicely preserved (and gentrifying) medieval neighborhood of **Parasio** that encircles the promontory of the same name. A network of stepped streets climbs the hill toward the tip-top **Piazza Chiesa Vecchia**, site where the *Paraxu* (the Genoese governor's palace) once stood. The piazza is named, however, for the church of San Maurizio that also once stood here, demolished around 1838. In contrast to the architecture of Porto Maurizio, testimony to its prominence under the Genoese Republic, Oneglia looks like a typical Ligurian fishing village. The porticoed waterfront **Calata Cuneo** is populated with fishmongers' shops and restaurants.

Duomo

Just outside the Parasio historical center, take the Via Acquarone from the Piazza del Duomo to reach its heart. Porto Maurizio's Duomo was designed and planned during the period of Genoese domination but not completed until the 18th-19th century (construction was active from 1781 to 1838). Inside are works from the 19th century and paintings and statues salvaged from the demolished church of San Maurizio that once stood at the pinnacle of Parasio.

Museo Navale Internazionale del Ponente Ligure

Sharing the Piazza del Duomo with the cathedral, Porto Maurizio's naval museum presents life aboard ship complete with cramped quarters. The museum is diminutive in size. Various objects, documents, models, uniforms, and books have been entrusted to the museum, founded in 1980 by Commander Flavio Serafini. (Open Wednesday-Saturday 3-7 pm; June-September 9-11 and 3-7 pm, ☎ 0183.651.541.)

Museo dell'Olivo

Perhaps the most fascinating museum in western Liguria, Oneglia's *Museo dell'Olivo*, founded in 1992, presents the 6,000-year history of olive cultivation, with special emphasis on olive oil production and its role in the economic, political, cultural, and artistic history of the western Riviera. Located in the Fratelli Carli oil-making plant on Via Garessio near the

train station, the museum has 18 rooms filled with ancient and modern objects that recount olive oil's role in ritual, trade, migration, and daily life. Beautiful photography and elegant displays create an instructive narrative. Outside are two 1,000-year-old trees and elements from an 18th-century Liguria mill and two Spanish olive oil presses from the 16th and 18th centuries. Afterwards, visit the Fratelli Carli facili-

Above: Artist's gallery, Bussana Vecchia
Below: Belltower and remains of the parish church, Bussana Vecchia

ties for a look at modern olive oil production. There's a café and shop featuring carved olive wood objects, oils, and olive oil-based cosmetics. (Open Monday-Saturday 9am-12:30 pm and 3-6:30 pm; advance booking required to visit Fratelli Carli plant, open December-March; ☎ 0183.295.762, www.museodellolivo.com; entrance free.)

Only in Imperia

Dolcedo

Inland from Porto Maurizio (take the road for Valle del Torrente Prino from the Via Aurelia) is the village of Dolcedo, a center for olive cultivation since the 13th century. Five bridges, including the Grande built by the Knights of Malta in 1292, cross the Prino stream that fed the olive mills. From the black-and-white parvis (courtyard) of the church of San Tommaso (where concerts are held in the summer season) a path leads to the **Sanctuary of Acquasanta di Lecchiore**, a pilgrimage site. The trail leads through olive groves and vineyards, making for a charming walk.

For Active Travelers

Spiaggia d'Oro

The "Golden Beach" of Porto Maurizio is named for the color of its sand, not necessarily its high caliber. But it's popular with water sports enthusiasts. Kite and wind surfers congregate here each year for the springtime Imperia Wind Festival. The beach is somewhat of a surf spot, too, and there are a few beach clubs.

Pieve di Teco

Prior to the 13th century Pieve di Teco was little more than a convenient rendezvous point for residents of the villages of the Upper and Middle Arroscia Valley, and travelers of the salt road between Liguria and Piedmont. Around 1232 several neighboring villages participated in the founding of Pieve di Teco, which was in a strategically important position geographically, and potentially beneficial to all its neighbors. The Clavesana, ruling family of the valley, consented to a village of "up to 300 hearths, with a Castle, Towers, and Embankments," and yielded property for the town site. In eight years the heart of Pieve di Teco had been built and settled.

Pieve di Teco

The linear plan of the village was c o m p l e t e l y altered after 1386, however, the year in which the Clavesana agreed to be vassals of Genoa and ceded the prosperous town to the Republic. Genoa, to counterbalance the growing threat of the House of Savoy in Piedmont to the immediate north, reorganized the administrative structure of the entire upper Arroscia Valley and made Pieve di Teco the seat of the military command of the region.

Its position at the crossroads between Liguria and Piedmont was indeed lucrative, and perilous. Commercial travelers of the salt road traditionally sojourned in the well-fortified town, where paper mills, rope-making workshops, tanneries, and silk- and cloth-making factories were flourishing. For nearly three centuries Genoa was able to thwart any attacks by Piedmont, but in 1625 the castle and the fortifications were destroyed during the first Savoyard war, in which Genoa ultimately prevailed. Then in 1672 tensions flared again in a proxy-battle between the nearby towns of Rezzo, controlled by Genoa, and Cenova, part of a Marquesate that belonged to the Savoy. Corsican mercenary troops fighting for Genoa waged battle with the Piedmontese throughout the valley.

Pieve di Teco was occupied by the Piedmontese again in 1744, and 50 years later was terrorized by the French, crossing through on their way to Piedmont during the Revolutionary Wars.

These days, however, Pieve di Teco's position on the SS28 between Liguria and Piedmont is again beneficial, as traffic has brought tourism and retained jobs that have become scarce in other inland villages. The town is still an artisan stronghold, and appreciated by visitors both for its architectural and culinary heritage.

Getting There

 By Train: The train stations at Imperia and Albenga are the most convenient for reaching Pieve di Teco. For schedules, see www.trenitalia.it.

 By Car: From the A10 exit Imperia Est and take the SS28 toward Colle di Nava. Alternately, exit at Albenga and take the SS453.

 By Bus: Local bus service is provided by **Riviera Trasporti** (www.rivieratrasporti.it). Buses from Imperia depart from the Oneglia train station.

Resources

- www.rivieradeifiori.org
- www.comunitamontanaarroscia.imperia.it
- **Tourist Office:** Piazza Brunengo, 1, ☎/fax 0183.364.53.

Being There

The heart of Pieve di Teco is the **Corso Ponzoni**, a tree-lined thoroughfare with a porticoed medieval piazza at either end. Clustered along the street are various shops selling some of the artisan products produced in the village, though their famed handmade hiking boots are getting harder and harder to find as traditional producers pass on. There are also *trattorie* where you can enjoy a meal washed down with the town's *Ormeasco* wine.

Santa Maria della Ripa

This 15th-century church has columns of black stone and pointed arches covered in black-and-white stripped stucco. Though no longer in popular use, the side door facing the village (with a large Gothic portal) was probably originally the main entrance. The slender, gabled bell tower has been recently restored. Internally the church is connected with the Oratorio of the Assunta, constructed at a later date to house the Confraternity of the Flagellants.

San Giovanni Battista

Pieve di Teco's parish church was planned by Gaetano Canoni and built in the early 19th century after the original building, said to have been built in 1234 but more likely in 1333, was demolished in 1785 for fear of its collapsing. The dome covering the sacristy, which is richly decorated with paintings by Genoese artist Michele Canzio, is a unique structure of whole bricks reinforced by projections along the principal beams and convex ring, a technique Cantoni borrowed from vaulted Roman mural structures. The method is repeated in the parish church at Porto Maurizio, Imperia, which Cantoni also designed and which is the only other example of this type of construction in all of Liguria. The balustrade of the altar of the Madonna del Rosario and the 15th-century baptismal fount were taken from the original church, and there are also sculptures from the Maragliano school and paintings by Giulio Benso, Domenico Piola, and Luca Cambiaso (to whom the *San Francesco di Paolo* is attributed). Behind the church, following the steep paved road past the convent of San Francesco, is a grove once belonging to the Capuchin monks, thickly planted with centuries-old trees.

Only in Pieve di Teco

Antique Fair

Antique vendors and artists can be found under the porticoes of the medieval central street on the last Sunday of each month, when Pieve di Teco holds an Antique and Craft Fair.

Colle di Nava

Continuing north on the SS 28 you reach this high mountain pass set amidst meadows and woods. The landscape is dotted with fortresses erected by the Savoy to guard this important passageway to their inland empire, and surrounding are fields of lavender that perfume the air and flavor the honey on offer at shops in the small town of Nava near the Ligurian border.

For Active Travelers

Trout Fishing

The Arroscia river is popular with anglers who ply the swift-moving waters or numerous calm "lakes" formed where the water pools in deeper depressions. This activity requires the proper permits, which can be applied for through the tourist office.

Paragliding

Northwest of Pieve di Teco is the mountain community of **Mendatica** and the **Colle San Bernardo**. This is an excellent launching spot for paragliders and hosts paragliding events and gatherings. The **San Bernardo Hotel** (☎ 0183.328.724) makes arrangements.

Hiking

An excellent, but easy, trail from Mendatica leads to the stunning **Arroscia Falls**, which cascade down the hillside in a series of rocky steps that are frequently navigated by climbers wearing wetsuits and special gear. Trails 7, 8, and 9 of the **Alta Via dei Monti Liguri** also pass nearby. Trail 7 – from Colle San Bernardo to Colle di Nava – is an easy trail split between a little-used paved road and a wooded mule track, all with views of the valley (time to travel, about 2½ hours). Trail 8 – from Colle di Nava to Passo di Prale – is a short and steep uphill on a mule track through the woods (time to travel, about two hours). Trail 9 – from Passo di Prale to Colle San Bartolomeo – is the most arduous, though still rated for average excursionists, with steep uphill and downhill sections that get tricky when the fog rolls in and visibility diminishes. For more information, see www.altavia-deimontiliguri.it.

Horseback Riding

The numerous paths and trails around the Colle di Nava are well suited for horseback riding, and the **Scuderia di Forte Pozzanghi** rents horses for guided treks in the area. Trails 7, 8, and 9 of the **Alta Via dei Monti Liguri** (from Colle San Bernardo to Passo di Prale) are also well suited for horseback excursions. Inquire at the stables.

■ Diano Marina - Pietre Ligure

Heading east around a villa-dotted promontory from Imperia is a stretch of coast that enjoyed the height of fame in the mid-19th century when its resorts became popular with post-WWII travelers to the Riviera. **Diano Marino** was once an important, if small, port, transporting olive oil from the many mills in the area. Almost completely destroyed by the earthquake of 1887, it was rebuilt in resort fashion and found its vocation as a tourist destination. The waterfront line of hotels, beach clubs, and restaurants continues almost unbroken through to Cervo, which is overlooked by a hilltop castle and the church of San Giovanni Battista. It is then on to **Alassio**, one of the loveliest towns of the western Riviera. The town's famous *muretto* is an homage to the celebrities who've been drawn to the town since the 1950s. Finally you reach **Albenga** sitting at the crux of a vast plain that, since Roman times when the town, with Ventimiglia, was the most important in western Liguria, has been a vital growing region. The walled medieval town is perfectly preserved and makes for fascinating exploring. It's amply populated with shops and restaurants.

Diano Marina

The resort town of Diano Marina has Roman roots, but even in the Imperial Age it was considered a place of leisure. The wood of *Lorcus Bormani*, dedicated to the pagan god Borman (who became Apollo under the Romans), was a resting place along the Via Julia Augusta. As olive cultivation became an important industry for this region of Liguria, Diano Marino developed a fleet and became a commercial center for the sea trading of olive oil.

In the Middle Ages the coast was repeatedly attacked by pirates, sending residents scurrying inland to the Diano Valley where they swelled the population of several other small towns, including Diano Castello, stronghold of the Clavesana family until Genoese domination in 1228, and eventually an independent commune and ally of the Republic.

In 1887 the same earthquake that completely destroyed the town of Bussana Vecchia rocked the town. Here, however, the residents decided to rebuild. By that date late in the 19th century other coastal towns of Liguria were catering to the British, German, and Russian tourists that were creating little colonies in San Remo, Bordighera, and other villages along the shore. Following suit, Diano Marina reinvented itself with Art Nouveau resort architecture, hotels, and a palm-lined seafront promenade.

Getting There

By Train: Diano Marina's **FS** station is located about two blocks inland from the seafront promenade on the western side of town. For schedules, see www.trenitalia.it.

By Car: Exit the A10 autostrada at Diano Marina.

By Bus: Bus service in the area is provided by **Riviera Trasporti** (see www.rivieratrasporti.it for timetables).

Resources

- www.golfodidiana.it
- www.rivieradeifiori.org
- **Tourist Office:** Corso Garibaldi, 60, ☎ 0183.496.956.

Being There

After the earthquake of 1887, the task of redesigning the town center was entrusted to engineer Giacomo Pisano, who established a plan of straight streets and buildings constructed only three

stories high (many have since scaled higher). Via Roma, running parallel to the waterfront is planted with orange trees, a nod to a town prefect with Sicilian roots, and the seafront promenade is lined with palms. In recognition of the importance of olive oil to the development of their town, residents still refer to Piazza Virgilio, once the commercial square for the trade, as *Piazza dell'Olio*. Diano Marino's beaches are relatively sandy in comparison with the pebbled beaches elsewhere in Liguria and the harbor is full of pleasure craft. The town is crowded the Sunday after Corpus Christi, 10 weeks after Easter, for the *Infiorata* when the streets are strewn with thousands of flower petals creating fragrant blooming carpets.

Museo Civico e Archeologico

Diano Marina's civic museum on Corso Garibaldi creates a narrative of the town's history through artifacts from its Roman and medieval periods, along with various objects from the Napoleonic era and the Risorgimento. Some of the Roman pieces (amphorae and other vessels) come from the undersea excavation of the *Pacata Felix*, a ship that sank just off the coast millennia ago. From the Middle Ages are *ziri* (containers for shipping grain overseas) and several objects related to the olive oil trade. The Risorgimento history glorifies Nicola Rossi, citizen of Diano Marina, who was friend and right-hand-man to Giuseppe Garibaldi and commander of one of the two steamers that took part in *The Thousand*, a pivotal moment in the unification of Italy. A statue of Rossi stands in Piazza Dante. (☎ 0183.497.621; open 9 am-12:30 pm and 3-5:30 pm daily; entrance fee €3 adults, children under 10 €1.)

Church of Sant'Antonio Abate

Constructed in 1862, the town's parish church has richly decorated side chapels, some with items from the previous parish church and friary of the Domenicans that was demolished at the end of the 18th century. On the right side aisle, the *Circumcision* in the first chapel is by Orazio de Ferrari, hanging over an altar dedicated to the archangel Raphael. In the last chapel, *Deposition from the Cross*, is by G.B. Casone from the first half of the 17th century. The painting above that, the *Baptism of Christ*, is attributed to Luca Cambiaso. On the left side aisle, the last altar is dedicated to St. Erasmo, patron saint of fishermen.

Only in Diano Marina

Infiorata

Celebrated 10 weeks after Easter on the Sunday following Corpus Christi, the *Infiorata* festoons the streets in colorful blooms artfully arranged into mosaics and painterly depictions. The same tradition is followed in neighboring Cervo, and the day's events include various processions and lively crowds. The *Infiorata* is uniquely Italian. The tradition originated in 1625, when the head of the papal flower nursery decided to commemorate the feast of Corpus Domini by covering the floor of the Vatican church with a mat of flowers. The event was perpetuated in Rome, and spread quickly to other areas. Obviously, it's a natural fit along the Riviera dei Fiori.

Diano Castello

The richly historical town of Diano Castello is located inland and uphill from Diano Marina. Once a stronghold of the Clavesana, who built the castle that gives the town its name, it has a lovely medieval center ringed by vineyards that produce celebrated Vermentino white wine (try it with fish). Sites include the Parish Church of San Niccolo, built in the early 18th century in Baroque style and missing the top to its bell tower, toppled in the earthquake of 1887. There's also a lovely fresco on an exterior wall of the Town Hall commemorating the Battle of Meloria in the 13th century, in which many men of the town took part on behalf of Genoa.

For Active Travelers

Windsurfing

Located at the Bagni Ponterosso, a full-service beach club, **Wind Surf Ponterosso** rents boards and offers windsurfing lessons for those new to the sport. (☎ 0183.401.300, www.bagniponterosso.it.)

Diving

The *Pacata Felix*, an ancient shipwreck off the coast, is a popular spot with divers; the sea bottom is colorful and varied with lots of life. *Eurosub* leads dives from Diano Marina and has lessons at all levels. (☎ 335.835.9710, eurosub@supereva.it.)

Cervo

The earthquake of 1887 that nearly leveled neighboring Diano Marina thankfully spared the town of Cervo, and so today there remains the charming medieval center surrounded by stone walls and ramparts overlooking the sea.

A Roman settlement built to protect the Via Julia Augusta, in the 11th century Cervo became a possession of the powerful Clavesana family that ruled this part of coastal Liguria before the surge in Genoese dominance from the 13th century onward. They built the castle that, after several refurbishments and renovations, still stands today. In 1172 Cervo entered a brief period of protectorship from Diano Marina, its neighbor to the west. But in the 13th century it formed an alliance with Genoa, who designated a podestà to oversee the town's governance in 1425.

Until 1720, a large part of the town's economy derived from the coral trade, and some of the profits from this lucrative activity were donated toward the construction of the Parish Church of San Giovanni Battista. The emblematic church with its concave façade is considered one of the best examples of Ligurian Baroque style and stands high up the hill overlooking the sea. The buildings behind, heading up toward the castle, are from the first periods of construction, and as the hill slopes toward the sea they are replaced by 17th-century structures.

Despite the modern presence of the neighboring resort town of Diano Marina, Cervo retains a sense of isolation derived from its geographical position, atop a seaside hill and backed by lush, unfettered vegetation that is crisscrossed with walking trails.

Getting There

 By Train: There is a train station for Cervo-San Bartolomeo, but only local trains make the stop (check the schedule). All trains on the Genoa-Ventimiglia line, however, stop at Diano Marina (three km/1.8 miles away), from where you can take the bus or taxi to Cervo. For schedules, see www.trenitalia.it.

By Car: Exit the A10 autostrada at San Bartolomeo or Andora and then continue along the Via Aurelia, which runs through town on the waterfront.

 By Bus: Bus service is provided by **Riviera Trasporti** (see www.rivieratrasporti.it for timetables).

Resources

■ www.cervo.com

■ www.golfodidiana.it

■ www.rivieradeifiori.org

■ **Tourist Office:** Piazza Santa Caterina, 2, ☎ 0183 408.197, infocervo@rivieradeifiori.org.

Being There

Cervo occupies a hill next to the sea, overlooked by the 12th-century Clavesana Castle and the Parish Church of San Giovanni Battista, colloquially known as the *Chiesa dei Corallini* for the patronage of the town's coral fishermen. Suitably, the church looks toward the sea and at night its floodlit façade is a stunning backdrop to the town. The medieval warren of carrugi or narrow alleys are primarily behind the church heading toward the castle and the Piazza Santa Caterina. Within the old streets, which are closed to all but pedestrian traffic, are numerous artist's workshops and small restaurants where you can taste fresh fish, dishes made with local olives, and the region's Vermentino white wine. Without sprawling beaches, sun worshippers and fans of aquatic activity make use of the small, rocky bays and coves that characterize the town's coastline.

San Giovanni Battista

The *Chiesa dei Corallini* was built under the direction of architect Giambattista Marvaldi and finished in the 18th century. The bell tower was constructed by Francesco Carrega, an architect and local painter from an artistic family credited with the decorations for many of the town's private palazzos (including the frescoes on the piano nobile of the Palazzo

Diano Marina – Pietre Ligure

Viale). The richly decorated interior has a *Crucifix* credited to Maragliano.

Clavesana Castle

Built in the 12th century when they were one of the most powerful families in Western Liguria, the castle – which has a vantage over the entire town and the coast – was the fortified residence of the Marquises of Clavesana. Later, it was used as an oratory and then a hospital, and today it houses the **Museo Etnografico del Ponente Ligure**. Figures, animations, and objects are used to recreate 19th-century life in the village. (☎ 0183.408.197; open every day 9 am-12:30 pm and 4-7:30 pm in summer, 9 am-6:30 pm in winter; entrance free.)

Only in Cervo

International Chamber Music Festival

Each summer the churchyard of the Chiesa dei Corallini is transformed into a stage for internationally-renowned artists in chamber music. Past performers have included pianists Richter, Michelangeli, Pollini, Argerich, Ciccolini, Badura-Skoda, and Schiff, and violinists Uto Ughi and Salvatore Accardo. Inquire at the tourist office regarding performance tickets.

For Active Travelers

Hiking

A well-maintained trail marked by a red circle and the number 1 begins where the medieval village meets the **Via Aurelia** that passes through Cervo. Heading east out of town it turns into a mule track that passes through lush vegetation and terraced olive groves. Eventually, the trail winds toward the town's *Ciapà* –

a protected green space on the hills behind Cervo – and then on to the **Castellareto Hill**. Onward through more olive terraces and past the remains of the ancient chapel of **San Giuseppe**, the itinerary leaves trail n°1 and joins trail n°21, which leads to **Via Solitario delle Alpi**, then through more olive terraces until ending at the square of the **Clavesana Castle**. Inquire at the tourist office for a trail map of this and other walks in the area.

Tennis

Swing your racket at the **Circolo Tennis Cervo**, a full-service club located between Cervo and San Bartolomeo al Mare, its modern neighbor full of vacation homes. Find the club at Via Steria, 49, a broad street before you cross the river into San Bartolomeo. (☎ 0183.402.392.)

Alassio

According to popular myth, the town of Alassio was founded in the 10th century when Adelasia, daughter of Holy Roman Emperor Otto I, fled Saxony – and her father – to marry Aleramo, a lowly cupbearer. The exiled lovers settled on the Ligurian coast and lived as charcoal burners until the Saracen invasions, when the Emperor, arrived to vanquish the marauders, was assisted in his task by the valiant Aleramo and his sons. The town's name, according to the story, derives from Adelasia, which became *Alaxia*, and then *Alassio*.

The lovely resort town with its history of celebrity visitors, their names enshrined on the town's famous *muretto*, inspires myth-making. But in its known history it was a possession of the Benedictines of the island of Gallinara (today a protected regional reserve lying just offshore). The monks exercised civil and religious authority over the inhabitants of Alassio until the government of Albenga annexed the city in 1303.

In the 16th century Alassio was claimed by Genoa and a podestà was named to head the local government. The town, with a large fleet of trading vessels and commercial ties to France, Spain, Portugal, the Netherlands, Sicily, and Sardinia, was a useful acquisition and to protect it an elaborate defense system was built. Noble residences such as the

Palazzo dei Marchesi di Ferrero and the **Palazzo Brea**, **Palazzo Morteo**, and **Palazzo Scofferi** also belong to this period.

Alassio's relationship with Genoa lasted until the declaration of the brief Ligurian Democratic Republic before the arrival of Napoleon and annexation to the French Empire.

The town's history began afresh in the late 19th century when, like other coastal towns in Liguria, it was "colonized" by wealthy English tourists, chief among them the Gibbs, the MacMurdos, and the Hanburys, escaping their island's dreary weather. Up on the hillsides overlooking the long, white-sand beach these expats built sumptuous villas surrounded by lush gardens. In the "new" town of straight streets along the waterfront, an Art Nouveau train station was erected to accommodate travelers to the posh resort, and nearby an Anglican church.

After WWII Alassio saw a resurgence in popularity. The *muretto* (and the Miss Muretto Beauty Pageant) on Corso Dante dates to this period, with its first three ceramic tiles added in 1951 and bearing the signatures of Ernest Hemingway, Quartetto Cetra, and Cosimo di Celie.

Getting There

By Train: The **FS** station in the heart of town is itself a tourist attraction. The first-class waiting room is furnished in Art Nouveau sofas, easy chairs, and period furniture and decorated with large mirrors and a Murano glass chandelier. For schedules, see www.trenitalia.it.

By Car: Exit the A10 autostrada at Albenga (east of town) or Andora (west of town) and then take the Via Aurelia toward Alassio.

By Bus: SAR provides bus service for towns between Andora and Savona. For more information and timetables, see www.sar-bus.com, ☎ 0182.215.44.

Resources

- www.comune.alassio.sv.it
- www.inforiviera.it
- **Tourist Office:** Piazza della Libertà, 5, ☎ 0182.647.027.

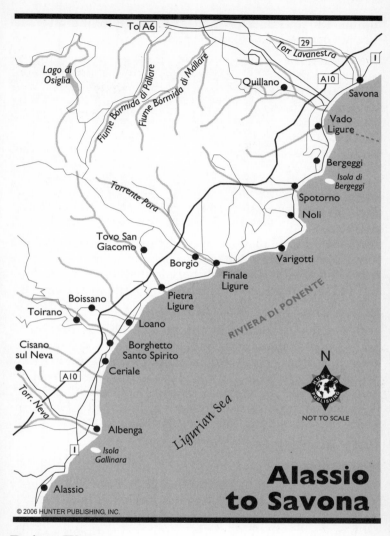

To A6

Torr. Lavanestra

29

A10

Lago di
Osiglia

Quillano

Savona

Fiume Bòrmida di Pàllare

Fiume Bòrmida di Màllare

Vado
Ligure

Bergeggi

Isola di
Bergeggi

Torrente Pora

Spotorno

Noli

Tovo San
Giacomo

Borgio

Varigotti

Finale
Ligure

RIVIERA DI PONENTE

Boissano

Pietra
Ligure

Toirano

Loano

Cisano
sul Neva

Borghetto
Santo Spirito

A10

Ceriale

Torr. Neva

N

NOT TO SCALE

Ligurian Sea

Albenga

Isola
Gallinara

**Alassio
to Savona**

Alassio

© 2006 HUNTER PUBLISHING, INC.

Diano Marina - Pietre Ligure

Being There

Visitors to Alassio will spend much of their time wandering the **budello**, the town's ancient alley (formally known as Via XX Settembre) that runs parallel to the waterfront. It's the shopping thoroughfare and separated from the beach by the line of hotels, restaurants, and other buildings that open directly onto the sand. From the budello take one of the narrow lanes to the **Passeggiata Italia**, the seafront promenade that includes Alassio's popular pier.

The beach itself runs over two miles and has fine white sand, where it can be seen under the ubiquitous beach chairs belonging to the multitude of clubs. Unlike many Ligurian beaches that seem to drop directly into deep water, creating a powerful shore break that can make entering and exiting the water a challenge, the water here is shallow for a long way out, and so standing about and walking in the surf is popular.

Parish Church of Sant'Ambrogio

Built in the 15th century on the site of a 10th-century building, Alassio's parish church, today on the Via Aurelia, received a 19th-century façade facelift but preserves the slate portal dating to 1511. It's decorated with depictions of *St. Ambrose, Christ and the Apostles* and *The Everlasting Father*. Within the Baroque interior are paintings by Giovanni Andrea de Ferrari and Bernardo Castello.

Only in Alassio
Miss Muretto

Alassio's end-of-summer beauty pageant, begun in the 1950s, is held each August. More risqué than an American pageant, it's sponsored by lingerie-maker DIM and, in addition to the swimsuit competition, has contestants clad in the company's scanty bustiers and undies. It's an important part of Alassio's summer scene, drawing celebrity judges and members of the glitterati to the resort for a number of special events held in sync with the contest.

Laigueglia

Just west of Alassio is the small fishing village of Laigueglia, which still retains its laid-back atmosphere. From the town you can walk (or drive, but it's a nicer walk) three km/two miles to **Colla Micheri**, a hillside village that was completely restored during the 1960s and 70s by Norwegian explorer Thor Heyerdahl of Kon-Tiki raft fame. Set amidst olive groves, the quaint hamlet has lovely views.

Isola Gallinara

Now a privately-owned but state-protected regional reserve, the island of Gallinara was once home to the Benedictine monks who for a time officiated over the surrounding territory. They built an abbey here in the eighth century that is now a villa for the island's owners. In summer (July-September) *Alimar* does boat trips around the island, offering a good vantage for viewing the lovely grottos on the southern side. Departures are from the end of the pier. (☎ 335.760.72.59, www.alimar.ge.it, alimarsrl@tin.it; fee €12 adults and €8 children.)

For Active Travelers

Water Sports

The sea is the star in Alassio and there are numerous ways to enjoy its beauty. Water-skiing has become a popular activity at the resort **Circolo Nautico al Mare** (☎ 0182.642.516) and **Club House** (☎ 0182.640.840), who charter ski boats. For a slower pace, try canoeing or kayaking. **Circolo Nautico al Mare** can also arrange rentals of those. If you're hoping to explore under the water, try **Centro Immersioni Continente Blu Alassio** (☎ 347.115.59.09, continenteblu@libero.it, www.continenteblu.com); **Centro Subacqueo "Essere-acqua"** (☎ 338.589.12.00, essereacqua@hotmail.com, www.essereacqua.com); or **Squama Diver Alassio** (☎ 0182.640.074).

Diano Marina – Pietre Ligure

Hiking

An easy, popular (but unmarked), and lovely hike in the area follows the Via Julia Augusta from Alassio to Albenga, making use of some public roads and mule tracks that now mimic the ancient thoroughfare. It begins at the church of Santa Croce on the far eastern side of town on the **Capo Santa Croce** (near the tourist port). From there the walk (sometimes known as the *Archaeological Walk* for the many Roman ruins it peruses) proceeds to the church of **San Martino di Albenga**, about three hours away. If you're fearful of getting lost, consider taking a guided hike instead. **Professor Bruno Schivo** works with the tourist office, leading hikes during the summer season and sometimes over the Christmas holidays that cover historical/ecological itineraries. One walk takes in the Via Julia Augusta; another traces the legacy of the English in Alassio while visiting villas, gardens, the library, and other buildings and institutions the colony left behind. The hikes are free. For more information, contact the tourist office (☎ 0182.648.142) or Professor Schivo (☎ 0182.640.351 or bruno.schivo@iol.it).

Whale Watching

During June, July, August, and September *Alimar* leads whale watching excursions to the sanctuary created off the Ligurian coast in 1999. (For more information, see *Cetacean Sanctuary*, page 203.) Among the cetaceans you're looking for are bottlenose dolphins, pilot whales, Risso's dolphins, sperm and fin whales, and even orcas (killer whales). Departures are from the end of the pier. (Reservations required, ☎ 335.760.72.59, www.alimar.ge.it, alimarsrl@tin.it; fee €25 adults and €15 children.)

Albenga

Centuries ago the flat land surrounding Albenga was a gulf into which the Arroscia and Nerva rivers flowed. But as the gulf silted up the geography was permanently altered, forming a broad plain of fertile soil through which a single river – the Centa – flowed, created from the confluence of the Arroscia and the Nerva.

It was here that the Roman settlement of *Albingaunum* was established after the defeat of the local *ingauno* people in 181 BC. With a natural harbor, vast lands under cultivation, and access to inland routes through the mountainous region's valleys, it quickly became (with Ventimiglia) the most important city of the Empire in Liguria. In the fifth century, after being sacked by the Goths and Vandals, it was rebuilt entirely by General Constance (who would later become Emperor).

Around that same time one of the most powerful dioceses in Liguria was established at Albenga in 451. The town's bishops would wield control throughout the surrounding territory for centuries, holding extensive feudal lands and governing in concert with some of the area's most powerful families.

For good or for bad, the Centa always figured in the town's fortunes. Particularly vulnerable to flooding, the town was swamped on several occasions, setting the conditions for malaria and other diseases to prey upon the populace. After a short stint as a free commune in the 11th century, with privileges afforded by its participation in the First Crusade, it was annexed to the Republic of Genoa in the 12th. Then, in the 13th century, around the same time that the town walls were rebuilt, the river changed course to the south of the town. The port began to silt up, signaling the end of Albenga's time as a maritime player, though not its relationship with Genoa.

Because of its agricultural activities and location on the salt routes through to Piedmont, Albenga remained a prosperous city. To this day, it's a flower- and vegetable-growing center. Its agricultural products are transported around Italy from the tiny airport at Villanova d'Albenga. Tourism has also become important to the local economy, as travelers arrive to explore the most perfectly intact medieval core on the western Riviera.

Getting There

By Train: The **FS** station is outside the medieval center on Piazza Matteotti near the waterfront. For schedules, see www.trenitalia.it.

By Plane: The small "international" airport of Villanova d'Albenga (at the northwest limit of the Albenga plain) is served by **AirOne** (flights to/from Rome) and **AirVallee** (flights to/from Sardinia).

By Car: Exit the A10 autostrada at Albenga and follow the signs toward the coast. The Via Aurelia passes behind the town – follow the signs marked *Centro Storico*.

 By Bus: SAR provides bus service between Andora and Savona. For more information and timetables, see www.sar-bus.com, ☎ 0182.215.44.

Resources

- www.inforiviera.it
- **Tourist Office:** Viale Martiri della Libertà, 1, ☎ 0182.558. 444.

Being There

Albenga's enticing medieval core is surrounded by a largely unexciting new town. Surrounded by 13th-century walls, the historic center is a bustling, mostly pedestrian-only area packed with monuments, some 50 distinctive tower houses, and other medieval buildings that now shelter cafés and shops. Its heart is the **Piazza San Michele**, once the center of civic and religious life. Around it the streets are organized according to the original Roman-imposed grid, and the broad, straight street of **Viale Martiri della Libertà** leads out of the old town and toward the waterfront and beach. The main shopping street is **Via Medaglie d'Oro**, which intersects **Via Enrico d'Aste** (which becomes Viale Martiri della Libertà at the Piazza del Popolo) just above the monument complex. **Via Bernardo Ricci** and **Via Cavour** are other lovely and evocative walking streets.

Cattedrale San Michele

Albenga's cathedral (seat of the powerful Bishops of Albenga) was originally built in the fifth century, around the time the ancient diocese was founded. Its Romanesque Baptistery survived the centuries intact (see below), but the church was extensively remodeled over the years resulting in something of a hodgepodge appearance. Inside, the roof over the nave has frescoes from the 19th century and an organ from that same period. There is also a 16th-century fresco of the *Crucifixion with Saints* over the central apse.

Baptistery

Probably the most famous monument of Albenga (and potentially Western Liguria), the 10-sided Baptistery was constructed in the fifth century by order of General Constance at the time of the town's rebuilding after the Goth and Vandal sackings. To reach the interior you descend a series of steps – a reminder that the town's terrain has changed markedly over the millennia due to flooding and subsequent silt deposits. Inside, the building is eight-sided and deco-

rated with Corsican granite columns, a few late medieval tombs, and an important fifth-century mosaic with the *Trinity and the Apostles*. Behind the cathedral and baptistery is the **Piazza dei Leoni**, named for its three stone lions, brought from Rome in the 17th century. Around the small square are several medieval tower houses that belonged to some of the town's wealthiest families.

Only in Albenga

Villanova d'Albenga

Founded by Albenga in the 13th century to protect the roads leading to the plain from the hinterland, the polygonal Villanova d'Albenga today is a delightful town to explore, surrounded by its original imposing walls and 10 defensive towers and accented by cheerful planters of blooming plants. Villanova's violets, which are shipped in distinctive clusters surrounded by their own leaves, are famous throughout Europe. The church of **Santa Maria del Soccorso** – just outside the town walls – was built in 1520 and is one of the few Italian churches with a round shape and an open-plan design.

Zuccarello

In 1625 this long, skinny walled village (founded in the 13th century by the Clavesana family) was the subject of a war between Genoa and the House of Savoy after the Del Carretto family, who had gained control in 1326, ceded a portion of feu-

dal control to the
Republic and the
rest to Savoy. The
town's ancient
structure survived
intact, however.
The ruins of the
castle built by the
Clavesana are on a
hill just outside the
town proper, and
the monumental
Del Carretto resi-

Zuccarello

dence is today a private villa. Zuccarello is remembered as the
birthplace of Ilaria Del Carretto who wed Paolo Guinigi of
Lucca – she married and died quite young and was honored by
a famous funeral monument in Lucca's cathedral built by
Jacopo della Quercia. (From Albenga, take the SS 582.)

Castelvecchio di Rocca Barbena

Steep, narrow, winding streets lead to the ancient Clavesana
castle that was established in the 12th century, making
Castelvecchio di Rocca Barbena the oldest feudal town of the
Val Neva. From a distance the town seems hewn of solid
stone, the hilltop castle ringed by houses barely differentiated
by their terraced rust-colored roofs. Numerous fountains
within the town were strategic during times of siege. Today
they are merely picturesque. The village passed from the
Clavesanas to the Del Carrettos, and fell to the Savoys in
1623 before eventually becoming part of the Republic of
Genoa. (From Albenga, take the SS 582.)

For Active Travelers

Golf

Opened in 1965, the **Garlenda Golf Club** in
Garlenda was designed by American architects
John Morrison and John Harris; it has 18 holes laid
out over a pristine landscape that the club's plan-
ners chose not to alter. Surrounded by olive groves and vineyards, it's a challenging course that demands strategy and
attention. (☎ 0182.580.012, fax 0182.580.561,

www.garlendagolf.it, info@garlendagolf.it; closed Wednesdays.)

Caving

 Taking the Via Aurelia east from Albenga to Borghetto Santo Spirito and then the provincial road heading inland, you arrive at the town of Toirano. From there taking the road for Bardineto you arrive at the **Grotte di Toirano**, Liguria's most famous cave complex. There are fantastic limestone and rock crystal formations, stalactites and stalagmites, underground lakes, and several evocative caverns named for the human and animal remains that have been found throughout. An archeological museum cataloging and explaining the precious finds is back in the town and included in the price of admission. (☎ 0182.980.62, fax 0182.921.903, www.toiranogrotte.it; open year-round; entrance fee €9 adults, €5 children six-14, under six free.)

■ Il Finalese: Finale Ligure - Bergeggi

The region known as *Il Finalese* – a long stretch of rugged coastline backed by the Manie plateau and the high inland region of the Val Bormida – has for centuries represented a kind of border. In its earliest history it was the dividing line between the *Ingauni* and *Sabazi* tribes of ancient Liguria. When the Romans arrived it became the frontier of the Vada Sabatia municipality. **Finale Ligure** is the modern combination of three separate towns, Final Marina, Finalborgo, and Final Pia, all at the western extreme of Il Finalese. For years this area was one of the greatest blockades to Genoese hegemony on the western Riviera.

Just to the east the town of **Noli** was a great maritime republic outfitted with a fine castle, fortified walls, and rich tower houses, a stalwart ally of Genoa. **Spotorno**, too, was under Genoese dominance, with a podestà established as the head of government. In the 13th century Noli pried the village from Savona, sworn foe of Genoa until the 16th century when it, too, was conquered and forced into vassalage by the Republic.

Bergeggi on the eastern edge of Il Finalese was acquired by Genoa in the 14th century and owes its present form, with fortress-houses and fortifications, to their influence.

But Finale Ligure fell to the Del Carretto family in the 13th century and for centuries thereafter was closely tied to Milan. The Del Carrettos were allies of the powerful Sforza of that city. Then, in the early days of the 17th century the Marquisate was sold to the Spanish royal family. It wasn't until 1748 – just a few decades before the establishment of the brief Ligurian Republic, followed by the years of French control and then the push for Italian unification – that Finale Ligure was overtaken by the Genoese.

Today the coastal towns are a splendid mix of the medieval and the modern, with Noli a standout for its picturesque walled core, towering castle, and lively carrugi (alleyways). The resorts here are less flashy than some of their counterparts elsewhere. Somehow they manage to be both quaint and cosmopolitan at the same time, evoking mid-century nostalgia and contemporary comfort in one fell swoop. The beaches, shallow bays, and turquoise coves are magnificent, with a lovely mile-long sand beach stretching west of Noli from the town of Varigotti.

Inland, the towns have a Piedmontese inflection, as does the cooking (making liberal use of mushrooms and the white truffles that are native to the Val Bormida). They're small and surrounded by wilderness that is popular for hiking, riding, and wind-born activities like paragliding from the peaks above the plateau.

Finale Ligure

Administratively speaking, Finale Ligure is one town (and has been since 1927). But the three villages of which it is composed – Final Marina, Finalborgo, and Final Pia – have separate personalities and identities, even separate histories.

At the western extreme is **Final Marina**, set right on the water and with a harbor given over to seafaring activities as its name implies. Its sailors took to trade and the town developed into a commercial center early in its history. In the 14th century there was a brief period of Genoese dominance, during which the Castelfranco was built.

But recognizing the strategic importance of an outlet for shipping and naval activities, the Del Carrettos – whose marquisate was based just inland at **Finalborgo** – seized Final Marina, incorporating it into their territory. Throughout the period of their dominance their Finalese holdings would be fiercely contested by the Genoese who sought to consolidate their hold on the western Riviera, culminating in a war between the two powers from 1447-1449. The Del Carrettos, allied with influential Sforza family of Milan, received protection from that wealthy northern city.

During the battle the marquisate's capital suffered great destruction, but the victorious Del Carrettos promptly rebuilt and Finale entered a period of prosperity and constructive fervor during which numerous churches and other important buildings were built or remodeled. It was during this time that **Final Pia** – also on the coast, across the river from Final Marina – took on its modern form, acquiring elegant residences adorned with slate portals.

By 1602 the fortunes of the Del Carrettos were on the decline, and the marquisate was sold to the Spanish royal family, becoming a linchpin to the crown's aspirations in greater Europe by giving them coastal access to Milan. Troops began to come and go through the town and in 1666 they built the Strada Berretta, providing an overland communication route to Milan. The Spaniards also strengthened the defensive system, making renovations to the Castelfranco and Castel Govone and such dramatic changes to the Castel San Giovanni that today it still appears a mishmash of medieval and Spanish architecture. In Final Marina and Final Pia they constructed distinctive residences, and in Marina an archway overlooking the sea dedicated to Marguerite of Spain.

In the first years of the 18th century, as the crisis over succession to the Spanish throne deepened, the territory was sold to its ancient enemy, the Genoese, spurring a series of revolts and popular uprisings that kept the Republic from formally taking possession until 1748. In 1795 the Ligurian Republic would be declared, followed by the arrival of Napoleon and years of French dominance and then the push to establish the Kingdom of Italy, which the three towns joined.

Getting There

By Train: The **FS** station is on the far western side of Final Marina on the Piazza Veneto, next to the riverbed of the Pora. For schedules, see www.trenitalia.it.

By Car: From the A10 autostrada exit at Finale Ligure. The Via Aurelia runs through the center of Final Marina and can be extremely slow during the summer season.

By Bus: SAR provides bus service for towns between Andora and Savona. For more information and timetables, see www.sar-bus.com, ☎ 0182.215.44. **ACTS** provides bus service for towns between Finale Ligure and Varazze. For more information and timetables, see www.acts.it, ☎ 019.220.12.31.

Resources

■ www.inforiviera.it

■ www.finaleligure.net

■ www.finalborgo.it

■ **Tourist Office:** Via San Pietro, 14 (Final Marina – open year round, ☎ 019.681.019); Piazza Porta Testa (Finalborgo – open seasonally, ☎ 019.680.954.)

Being There

The district of **Final Marina** is the seaside resort and destination for holidaymakers and sun worshippers. Here you'll find beach clubs and nightlife, hotels, and restaurants catering to travelers. **Final Pia** retains a rustic ambiance influenced by the terraced hillsides that surround it, covered with olive groves and vineyards. It is much quieter than Final Marina, with 16th- and 17th-century villas surrounded by cultivated land. **Finalborgo** is the medieval gem, though hardly as visited as coastal Marina. Completely encapsulated by its intact 15th-century walls, it has straight streets laid in a grid pattern punctuated by several piazzas, around which the churches and noble residences are found. Craft workshops and shops selling traditional ceramic ware, glass, and items of olivewood and iron populate the narrow alleys.

Church of San Biagio

Members of the Del Carretto family are prominently depicted in a 16th-century painting of *Our Lady of the Rosary*, housed in this church located at the **Porta Reale**, an ancient door through the city walls. The octagonal bell tower of the church rises above the town walls, emerging from a defensive tower.

Convent of Santa Caterina

At another door to the city, the west-facing **Porto Testa**, is the Piazza Santa Caterina, named for the convent dedicated to the saint of the same name. The Del Carrettos founded the convent in 1359, but the cloisters that today host the **Museo Archeologico del Finale** date to the 15th century. Deconsecrated in the mid-19th century, the convent was used as a penitentiary for 100 years, reverting to civic cultural use in 1965. The museum houses a collection of prehistoric, Roman, and medieval items from the surrounding territory. (☎ 019.690.020, www.museoarcheofinale.com; open Tuesday-Sunday July-August 10 am-12 pm and 4-7 pm; September-June 9 am-12 pm and 2:30-5 pm; entrance fee €3.)

Church of Santa Maria di Pia

The nucleus of the ancient village of Pia, a small chapel already existed here in the 12th century and was transformed in the 16th to accommodate the adjoining Benedictine monastery. Inside the abbey are some fine terracottas credited to the Della Robbia School.

Only in Finale Ligure

Antique Market

On the first Saturday and Sunday of each month (from 10 am-10 pm in the summer season), Finalborgo hosts a lively antique market featuring vendors with everything from clothing and jewelry to furniture and memorabilia.

Perti

Traveling inland from Finaleborgo up the Aquila River valley, or hiking the 17th-century Strada Beretta that departs from the town center, you reach the small hamlet of Perti. Here

Il Finalese

you'll find the remains of **Castel Gavone**, constructed in the 12th century by Henry II (*Enrico* in Italian), son of *the Guercio* who established the Del Carretto family coat-of-arms around 1142. The construc-

Castel Gavone

tion of the fortress at the base of the rocky spur of the Bechignolo marked the founding of the Finale. Once the most refined military residence in western Liguria, in 1448 the castle was sacked by the Genoese near the end of the two-year war that raged between the Republic and the Del Carrettos. When the Finalese family emerged victorious in 1450 (it is said that the tide of battle turned in one night), the castle was rebuilt by Giovanni I Del Carretto. But when the Genoese took possession of Finale Ligure from the Spanish in the 18th century, they symbolically destroyed and dismantled the castle, leaving only the lovely **Torre dei Diamanti** (Tower of Diamonds). Also nearby, surrounded by olive groves, is the **Church of Nostra Signora di Loreto**, known as the "church of the five bell towers" for the Renaissance structure that crowns the cupola.

Varigotti

In the mid-14th century – seeking to inhibit its navy and punish the town's alliance with the Del Carretto – Genoa destroyed and buried the port of Varigotti, Finale Ligure's immediate neighbor to the east. Sections of stone wharves can still be seen below the waters of the Baia dei Saraceni, an excellent place for snorkeling. The charming and chic little village has buildings painted in shades of yellow, orange, pink, and red that open directly onto the mile-long sand beach – one of the finest in Liguria.

For Active Travelers
Rock Climbing

The climbing around Finale Ligure is legendary, with 36 linear miles of sport climbing and 2,000 bolted routes ranging in difficulty from 4 to 8c (5.5 to 5.14b in the American system). With so many locations to choose from, your best option is to hire a guide. **BluMountain** leads full-day excursions for around $200 per person. Make arrangements through **Rockstore** on the piazza in Finalborgo (☎ 019.690.208, www.rockstore.it, www.blumountain.it). Rockstore also maintains a message board where experienced climbers can hook-up with partners for excursions.

Mountain Biking

An extensive network of trails branches out around Finale Ligure, with diverse terrain that includes alpine forest, seaside scrub, and olive orchards. In fact, the town hosts an annual **24h of Finale** mountain biking competition each fall, drawing riders from all over Europe (www.24hfinale.com). The **Outdoor Café** in Finalborgo is the headquarters of the International Mountain Biking Association in Italy; it provides trail maps (and guides), does rentals, and has a mechanic available (☎ 019.680.564). The **Medusa Hotel** is another hub, with a bike room for storage and maintenance and trail maps at the front desk. Maps and information on the trails are also available from their website, www.medusahotel.it.

Paragliding

The plateaus above Finale Ligure are a favorite launching point for paragliders. Hook up with the school **Ponente Fly** for a flight over the sea and Mediterranean landscape (☎ 019.692.219).

Windsurfing

Between Finale Ligure and Noli (the next town heading east from Varigotti) is a stretch of turquoise sea that is home to world-class windsurfing. Fabrizio Amarotto, one of Italy's best at the sport, makes his home here to be near the action. In summer, expect a constant breeze blowing at just under 15 miles per hour. But if you're looking for a challenge, in October the *Tramontana* begins to blow from the north, producing winds of up to 30 miles per hour, especially at sunrise and sunset. During summer there are board rentals and lessons (group and private) offered by the **Varigotti Windsurfing School** at the Bagni Mariella beach club in Varigotti. Amarotto is on the staff. (☎ 019.698.760, www.bagnimariella.it.)

Noli

Situated on a gorgeous, sand-bottomed turquoise bay between Capo Noli and the Punta del Vescovo, Noli might be the most charming town of the western Riviera. Medieval defensive walls climb the surrounding castle-topped hillsides and a palm-lined promenade fronts the beach. Directly behind is the old town and its network of cobbled carrugi (narrow alleyways) populated by tower residences, gelaterias, restaurants and wine bars, chic boutiques, and food shops with some of the region's delicious specialties available for take-away picnics on the beach.

It's probable that Noli was a small village during the Imperial Age, but certain that in the seventh century the town – then known as *Naboli* – was destroyed during the Lombard invasions and rebuilt. By the 11th century it was a possession of the Del Carretto family, with whom it took part in the First Crusade in 1097, sending men and ships.

The Crusades turned the town's fortunes, as its distinguished participation earned Noli many political and commercial privileges from the King of Jerusalem. Noli seized the opportunity to establish itself as an important seaport, and with its riches eventually won independence from the Del Carrettos and established itself as a free commune in 1192.

To do so it relied heavily on Genoa who, faced with fierce opposition from the Del Carrettos to their intended hegemony in Western Liguria, were happy to have Noli as a an ally and to support the town's aspirations to become a grand maritime republic. In 1202 an official alliance was signed between the Republic and Noli, an act that brought down the wrath of neighboring Savona. However the town was well buffered by its powerful protector, as Genoa used the port to shelter some of the ships of its massive navy.

Thus Noli grew and prospered, and retained its independence until Napoleon's invasion in 1797. Within the old town, surrounded by three of its original walls, the architecture has been influenced by the Genoese. At one time, 72 tower residences rose high above the skyline, but only eight remain today, including the entirely intact Communal Tower. On the waterfront, an arcade mimicking the *Ripa* (that city's waterfront colonnade) once stretched uninterrupted, providing a passageway for pedestrians and a place to shelter the boats of the town's fishermen. Today the beach is dotted with fishing boats. A section of arcade remains near the Porta Piazza, over which a fresco of the Madonna surveys the sea.

Getting There

By Train: Noli's **FS** station is located at the backside of the old town, near the church of *San Paragorio*. For schedules, see www.trenitalia.it.

By Car: Exit the A10 autostrada at Spotorno and then take the Via Aurelia in the direction of Finale Ligure. The Via Aurelia passes through the town as Corso Italia.

By Bus: SAR provides bus service for towns between Andora and Savona. For more information and timetables, see www.sar-bus.com, ☎ 0182.215.44. **ACTS** provides bus service for towns between Finale Ligure and Varazze. For more information and timetables, see www.acts.it, ☎ 019.220.12.31.

Resources

- www.inforiviera.it
- www.noli.it
- **Tourist Office:** Corso Italia, 8, ☎ 019.749.90.03

Being There

Noli's vibe is relaxed and informal, but with a sophisticated edge. A favorite holiday destination for Italians, its beach clubs are packed with ultra-tan men and women lounging under umbrellas and bronze children playing along the shore. Inside the old town, the streets are lively with pedestrians, especially along **Via Manin** (which leads into the heart of the town from the Porto

Noli Bay

Piazza) and shop-lined **Via Colombo** (the buildings are converted palaces). On summer evenings there's a party atmosphere as vacationers stroll along the palm-lined promenade, dine *al fresco* at any of the town's many restaurants, and dance into the wee hours to live bands playing at some of the waterfront hotels.

Cathedral of San Pietro

Noli's cathedral (the town was named a diocese by Genoa in 1239) is tucked amidst medieval houses and towers near the waterfront, just off Via Vignolo that leads from the *Ripa*-styled arcade to Via Colombo and the Piazza Morando. Built in the 13th century, its Baroque alterations don't entirely conceal its original medieval form. A Roman sarcophagus is used as the altar, and the relics of the town's patron saint – Sant'Eugenio – have rested here since they were moved from the island of Bergeggi where he lived during fifth century.

Church of San Paragorio

Surprisingly, the bishop's throne is found here, rather than in San Pietro Cathedral. But this Romanesque church – built around 1000 on the site of an eighth- century church – is one of the most important churches in Liguria because of its age and unadulterated form. The façade faces the hills and the exterior is decorated with precious Islamic majolica works, blind arches and pilaster strips in the Lombard style. The crucifix and altar date to the time of the church's construction, while the frescoes were added in the 15th century. Other treasures include a wooden copy of the *Volto Santo* at Lucca.

Noli Castle

It's lovely walk up the **Strada Panoramic di Monte Ursino** to Noli Castle, constructed by the Del Carrettos in the 12th century and altered over the centuries. The medieval wall with its defensive towers leads from here downhill toward the town and is one of the most famous features of Noli. The view from the top of Mt. Ursino – which is said to have inspired Dante's vision of Purgatory – is breathtaking.

Only in Noli

Regatta dei Rioni

Held the second Sunday in September, Noli's regatta pits the town's four *borgos* (Burgu, Maina, Classa, and Purtellu) against one another. The event celebrates Noli's history as a mighty, albeit the smallest in Italy, maritime republic and features historical costumes and a procession in addition to the sailing competition and accompanying festival.

For Active Travelers

Sailing

As Italy's Fifth (and smallest) Maritime Republic, Noli has a rich sailing tradition. If this prompts you to do a little navigating yourself, the **Lega Navale Italiana Noli** has lessons and rents catamarans, sailboats, and windsurfing equipment (☎ 019.748.335, Via Aurelia, 1, www.leganavale.it/noli, noli@leganavale.it).

Spotorno

During the 11th century the once-humble fishing village of Spotorno found itself in an uncomfortable position, wedged between mighty Noli – a staunch ally of Genoa – and Savona, a contentious rival of the Republic. At the time, the village was a possession of the bishops of Savona, who built the Vecovile Castle slightly above the town as a residence for the bishop around 1180.

In 1227 the town was completely destroyed by Noli and in the 14th century was given to the Republic of Genoa by Pope Urbano VI. Genoa made Spotorno a headquarters of the podestà (their local governor) and invested in the town's marine industry and commerce. For defensive purposes it built the watchtowers of Correallo and Sant'Antonio.

The medieval layout of the old *borgo* is today marred by modern buildings erected since the 1960s, when the town began to reinvent itself as a center for tourism. With this new emphasis have come plenty of resort amenities, from beach clubs and tennis courts to luxury hotels and restaurants.

Getting There

 By Train: The **FS** station is located behind the town on the Piazza S. Barbaro. For schedules, see www.trenitalia.it.

 By Car: Exit the A10 autostrada at Spotorno. The Via Aurelia runs through town.

 By Bus: SAR provides bus service for towns between Andora and Savona. For more information and timetables, see www.sar-bus.com, ☎ 0182.215.44. **ACTS** provides bus service for towns between Finale Ligure and Varazze. For more information and timetables, see www.acts.it, ☎ 019.220.12.31.

Resources

- www.inforiviera.it
- www.infospotorno.com
- **Tourist Office:** Piazza G. Matteotti, 6, ☎ 019.741.50.08.

Being There

There are a handful of sites to visit in Spotorno, but mostly people come to relax on the long sandy beach, from which there is a lovely view of the island of **Bergeggi**. Beach clubs populate the area immediately off the promenade. Head west to find the free public beach. The old town still has the layout of a Ligurian fishing village with its main streets – **Via**

Cavour and **Via Garibaldi** – running parallel to the waterfront, which sports the ubiquitous palm-lined promenade, here named for President John F. Kennedy. Narrow alleyways run

Spotorno

between the main street and the promenade. The village is backdropped by its castle, but you'll have to walk uphill through the most recently developed part of town to reach it. Back beyond that, the hills are covered in orchards, mostly fruit trees, especially apricots, and vineyards that produce Buzzetto and Vermentino white wines.

Church of the Assunta

Spotorno's 17th-century parish church stands on its ancient thoroughfare and is instantly recognizable for its colorful trompe l'oeil facade. Inside are paintings by Giovanni Andrea de Ferrari, Domenico Piola, and a crucifix from the Maragliano school.

Oratory of the Annunziata

Probably constructed near the beginning of the 17th century, this oratory on the Piazza Aonzo has several paintings and sculptures from the period, and a collection of votary objects left by sailors and fishermen seeking benevolent intercession on the seas.

Only in Spotorno

Spotornocomics

At the end of August Spotorno hosts cartoonists and illustrators from all over Italy for an event highlighting the craft of humorous illustration. Tables and booths are set up around town and cartoonists literally draw their subjects from the audience. Exhibits display illustrations past and present.

For Active Travelers

Diving

The sea surrounding the island of Bereggi, soon to be established as a marine protected area, is a favorite with divers, and sub operators from up and down the coast make regular trips. Night trips are particularly popular. The island is just off the coast of Spotorno, and several outfitters lead dives to explore the varied aquatic terrain between the island and the Punta delle Grotte. **NereoSub** (☎ 019.741.43.4, Via Berninzoni, 124, www.nereosub.com) is a full-service dive shop that offers lessons and certification in addition to leading trips to the waters of Bereggi and other locales. As the name implies, **Bergeggi Diving School** (☎ 019.85.99.50, Punto Mare, Bagni Cormorano, www.bergeggidiving.it) specializes in trips around the island.

Sailing

The Spotorno branch of the **Lega Navale Italiana** is the place to go for information on boat rentals, sailing lessons, and charters. They're located on the wharf at the Via Aurelia. (☎ 019.747.196, www.leganavale.it/spotorno.)

Tennis

In true resort-town fashion, Spotorno has not one, but two tennis clubs. Practice your serve at **Tennis Club Spotorno** (☎ 019.745.843, Via Serra, 2), or take in a game at **Tennis Club Aranci** (☎ 019.743.111, Via Maremma, 26).

Bergeggi

In ancient times it's possible that the *isola* of Bergeggi – a cone-shaped mass some 200 yards off the coastline – was connected to the mainland by a narrow, rocky tongue. However, if true, the link disappeared millennia ago. Today, the name *Bergeggi* refers to the island and to the small village that sits in a panoramic position above the sea, and also to the regional natural reserve that was established in 1985 to protect the *isola* and the environment of chalky cliffs, partially submerged grottoes, and tiny beaches that line the coast between Bergeggi and Spotorno.

Evidence of man's presence in Bergeggi dates to Neolithic times, when the grottoes along the shore were probably much higher above sea level than they are today, owing to the effects of glaciation. Inside Bergeggi's famed **Marine Cave**, researchers have found a square-lipped vase and other materials dating to 5000-2000 BC, when the caves probably served as primitive shelters.

Prior to the Imperial Age, the Ligurian Sabazi tribe was established in the area, evidenced by the remains of a structure built on Monte Sant'Elena as a sort of lookout. They were vanquished by the Romans, who constructed the port of Vada Sabatia and the Via Julia Augusta that was an important communication and transport route along the Ligurian coast. It's theorized that the most ancient structural remains found on the island are the ruins of a Roman lighthouse built to guide ships safely to shore, past the treacherous rocky cliffs.

Isola Bergeggi's isolation lent itself naturally to monastic life, and in the fifth century Sant'Eugenio of Carthage arrived here during his flight from the Vandals. He lived here as a hermit until his death and his remains were buried on the island for 800 years before being moved to the cathedral at Noli. In 922 a monastery was constructed by the Bishop of Savona and given to the Benedictine monks from Lérins, France. They stayed until the 13th century, leaving behind the remains of two churches. Today the island is once again submerged in solitude. Since the establishment of the regional reserve, the only creatures allowed to set foot on its rocky shores are the seagulls.

The town at the base of Mont Sant'Elena developed during medieval times, but even after its annexation by Genoa in 1385 continued to be a loosely linked conglomeration of neighborhoods. Today the old districts of Gastaldi, Broxea, and Negli have been joined by the resort *borgo* of **Torre del Mare** on the Capo Maiolo promontory. The town's newest residences are here, and most of the tourist amenities, but Bergeggi's life is lived on the many beaches – public and private, accessible and isolated – that dot the coastline.

Getting There

By Train: Bergeggi has no train station. Travelers must get off in Savona or Spotorno and then take a taxi or bus into town. For schedules, see www.trenitalia.it.

By Car: Exit the A10 autostrada at Spotorno and head toward Savona.

By Bus: SAR provides bus service for towns between Andora and Savona. For more information and timetables, see www.sar-bus.com, ☎ 0182.215.44. **ACTS** provides bus service for towns between Finale Ligure and Varazze. For more information and timetables, see www.acts.it, ☎ 019.220.12.31.

Resources

- www.inforiviera.it
- www.parks.it/riserva.bergeggi
- **Tourist Office:** Via Aurelia, ☎ 019.859.777

Being There

Between the grottoes, terraced hillsides, beaches, cork forest, and pristine protected environment of the island, Bergeggi is a nature-lover's paradise, and really the whole reason to visit is to indulge in the great outdoors. The district of Torre del Mare typifies Ligurian resort style and the old neighborhoods, while charming, have few sites of historical significance. There is no public access to the island since the establishment of the regional reserve 20 years ago, but the dive shops run a regular trade in excursions to its underwater caves and the seabeds surrounding.

Marine Cave of Bergeggi

First discovered in 1881 and explored extensively in the 1960s, this grotto is visible from the Via Aurelia but only accessible by boat. Neolithic artifacts found in the cave indicate that it was used as a shelter for primitive man at a time when the sea level was much lower. However, the presence of several holes produced by ancient lithophagous molluscs point to another period since when the cave was deeply submerged. To the south, beyond

Punta Predani, is the **Grotto delle Sirene** (Cave of the Mermaids), also accessible by boat.

Natte Cork Tree Forest

These woods, which are on private property, represent the largest cork tree forest in middle-western Liguria and will soon become a provincial protected area. Located on the slopes of Mt. Rocchetto, the trees, some of which reach 10 m/30 feet high, are clustered in groves. Cork trees only grow under certain climatic and ecological conditions and their presence in the Mediterranean is very rare.

For Active Travelers

Hiking

A **botanic trail** has been established through the coastal area of the Bergeggi regional preserve with trailheads at **Torre d'Ere** and **Gola San'Elena** where you can pick up route maps. Along the way representative flora indicated by educational signage. Some typical examples, which are probably familiar to anyone who's done much hiking through the Mediterranean maquis, include sage-leaved rockrose, ilex, myrtle, olives, and aleppo pine.

Il Finalese

Snorkeling/Diving

Snorkelers won't be disappointed by the variety of sealife found along the rocky coastline, in particular adjacent to some of the beaches tucked away among the cliffs and accessible only by boat. Bring equipment with you. Head back to Spotorno to connect with **NereoSub** (☎ 019.741.43.4, Via Berninzoni, 124, www.nereosub.com) or **Bergeggi Diving School** (☎ 019.85.99.50, Punto Mare, Bagni Cormorano, www.bergeggidiving.it) if you want to explore the underwater itineraries around *isola* Bergeggi. Three routes – *Il Pifferaio* (the Piper), *La Franata* (the Landslide), and *Il Canalone* (the Gully) are organized by the association **Sentiero Blu**. The first, down to a depth of 18-20 m/54-60 feet and popular at night, takes in the seafloor surrounding the west-facing side of the island. A highlight here is *Oculina Patagonica*, a species of tropical coral that can only be found in the Mediterranean in this one location. Snorkelers can also generally find it at a depth of around two m/six feet. The second dive, from the southeastern side of the island, is considered the archeological itinerary for the fragments of amphorae that litter the bottom. Finally, expert divers can take in the gully where a rock wall is entirely covered in sea anemone and where lobsters, conger eels, and scorpion fish congregate. Monkfish are a rare sight, and at 20 m/60 feet it's possible to find large groupers.

■ Savona - Varazze

As you approach Savona from the west there's an almost palpable tug exerted by Genoa, which is now just a short distance away. Akin to the suburbs of Genoa, the outskirts of Savona (the largest town on the western Riviera) are framed in factories and modern construction that shroud the beautiful and ancient medieval center on the waterfront. Historically, too, Genoa's influence was strongly felt in Savona, which for centuries fiercely opposed the Republic's intended hegemony.

Heading inland from Savona, however, you abruptly re-enter rural Liguria. The village of Sassello is perched on the edge of the Beigua Regional Park, and the town's alpine feel is rein-

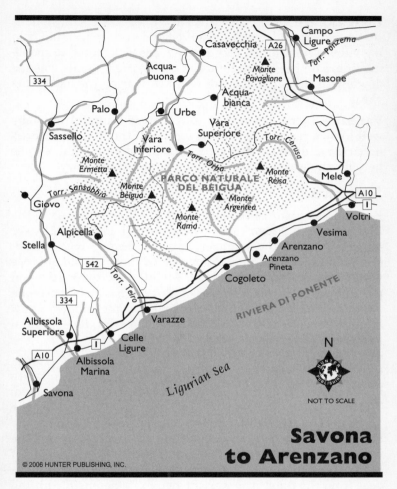

Savona to Varazze

Savona to Arenzano

NOT TO SCALE

© 2006 HUNTER PUBLISHING, INC.

forced by the surrounding woods where hiking is a popular pastime.

Back on the waterfront is a string of lovely resorts. **Albissola Marina** has, for centuries, been identified with artisan ceramics and has a promenade paved in handmade mosaics by prominent artists. Boutiques and galleries around the town display works of stunning beauty, including various pieces done in the monochromatic pale blue that is a hallmark of Albissola.

Celle Ligure has two distinct neighborhoods; the modern resort district and a well-preserved and atmospheric old fishing village. It's a quiet, lazy sort of place well suited to spending hours on the beach followed by leisurely meals washed down with the *Lumassino* or *Rollo* wine from the local vineyards.

Varazze, by contrast, has much more bustle and is the well-known resort town of this stretch of the Riviera. There's a marina and a mile-long sandy beach, but many others come here for the waves: It's a popular spot with surfers.

Savona

Established prior to the arrival of the Romans, during the Imperial Age, *Saona* (as it was known then) was of lesser importance than the neighboring port of *Vada Sabatia* (modern Vado Ligure). In part this reflected Savona's old alliance with Carthage, which had been defeated by Rome. In equal part, however, it was a matter of geography. Ancient Savona clustered on the hill where the Priamar fortification now stands. By contrast, Vada Sabatia was on flat, level ground and was therefore easier to develop.

The fall of the Empire turned the tide of Savona's fortunes. The Roman roads, which passed through *Vada*, fell into disrepair, lessening the preeminence of towns they connected. Then, in the eighth century (according to tradition) the Longobards were defeated on the plane of Vada by the Franks, who proceeded to destroy the town in 774. During the frequent Saracen attacks that characterized the later half of the first millennium, Savona began to be populated by refugees from the coast who were drawn to its defensible hilltop position.

Perhaps the most auspicious event in Savona's history, however, was the 10th-century transfer of the Bishop's See, previously established in Vada in the seventh century. This honor brought tremendous wealth, power, and prestige to the town, which it wielded to garner economic, military, and political influence. Situated on an overland trade route to the Po Valley and onward to northern Europe, Savona became an important port for Piedmont and enjoyed good relations therefore with the French.

In Genoa, Savona was perceived as a gathering threat, especially as the Republic sought to extend its hegemony in western Liguria through allegiance and territorial concessions. In 1153 it pressured Savona's governors to sign a convention that severely limited Savona's business activities, laying the foundation for the intense rivalry that would develop between the two powers.

In 1191, with the help of the Church, Savona appealed for and was granted independence from the marquis and became a free commune. Its freedom from Genoa, however, was politically uncertain during politically tumultuous times. Throughout the 13th, 14th, and 15th centuries it would have periods of independence interspersed with periods of subjugation. But in 1528, when Andrea Doria implemented his coup and obtained from Charles V recognition of the Republic of Genoa's autonomy and territorial integrity in Liguria, Savona was finally vanquished. Doria ordered the sinking of several large vessels filled with stones at the mouth of Savona's port, and the town found itself in humbling vassalage.

Savona was finally freed from Genoa's yoke with the establishment of the Kingdom of Italy. It resumed its commercial relationship with Piedmont and, with ships moving in and out of the port, began to prosper. The gridded streets just outside of Savona's medieval core reflect this period of 19th century growth. Farther out, the industrial areas reflect the period of development just after WWII. Like Genoa, the Savona of the 21st century is a city in the midst of transforming itself, struggling to develop its opportunities in both business and tourism. It hasn't made the same progress as Genoa in terms of appealing to travelers, but visitors who invest the time and energy don't leave disappointed.

Getting There

 By Train: Savona's **FS** station is inland in the Mongrifone district, near the Piazza di Nazioni. Of interest, the station was designed by the famous Italian architect Pier Luigi Nervi. For schedules, see www.trenitalia.it.

By Car: Exit the A10 autostrada at Savona-Vado and head east towards Savona.

By Bus: SAR provides bus service for towns between Andora and Savona. For more information and timetables, see www.sar-bus.com, ☎ 0182.215.44. **ACTS** provides bus service for towns between Finale Ligure and Varazze. For more information and timetables, see www.acts.it, ☎ 019.220.12.31.

Resources

- www.inforiviera.it
- www.comune.savona.it
- **Tourist Office:** Corso Italia, 157r, ☎ 019.840.2321.

Being There

Savona isn't an easy town to penetrate, shrouded as it is in the trappings of a modern port (albeit one that has seen its activity decline in recent years). Its most interesting sights, however, are clustered in a small area near the waterfront where the town began. Here you'll find a core reminiscent of Genoa, the town's ancient rival, and well equipped with restaurants and shops. The western part of town features some interesting modern architecture by **Pier Luigi Nervi**, the Italian architect who was a pioneer in the use of reinforced concrete. Design buffs will appreciate his work on Savona's main railway station and the **Palazzo della Provincia**, both completed during the 1960s.

Fortezza del Priamar

When the Genoese finally and ultimately conquered Savona in 1528, they ordered the razing of the hilltop where Savona's ancient castle and first cathedral stood. In their place they constructed this massive fortress, which served as a garrison and prison (Giuseppe Mazzini was held here between 1830-31) and a constant reminder of Genoa's supremacy over the once-rebellious Savonese. In recent years the stronghold has been converted to a museum complex. A garden adjoins the fortress and the Corso Italia – a 19th-century street that is now lined with elegant shops – leads away toward the old town.

The **Museo Storico-Archeologico** on the lower floor presents Savona's ancient history through objects and artifacts recovered in the vicinity, including a sixth-century necropolis that is enshrined in situ. Also of interest are lovely North African mosaic floors from the third and fourth centuries. (Open June-September, Tuesday-Saturday 10 am-12 pm and 5-7 pm, Sunday 5-7 pm; October-May, Tuesday-Friday 9:30 am-12:30 pm and 3-5 pm, Saturday 10 am-12 pm and 3-5 pm, Sunday 3-5 pm; ☎ 019.822.708; entrance fee €2,10).

On the ground floor the **Museo d'Arte Sandro Pertini** is a contemporary museum showcasing the art collection of the former Italian President, a Savona native. There are works by Miró, Morandi, Rosai, de Chirico, and others. (Open Saturday and Sunday 10 am-12 pm, ☎ 019.854.565; entrance fee €2,10).

Located on the second and third floors, the **Pinacoteca Civica** is the place to go for a comprehensive lesson in Ligurian painting and painters from the Middle Ages through the 18th century. Names you've encountered in churches and palaces throughout the region are illuminated here, and there is also an impressive collection of ceramics that underscores the importance of this craft in the area. A contemporary gallery presents some modern works by Picasso, Magritte, de Chirico, Twombly and others. (Open October-March, Monday, Wednesday, Friday 8:30 am-1 pm; Tuesday, Thursday 2-7 pm; Saturday 8:30 am-1 pm and 3:30-6:30 pm; Sunday 9:30 am-12:30 pm. June-September, Monday, Wednesday, Friday 8:30 am-1 pm; Tuesday, Thursday 2:30-5 pm; Saturday 8:30 am-1 pm, 8-11 pm; Sunday 8-11 pm; ☎ 019.811.520; entrance fee €4.)

Duomo

Genoa's first cathedral – which formerly stood on the site of the Priamar fortress – was razed by the Genoese when Savona finally capitulated in 1528. The cathedral of **Santa Maria Assunta**, center of the Duomo complex, was built at the end of the 16th century. Inside is Albertino Piazza's *Enthroned Madonna and Child with St. Peter and St. Paul*. Other valuable paintings are kept in the *Museo del Tesoro della Cattedrale* (open on request), including Lodovico Brea's 15th century *Assumption*

and Saints. Also in the treasury are the cathedral's riches in silver and gold work.

Thanks to Francesco della Rovere – a member of Savona's most powerful 15th-century family, who became Pope Sixtus IV (another della Rovere, Giuliano, had been Pope Julius II and built the original cathedral) – Savona has it's own Sistine Chapel, also with magnificent ceiling decoration. To be fair, however, it pales in comparison with Michelangelo's work in Rome. Built as a monument to his parents, the chapel (open Saturdays 4-6 pm) was redesigned in the 18th century in Rococo style.

Palazzo della Rovere

Giuliano della Rovere – the future Pope Julius II – had this palace on the Via Pia (old Savona's main thoroughfare, today lined with shops and other monumental buildings) built at the end of the 15th century. Unfortunately, the original decorations by Semini, deemed too secular, were destroyed when the palace was converted into a convent in 1673. The palace is closed to the public, but some vestiges of its original splendor can be glimpsed in the post office at the rear of the courtyard, which is open for visitors.

Medieval Towers

Several towers rise around Savona. The **Torre del Brandale** was built in the 12th century and is decorated with a ceramic *Visitation* on its exterior and with frescoes inside. The **Torre di Leon Pancaldo** on the waterfront is emblematic of Savona. Built in the 14th century, it is named for the Savonese navigator who accompanied Magellan on his trip around the world in 1521. The Latin inscription on the side reads, "In this raging sea,

this sudden storm, I beseech thee, oh guiding star." The tower stands at the foot of Via Paleocapa, a good shopping street.

Only in Savona

Holy Friday Procession

Since the 12th century – when penitents marched, striking themselves with rods or whips – Savona has observed Holy Friday (two days before the celebration of Easter) with a solemn procession. Today the event is held every other year. Members of the confraternities carry massive *casse* – wooden monuments depicting episodes from the Passion of Jesus Christ. The final *casse*, depicting the *Ark of the Holy Cross*, is said to contain a piece of the true cross.

Fair of Saint Bartolomeo of the Forest

Held annually in September (with expositions on the grounds of the Priamar fortress), this agricultural fair features cattle, pigs, sheep, goats, even ostriches, along with produce (wine, honey, cheese, etc.) from the region surrounding Savona.

Altare

Heading up the A6 from Savona you arrive at Altare, where Benedictine monks from Bergeggi introduced the art of glass blowing in the 12th century. Today the practice lives on in the craftsmen's workshops and art galleries, and the town's **Glass Museum** (open Monday-Friday 3-6 pm), which presents valuable pieces and illuminates the history of glass production in Altare.

Corsica & Sardinia

Corsica Ferries and **Sardinia Ferries** operate out of the new ferry terminal at Vado Ligure and have service to Bastia in Corsica and Calvi in Sardinia. (Twice daily departures in the summer season, less frequent in the fall, winter, and spring.) For schedules and ticketing information, see www.porto.sv.it/english/Cruises/index.htm.

For Active Travelers

Mountain Biking

An extensive network of mountain bike trails exists in the area surrounding Savona and Vado Ligure. Stop at the tourist office to inquire about rentals and trail maps. At least two trails (ascent to Naso di Gato and ascent to Colle di Cadibona) depart from Savona using the asphalt road to Turin.

Sassello

There's a distinctly alpine feel to the village of Sassello, located inland from Savona and surrounded by the protected forests and fields of Mt. Beigua Regional Nature Park. Even in summer a cool breeze blows and the air is scented with the perfume of rich earth and trees, augmented with the smell of *amaretti* – the town's famous almond cookies – baking at the town's numerous pasticcerie and food shops.

Sassello is first mentioned around 1273, when the land was sold to a branch of the Doria family, though there is archeological evidence that the region was settled in prehistoric times. These Doria built the **Bastia Soprana** (now in ruins) as a

Above: Doria Castel, Dolceacqua
Below: The medieval bridge and Doria Castel, Dolceacqua

Above: Piazza Garibaldi, Dolceacqua
Below: Approaching Castel Vittorio

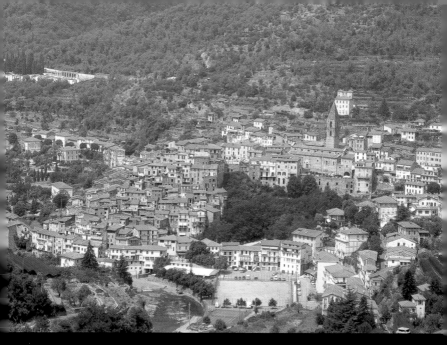

Above: Looking down from Castel Vittorio at Pigna
Below: Isolabona in the Val Nervia, where the road diverges to Apricale

defensive fortification and used the town as a base for raids on Genoa, against whom they were openly rebellious. The schisms in the Doria clan were notorious in this period of history. Around 1450 Filippo Doria – who was on better terms with the powerful family of Genoa – acquired the territory and built the *Bastia Sottana*, moving the town's center within its new defensive walls.

In the early 17th century Sassello came under the dominion of Genoa and entered a period of prosperity founded on the town's iron and coal industry, which Genoese ships carried from the coast to markets on the Mediterranean. Later that century, however, during the Savoy Wars, the town was destroyed by fire. Thus the village as it appears today – with its buildings in stone and limestone connected by narrow alleys and lovely porticos – is a product of that late period.

Today, Sassello is a sleepy hamlet that is popular with hikers and other outdoor enthusiasts, and was the first town in Liguria to be awarded an 'Orange Flag' for promoting environmentally responsible tourism.

Getting There

By Train: There is no direct rail service to Sassello. Instead, get off at Varazze and take the **ACTS** bus. For schedules, see www.trenitalia.it.

By Car: Exit the A10 autostrada at Albisola and then take the SS334 inland.

By Bus: ACTS provides bus service for towns between Finale Ligure and Varazze. For more information and timetables, see www.acts.it, ☎ 019.220.12.31.

Resources

- www.inforiviera.it
- www.comunesassello.it
- **Tourist Office:** Via G.B. Badano, 45 , ☎ 019.724.020 (open seasonally).

Being There

The air is noticeably crisper in Sassello, especially if you're traveling in summer from the coast. The village has an alpine feel with buildings that call to mind mountain chalets. Inside the town center cobbled streets wind around a network of church-fronted piazza, while outside the village is encircled by pristine forests of beeches, oak, and chestnuts. A highlight of Sassello is tasting some of its *amaretti* cookies (you can buy them by the sack at numerous pasticcerie) and enjoying a picnic composed of some of the local cheeses and specialty cured meats available from the *salumeri*. The ideal location for this *al fresco* meal? The **Beigua Regional Park**, which has loads of trails and scenic locales.

Church of the Holy Trinity

Sassello's Baroque-style parish church was consecrated in the 18th century, and was only built after much controversy. Reflecting power struggles, the building was opposed by the friars of the church of San Giovanni, the oldest in Sassello, even though by the 17th century the swelling population required another house of worship. After a minor miracle in the midst of the Savoy War, however, the priests consented to the construction of a new church, but building and consecration took nearly another century.

Church of the Immacolata Concezione

Standing opposite the town hall is the rather plain but lovely Church of the Immaculate Conception, built between 1582 and 1584. The painting of the *Virgin and Child with Saint Antonio of Padua* in the third chapel on the right is by Lorenzo de Ferrari.

Museo Perrando

The former *palazzo* of the Perrando family houses the archaeology and local history museum and the Sassello library and cultural center. The varied collection consists of several prehistoric artifacts found in the region of Sassello and Mount Beigua, in addition to items from the Bastia Soprano, and furnishings, books, Albisola ceramics, and a collection of paintings from the 17th and 18th centuries that were the holdings of the Perrandos. A newer ethnographic section recreates the atmosphere of an ironworks and an amaretti factory. (Open June-September on Wednesday, Saturday, and Sunday 10 am-12 pm and 5-7 pm; October-June on Saturday 10 am-12 pm and 3-5 pm, ☎ 019.724.1000.)

Only in Sassello

Beigua Regional Nature Park

Liguria's largest natural park also boasts the richest biodiversity. Beigua has a stunning variety of environments (forests, peat bogs, river gorges, meadows, wetlands) and – from certain vantages – panoramic views that, on a clear day, extend as far as the island of Corsica. In addition, the park is home to ample evidence of man's prehistoric presence in this pristine area, ranging from rock etchings to ancient cave shelters, and tools, bones, and decorative items found in the collections of a sprinkling of small museums in the park's villages. Wildlife in the park includes wild boar, river otters, and an impressive number of birds of prey that visit the park on their annual migrations.

There are some 500 km/300 miles of well-maintained trails marked throughout the park, passing through chestnut and beech forests on the inland side of the Beigua massif and through Mediterranean maquis on the seaward side. The trails are open for hiking, mountain biking, and horseback riding. For more information, see www.parks.it/parco.beigua or www.parcobeigua.it. On the website you'll also find a list of guided nature hikes, each organized around a theme and costing about €5 per person to participate (English-speaking guides available).

For Active Travelers

Hiking

The area of the Beigua is traversed by some 500 km/300 miles of trails. Just outside Sassello is a loop (hiking time about 3½ hours) that passes through Norway spruce and Douglas fir, fragrant daphne, and forests of beech and chestnut before ending near the Bellavista Castle. Get a map of this and other trails at the headquarters of the **Beigua Regional Nature Park** in

Savona, Corso Italia, 3, ☎ 019.841.873.00; or at the tourist office in Sassello.

Sassello is also near trails 19 and 20 of the Alta Via dei Monti Liguri. These are both demanding hikes, and nº19, in particular – which climbs up Monte Beigua – is steep and requires great endurance. But from the top, on a clear day you can see Corsica and perhaps even as far as the archipelago off the coast of Turkey. Trail nº20 takes in the heart of the Beigua Regional Park, where the mountains have a harsh appearance due to the presence of *serpentinite*, a rock that came from the bed of an ancient ocean and is toxic to many species of plants. The environment is therefore unique, with such rare species of plant-life as the Bertoloni violet and the scented daphne. For more, see www.altaviadeimontiliguri.it. (The Alta Via is covered in its entirety starting on page 212.)

● **Trail nº19**
- Starting Point: Il Giova.
- Ending Point: Prato Rotondo.
- Distance: roughly 12 km/7.2 miles.
- Average travel time: 3½ hours.
- Link up trails: From Costa del Giancardo (midway through the hike) to Sassello, uphill, an additional 2½ hours.

● **Trail nº20**
- Starting Point: Prato Rotondo.
- Ending Point: Passo del Faiallo.
- Distance: roughly 10 km/six miles.
- Average travel time: 2½ hours.

Snow Skiing

Sassello is (sometimes) transformed into a snowy wonderland in the winter and then skiing – both downhill and cross-country – become popular activities. **Alberola** is the resort in the area, with two lifts serving five trails. It's not Aspen, but it'll do in a pinch.

Albissola Marina

The town of Albissola Marina, identified with its ceramic works since the 16th century, started life as the Borgo Inferiore of a larger settlement of Albissola belonging to the Benedictines and supported by Savona. The other half, Borgo d'Alto, is modern-day Albisola Superiore which begins inland and stretches to the sea just east of Albisola Marina.

The Genoese intervened in Albissola in the 14th century, bringing it under administrative control of the podestà established at Varazze. In 1615 Albissola Marina officially separated from Albissola Superiore and became a free commune, though still dependent for protection on Varazze and, to a degree, Savona. It was during this period that the ceramics industry began to flourish. Quarries of red earth and white stone were established inland to provide raw materials for the craft, communal kilns were opened, and final products were shipped to destinations all across Europe and the Mediterranean. The most sought-after pieces were in Albissola Marina's signature majolica – a monochrome pale blue. In the 20th century the industry thrived again when artists began producing pieces in Art Nouveau and Futurist styles.

The construction of the Via Aurelia severed the physical connection of the town center, site of the kilns and workshops, to the beach, where once ceramics were left to dry and harden on the sand. In the 1960s, a collaboration of artists responded with the creation of the **Passeggiata degli Artisti**, an original work of mosaic panels that makes for one of the most beautiful promenades on the Italian Riviera.

Getting There

By Train: A single **FS** station serves both Albissola Marina and Albisola Superiore, located near the Piazza Giulio II off Via Mazzini under the autostrada. For schedules, see www.trenitalia.it.

By Car: Exit the A10 autostrada at Albissola. The Via Aurelia passes through town.

By Bus: ACTS provides bus service for towns between Finale Ligure and Varazze. For more information and timetables, see www.acts.it, ☎ 019.220.12.31.

Resources

- www.inforiviera.it
- www.albissola.com
- **Tourist Office:** Corso Ferrari, Passeggiata a Mare, ☎ 019.400.2008.

Being There

It's practically impossible not to visit both Albissola Marina and Albisola Superiore at the same time, as the two blend almost seamlessly, the Sansobbia river being the geographic delineation. The *Passeggiata degli Artisti* is at the western extreme of Albissola Marina, but you'll find artistic testimonies large and small all over both towns. The oldest quarter of Albissola Marina is on the waterfront behind the promenade, but to find the medieval section of Albisola Superiore, head inland and uphill toward the church of San Nicolo on the square of the same name.

Nostra Signora della Concordia

Albissola's parish church was founded in 1590 when the churches of San Benedetto and San Antonio were united. The church, which sits on a lovely black-and-white cobbled *parvis* or courtyard, counts among its treasures a polychrome wood group by Maragliano and a majolica-decorated altarpiece entitled *Adoration of the Shepherds* from 1576, produced in Albisola.

Villa Faraggiana

Situated among gardens on the northeast side of town, the villa was built in the early 18th century as a holiday residence for Gerolamo Durazzo of Genoa. It was sold in 1821 to the Faraggiana family, who bequeathed the villa to the city in 1961. Within the sumptuously decorated rooms are a priceless collection of sculptures by Filippo Parodi, majolica, and period furniture including pieces by the cabinetmaker E.T.

Peters. (Open March-September, 3-7 pm with final tour beginning at 6:15 pm, www.villafaraggiana.it.)

Fabbrica Casa Museo G. Mazzotti

This working factory and museum on the Viale Matteotti was established in 1903 when Giuseppe Mazzotti rented rooms in the Pozzo Garitta village – site of the ancient furnaces – and began manufacturing ceramics. In the 1930s the factory was associated with Italian Futurism and the underwriters of the Futurist Manifesto, and in the 1950s with such artists as Fontana, Jorn, and Sassu. The museum displays pieces from Albisola's long history of ceramic production, and the factory offers a glimpse of the intricate process of forming, firing, and glazing. (Open 10 am-12 pm and 4-6 pm, ☎ 019.489.872.)

Only in Albisola Marina

Albisola Superior

Established in Roman times, the town of Albisola Superior (then known as *Borgo d'Alto*) grew up around the church of San Nicolo and a ninth-century castle built on top of Monte Castellaro by Bonifacio del Vasto. The town's districts stretch along the road to Sassello from the inland hilltop to the sea. Its prosperity, like Albisola Marina, has been linked to ceramic production and, more recently, to tourism. The ceramic art museum of **Museo Manlio Trucco** is worth visiting and there are several lovely 16th-century villas (all private property) surrounded by gardens.

Ceramics Shopping

Find shops, galleries, and work-shops throughout Albisola Marina and Albisola Superior selling ceramic wares in a variety of styles and forms, including some antique pieces of great value. Note that ceramics produced under specified conditions in Albissola Marina are guaranteed by D.O.C. specification and/or marked "Albissola Origin." The *Associazione Ceramisti* on Via dell'Oratorio organizes  expositions and fairs and has a registry of craftsmen producing in Albissola, Savona, and Genoa.

For Active Travelers

Diving

Abysso International Diving Center in Albisola Superiore takes divers to the area surrounding the Island of Bergeggi and to other sites around Albisola, including to a couple of shipwrecks off the coast (including the *Haven*, the largest accessible wreck in the Mediterranean). The center does diving certification and also teaches a course on snorkeling for adults and children, and can provide all equipment and transportation. (☎ 019.481.451, www.sub-abysso.com, info@sub-abysso.com)

Golf

Hit the links in Albisola Superiore at the **Filanda Golf Club**, where 18 holes are spread over a lovely landscape between the Sansobbia river and the Erchi hill. There's a clubhouse, driving range, spa, and restaurant. (☎ 019.484.857, fax 019.400.31.33, Via Csarino, 143, www.filanda.org.)

Celle Ligure

Before its acquisition by the Republic of Genoa in 1343, the town of Celle Ligure was under several different dominions. In the 11th century, according to the historical accounts of Emperor Enrico II, Celle was a part of the Marca Aleramica with nearby Varazze and Albisola. The name Celle is said to derive from the old word Cellae used to describe huts where boats and fishing tools were stored. Early in its history Celle Ligure was little more than a fishing village with a small population.

Soon after, however, it passed under the control of the Marquis of Ponzone, then Malocelli, then Doria, and then to Genoa at the same time as the Republic took acquisition of Albisola and Varazze. The three towns were treated as separate entities and drew their own municipal statutes. Those of Celle Ligure were recognized in 1414.

By the 17th and early 18th century Celle Ligure was prospering from sea trade conducted with Spain, France, and the

Americas, but with the arrival of Napoleon and the intrusion of the French customs system lost many of its ships. When the railroad was built in the mid-19th century, Celle Ligure embraced the new industry of tourism with great success, building a lovely promenade that links Centre and Piani, the most modern district that is the center for hotels and tourist activities.

Getting There

 By Train: The FS station is located in Centre, just a few blocks off the waterfront near Piazza Volta. For schedules, see www.trenitalia.it.

 By Car: Exit the A10 autostrada at Celle Ligure.

 By Bus: ACTS provides bus service for towns between Finale Ligure and Varazze. For more information and timetables, see www.acts.it, ☎ 019.220.12.31.

Resources

- www.inforiviera.it
- www.celleligure.com
- **Tourist Office:** Via Boagno, Palazzo Comunale, ☎ 019.990.021.

Being There

The town of Celle Ligure is split into two districts. The atmospheric *centro storico* is at *Centre*, first developed in the Middle Ages in rows of buildings on either side of the main road, **Via Aicardi**. Moving east you find **Piani**, the modern half of town where hotels and services are clustered. The lovely **Parco Bottini** is on the far west side of town on a headland with panoramic views over the water. Behind the town are vineyards where the grapes for local *Lumassino* and *Rollo* wines are cultivated.

San Michele Arcangelo

Celle Ligure's 17th-century parish church stands away from the coast up a steep flight of steps. Built over a 12th-century structure of which only the cusped bell tower remains, the interior is decorated with frescoes and sculptures by Maragliano. The 16th-century **Oratorio dei Disciplinati** next door has a wooden statue of St. Michael, also by Maraglino. Other artistic treasures include Perin del Vaga's 16th-century polyptych *St. Michael, St. Peter, and John the Baptist* and 17th-century paintings by Domenico Fiasella, Domenico Piola, and G.B. Carbone. The sacristy holds one of the oldest existing processional chests, dated to 1481.

Only in Celle Ligure

Antique Market

Every second Sunday the streets of *Centre* are enlivened with vendors who come to sell a variety of antiques (clothing, objects, furniture, jewelry) to the visiting crowds. On Friday mornings is the regular traveling market – with produce and a wide range of merchandise – that moves from village to village along the coast throughout the week.

For Active Travelers

Sailing & Windsurfing

 Check in with Celle's **Club Nautico** for information on sailing or windsurfing (classes are available) off the coast of Celle Ligure. (open seasonally on Lungomore Crocetta, www.clubnauticocelle.it, clubnauticocelle@tiscali.it.)

Varazze

During the Imperial Age, *AD Navalia* was associated with shipbuilding (a reputation that persisted through the Middle Ages), making use of the thick timber that covers the hillsides behind the town and the beaches that are perfect launching points. Today, it's better known as a tourist resort and as a popular spot with surfers along the Ligurian coast. The forests are a favorite with hikers.

It's also remembered as the home of Jacopo da Varagine, a Domenican friar and archbishop of Genoa who authored *The*

Golden Legend, a medieval bestseller that was a compilation of the lives of the saints. His greatest contribution to his times, however, might have been his role as peacemaker between the Guelphs and Ghibellines. He's remembered as such in depictions in the churches of Sant'Ambrogio and Santi Nazario e Celso.

The town was part of the *Marca Aleramica* with Celle Ligure and Albisola, and then dominated by the Marquis of Ponzone, then the Del Bosco, then the Malocelli, before coming under Genoese control. During the Middle Ages extensive ramparts encircled and protected the town, but only the northern sections are still standing. Incorporated into the ramparts was the 12th-century Romanesque church of Sant'Ambrogio, which now stands in a state of graceful ruin.

Varazze is the big tourist resort of this section of the Riviera, with a large marina, a sandy beach, and a seafront walk (the *Lungomare Europa*) that extends for five km/three miles and is crowded in the early evenings when the town comes out for a stroll. Another long path, the *Piani d'Invrea* that winds eastward from the town center to the mouth of the river Arrestra, grants access to a series of tiny coves that make for some of the nicest sunbathing and swimming in Varazze.

Getting There

 By Train: Varazze's **FS** station is on the western extreme of town, just off the Via Aurelia. For schedules, see www.trenitalia.it.

 By Car: Exit the A10 autostrada at Varazze. The Via Aurelia runs through town.

 By Bus: ACTS provides bus service for towns between Finale Ligure and Varazze. For more information and timetables, see www.acts.it, ☎ 019.220.12.31.

Resources

■ www.inforiviera.it
■ **Tourist Office:** Viale Nazioni Unite, 1, ☎ 019.935.043.

Being There

Varazze is rather a long and skinny town, with most of its atmospheric streets packed in between the Via Aurelia and the long street along the waterfront that changes name in several spots (from west to east it's known as the Via Savona, then Via Torino, then Corso Colombo, then Corso Matteotti, then finally Via S. Caterina). The marina and yacht-building center are on the western side of town.

Churches of Saint Ambrose

The original church of Sant'Ambrogio is the 12th-century Romanesque building, now in ruins, that stood outside town but was incorporated into the medieval ramparts when the northern section was built in 1370. In 1535 the Collegiate Church of Saint Ambrose was begun on the foundations of a 14th-century building. Inside, the church has works by Luca Cambiaso, Francesco Schiaffino, Giovnni Barbagelata, and a statue of *Saint Catherine of Siena* by Maragliano. Saint Catherine is said to have lifted a plague from Varazze when she passed through the town, returning from Avignon, and stopped to pay honor to the memory of Jacopo da Varagine.

Only in Varazze

Osho Meditation

Feeling a little stressed out and world-weary from all your traveling? The hills above Varazze are home to the **Osho Arihant Meditation Center**, one of several such centers around the world dedicated to the forms of meditation and spiritual practice taught by Osho, also known as Zorba the Buddha. There are accommodations and a vegetarian kitchen, but the facility is also open to visitors who come just for Dynamic and Kundalini Meditation. For more information, see www.oshovarazze.com.

Town of the Women

During the spring months Varazze turns its attention to the ladies, hosting a series of exhibitions, fashion shows, cultural meetings, sports events, and other entertainment all geared toward women.

For Active Travelers

Botanical Trail

 If you're feeling up to the challenge, you can reach the botanical path that winds around the Desert Hermitage of the Barefoot Carmelites by hiking about 18 km/11 miles uphill from Varazze. The path starts on the eastern side of the Teiro river heading toward Alpicella, then turns off to the right at Casanova and continues to the hermitage. The botanical trail passes through groves of holm oaks, beech trees, and cypress, calling out interesting specimens amid the flora. Inside the hermitage, known for its lovely architecture, is a beautiful ivory statue of the Crucifixion.

Surfing

 Varazze is one of the few good surf spots on the western Riviera. If you forgot your board, or you're looking for some good info on when and where to try the waves, head to the **Varazze Surf Shop** (Via Campana, 44, ☎ 019.931.18.18, www.varazze-surfshop.net). They can also equip you for skim or boogie boarding, or fit you up with a righteous skateboard, because cobblestone streets are the *best* for skateboarding.

Where to Stay

The following list of places to stay includes hotels (*alberghi* or *pensione*), bed & breakfasts, and a few *agriturismo* locations – working farms or vineyards that provide comfortable rooms in a rural setting.

For booking purposes, I recommend contacting the hotels directly either by phone or e-mail. If you're calling, you'll often be asked to send a fax confirming the details of your trip (arrival and departure dates) and the type of accommodation you're requesting. The hotel will then respond with a fax confirming your reservation and the room rate. It's always a good idea to have copies of these "receipts" with you when arriving to check-into your room, especially if you've been promised a room with a view or a balcony, etc., or a particularly good rate. The same applies when arrangements have been made by e-mail. Print out copies of your confirmation and bring them with you.

Those who prefer using an online booking service might try **www.venere.com**, which books hotels, B&Bs, and apartments throughout Liguria, though not generally for small locations in the small towns. For agriturismo bookings, in English generally referred to as "farm stays," try **www.agriturismo.it**, which is available in English. This is particularly useful if you're looking for a place to stay in the hinterland where big hotels are largely unheard of.

Be advised that many hotels charge by the person, not by the room. The listings below are all based on a double room with two people. Children under age five are not generally counted, but there may be an additional fee if you're requesting a crib or child's cot. Finally, there is a difference in rate depending on whether you're booking standard board, which usually includes breakfast and is sometimes called the "bed and breakfast" rate, or half-board or full-board, which includes most or all of your meals. There are so many wonderful places to eat on the Riviera, it would be a shame to squander precious euros on half- or full-board. Take the standard room rate and enjoy your typical Italian breakfast – espresso, juice, fococcia, bread, or rolls, slices of ham, cheese, yogurt, and muesli.

Hotels vary their room rates by the season, and the most expensive season is the summer months of June, July, August, and September. Rates are also generally higher at Christmas and Easter. The range of prices given in these listings (which are, of course, subject to change) reflect the differences in low and high season rates.

Alassio

Hotel Savoia

Via Milano, 14, 17021 Alassio

☎ 0182.640.277, fax 0182.640.125, info@savoiahotel.it, www.savoiahotel.it

€58-116

35 rooms

AE, MC, V, DC

Parking available

This modern hotel in an excellent, central location has a private beach and spacious rooms, several with airy balconies. For the most magnificent view, request one of the corner rooms on the tower side. The terrace is a fine spot for lounging, and three hotel restaurants serve typical Ligurian cuisine with an emphasis on seafood.

Diana Grand Hotel

Via Garibaldi, 110, 17021 Alassio

☎ 0182.642.701, fax 0182.640.304, hotel@dianagh.it, www.hoteldianaalassio.it

€130-220

57 rooms, 4 suites

AE, MC, V, DC

Parking available

A high-rise luxury hotel on the eastern side of the town, the Diana Grand has spacious, tastefully decorated rooms and a private beach with full club amenities. A heated indoor pool opens onto a private garden and solarium where guests can relax in the Jacuzzi after spa treatments.

Hotel Beau Rivage

Via Roma, 82, 17021 Alassio

☎ 0182.640.585, fax 0182.640.585, b.rivage@libero.it, www.hotelbeaurivage.it

€120-200

Closed October 9-December 25

20 rooms

Housed in a late 19th-century building on the seafront, this elegant little family-run hotel is a little out of the way on the far western side of town. Rooms are on the plain side, but the small dining room (which boasts an excellent wine list and typical Ligurian cuisine) has a lovely frescoed ceiling.

Villa Firenze

Via Dante, 35, 17021 Alassio

☎ 0182.661.11, fax 0182.661.1601, villafirenze@alassio.it, www.residencevillafirenze.it

€320-750

Make Alassio your home base on the Riviera and book an apartment in this converted 19th-century villa in the heart of the village. Rates are based on a Saturday-Saturday stay and include room amenities (including cooking facilities and a refrigerator), Internet access, cleaning, and your favorite newspaper and hot croissants delivered fresh each morning.

Hotel Lamberti

Via Gramsci, 57, 17021 Alassio

☎ 0182.642.747, fax 0182.642.438, hotellamberti@libero.it, www.hotellamberti.it

€100-200

Closed October-December 18

This small hotel near the Piazza San Francesco on the eastern side of town is in a prime location for the beach and excursions to the shops of the *budello*. Recently redecorated rooms are spacious and there's a cozy sitting area adjacent the dining room where guests can relax.

Where to Stay

Albenga

Sole Mare

Lungomare Cristoforo Colombo, 15, 17031 Albenga
☎ 0182.518.17, fax 0182.545.212, hotelsolemare@tiscali.it
€100-125
Closed December 8-25

Located on Albenga's waterfront, the Sole Mare is a bit of a distance from the Centro Storico but well situated to enjoy the beach. Plain but nicely proportioned rooms, many with sea views.

Hotel Italia

Viale Martiri della Libertà, 8, 17031 Albenga
☎ 0182.504.05

An ideal location near the Piazza del Popolo and the Centro Storico makes up for the lack of charisma in this one-star hotel. There's a bar and restaurant but opt instead for meals in the old town.

Hotel Cà di Berta

Località Cà di Berta, 5, I - 17031 Salea
☎ 0182.559.930, fax 0182.559.888, info@hotelcadiberta.it, www.hotelcadiberta.it
€110-210
Closed November

Surrounded by palms and olive trees on the plateau less than 10 km/six miles outside Albenga, the Hotel Cà di Berta boasts lovely, park-like grounds and large but reasonably priced suites. The stone-rimmed swimming pool is an oasis of calm and a great place for an evening cocktail. This is in a prime location for excursions to the inland areas of the Albenga plain.

Albissola Marina

Hotel Garden

Viale Faraggiana, 6, 17012 Albissola Marina
☎ 019.485.253, fax 019.485.255, garden@savonaonline.it,
www.hotelgardenalbissola.com
€100-150

A comfortable hotel with a pool and private beach, the Hotel Garden has a permanent contemporary art collection displayed in its modern interior. Rooms are a little bland, but are soundproofed and air-conditioned and offer balconies with sea views and bathrooms with Jacuzzi tubs.

Apricale

La Favorita

Strada San Pietro, 1, 18035 Apricale
☎ 0184.208.186, fax 0184.208.247,
info@hotelristorantelafavorita.com,
www.hotelristorantelafavorita.com
€70

At the bottom of the village overlooking the valley, La Favorita earns its title with tidy, comfortable rooms, ceiling frescoes and a large terrace where inland-inflected Ligurian cuisine is served with a panoramic view.

Locanda dei Carugi

Via Roma 12/14, 18030 Apricale
☎ 0184.209.010, fax 0184.209.942, carugi@masterweb.it,
www.locandadeicarugi.it

A 15th-century stone building in the heart of medieval Apricale is a romantic setting for this small, rustic getaway hotel. Antique furnishings lend charm to the rooms and interiors: The Attico di

Lucrezia is particularly lovely and spacious with wood-beamed ceilings and large windows that invite the alpine breeze.

Bergeggi

Hotel Claudio

Via XXV Aprile, 37, 17028 Bergeggi
☎ 019.859.750, fax 019.859.750, info@hotelclaudio.it
€130-180
closed January and February

Chef/owner Claudio Pasquarelli presides over this elegant hotel high upon a cliff overlooking the wild Bergeggi coastline. The restaurant has earned a Michelin star, and equal attention has been paid to the comforts provided to guests. Twenty deluxe rooms and six suites open onto a terrace equipped with pool and solarium. Far below, the hotel has a private beach.

Bordighera

Villa Elisa

Via Romana, 70, 18012 Bordighera
☎ 0184.261.313, fax 0184.261.942, info@villaelisa.com, www.villaelisa.com
€110-165

The reputation of the Villa Elisa was established in the early 20th century when British tourists discovered the hotel's serene atmosphere. Today it's in an ideal location in the old town, surrounded by a Mediterranean garden of flowers, oranges, lemons, and olives. Rooms are classically elegant.

Grand Hotel del Mare

Via Portico della Punta, 34, 18012 Bordighera
☎ 0184.262.201, fax 0184.262.394, info@grandhoteldelmare.it
€280-310
Closed October 11-December 22

This modern hotel complex occupies a picturesque curve of coastline and has a small private beach for guests not satisfied with the saltwater pool surrounded by sloping gardens. Complete spa facilities and a refined restaurant complete the package. Rooms are smartly furnished, many with stunning views.

Hotel Parigi

Lungomare Argentina, 16/18, 18012 Bordighera

☎ 0184.261.405, fax 0184.260.421, direzione@hotelparigi.com, www.hotelparigi.com

€90-280

A location on the palm-lined promenade is one of the highlights of this turn-of-the-century hotel. The fifth-floor spa is another, with massage, sauna, Turkish bath, hydromassage, and a pool filled with warm, purified seawater under a glass roof. Rooms are tastefully decorated.

Aurora

Via Pelloux 42/b, 18012 Bordighera

☎ 0184.261.311, fax 0184.261.312, www.hotelaurora.net, info@hotelaurora.net

€120-180

An alternative to waterfront lodgings, the Aurora – built in the 1920s – is a short distance from the old town and boasts a rooftop terrace/solarium and an interior adorned by ceiling frescoes. Located in the villa district.

Bussana Vecchia

Apriti Sesamo

Via Alla Chiesa, Bussana Vecchia di San Remo

☎ 0184.510.022, fax335.231.794, info@ristorantenaturale.it, www.ristorantenaturale.it

From €60

At the top of the village, adjacent to the ruins of the church, this bed & breakfast has double, spartan double, triple, and quad rooms with en suite bathrooms and sea views. Organic meals are served at the restaurant, with vegans, vegetarians, and macrobiotic dieters happily accommodated. Families encouraged.

Camogli

Cenobio dei Dogi

Via Cuneo, 34, 16032 Camogli

☎ 0185.724.1, fax 0185.772.796, www.cenobio.it, reception@cenobio.it

€150-300

Where to Stay

This gracious villa above the fishing village was built by an aristocratic family of doges in the 16th century and converted to an exclusive hotel in 1956. The room décor is somewhat corporate (and indeed the hotel is popular with conventions and business travelers), but the rooms with balconies have unparalleled views of the port. The range of amenities includes a restaurant, private garden, tennis court, pool, and shuttle service to the private beach.

La Camogliese

Via Garibaldi, 55, 16032 Camogli
☎ 0185.771.402, fax 0185.774.024, info@lacamogliese.it, www.lacamogliese.it
€65-100

Family-run and so close to the water you can hear the pounding surf from some of the rooms, this central hotel is an exceptional value on the high-priced Portofino Promontory.

Hotel Augusta

Via Schiaffino, 100, Camogli 16032
☎ 0185.770.592, fax 0185.770.593, info@htlaugusta.com, www.htlaugusta.com
€55-105

A short walk from the Piazza Colombo is this family-run hotel recently renovated to produce pleasant, parquet-floored rooms, all with en suite bathrooms. Large family rooms available.

Camporosso

La Palma Bed & Breakfast

Strada degli Olandesi, 239, 18033 Camporosso
☎ 0184.252.299, palma02@libero.it, www.bblapalma.it
From €60

Rooms are plain but the garden is lovely and the property is near hiking trails through olive groves and vineyards.

Agriturismo Il Bausco
Localita Brunetti
☎ 0184.206.013/312.31, fax 0184.206.851, www.ilbausco.com
€45-50

Three atmospheric stone
cottages are near the hiking trails of the Alta Via.
Rooms are simple, but
clean and comfortable and
all have equipped kitchens.
The two-bedroom Casolare
Bausco also has a fireplace
and rooftop terrace. The
farm produces organic

fruits and vegetables, the regional Rossese wine, and extra
virgin olive oil, all available for purchase during your stay.

Castel Vittorio

Agriturismo Il Rifugio
Localita Langan
☎ 0184.241.661
€80-100

This working farm in the countryside near Castel Vittorio has
four double rooms with bathrooms, a play area for children,
and a dining room serving dishes made with such mountain
delicacies as wild boar, goat, and rabbit. Fresh cheese made
on the premises is served with meals and available for purchase.

Celle Ligure

San Michele
Via Monte Tabor, 26, 17015 Celle Ligure
☎ 019.990.017, fax 019.993.111, info@hotel-sanmichele.it,
www.hotel-sanmichele.it
€140-170
Open May-September

Rooms are simple and plain, but the location – just a few
blocks from the sea – is good and there's a nice pool and private garden.

Hotel La Giara

Via Dante Alighieri, 3, 17015 Celle Ligure

☎ 019.993.773, fax 019.993.973, www.lagiarahotel.it, info@lagiarahotel.it

€90-110

Closed December 15-27

A well-priced and well-decorated small hotel off the waterfront. Extended stays available for reasonable rates if you plan to make Celle Ligure your home base on this part of the Riviera.

Cervo

San Giorgio

Via Alessandro Volta, 19, 18010 Cervo

☎ 0183.400.175, fax 0183.400.175

€130-180

Two rooms available on the property of the town's most celebrated restaurant. Excellent location adjacent the castle and old village.

Chiavari

Torino

Corso Colombo, 151, 16043 Chiavari

☎ 0185.312.231, fax 0185.312.233, info@hotel-torino.net, www.hotel-torino.net

€75-120

On the promenade near the tourist port, the Torino is a modern hotel with comfortable, if unremarkable, rooms. Sea views available.

Monte Rosa

Via Monsignor Marinetti, 6, 16043 Chiavari

☎ 0185.314.853, fax 0185.312.868, info@hotelmonterosa.it, www.hotelmonterosa.it

€140-150

Located in the medieval center near the monthly antique market, since the turn of the century the Monte Rosa has enjoyed a good reputation with travelers thanks to its gracious hospitality and excellent dining room. During the summer season, tours of Chiavari are offered to guests illuminating the history and craft traditions of the town.

Mignon

Via Salietti, 7, 16043 Chiavari
☎ 0185.309.420, fax 0185.309.420
From €75

Near the Piazza Cavour and Piazza Roma in the city center, the Mignon, which means "cute" in French, doesn't quite live up to its name (rooms are very standard), but there is a tiny garden where guests can have breakfast in the mornings and the price is right.

Corniglia

La Posada Restaurant & Rooms

Via Fieschi, 121, 19010 Corniglia
☎ 0187.812.384, fax 0187.821.174, la_posada@libero.it,
www.cinqueterre-laposada.com
Open March to October

Take a room with a sea view for a short stay, or one of La Posada's lovely apartments for an extended vacation. The Aurora occupies two floors, has stone accents, a kitchen, and a big terrace overlooking the terraced vineyards around Corniglia. The Sole & Luna is a two-bedroom with a large terrace hanging over the turquoise sea. Freshly caught fish served in the restaurant.

Ristorante Pensione Cecio

Via Serra, 58, 19010 Corniglia
☎ 0187.812.043, fax 0187.812.138, simopank@libero.it,
www.cecio5terre.com
From €60

Family-run and well situated, this restaurant/inn has rooms with private bath and large windows overlooking the sea.

Diano Marina

Villa Igea

Via Sant'Elmo, 1, 18013 Diano Marina
☎ 0183.495.100, fax 0183.494.107, info@hotelvillaigea.com,
www.hotelvillaigea.com
€75-150

The Bracco family has run this converted villa in the residential section of Diano Marina as a gracious hotel for three generations. A great location for families, the villa has a playground and a small children's pool next to the large pool on the terrace.

Hotel Bellevue et Mediterranee

Via Generale Ardoino, 2, 18013 Diano Marina
☎ 0183.40.93, fax 0183.409.385
postmaster@bellevueetmediterranee.it
www.bellevueetmediterrranee.it
€100-150

This large, modern hotel on the waterfront is short on charm but has some interesting features, like rooms with sea views from enclosed private solariums. An elevator provides access to the private beach with club amenities, or there's a heated saltwater pool.

Hotel Arc en Ciel

Viale Torino, 21, 18013 Diano Marina
☎ 0183.495.283, fax 0183.496.930, hotelarcenciel@hotelarcenciel.it,
www.hotelarcenciel.it
€75-100
Open Easter through October 15

This lovely little hotel on the waterfront is an excellent bargain. Surrounded by pines and palms, it has an air of isolation in an otherwise bustling resort town. Breakfast served on the terrace overlooking the Gulf of Diana.

Hotel Torino

Via Milano, 42, 18013 Diano Marina
☎ 0183.495.106, fax 0183.493.602, info@htorino.com,
www.htorino.com
From €95
Closed November and December

A garden atmosphere prevails at this small hotel off the waterfront in the city center. A beautiful pool has a large Jacuzzi and there's a private disco for nighttime revelry.

Grand Hotel Diana Majestic
Via degli Oleandri, 25, 18013 Diano Marina
☎ 0183.402.727, fax 0183.403.040, grandhotel@dianamajestic.com, www.dianamajestic.com
€210-220

A private park surrounds this luxurious hotel with century-old olive trees opening directly onto a private sandy beach. Bathrooms are finished in white Carrara marble and there are other elegant touches. Two casual restaurants, one candle-lit fine-dining establish-  ment, and a poolside venue for snacks and light meals cater to gourmet guests.

Dolceacqua

B&B The Cereghetti
Centro Storico, Dolceacqua
☎ 3322.16.59, elena.perno.landi@virgilio.it

One lovely apartment with coved ceilings and stone accents available in the Centro Storico. Fireplace and equipped kitchen.

B&B Il Gato et La Volpe
Via Monsignor Laura, 2, 18035 Dolceacqua
☎ 0184.206.267, 348.067.97.62, 349.318.68.81

One apartment in a historic building overlooking the river and the town's famous Roman bridge. Equipped kitchen.

Agriturismo Terre Bianche
Località Arcagna Est, 18035 Dolceacqua
☎ 0184.314.26, fax 0184.312.30, terrebianche@terrebianche.com, www.terrebianche.com
€140-160
Closed November

Working winery producing Rossese di Dolceacqua, Vermentino, and Pigato wines has comfortable double rooms with en suite bathrooms in stone country houses situated amidst the olive trees and vines. Meals feature produce from the farm and a riding school on the premises arranges treks on horseback.

Finale Ligure

Punta Est
Via Aurelia, 1, 17024 Finale Ligure
☎ 019.600.611, fax 019.600.611, info@puntaest.com, www.puntaest.com
€160-230
Open April-October

A converted 18th-century villa, the Punta Est has park-like grounds with olive groves, terraces, and shaded walkways. Rooms are tastefully furnished to create a period ambiance. The grotto with its stalactites and stalagmites is an unforgettable place for a drink or one of the performances the hotel sponsors during the season.

Medusa

Vico Bricchieri, 7, 17024 Finale Ligure
☎ 019.692.545, fax 019.695.679, mail@medusahotel.it, www.medusahotel.it
€100-150

Popular with mountain-bikers who come for the extensive network of trails outside town, the Medusa is friendly and accommodating. A bike room is available for storage and maintenance and the desk distributes maps. Despite the sporty reputation, rooms are elegantly furnished. Excellent choice for families.

Hotel Rosita

Via Mànie, 67, 17024 Finale Ligure

☎ 019.602.437, fax 019.601.762, rositafinale@supereva.it, www.hotelrosita.it

€80-100

Closed in January

Spacious rooms are equipped with balconies overlooking the sea from the hill of Le Mànie where this small hotel is located. The restaurant has a pretty terrace for outdoor dining in the summer.

Hotel Moroni

Via Lungomare San Pietro, 38 17024 Finale Ligure

☎ 019.692.222, fax 019.680.330, info@hotelmoroni.com, www.hotelmoroni.com

€150-220

A modern hotel on the palm-lined promenade has a private beach and rooms with balconies.

Genoa

Agnello D'Oro

Via Monachette, 6

☎ 010.246.20.84, fax 010.246.23.27, hotelagnellodoro@libero.it, www.hotelagnellodoro.it

€90-130, includes breakfast

Parking available, €13

The rooms are spare, but spacious, clean and full of character. Plus the price and location of this family-run hotel can't be beat, nor the warmth of reception. Via Monachette is a "typical" Genoese ally – entering and exiting by car is hair-raising – in the Principe adjacent to the Via Balbi, with its museums, and in close proximity to Via Garibaldi, the Porto Antico, and the Centro Storico. For maximum character, ask for a room in the old wing.

Bristol Palace

Via XX Settembre, 35

☎ 010.59.25.41, fax 010.56.17.56, info@hotelbristolpalace.com, www.hotelbristolpalace.com

€150-€370

Parking available, €20

An elegant spiral staircase winds upward through what was formerly a private 19th-century mansion. Rooms and suites are spacious, with antiques and chandeliers adding to the period ambiance. Modern comfort is found in whirlpool tubs and en suite amenities. Excellent location for proximity to restaurants, shopping, and the Centro Storico.

Locanda di Palazzo Cicala

Piazza San Lorenzo, 16
☎ 010.251.88.24, fax 010.246.74.14, palazzocicala@mentelocale.it, www.palazzocicala.it
€140-190 double
Parking available

The fashionable Locanda di Palazzo Cicala – the 16th-century private palace of the Cicala family – has received an exterior facelift and an interior renovation. Aficionados of modern design will recognize fixtures and furniture by such luminaries  as Phillipe Stark, Flos, and Cappellini. Excellent location on the Piazza San Lorenzo is central to sites and shopping, while retaining a peaceful palazzo ambience. Book well in advance as the hotel is extremely popular, especially with upscale business travelers.

Hotel Cairoli

Via Cairoli, 14/4
☎ 010.246.14.54; 010.246.15.24, fax 010.246.7512, info@hotelcairoligenova.com, www.hotelcairoligenova.com
€70-€90 double, breakfast for additional €8
Parking available

If you're looking for an inexpensive, centrally located yet peaceful and quiet hotel, this one's for you. Near the foot of the Via Balbi on a pedestrian-only street, the Hotel Cairoli has sound-proofed rooms and a rooftop terrace where you can enjoy an espresso or aperitif. Another plus, pets are welcome if you're traveling with your canine or feline companion.

Best Western City Hotel

Via San Sebastiano, 6

☎ 010.5545; toll-free reservations from US 1-800-780-7234

fax 010.586.301, city.ge@bestwestern.it, www.bestwestern.it/city-ge

€140-€220 double; €200-€320 suite; breakfast included

Parking available, €20

Don't fret the bland exterior or the affiliation with a large hotel chain. Instead, appreciate light, modern, soundproofed rooms with parquet floors and a location at the intersection of old and new Genoa. The City is located one block from the Piazza de Ferrari, within easy walking distance of the theater, Via Garibaldi, and shopping on Via Roma. The hotel's restaurant, Le Rune, serves regional fare in a medieval hall setting.

Bed & Breakfast Columbus Village

☎ 010.377.72, fax 010.377.72, info@columbusvillage.com, www.columbusvillage.com

From €60 for a basic apartment, double with private or shared bath, to €155 for a "charming" private home – both in center city and suburban Genoa

An association of bed & breakfast establishments around Liguria, Columbus Village maintains 16 properties in Genoa, some in the historic city center. Accommodations range from rooms in a private home with shared bath, to a rustic cottage with gardens in Nervi (the eastern district of Genoa). In the *centro storico*, flats in the Casa degli Affreschi have restored ceiling frescos and are close to Via Garibaldi, while Casa La Cabotina is a stone's throw from the Cathedral of San Lorenzo. Ask loads of questions on booking, including whether apartments have elevators, and check addresses online for proximity to sites and/or transportation.

Jolly Hotel Marina

Molo Ponte Calvi, 5, Porto Antico, 16124 Genoa

☎ 010.253.91, fax 010.251.13.20, genova_marina@jollyhotels.it, www.jollyhotels.it

€250-320 double w/breakfast

Parking available

Though expensive, a particularly good choice for those traveling with children thanks to its location on a pier of the Porto Antico. The Acquario di Genova, Citta dei Bambini, and Bigo

Where to Stay

are all a short walk away, as are a small playground and several pizzerie. Those without children will obviously also appreciate the Old Port location and its amenities, as well as the Jolly Marina's decor, which is reminiscent of an old sailing ship outfitted in mahogany and brass. The restaurant has views over the water.

Hotel Vittoria

Via Balbi, 33-45
☎ 010.261.923, fax 010.246.26.56, www.vittoriaorlandini.com
€85-105 double
Parking available

In the Principe neighborhood, close by the railway station, this hillside hotel is at the top of Via Balbi — a quick walk to the Palazzo del Principe and Palazzo Reale. Smallish rooms are nothing to write home about, but the price for the location is good, and the hotel is well buffered from noise, owing to its perch and surrounding buildings. Many rooms have balconies.

Best Western Hotel Metropoli

Piazza Fontane Marose
☎ 010.246.88.88, fax 010.246.86.86, metropoli.ge@bestwestern.it, www.bestwestern.it
€108-180
Parking available

The Best Western chain scores a second success with this comfortable and handsome hotel on a piazza at the foot of Via Garibaldi. The hotel has been recently renovated and boasts of "constant improvement," which probably includes the tasteful room décor – a pleasant break from the

usual humdrum corporate look of a chain hotel. Well located for exploring the Centro Storico.

Imperia

Relais San Damian

Strada Vasia, 47, 18100 Imperia

☎ 0183.280.309, fax 0183.280.571, info@san-damian.com, www.san-damian.com

€120-140

In the hills behind Imperia, surrounded by olive groves, the Relais San Damian offers three handsome suites outfitted with fireplaces and chic furnishings. An infinity-edge pool has a lovely view. Excellent value for understated luxury.

Hotel Croce di Malta

Via Scarincio, 148, 18100 Porto Maurizio

☎ 0183.667.020, fax 0183.636.87, info@hotelcrocedimalta.com, www.hotelcrocedimalta.com

€80-110

A modern hotel in an excellent location right on the marina by the Spiaggia d'Oro in Porto Maurizio. Clay tennis court for guests and the hotel can arrange scuba or sailing lessons or excursions.

Kristina

Spianata Borgo Peri, 8, 18100 Imperia

☎ 0183.293.564/0183.297.434, fax 0183.293.565, info@hotelkristina.com, www.hotelkristina.com

€75-100

On the promenade near the old town of Oneglia, the family-run Kristina has a private beach and comfortable, if unmemorable, rooms.

La Spezia

Jolly Hotel La Spezia

Via XX Settembre, 2, 19124 La Spezia

☎ 0187.7555, fax 0187.221.29, la-spezia@jollyhotels.it, www.jollyhotels.it

€150-200

A modern high-rise hotel with panoramic views near the train station, the Jolly La Spezia is popular with business travelers and conventions.

Hotel Firenze & Continentale
Via Paleocapa, 7, 19122 La Spezia
☎ 0187.713.210/0187.713.200, fax 0187.714.930
hotel_firenze@hotelfirenzecontinentale.it,
www.hotelfirenzecontinentale.it
€125-250

The hotel's proximity to the train station makes the Hotel Firenze & Continentale a convenient home base while exploring the Gulf of Poets. A recent renovation has recreated a period atmosphere.

Albergo Teatro
Via Carpenino, 31, 19121 La Spezia
☎ 0187.731.374, fax 0187.731.374, antonio@albergoteatro.it,
www.albergoteatro.it
€90-120

Located in a pedestrian district of the old town near the Arsenale, the hotel is inexpensive and well-situated, if a tad shabby. Request a room with bathroom. Good home base while visiting other towns around the Bay.

Lavagna

Hotel Villa Fieschi
Via Rezza, 12, 16033 Lavagna
☎ 0185.304.400, fax 0185.313.809, info@hotelvillafieschi.it,
www.hotelvillafieschi.it
€100-170

The converted 19th-century villa is elegantly turned out with pretty rooms overlooking the park-like grounds. Traditional Ligurian cuisine prepared by the chef/owners is served in the dining room.

Le Grazie

Hotel Della Baia

Via Lungomare, 111, 19022 Le Grazie

☎ 0187.790.797, fax 0187.790.034, baia@baiahotel.com, www.baiahotel.com

Fronted by strands of palms that line the harbor, the Hotel Della Baia offers tranquility and proximity to La Spezia and Portovenere. Clean, stylish rooms – with original paintings and some custom furniture by regional artists – have views, terraces, and a plethora of amenities, including Internet connectivity. Relax by the pool in-between excursions. The restaurant is noteworthy.

Hotel Le Grazie

Via Roma, 43, 19022 Le Grazie

☎ 0187.790.017, fax 0187.792.530, info@hotellegrazie.com, www.hotellegrazie.com

€95-135

Close by the sea is this small hotel, featuring a bar and restaurant and tidy, if unremarkable, rooms, many with balconies and sea views.

Lerici

Hotel Shelley e Delle Palme

Lungomare Biaggini, 5, 19032 Lerici

☎ 0187.968.205, fax 0187.964.271, info@hotelshelley.it, www.hotelshelley.it

€130-170

This modern hotel on the promenade has a private beach and comfortable, pleasant rooms.

Where to Stay

Hotel Europa

Via Carpanini, 1, 19032 Lerici

☎ 0187.967.800, fax 0187.965.957, europa@europahotel.it, www.europahotel.it

€140-170

A flight of about 100 stairs leads down to the heart of Lerici from the hotel's hilltop location. Well-decorated rooms and a private garden.

Fiascherino

Via Byron, 13, 19030 Fiascherino

☎ 0187.967.283, fax 0187.964.721, hotelfiascherino@libero.it, www.hotelfiascherino.it

€150-210

A lovely location in the fishing village of Fiascherino outside Lerici, with a beautiful pool and terraces for al fresco dining. All rooms have small balconies. The hotel arranges sailing trips (with dinner in the summer season) aboard the *Zigoela*.

Miramare

Via Fiascherino, 22, 19030 Tellaro

☎ 0187.967.589, fax 0187.966.534, info@pensionemiramare.it, www.pensionemiramare.it

€45-75

A guesthouse at the top of the small fishing village of Tellaro has a panoramic view from the rooftop terrace and simple, tidy rooms, some with balconies.

Levanto

Hotel Nazionale

Via Jacopo da Levanto, 20, 19015 Levanto

☎ 0187.808.102, fax 0187.800.901, hotel@nazionale.it, www.nazionale.it

€70-100

Centrally-located near the waterfront, this family-run hotel has pleasant rooms and meals served on an outdoor terrace.

Agriturismo Villanova

Località Villanova Est, 19015 Levanto

☎ 0187.802.517, fax 0187.803.519, massola@iol.it, www.agrivillanova.com

€85-135

Olive oil, wine, and honey are cultivated and produced on this working farm where guests stay in tasteful rooms in the main villa or a 19th-century stone building on the property. For longer stays, book an apartment in the 17th-century villa or rectory. There's a carefully cultivated period ambiance and gorgeous, lush surroundings. Organic breakfast buffet included in room rate.

Manarola

Ca' D'Andrean
Via Discovolo, 101, 19010 Manarola
☎ 0187.920.040, fax 0187.920.452, cadandrean@libero.it, www.cadandrean.it
€75-90

Spacious rooms (some with terrace) in a small, family-run hotel. Breakfast served amid lemon trees in the garden. No sea views, but private bar with fireplace for guests' use.

Marina Piccola
Via Birolli n°120, 19010 Manarola
☎ 0187.920.103, fax 0187.920.966, info@hotelmarinapiccola.com, www.hotelmarinapiccola.com

Simple rooms, some with view, and a restaurant serving fresh seafood and wines from the Cinque Terre.

La Torretta
Piazza della Chiesa - Vico Volto, 20, 19010 Manarola
☎ 0187.920.327, fax 0187.760.024, torretta@cdh.it
Closed January and February

An appealing bed & breakfast with sea views and a terrace for dining.

Luna di Marzo
Via Montello, 387/C, 19019 Volastra (Manarola)
☎ 0187.920.530, fax 0187.920.530, info@albergolunadimarzo.com, www.albergolunadimarzo.com
€90-100

Up the terraced hillsides in Volastra (a good vantage for hiking the upper trails), a small hotel with sunny terraces and pretty grounds but somewhat standard rooms.

Moneglia

Villa Edera
Via Venino, 12/13, 16030 Moneglia
☎ 0185.492.91, fax 0185.494.70, info@villaedera.com, www.villaedera.com
€98-130

Located up the hill, 200 m/600 feet from the sea on the eastern side of town, the Villa Edera has individually decorated rooms with views of the pool or the surrounding hillsides. The property is ringed by a Mediterranean garden.

Castello di Monleone
Via Venino, 3, 16030 Moneglia
☎ 0185.492.91, fax 0185.494.70, info@castellodimonleone.com, www.castellodimonleone.com

A 19th-century castle built by the Marchese de Fornari now functions as a bed & breakfast with five rooms (adults and children over 15 only) decorated with ceiling frescos and antique furnishings. Guests have access to all the facilities of the nearby Villa Edera (operated by the same family) as well as the park grounds with gardens, man-made caves, and statues.

Piccolo Hotel
Corso Longhi, 19, 16030 Moneglia
☎ 0185.493.74, fax 0185.401.292, laura@piccolohotel.it, www.piccolohotel.it
€110-140

On the Viale delle Palme, this cheerful establishment caters to families with activities and facilities for children. Comfortable, if unimaginative, room décor.

Montemarcello

B&B Armelina
Via Corvo, 1, 19031 Ameglia
☎ 0187.600.450, fax 0187.625.965

Lemon trees and other Mediterranean greenery grow on the grounds of this tucked-away bed & breakfast within walking distance of a shingle beach. Rustic, simple décor. The small summer house has a vine-covered pergola, kitchen, and BBQ. No children under 14. Mountain bikes available.

Paracucchi-Locanda dell'Angelo
Viale XXV Aprile, 60, 19031 Ameglia
☎ 0187.643.91, fax 0187.643.93, info@paracucchilocanda.it, www.paracucchilocanda.it
€100-150

A contemporary hotel designed by Vico Magistretti and featuring modern artworks displayed throughout the interiors. Chef/owner Angelo Paracucchi (who spends part of the year working in Paris) leads the kitchen and has won wide acclaim for his updated renditions of Ligurian cuisine. Week-long cooking seminars offered on the premises with Paracucchi and other Michelin-starred chefs.

Monterosso al Mare

Hotel La Collina
Via Zuecca, 6, 19016 Monterosso al Mare
☎ 0187.817.439, fax 0187.817.788, info@lacolonninacinqueterre.it, www.lacolonninacinqueterre.it
Contact hotel for rates

Excellent location in a pedestrian-only zone away from the waterfront. A lovely garden encloses the outdoor terrace. Rooms tastefully and individually decorated.

Locanda Il Maestrale

Via Roma, 37, 19016 Monterosso al Mare

☎ 0187 817013, fax 0187 817084, maestrale@monterossonet.com, www.locandailmaestrale.it

€75-130

Book one of the suites named for the towns of the Cinque Terre and enjoy frescoed ceilings and period furniture. Double rooms and one single also available, and decorated with equal dedication to style. Breakfast served outdoors on the terrace. Quiet location away from the waterfront.

Hotel Cinque Terre

Via IV Novembre, 21, 19016 Monterosso al Mare

☎ 0187.817.543, fax 0187.818.380, info@hotel5terre.com, www.hotel5terre.com

€130-150

Close by the waterfront off the Piazza Cavour, this modern hotel has a game-room, restaurant, pub, and two small gardens.

Hotel Porta Roca

Via Corone, 1, 19016 Monterosso al Mare

☎ 0187.81.75.02, fax 0187.81.76.92, portoroca@cinqueterre.it, www.portoroca.it

€165-280

There's a stunning view from the terrace garden of this large hotel near the hiking trail to Vernazza. Private beach below on the shore. Rooms have standard décor.

Hotel Baia

Lungomare Fegina, 88, 19016 Monterosso al Mare

☎ 0187.817.512, fax 0187.818.322, info@baiahotel.it, www.baiahotel.it

€110-150

Waterfront hotel has standard hotel rooms. Good location for enjoying the beach. Hotel arranges sailboat charters for trips around the Cinque Terre and Bay of La Spezia.

Nervi

Hotel Bonera

Via Sarfatti, 8 16100 Nervi

☎ 010.372.61.64, fax 010.372.85.65, info@villabonera.com, www.villabonera.com

€106-125 (rate for two people, double)

Parking available, included in room fee

The 16th-century Villa Bonera, situated amid private gardens, has been operating as a hotel since the 19th century and the service remains smooth and hospitable. The villa is within walking distance of Nervi's small port and the Serra Gropallo Park, and public transport is readily available for excursions to Genoa's city center or, by ferry, to Camogli and Portofino down the coast. Full- and half-board requires a three night stay, but bed and breakfast is a bargain (charged per room instead of per person) and there's no minimum. Request a room with bathroom and ceiling frescoes.

Romantik Hotel Villa Pagoda

Via Capoluogo, 15 16167 Nervi

☎ 010.372.61.61, fax 010.321.218, info@villapagoda.it, www.villapagoda.it

€145-770

A stand-out among hotels of the Italian Riviera, the Romantik Hotel Villa Pagoda was built by an 18th-century Genoese merchant as a romantic tribute to a Chinese girl he fell in love with during one of his voyages. Carerra marble floors, Murano chandeliers, antique furniture, and luxuri-

ous, precious fabrics augment oriental-inspired architecture. All who stay here will feel pampered and privileged, but for ultimate luxury book one of two deluxe suite tower rooms, each with a panoramic view over the turquoise sea. The restaurant "Il Roseto" is acclaimed for innovative, modern Italian cuisine.

Hotel Esperia
Via Val Cismon, 1 16167 Nervi
☎ 010.372.60.71, fax 010.329.10.06, info@hotelesperia.it, www.hotelesperia.it
€110-160
Parking available

Weary travelers can relax in the hotel's private garden or take a short walk to the nearby Nervi Park or Passegiata a Mare. Rooms are well-lit by large windows with nice views, and are comfortably furnished. The hotel restaurant offers simple, light meals emphasizing Ligurian and Genoese specialties.

Hotel Marinella
Passeggiata A. Garibaldi, 18 16167 Nervi
☎ 010.321.429, fax 010.329.82.48, brunomore@tiscalinet.it, www.genovabynet.it/marinella
€75-140

If this hotel were any closer to the water, you'd be awakened by the waves breaking over your bed, rather than the smell of fresh fococcia baking at the hotel's pasticceria. This reasonably-priced hotel is on the Passeggiata a Mare, an excellent splace for seaside promenades. It's also next to the train station, which, while convenient for travelers, also means more noise than elsewhere in this otherwise quiet suburb of Genoa.

Noli

Miramare
Corso Italia, 2, 17026 Noli
☎ 019.748.926, fax 019.748.927, hotelmiramarenoli@libero.it, www.hotelmiramarenoli.it
€110-175

Convenient and pleasant hotel on the promenade, a short walk from the Porta Piazza that leads to the charming medieval town. Spacious, if standard rooms, some with balconies or large terraces.

Ines

Via Vignolo, 1, 17026 Noli
☎ 019.748.54.28, fax 019.748.086
From €65

A small hotel next to St. Peter's Cathedral and centrally located for visiting the beach or the old town.

Residenza Palazzo Vescovile

Via al Vescovado, 13, 17026 Noli
☎ 019.749.90.59, fax 019.749.90.59, info@vescovado.net, www.vescovado.net
€190-220

On the edge of the village, the former Bishop's Palace is converted to an elegant hotel with gorgeous interiors and several rooms with frescoed  ceilings and period furniture. Expansive views up and down the coast from its hillside vantage.

Hotel Italia

Corso Italia, 21, 17026 Noli
☎ 019.748.971, www.hotelitalianoli.it
€125-140

Waterfront hotel has a pleasant terrace and excellent location. Rooms are somewhat inconsistent – some interesting with coved ceilings, others very standard.

Perinaldo

La Riana

Via Genova, 12, 18032 Perinaldo
☎ 0184.672.015/0184.672.433, www.hotel-lariana.com
Contact hotel for rates

German-run hotel with a special connection to the scientific community that gathers in Perinaldo, La Riana sits on the south slope of the town with views over olive trees and cypresses. Attention paid to decoration and detail.

Pieve di Teco

Hotel Negro

Via Canada, 10, 18020 Cenova
☎ 0183.340.89, fax 0183.324.800, hotelnegro@libero.it
From €70

In the small hamlet of Cenova a short distance from Pieve di Teco, this restaurant/inn has tidy, fresh rooms with exposed wooden ceilings and whitewashed walls. The fireplace-warmed dining room has vaulted ceilings and serves mountain-inflected Ligurian cuisine.

Ponte di Nava-da Beppe

Frazione Ponte di Nava, 32, 12070 Ponte di Nava
☎ 0174.399.924, fax 0174.399.007, albergopontedinava@cnnet.it
Closed January 7-February 7, last week June, Wednesdays
From €60

This establishment in a mountain hamlet near the Piedmont border has 15 rooms and an acclaimed restaurant.

Pigna

Grand Hotel Terme di Pigna

Regione Lago Pigo, 18037 Pigna
☎ 0184.240.010, fax 0184.240.949, info@termedipigna.it, www.termedipigna.it
€110-170

On the valley floor below the village, this luxury hotel/spa has natural sulphur and thermal-fed pools and offers an extensive and well-priced range of body treatments ranging from massage and mud treatments to facials and aromatherapy.

La Casa di Giacomo

Loc. Madonna di Campagna, 18037 Pigna
☎ 0184.241.585, fax 3613.25.42
bedpigna@libero.it, www.lacasadigiacomo.it
Contact hotel for rates

Nature lovers and outdoor enthusiasts will appreciate the range of activities organized by this friendly bed & breakfast outside the village of Pigna. Excursions include hiking trips, quad rides, and visits to a nearby lake. Good location for exploring the trails of the Val Nervia.

Portofino

Piccolo Hotel

Via Duca degli Abruzzi, 31, 16034 Portofino
☎ 0185.269.015, fax 0185.269.621, piccolo@domina.it, www.dominapiccolo.it
€235-360

A charming hotel situated just outside the village of Portofino and a great value for the town. Splendid views over cove of majestic beauty. Pleasant reception and small restaurant serving typical Ligurian cuisine. Private pebble beach with stone terraces and lounge chairs. Pleasant path through greenery leads to the heart of Portofino.

Hotel Splendido

Viale Baratta, 16, 16034 Portofino
☎ 0185.267.801, fax 0185.267.806, reservations@splendido.net, www.hotelsplendido.com
€850-1,400

One of the most exclusive hotels in the world and a favorite haunt of celebrities since the 1950s. Boasting spectacular views from its rarified perch above the village, the Splendido provides every comfort and caters to guests' every whim.

Splendido Mare

Via Roma, 2, 16034 Portofino
☎ 0185.267.806, fax 0185.267.806, reservations@splendido.net, www.hotelsplendido.com
€475-800

A value option for guests craving the luxury of the Splendido without the pricetag. Located on the charming Portofino piazzetta, the boutique hotel has a handful of rooms and suites – most with terrace or balcony – and a lively restaurant that is part of the scene.

Hotel Eden

Vico Dritto, 20, 16034 Portofino
☎ 0185.269.091, fax 0185.269.047,
e d e n p o r t o f i n o @ y a h o o . i t,
www.hoteledenportofino.com
€120-220

Tucked-away on a side street off the piazzetta, the Hotel Eden has a small garden where meals are served *al fresco*. Pretty rooms and excellent proximity to all the pleasures of Portofino.

Paraggi

Lungomare Paraggi, 17, 16038
☎ 0185.289.961, fax 0185.286.745, hotelparaggi@libero.it,
www.hotelparaggi.it
€210-370

This contemporary hotel with sophisticated charm dominates the gorgeous green cove of Paraggi – between Portofino and Santa Margherita Ligure. The beach club has all amenities for enjoying the crystalline waters.

Portovenere

Grand Hotel Portovenere

Via Garibaldi 5, 19025 Portovenere
☎ 0187.792.610, fax 0187.790.661, ghp@village.it,
ghp@rphotels.com, www.rphotels.com

The serenity of this harbor-front hotel reminds one that it was previously a Franciscan monastery. Now part of a large Ital-

ian hotel group, the décor is corporate but pleasant in shades of blue and white that bring the brilliance of the Gulf of Poets indoors. Conveniently located for enjoying the lively waterfront or excursions via the boats that launch from the quay. Rooms with balconies have exceptional views, as does the restaurant terrace, where you can dine on fresh seafood and local specialties.

Royal Sporting Hotel

Via dell Olivio, 345, 19025 Portovenere
☎ 0187.790.326, fax 0187.777.707, royal@royalsporting.com, www.royalsporting.com
€120-200

This waterfront hotel sits just outside the city center and is a travelers' favorite. Large, but not imposing, it has a purified saltwater pool overlooking the Golfo dei Poeti or, if you prefer, a private beach with club amenities. Breakfast and lunch are served poolside. For dinner in the dining room try a dish prepared with local mussels. Check out balls and rackets at the reception desk for a game on the grass tennis court (they'll even provide you with a partner if need be).

Hotel Belvedere

Via Garibaldi, 26, 19025 Portovenere

☎ 0187.790.608, fax 0187.791.469, info@belvedereportovenere.it, www.belvedereportovenere.it

€75-145

Closed November

This waterfront hotel/restaurant was built at the turn of the century but has been completely renovated in smart Liberty/Art Deco style. Request a room with a sea view, and enjoy Ligurian dishes – emphasis on seafood – served on the restaurant terrace.

Albergo Genio

Piazza Bastreri, 8, 19025 Portovenere

☎ 0187.790.611, fax 0187.790.611

€ 90-100

A central location at the base of the Carrugio is a highlight of this small hotel, which also boasts a terrace bar and restaurant with views over the harbor and piazza. The staff are friendly and helpful, but Italian is definitely the language of the house. A phrasebook is helpful, though good gesturing goes a long way, especially if you're indicating another bottle of vino while dining at the restaurant.

Albergo Paradiso

Via Garibaldi, 34-40, 19025 Portovenere

☎ 0187.790.612, fax 0187.792.582, info@paradisohotel.net, www.paradisohotel.net

Contact hotel for rates

Centrally located above the harbor, all the rooms of the Albergo Paradiso have sea views looking toward Palmaria Island and the Apuan Alps. Rooms are furnished in typical Mediterranean style and breakfast is served  every morning on the terrace. The restaurant features regional cuisine with an emphasis on fresh seafood.

He

Locanda Lorena

Corso Cavour, 4, 19025 Isla Palmeria, Palmeria
☎ 0187.792.370, fax 0187.766.077, www.locandalorena.it
Contact hotel for rates

Celebrated for its food, which makes use of fresh local seafood and shellfish, this bed & breakfast/restaurant is considered one of Liguria's regional treasures (culinary tours make it a destination). Rooms are small but comfortable, though only three are equipped with private bath. Some have views of the bay and the mussel beds at Seno del Terizzo, others of the small garden. If you require larger accommodations, book the *Villino* – a small,  self-contained villa nearby. The hotel runs its own taxi-boat service for guests from Portovenere.

Rapallo

Excelsior Palace Hotel

Via San Michele di Pagana, 8, 16035 Rapallo
☎ 0185.230.666, fax 0185.230.214, excelsior@thi.it, www.excelsiorpalace.thi.it
€475-720

The original mecca for early 19th-century tourism has been recently renovated and rooms are lavishly decorated to create a period ambiance. Spa facilities, Lord Byron and Eden Roc restaurants, and a private beach cater to guests.

Europa

Via Milite Ignoto, 2, 16035 Rapallo
☎ 0185.669.521, fax 0185.669.847, info@hoteleuropa-rapallo.com, www.hoteleuropa-rapallo.com
€137-185

The 18th-century Palazzo Serra saw guests like Victor Emmanuel I and Giuseppe Mazzini before it was converted to a high-class hotel in 1901. Now fitted-out with comfortable, modern rooms in a central location.

Hotel Astoria

Via Gramsci, 4, 16035 Rapallo

☎ 0185.273.533, fax 0185.627.93, astoriarapallo@mclink.it, www.dominahotels.com

€120-175

A small Art Deco hotel on the waterfront, refurbished to provide comfortable, elegant rooms. Near the marina and several beach resorts.

Hotel Stella

Via Aurelia Ponente, 6, 16035 Rapallo

☎ 0185.503.67, fax 0185.272.837, reservations@hotelstella-riviera.com, www.hotelstella-riviera.com

€75-110

A good value for a pleasant, central hotel on the western side of town. Rooftop solarium and clean, well-maintained rooms.

Riomaggiore

Cinque Terre Residence

Via De Battè, 19017 Riomaggiore

☎ 0187.605.38, fax 0187.760.564, customer-care@cinqueterreresidence.it, www.cinqueterre-residence.it

€85-100

Away from the village center, a cluster of eco-friendly buildings houses double and triple rooms, all with en suite bathroom, and two suites with kitchens. Hillside location affords nice views of the village, vineyards, and sea.

Il Saraceno

19010 Volastra

☎ 0187.760.081, fax 0187.760.791, hotel@thesaraceno.com, www.thesaraceno.com

€85-90

A new hotel in Volastra on the trail of the Sanctuaries has paid particular attention to comfort and convenience in rooms named for the villages of Cinque Terre. Nice breakfast room and convenient parking garage.

Locanda Ca dei Duxi

Via Colombo, 36/Via Pecunia, 19, 19017 Riomaggiore
☎ 0187.920.036, fax 0187.920.036, info@duxi.it, www.duxi.it
€60-120

Outside the center of the village, a 15th-century building preserves its historical integrity and presents plainly furnished rooms, all with en suite bathrooms.

San Remo

Royal Hotel

Corso Imperatrice, 80, 18038 San Remo
☎ 0184.53.91, fax 0184.66.14.45,
reservations@royalhotelsanremo.com, www.royalhotelsanremo.com
€215-395

San Remo's premier hotel since the mid-19th century, today the Royal Hotel is situated in a subtropical park with a heated free-form saltwater pool. The sumptuous lobby gives way to elegantly-decorated rooms and suites with panoramic views.

Hotel Paradiso

Via Roccasterone, 12, 18038 San Remo
☎ 0184.571.211, fax 0184.578.176, paradisohotel@sistel.it, www.paradisohotel.it
€100-150

Located above the park off the Corso Imperatrice, a short distance from the Casino and shopping streets, the Hotel Paradiso has quiet, tastefully-decorated rooms.

Lolli Palace Hotel

Corso Imperatrice, 70, 18030 San Remo
☎ 0184.531.496, fax 0184.5415.74,
info@lollihotel.it, www.lollihotel.it
Closed November 4-December 20
€85-150

A Liberty-style (Art Deco) hotel on the promenade just a short stroll from the Casino, the Lolli Palace offers friendly service and rooms that are nicely decorated, if a bit dark. Small balconies provide views of the sea.

Nazionale

Via Matteotti, 3, 18038 San Remo
☎ 0184.577.577, fax 0184.541.535, nazionale.in@bestwestern.it, www.hotelnazionalesanremo.com
€140-220

This very central hotel, part of the Best Western chain, has recently-renovated rooms, fitness facilities, and the Rendez-Vous Restaurant. Recently-added suites are lavishly decorated.

Eveline-Portosole

Corso Cavallotti, 111, 18038 San Remo
☎ 0184.503.430, fax 0184.503.431, hotel@evelineportosole.com, www.evelineportosole.com
€100-300

The exterior of this hotel near the marina is pretty though unremarkable, but inside are individually- and lavishly-decorated rooms and suites making ample use of flowing fabrics. The Japan Imperial Suite has a hammam soaking tub.

Santa Margherita Ligure

Imperial Palace Hotel

Via Pagana 19, 16038 Santa Margherita Ligure
☎ 0185.288.991, fax 0185.284.223, info@hotelimperiale.com, www.hotelimperiale.com
€267-420

A landmark hotel on the eastern edge of Santa Margherita Ligure. The late 19th-century building has a wedding-cake façade and a gilded interior with chandeliers and ceiling frescoes. Spa facilities and a shapely saltwater pool.

Fiorina

Piazza Mazzini, 26, 16038 Santa Margherita Ligure

☎ 0185.287.517, fax 0185.281.855, fiorinasml@libero.it

€95-125

The Fiorina has earned a loyal following of guests who appreciate the excellent location – close by the Via Palestro and the grounds of the Villa Durazzo. Simple rooms and good value.

Albergo Fasce

Via Bozzo, 3, 16038 Santa Margherita Ligure

☎ 0185.286.435, fax 0185.283.580, hotelfasce@hotelfasce.it, www.hotelfasce.it

From €100

Family-run and friendly with a garden atmosphere and pretty, simple rooms.

Continental

Via Pagana, 8, 16038 Santa Margherita Ligure

☎ 0185.286.512, fax 0185.284.463, continental@hotel-continental.it, www.hotel-continental.it

€120-200

A short walk from the town center on the eastern side of Santa Margherita Ligure, the Continental is surrounded by a lush park and has nicely decorated rooms, many with sea views from balconies or terraces.

Metropole

Via Pagana, 2, 16038 Santa Margherita Ligure

☎ 0185.286.134, fax 0185.283.495, hotel.metropole@metropole.it, www.metropole.it

€140-215

There's a private beach at the end of the sloping palm-filled park that surrounds the turn-of-the-century Hotel Metropole. Rooms in shades of blue evoke the sea.

Sarzana

La Villetta

Via Sobborgo Emiliano, 8, 19038 Sarzana

☎ 0187.620.195, fax 0187.187.88.41, lavilletta@luna.it

From €60

Very plain rooms in an unremarkable hotel, but excellent location just outside the medieval town walls near the Piazza

Vittorio Venetto. Good venue for exploring the medieval village.

Agriturismo La Cascina dei Peri

Località Montefrancio, 71, 19030 Castelnuovo Magra

☎ 0187.674.085, fax 0187.674.085, info@cascinadeiperi.com, www.cascinadeiperi.com

From €75

Situated in the Lunigiana hills outside of Sarzana in Castelnuovo Magra, a holiday farm with lots of greenery, flocks of chickens, and plain rooms. Olive oil and wine produced on the premises.

Sassello

Agriturismo Francesco Romano

Loc. Albergare, 4, 17046 Sassello

☎ 019.724.527, agriturismo.romano@libero.it, www.parks.it/agr/romano.francesco

€55-65

Enjoy fishing, horseback riding, and mushroom hunting while staying on this farm that produces fruit and vegetables and breeds cattle, pigs, and sheep. Simple rooms with exposed wooden ceilings.

Bed & Breakfast di Stafnia Pesce

Viale Rimembraza, 11, 17046 Sassello

☎ 019.724.180, stefi.pesce@tiscali.net

Contact hotel for rates

Stay here to make the medieval village of Sassello your home base while exploring the Beigua.

Savona

Mare Hotel

Via Nizza, 89r, 17100 Savona

☎ 019.264.065, fax 019.263.277

From €100

The hotel, outside of town to the west, has a private beach and a beautiful pool. Modern rooms.

Il Respiro del Tempo Bed & Breakfast

Via Don Peluffo, 8, Quiliano 17040

☎ 019.887.87.28, ilrespirodeltempo@libero.it,
www.ilrespirodeltempo.com

€60-90

A charming bed & breakfast in the wine-making town of
Quiliano just seven km/four miles outside Savona. Frescoed,
gilded ceilings and period décor create the ambiance.

Sestri Levante

Grand Hotel dei Castelli

Via alla Penisola, 26, 16039 Sestri Levante

☎ 0185.487.020, fax 0185.447.67, info@hoteldeicastelli.com,
www.hoteldeicastelli.com

Contact hotel for rates

A complex of castles built in the early 20th century houses
this luxury hotel, the grounds of which form the Parco dei
Castelli – site of the Marconi Tower. They take up the majority of the headland. Sophisticated, elegant rooms and surroundings and private beach.

Grand Hotel Villa Balbi

Viale Rimembranza, 1, 16039 Sestri Levante

☎ 0185.429.41, fax 0185.482.459, villabalbi@villabalbi.it,
www.villabalbi.it

Contact hotel for rates

An aristocratic ambi-
ance is preserved at the
16th-century villa of the
powerful Balbi family.
Chandeliers, painted
ceilings, rich woodwork,
and gilding character-
ize the public areas and
spacious rooms have
parquet floors and fine
furnishings. Set in a
garden park with a
heated swimming pool.

Grande Albergo Sestri Levante

Via Vittorio Veneto, 2, 16039 Sestri Levante

☎ 0185.450.837, fax 0185.450.54,
info@grandalbergo-sestrilevante.com,
www.grandalbergo-sestrilevante.com
€140-200

The historic Grande Albergo has been recently renovated to create pretty, feminine rooms. The hotel arranges sporting activities including paragliding, horseback riding, squash, and tennis.

Due Mari

Vico del Coro, 18, 16039 Sestri Levante

☎ 0185.426.95, fax 0185.426.98, info@duemarihotel.it
€110-150

Located in a 17th-century building in the old town on the isthmus, there are views of the Baia del Silenzio, indoor and outdoor pools, and elegantly furnished rooms.

Hotel Helvetia

Via Cappuccini, 43, 16039 Sestri Levante

☎ 0185.411.75, fax 0185.457.216, helvetia@hotelhelvetia.it,
www.hotelhelvetia.it
€115-155

Quiet, peaceful location on the Baia del Silenzio. Sunny rooms with lovely garden and sea views. Private beach and terrace.

Spotorno

Riviera

Via Berninzoni, 24, 17028 Spotorno

☎ 019.745.320, fax 019.747.782, info@rivierahotel.it,
www.rivierahotel.it
From €100

This modern hotel is well situated just off the promenade on the waterfront with a pool, garden, and comfortable rooms.

La Perla

Via Lombardia, 6, 17028 Spotorno

☎ 019.746.223, fax 019.741.59.23, info@hotellaperlaspotorno.com, www.hotellaperlaspotorno.com

€80-120

This family-run hotel is attentive to guests' needs and comforts. A bright little restaurant serves typical Ligurian cuisine. Located away from the sea but a short walk from the beach and town center. Single night reservations not accepted.

La Torre

Via Alla Torre, 25, 17028 Spotorno

☎ 019.745.390, fax 019.746.487, www.hotellatorre.it

€100-130

The Maio family has been managing this property on the green hillside above Spotorno since its opening. Basic rooms, all with terrace and view. Restaurant serves Ligurian cuisine based on locally-produced olive oil, fresh fish, and homegrown vegetables.

Taggia

B&B La Capannuccia

slowbrock@libero.it, www.capannuccia.it

€60-70

Three rooms available in a 19th-century villa in a convenient location for exploring the old town of Taggia.

Triora

Colombo D'Oro

Corso Italia, 66, 18010 Triora

☎ 0184.940.51, fax 0184.940.89, colombadoro@libero.it, www.colombadoro.it

€60-100

The breakfast spread includes fresh-baked foccocia and biscotti along with locally produced jams and honey at this bed & breakfast with quiet rooms and views of the Valle

where to stay

Argentine or the old town of Triora. The restaurant serves typical Ligurian dishes from the hinterland.

Varazze

Hotel Cristallo

Via Cilea, 4, 17019 Varazze

☎ 019.972.64, fax 019.935.57.57, info@cristallohotel.it, www.cristallohotel.it

€65-110

Located a short walk from the waterfront. Modern hotel with comfortable, if standard, rooms.

Villa Elena

Via Coda, 16, 17019 Varazze

☎ 019.975.26, fax 019.934.277, info@genovesevillaelena.it, www.genovesevillaelena.it

Closed October to Christmas

Contact hotel for rates

Attractive Art Deco villa steps from the promenade has pretty rooms with modern amenities. Rooms in the Villetta – located in the garden – are equally attractive, but without air conditioning.

Varigotti

Hotel al Saraceno

Via del Capo, 2, 17029 Varigotti

☎ 019.698.81.82, fax 019.698.81.85, hotelalsaraceno@libero.it, www.hotelalsaraceno.com

€130-200

The color scheme of this smart, modern hotel mimics the town's ochre and blue tones. Excellent location opening directly onto Varigotti's sand beach.

Al Capo

Vico Mendaro, 3, 17029 Varigotti

☎ 019.698.80.66, fax 019.698.80.66, hotelalcapo@tiscalinet.it

From €110

Friendly atmosphere at a family-friendly hotel in a good location off the Via Aurelia, a short distance from the beach.

Ventimiglia

Baia Beniamin
Corso Europa, 63, 18039 Ventimiglia
☎ 0184.38.002, fax 0184.38.027, www.baiabeniamin.it
€200-230

Five elegant rooms are available at this establishment on the French frontier, in a building surrounded by a lush tropical garden and with expansive views along the coast. The restaurant is famed for its fine cuisine.

Sea Gull
Via Marconi, 24, 18039 Ventimiglia
☎ 0184.351.726, fax 0184.231.217, info@seagullhotel.it, www.seagullhotel.it
€75-115

Request a room with a view at this hotel near the edge of the Rola and not far from the waterfront. Exterior very standard, but inside interesting architectural details and period furniture create a homey environment. Rooms, however, rather standard.

Hotel Sole Mare
Via Marconi, 22, 18039 Ventimiglia
☎ 0184.351.854, fax 0184.230.988, info@hotelsolemare.it, www.hotelsolemare.it
€72-120

Spacious rooms with sea-view balconies directly on the promenade. Private beach with club amenities.

Vernazza

Albergo Barbara
Piazza Marconi, 21, 19018 Vernazza
☎ 0187.812.398, fax 0187.812.398
From €55

Fabulous location on Vernazza's little beachfront piazza. Rooms all have shared bathroom and you'll carry your luggage up several flights of stairs, but the views from the spacious seafront rooms are worth it.

Gianni Franzi
Piazza Marconi, 5, 19018 Vernazza
☎ 0187.812.228/0187.821.003, fax 0187.812.228
From €65

One of the best restaurants in Vernazza also has rooms up a steep flight of stairs between the waterfront and the castle. Gorgeous location and sweetly decorated rooms.

L'Eremo Sul Mare
Via Gerai, 18019 Vernazza
☎ 3268.56.17, www.eremosulmare, info@eremosulmare.com
From €82

The location of this lovely restored villa nestled on a rocky promontory high above the village is ideal and picturesque, but necessitates hiking uphill with your luggage. Pack lightly.

Villanova d'Albenga

Hotel Hermitage
Via Roma, 152, 17038 Villanova d'Albenga
☎ 0182.582.976, fax 0182.582.975
Contact hotel for rates

Recently refurbished family-run hotel has nice rooms on a property with garden.

Zoagli

Le Palme
Via Aurelia Orientale, 166, 16030 Zoagli
☎ 0185.258.071/0185.259.042, fax 0185.259.042,
lepalme@hotmail.com, www.lepalmehtl.it
€105-125

A private park surrounds this converted villa a stone's throw from the waterfront. Rooms with en suite bathroom. Ligurian cuisine served in the terrace restaurant.

Where to Eat

Liguria is the place to realize your fantasy of eating your way across Italy. It's on a smaller scale – which promises to go lightly on your waistline – and presents great variety of cuisine. (For more on regional dishes, see page 21, *Cuisine of the Italian Riviera*.) You'll find that dishes vary between the inland hamlets and the villages along the coast, but that in general the Ligurian diet is very healthful and based on fresh fish and vegetables with very little meat.

As everywhere, there are fantastic restaurants in every city of Liguria, and plenty of mediocre ones. The restaurants listed below are standouts where you will get a true taste of the cooking. They are coded for price as follows:

€ = excellent value

€€ = moderately expensive

€€€ = splurge

Alassio

La Prua
Passeggiata Baracca, 25, 17021 Alassio
☎ 0182.642.557, fax 0182.640.277
€€€

Whitewashed walls and exposed-stone ceilings lend character at this waterfront restaurant specializing in seafood. Service on the terrace in summer.

Palma
Via Cavour, 11, 17021 Alassio
☎ 0182.640.314, fax 0182.640.314
€€€

Make reservations for a special night out at this celebrated, central restaurant specializing in Ligurian and Provençal cuisine.

Albenga

Pernambucco
Viale Italia, 35, 17031 Albenga
☎ 0182.534.58, fax 0182.534.58
€€

Don't be distracted by the location within the Minisport recreation park. This restaurant serving seafood specialties is a favorite in the town.

Antica Osteria dei Leoni
Via Lengueglia, 49, 17031 Albenga
☎ 0182.519.37
Closed second and third weeks January, mid-end October, Mondays
€€

A restaurant serving fish and seafood in an atmospheric corner of Albenga's lovely Centro Storico.

Da Puppo
Via Torlaro, 17031 Albenga, fax 0182.518.53
€

Very popular little restaurant serving traditional, informal dishes like farinata and tortas, with a wood-burning oven for pizza.

Albissola Marina

Al Cambusiere
Via Repetto, 86, 17012 Albissola Marina
☎ 019.481.663, fax 019.486.866, info@cambusiere.it, www.cambusiere.it
€€

Chef Ignazio Benenati serves seafood dishes in the dining room of this 17th-century building in the historical heart of the seaside resort. Rooms available.

Ristorante Da Mario
Corso Bigliati, 70, 17012 Albissola Marina
☎ 019.481.640
€€

A beautiful, sunny terrace is available for outdoor dining overlooking the sea. For three generations serving Ligurian seafood specialties.

Ameglia

Locanda delle Tamerici
Via Litoranea, 106, loc. Fiumaretta di Ameglia 19031
☎ 0187.642.62, fax 0187.646.27, locandadelletamerici@tin.it
Closed Mondays, Tuesdays, December 24-January 15
€€€

The rustic dining room is a contrast to the elegant, modern meals prepared by this Michelin-starred kitchen. Seasonal, local ingredients inform the changing menu.

Apricale

Le Grotte della Locanda
Via Roma, 1, 18030 Apricale
☎ 0184.208.5222
Closed Thursdays
€

A stone-vaulted grotto is the setting for a wine bar with an extensive list and menu of simple dishes.

La Capanna da Baci
☎ 0184.208.139, fax 0184.209.977
Closed Tuesdays, Monday dinner
€

Atmospheric setting with stone walls and a terrace with panoramic valley view. House-made pastas and roasted meat dishes.

La Favorita
Strada San Pietro, 1, 18035 Apricale
☎ 0184.208.186, fax 0184.208.247
Closed last week June-first week July, Tuesday dinner, Wednesdays except July-September, info@hotelristorantelafavorita.com, www.hotelristorantelafavorita.com
€

A standout for Ligurian dishes with a mountain inflection. Rustic dining room and terrace with magnificent view.

Where to Eat

Bergeggi

Claudio

Via XXV Aprile, 37, 17028 Bergeggi
☎ 019.859.750, fax 019.859.750, info@hotelclaudio.it,
www.hotelclaudio.it
Closed January, February, Mondays, weekday lunch
€€€

Chef/owner Claudio Pasquarelli presides in this celebrated
kitchen, turning out impeccable seafood dishes. Lovely view
from the terrace. Inquire about meals served aboard the
hotel/restaurant's 22-m/66-foot sailing cutter.

Bordighera

Magiargè Vini e Cucina

Piazza Giacomo Viale, 18012 Bordighera
☎ 0184.262.946, fax 0184.262.946, viniecucina@magiarge.it,
www.magiarge.it
Dinner only July-August, closed Monday, Tuesday lunch
€

Tucked-away rustic restaurant is a locals' choice for simple
but perfectly prepared meals.

Piemontese

Via Roseto, 8, 18012 Bordighera
☎ 0184.261.651, fax 0184.261.651
Closed November, Tuesdays
€

Winter visitors get to sample the cuisine of neighboring
Piedmont while fish and Ligurian specialties are on the menu
during summer.

La Via Romana

Via Romana, 57, 18012 Bordighera
☎ 0184.266.681, fax 0184.267.549
viaromana@masterweb.it, www.laviaromana.it
€€€

This elegant, Liberty-style (Art Deco) dining room in the
Grand Hotel Londre has earned a Michelin star for its
fine-quality seafood and meats.

Bussana Vecchia

Apriti Sesamo
Via Alla Chiesa, Bussana Vecchia di San Remo
☎ 0184.510.022, 335.231.794, info@ristorantenaturale.it,
www.ristorantenaturale.it
€

Organic meals prepared using locally sourced ingredients,
including fresh-caught fish delivered each morning. Charming artistic atmosphere amid the ruins.

Camogli

Rosa
Largo Casabona, 11, Camogli 16032
☎ 0185.773.411, fax 0185.771.088
Closed mid-January through first week February, mid-November
through first week December, Tuesdays, Wednesday lunch
€€

In summer, book a table on the terrace to watch the sunset
while you dine on fresh fish prepared in proprietor Maria
Rosa Costa's acclaimed kitchen.

Da Paolo
Via San Fortunato, 14, 16032 Camogli
☎ 0185.773.595
Closed mid-end February, Mondays, Tuesday lunch
€€

The best fresh, local seafood on the waterfront is to be had
here, in a family-run restaurant with a rustic atmosphere.

Da Giovanni
San Fruttuoso, 16030 San Fruttuoso
☎ 0185.770.047, fax 0185.770.047
Closed November, weekdays December-February
€€

Seafood served in the most rarified of environments on the
Portofino Promontory, overlooking the beach of San
Fruttuoso. Ferry service from Camogli or Portofino.

Where to Eat

Camporosso

Manuel
Corso Italia, 265, 18033 Camporosso
☎ 0184.205.037, fax 0184.205.037
Closed Mondays, Tuesday lunch
€€

Meals begin with local Taggiasca olive oil and fresh-baked foccocia and are enlivened by a well-selected wine list. Classic Ligurian dishes.

Castel Vittorio

Ristorante Italia
Corso Umberto I
☎ 0184.241.694
€

Rustic restaurant in the old town serves wild game and pasta dishes.

Celle Ligure

Ristorante Mosè
Via Colla, 30, 17015 Celle Ligure
☎ 019.991.560, fax 019.991.560, ristorantemose@tiscali.it, www.ristorantemose.it
Closed mid-October to mid-December, Wednesday
€€

Converted from an 18th-century palace chapel, this family-run restaurant features fresh locally-caught seafood. *Ciuppin alla Ligure* available with one-day's notice.

Cervo

San Giorgio
Via Alessandro Volta, 19, 18010 Cervo
☎ 0183.400.175, fax 0183.400.175
Closed mid-end January, November, Monday dinner and Tuesday from mid-October to Easter, Tuesday lunch from mid-June to mid-September
€€

Chef/owner Caterina Barla presents healthful Ligurian dishes based on local and seasonal fish and produce. Good location at the top of the medieval town near the castle.

Chiavari

Lord Nelson
Corso Valparaiso, 27, 16043 Chiavari
☎ 0185.302.595, fax 0185.310.397
Closed mid-end November, Wednesdays
€€

A stylish restaurant on the promenade that pays particular attention to the pairing of food and wine, featuring classic cuisine. Wine bar.

Da Felice
Via Risso, 71, 16043 Chiavari
☎ 0185.308.016, fax 0185.304.730
Closed lunch mid-June to mid-September, Mondays
€

Dishes based on market-fresh produce served in this small trattoria near the promenade.

Cà Peo
Via dei Caduti, 80, Località Leivi, 16043 Chiavari
☎ 0185.319.696
Closed November, Mondays, Tuesday lunch
€€€€

Franco and Melly Solari have only nine tables in this old farmhouse cum restaurant in the hills above Chiavari. Chef Melly turns out contemporary cuisine with local ingredients.

Corniglia

A Cantina de Mananan
Via Fieschi, 117, Corniglia
☎ 0187.821.166
€

A husband and wife team works the cozy stone dining room where the menu – all regional dishes – is part of the wall art.

Diano Marina

Il Caminetto
Via Olanda, 1, 18013 Diano Marina
☎ 0183.494.700, ristcaminetto@libero.it,
www.ristoranteilcaminetto.it
Closed mid-November to mid-December, Mondays in non-summer months
€€

In summer months dine under umbrellas in the garden of this out-of-the-way restaurant specializing in seafood and Ligurian dishes.

Dolceacqua

Enoteca Trattoria Re
Via Patrioti Martiri, 26, 18035 Dolceacqua
☎ 0184.206.137, fax 0184.206.137
Closed January, last week September, Thursdays
€

In the old part of town. Simple, regional meals punctuated by selections from the extensive wine list.

Finale Ligure

La Lampara
Vico Tubino, 4, 17024 Finale Ligure
☎ 019.692.430
Closed November to mid-December, Wednesdays
€€

Central location for trattoria with fish dishes.

Ai Torchi
Via dell'Annunziata, 12, 17024 Finalborgo
☎ 019.690.531, fax 019.690.531
Closed first week January to first week February, Tuesdays
€€

Atmosphere of an ancient olive mill preserved in the décor of this seafood restaurant.

Genoa

La Buca di San Matteo
Via David Chiassone, 5/7r, 16100 Genoa
☎ 010.869.06.48
Closed Sunday lunch
€€

Close by the Palazzo Ducale, this Tuscan restaurant is the place to take yourself when you're ready for a carnivorous feast (or just can't face yet another piece of fish). Atmospheric, with wooden beams overhead and chefs working busily in the open kitchen. Salami from Siena is a treat, as are T-bone steaks grilled in the Florentine style.

Papageno
Via Assarotti, 60/r, 16100 Genoa
☎ 010.839.29.29
Closed 1-7 January, 10-20 August, Saturday lunch
€€

Ligurian cuisine is evolving at this small restaurant, where minimalist furnishings keep the spotlight on the food. Popular with locals of the upscale neighborhood, it is stylishly informal. Menu changes seasonally. Make reservations as seating is limited.

I Tre Merli
Porto Antico, 16100 Genoa
☎ 010.246.44.16, fax 010.246.54.66, info@itremerli.it, www.itremerli.it
€€

Though located on the Old Port – the center of tourist activities – I Tre Merli is as authentically Genoese as a restaurant chain with three New York City outposts can be. Fresh fish here is delicious, enjoyed outside on the patio or indoors amid the black-and-white-striped columns that evoke the architecture of San Lorenzo. Good wine list and friendly service.

Lupo Antica Trattoria
Via Monachette, 20, 16100 Genoa
☎ 010.26.70.36, fax 010.26.70.36, info@lupoanticatrattoria.it, www.lupoanticatrattoria.it
Closed Christmas
€€

Where to Eat

Refined versions of Genoese and Ligurian specialties are on offer at this stylish, but moderately priced, trattoria in the Principe. The restaurant's strict dedication to regional, artisan products and ingredients has earned a following among foodies, who especially acclaim the pesto. Various dishes make use of impeccably fresh seafood, but meat lovers will not be disappointed in the *filetto*, here with a red wine sauce. Ask for assistance with the excellent wine list.

Mentelocale Restaurant/Café

Palazzo Ducale, 16100 Genoa
☎ 010.596.96.98, fax 010.868.16.15, info@mentelocale.it, www.mentelocale.it
€

The hip and culturally literate of Genoa come for brunch on Saturday (12-3 pm) or Sunday (11-5 pm), then a browse through the of-the-moment exhibits at the Palazzo Ducale (you can sometimes buy brunch and an exhibition ticket for a reduced combined price). The informal café and its patio on the Piazza de Ferrari is also open daily for sandwiches, salads, and desserts, and in the evening for aperitifs or after-theater snacks. The recently opened Mentelocale Restaurant has innovative cuisine based on fish and vegetables. The Mentelocale website (in Italian only) presents a hipster's view of events around the city.

Al Teatro di Campopisano

Vico Campopisano, 15r, 16100 Genoa
☎ 010.251.18.29
€

Near the eponymous Teatro di Campopisano, this trendy new restaurant serves small plates at lunch and attracts a hip crowd at night for a fixed-price menu featuring pastas, fish, and game. The ambiance is artistic, with music, cabaret, and actors doing live improv the first Thursday night of each month.

Antica Osteria di Vico Palla

Vico Palla, 15/r, 16128 Genoa
☎ 010.246.65.75, fax 010.362.44.58
Closed Mondays, 10-20 August, Christmas, New Years
€

After taking in the panoramic views from the Bigo or spending time with the sea life at the Acquario, a short walk along the old pier leads to this rustic family-run restaurant. Traditional regional cuisine is served; stockfish and salted cod are house specialties. Reservations suggested for dinner.

Zeffirino

Via XX Settembre, 20

☎ 010.591.990, fax 010.586.464, info@ristorantezeffirino.it, www.ristorantezeffirino.it

€€€

Considering the ancient rivalry between the two cities, it's ironic that *Zeffirino* was the "celebrity" Italian restaurant that the *Venetian* in Las Vegas chose to replicate for the casino. Family-run by the Belloni's since 1939, the restaurant is a veritable institution of Italian cuisine with a following that includes such luminaries as the Pope (check out the gilded chair His Holiness sat in upstairs) and the late Frank Sinatra (Papa Zeffirino was once his personal chef). Several prix-fix menus to choose from and a nice wine list. For entertainment, watch the Italian ladies preparing the restaurant's handmade pastas in the restaurant front window.

Rina

Via Mura delle Grazie 3/r, 16128 Genoa

☎ 010.246.64.75, fax 010.246.64.75

Closed Mondays

€€

A favorite with locals, Rina is also the place to dine if you didn't get enough of Italian celebrity gawking in Portofino. Seated under the 15th-century vaulted ceiling you'll dine on fresh fish dishes, which have been the restaurant's specialty since it opened in 1945.

Da Maria

Vico Testadoro 14r, 16100 Genoa

☎ 010.581.080

€

Not far from the Piazza de Ferrari, on the corner with XXV Aprile, you'll find this no-frills trattoria serving exceptional versions of classic Ligurian dishes such as torta pasqualina. It's popular with locals and a participant in the Slow Food movement, which emphasizes commitment to quality and regional integrity.

Imperia

Chez Braccio Forte
Via Des Genejs, 46, 18100 Oneglia
☎ 0183.294.752
Closed January, Monday
€€

Superb waterfront Oneglia location for a seafood restaurant with a maritime-themed interior.

Salvo Cacciatori
Via Vieusseux, 12, 18100 Oneglia
☎ 0183.293.763, fax 0183.765.500, ristorantecacciatori@virgilio.it
Closed last week July to first week August, Mondays, Sunday dinner
€€

Near the Piazza Dante, a family restaurant with traditional Ligurian dishes served from an open kitchen.

Al Gambero
Borgo Marina Via Scarincio, 16/18, 18100 Porto Maurizio
☎ 0183.667.413, fax 0183.667.413
Closed mid- to end January, Mondays
€€

Near the Duomo with a sea view, a small family-run restaurant prepares seafood dishes in classic style.

Lanterna Blu da Tonino
Via Scarincio, 148, 18100 Porto Maurizio
☎ 0183.638.59
Closed Christmas, mid-October to mid-November, second and third weeks of June, non-summer Wednesdays, July-August lunch
€€€

The Fiorillo family sends seafood dishes to the table that reveal the family's Neopolitan/Sicilian roots.

La Spezia

Antica Hostaria Secondini
Via Montalbano, 84, 19124 La Spezia
☎ 0187.701.345
Closed September, Wednesdays
€

Since 1953 this family-run establishment has served simple dishes based on traditional recipes. Excellent value for the money.

Il Forchettone

Via Genova, 288, 19124 La Spezia

☎ 0187.718.835

Closed June, Sundays

€€

Ligurian seafood dishes complemented by some Sicilian preparations in this intimate restaurant.

Lavagna

Il Gabbiano

Via San Benedetto, 26, 16033 Lavagna

☎ 0185.390.228, fax 0185.390.228

ristgabbiano@libero.it, www.ristoranteilgabbiano.com

€

The terrace of this hillside restaurant is the perfect spot for watching the sunset while dining on well-presented seafood dishes.

Lerici

Due Corone

Via Vespucci, 1, 19032 Lerici

☎ 0187.967.417, fax 0187.967.417

Closed for Tuesday lunch July-August

€€

A nice location on the promenade for a seafood restaurant that gets away from standard interpretations.

La Calata

Via Mazzini, 7, 19032 Lerici

☎ 0187.967.143, fax 0187.969.616

Closed Tuesdays, December

€€

Fabulous view over the port from the sunny terrace. Local seafood is the main attraction.

Where to Eat

Il Frantoio

Via Cavour, 21, 19032 Lerici
☎ 0187.964.174, fax 0187.952.227
€€

Closed mid-end February, mid-end July, Mondays

Whitewashed, wood-beamed dining area and a central location for enjoying seafood dishes.

Levanto

Osteria Tumelin

Via Grillo, 32, 19015 Levanto
☎ 0187.808.379, fax 0187.808.088, info@tumelin.com
Closed from January 7 to February 7, non-summer Thursdays
€€

In the heart of Levanto the restaurant serves classic fish dishes, including a mixed seafood antipasto that is the specialty of the house.

Locanda La Loggia

Piazza del Popolo, 7, 19015 Levanto
☎ 0187.808.107, fax 0187.808.107, locandalaloggia@hotmail.it
Closed mid-January to mid-February, last two weeks November
€€

Porticoed 13th-century building in the Centro Storico serving seafood dishes in a friendly atmosphere.

Manarola

Marina Piccola

Via Lo Scalo, 16, 19010 Manarola
☎ 0187.920.103, fax 0187.920.966, info@hotelmarinapiccola.com,
www.hotelmarinapiccola.com
Closed November, Tuesdays
€€

Terrace dining during the summer months. Menu pairs fresh seafood and regional wines.

Monegli

La Campana d'Angiò
Località Pero - Via Aurelia, 7
Moneglia (GE)
☎ 0185/49741
€

Closed for lunch (except Saturdays and holidays), every Monday, February 15-28

Restaurant specializing in seafood.

Montemarcello

Dai Pironcelli
Via delle Mura, 45, 19030 Montemarcello
☎ 0187.601.252
€

Closed January. Closed Wednesdays. June-September closed for lunch.

A rustic trattoria in Montemarcello that is recommended by Slow Food for their dedication to preserving the traditional cuisine of Liguria.

Pescarino-Sapori di Terra e di Mare
Via Borea, 52, 19030 Montemarcello
☎ 0187.601.388, fax 0187.603.501
Closed mid-end January, mid-end June, Mondays and Tuesdays, weekday lunch.
€

On the edge of Montemarcello, a simple dining room serving creative meat and seafood dishes.

Monterosso al Mare

Miky
Via Fegina, 104, 19016 Monterosso al Mare
☎ 0187.817.608, fax 0187.817.608, miky@ristorantemiky.it, www.ristorantemiky.it
Closed Tuesdays

Fresh fish and shellfish – including local lobsters kept in the garden aquarium – are the backbone of the menu, but there's also a wood-fired pizza oven.

Nervi

La Ruota
Via Oberdan, 215r, 16167 Nervi
☎ 010.372.60.27, fax 010.372.60.27
Closed first two weeks August, Mondays
€
A family-run trattoria serving seafood dishes.

Noli

Ristorante Italia
Corso Italia, 23, 17026 Noli
☎ 019.748.971, fax 019.749.18.59, info@hotelitalianoli.it,
www.hotelitalianoli.it
€€
On the promenade, this hotel dining room with a
glass-fronted terrace prepares traditional Ligurian dishes.

Malafemmina
Piazza Garibaldi, 4, 17026 Noli
☎ 019.748.825
€€
In the heart of the Centro Storico, a contemporary restaurant
and wine bar serving modern dishes.

Da Pino
Via Cavalieri di Malta, 37, 17026 Noli
☎ 019.749.00.65
Closed November, Mondays, Tuesday lunch
€€
Away from the waterfront a family-run restaurant bases
dishes on the local catch.

Pieve di Teco

Negro
Via Canada, 10, 18020 Cenova
☎ 0183.340.89, fax 0183.324.800, hotelnegro@libero.it
Closed January-Easter, non-summer Wednesdays
€€
In the small hamlet of Cenova a short distance from Pieve di
Teco, the fireplace-warmed dining room has vaulted ceilings
and serves mountain-inflected Ligurian cuisine.

Ponte di Nava-da Beppe

Frazione Ponte di Nava, 32, 12070 Ponte di Nava
☎ 0174.399.924, fax 0174.399.007, albergopontedinava@cnnet.it
Closed January 7-February 7, last week June, Wednesdays
€

Traditional cuisine reflecting the proximity to Piedmont served in a traditional dining room.

Pigna

Terme

Via Madonna Assunta, 18037 Pigna
☎ 0184.241.046, fax 0184.241.046, cllante@tin.it
Closed mid-January to mid-February, Wednesdays except August, November-March dinner by reservation only
€

Family-run trattoria offers rustic renditions of Ligurian fare.

Il Castellana

Regione Argeleo, 18037 Pigna
☎ 0184.241.014
Closed Mondays, November
€€

On a hillside perch off the road before Pigna, overlooking the valley, a rustic stone building with handsome dining room serves seasonal dishes based on local ingredients.

Portofino

Da Puny

Piazza Martiri dell'Olivetta, 5, 16034 Portofino
☎ 0185.269.037
Closed Thursdays
€€

Make reservations well in advance and bring cash (no credit cards accepted) to Portofino's most popular piazzetta restaurant. Dine on traditional dishes while rubbing elbows with VIPs and celebrities.

Taverna del Marinaio

Piazza Martiri dell'Olivetta, 36, 16034 Portofino
☎ 0185.269.103
Closed Tuesdays
€€

Where to Eat

Requisite location on the piazzetta with the added bonus of excellent seafood dishes served in a lively dining room or at outdoor tables.

La Terrazza

Hotel Splendido
Viale Baratta, 16, 16034 Portofino
☎ 0185.267.801, fax 0185.267.806, www.hotelsplendido.com
€€€

Light lunches and late suppers graciously accommodated either in the elegant dining room or spectacular, panoramic terrace.

Chuflay Bar Restaurant

Splendido Mare
Via Roma, 2, 16034 Portofino
☎ 0185.267.806, fax 0185.267.806, www.hotelsplendido.com
€€

Breakfast, lunch, snacks, high tea, dinner, and late suppers served at the piazzetta restaurant of the Splendido Mare.

Portovenere

Le Bocche

Calata Doria, 102, 19025 Portovenere
☎ 0187.790.622, fax 0187.766.056, pbercini@tin.it
Closed November, December, non-summer Tuesdays
€€€

A sleek, contemporary restaurant in the ramparts of the 12th-century fortress has an amazing view and menu dedicated to fresh ingredients. Live lobster and oyster tank. Gorgeous terrace.

Trattoria La Marina-da Antonio

Piazza Marina, 6, 19025 Portovenere
☎ 0187.790.686, fax 0187.790.686
Closed November, Thursdays
€€

There are views of the Marina from this family-run trattoria serving fish dishes.

Olioteca Bansigo

Via Capellini, 95, 19025 Portovenere
☎ 0187.793.045
€

After receiving an excellent education on Ligurian olive oils, take a minute to sign the stylish glass wall where other happy patrons have left their praiseful grazie. Bottles or tins can be filled with your pick of oil – make a decision after tasting several – and taken-away or shipped. There are also light food items, perfect for a nibble, or antipasti.

Bajeico - la Bottega del Pesto

Via Capellini, 70, 19025 Portovenere
☎ 0187.791.054
€

This shrine to artisan pesto is sleek and modern, but devoted to the most traditional of Ligurian condiments. Baskets of fresh basil scent the air and generous tastings are offered. Fresh pesto can be slathered on bread for takeaway, or purchase a container for prolonged enjoyment.

Locanda Lorena

Corso Cavour, 4, 19025 Isla Palmeria, Palmeria
☎ 0187.792.370, fax 0187.766.077, www.locandalorena.it

Mussels from the beds at Seno del Terizzo feature prominently on the menu of this culinary haven, also known for its use of fresh local seafood and shellfish.

Rapallo

Luca

Via Langano, 32, 16035 Rapallo
☎ 0185.603.23, fax 0185.603.23
ristoranteluca@yahoo.it
Closed Tuesdays
€€

A seafood restaurant on the waterfront has a friendly atmosphere and well-prepared dishes.

Eden

Via Diaz, 5, 16035 Rapallo
☎ 0185.505.53, fax 0185.50553, w.eden@tin.it
Closed Christmas week, last three weeks February, Wednesday lunch July-August
€€

Popular with visitors and locals alike, just off the waterfront serving seafood.

Ü Giancu
Via San Massimo, 78, 16035 Rapallo
☎ 0185.261.212
Closed Wednesdays, weekday lunch
€€

Fun atmosphere established by cartoon-decorated walls. Traditional Ligurian fare.

Recco

Ristorante Manuelina
Via Roma, 278, 16036 Recco
☎ 0185.720.779, fax 0185.721.095
manuelina@manuelina.it, www.manuelina.it
€€

Legend holds that Recco's famous bread, *focaccia al formaggio*, was invented here in 1885 to serve hungry locals returning from the Genoa opera. The focacceria still turns out the specialty while the kitchen prepares outstanding Ligurian dishes.

Vitturin
Via dei Giustiniani, 48, 16036 Recco
☎ 0185.720.225, fax 0185.723.686, vitturin@libero.it
Closed second week February, Mondays
€

Regional dishes served in a family-run establishment with veranda.

Da ö Vittorio
Via Roma, 160, 16036 Recco
☎ 0185.740.29, fax 0185.723.605, info@daovittorio.it
www.daovittorio.it
Closed last week November to mid-December, Thursdays
€

Excellent value for regional fare served in a classically styled dining room.

Riomaggiore

Ripa del Sole
Via de' Gaspari, 282, 19017 Riomaggiore
☎ 0187.920.143
Closed mid-January to mid-February, Mondays November-March
€

Shellfish features prominently on the good-value menu of this typical restaurant.

San Remo

Paolo e Barbara

Via Roma, 47, 18038 San Remo

☎ 0184.531.653, fax 0184.545.266, paolobarbara@libero.it,
www.paolobarbara.it

€€€

Paolo Masieri earned a Michelin star at 25 and continues to
shine, turning out contemporary Ligurian cuisine based
impeccably fresh ingredients including locally sourced
organic meats and fish, wild game, and produce cultivated on
the Masieri farm near Castel Vittorio.

Il Bagatto

Via Matteotti, 145, 18030 San Remo

☎ 0184.531.925, fax 0184.531.925

Closed July, Sundays

€€

Splendid location in the Palazzo Borea d'Olmo. Family-run
and featuring fish and meat dishes based on classic Ligurian
preparations.

Cantine Sanremese

Via Palazzo, 7, 18030 San Remo

☎ 0184.572.063

Closed November, last week June

€

Convivial atmosphere in a wine cellar where the chef/owner
presents simple, classic Ligurian fare and wine by the glass.

Ristorante L'Airone

Piazza Eroi Sanremesi, 12, 18030 San Remo

☎ 0184.531.469

€

Good location on a pedestrian-only street in the old part of
town with tables on the piazza or in a small garden in summer
months. Ligurian cuisine and pizza.

Santa Margherita Ligure

Trattoria Cesarina

Via Mameli, 2/c, 16038 Santa Margherita Ligure

☎ 0185.286.059

Closed last weeks December, Tuesdays, lunch July-August

€€

Tables under the porticoes or in the traditional dining room.
Seafood dishes.

Skipper
Calata del Porto, 6, 16038 Santa Margherita Ligure
☎ 0185.289.950, fax 0185.289.950
Closed February, Wednesdays, lunch Tuesdays and Wednesdays July and August
€€
Seafood is the obvious choice when dining at this restaurant on the wharf, or on the establishment's floating venue.

Oca Bianca
Via XXV Aprile, 21, 16038 Santa Margherita Ligure
☎ 0185.288.411, fax 0185.288.411
Closed first week January to mid-February, Mondays, lunch Tuesday-Thursday
€€
When you've had your fill of seafood, head to this restaurant dedicated to all things not fish, including meat dishes, Italian cheeses, and local produce.

Il Frantoio
Via Giuncheto, 23a, 16038 Santa Margherita Ligure
☎ 0185.286.667
Closed weekday lunch
€€
Wood-fired pizza and Ligurian dishes served in the former oil mill of the Villa Durazzo.

Sarzana

La Giara
Via Bertoloni, 35, 19038 Sarzana
☎ 0187.624.013
Closed Tuesdays, Wednesday lunch
€
An excellent value for home-style cooking in a pleasant, informal setting.

Taverna Napoleone
Via Bonaparte, 16, 19038 Sarzana
☎ 0187.627.974, taverna.napoleone@libero.it
Closed February 7-14, Wednesdays, lunch
Near its namesake's ancestral home, a rustic restaurant with good wine list.

Sassello

Pian del Sole

Località Pianferioso, 23, 17046 Sassello
☎ 019.724.255, fax 019.720.038, info@hotel-piandelsole.com,
www.hotel-piandelsole.com
€

Spacious dining room prepares inland Ligurian cuisine with
local specialties like wild mushrooms, game, and truffles.
Enjoy *Amaretto* cookies with your espresso.

Savona

L'Arco Antico

Piazza Lavagnola, 26r, 17100 Savona
☎ 019.820.938, fax 019.820.938, arcoantico@lycos.it
Closed Sundays, lunch by reservation only
€€

Creative, seasonal seafood dishes have earned this restaurant on the outskirts of town its Michelin star.

Osteria Bacco

Via Quarda Superiore, 17r, 17100 Savona
☎ 019.833.5350

Stimulating décor primes the palate for Ligurian dishes at
this waterfront restaurant.

Sestri Levante

Rezzano Cucina e Vino

Via Asilo Maria Teresa, 34, 16039 Sestri Levante
☎ 0185.450.909, fax 0185.450.909, rezzanocucinaevino@libero.it
Closed Mondays, lunch June-September
€€

Minimalist setting lets the seafood dishes shine.

Portobello

Via Portobello, 16, 16039 Sestri Levante
☎ 0185.415.66
Closed January, February, November, non-summer Wednesdays
€€

Gorgeous location on the Baia del Silenzio. Dine on the beach
in summer.

Where to Eat

Bottega del Vino
Via Nazionale, 530, 16039 Sestri Levante
☎ 0185.433.49
€

Popular and fun winebar has extensive selection to enjoy by the glass with simple dishes.

Spotorno

A Sigögna
Via Garibaldi, 13, 17028 Spotorno
☎ 0197.450.16
Closed end-October to December, non-summer Tuesdays
€€

Enjoy seafood dishes at this family-run restaurant.

Taggia

Germinal
Via Gastaldi, 15 b
☎ 0184.411.53
€

A typical osteria with a pub atmosphere (sometimes with live music) appreciated for its history and its dedication to traditional fare.

La Conchiglia
Lungomare, 33, 18011 Arma di Taggia
☎ 0184.431.69, fax 0184.428.72
Closed Wednesdays, Thursday lunch
€€

Elegant atmosphere for a fine-dining establishment using regional ingredients to create modern cuisine.

Tellaro

Nta' Grita
Piazza Figoli, 3, 19030 Tellaro
☎ 0187.964.713, roberto@ntgagrita.it, www.ntagrita.it
€

Market fresh, seasonal produce and local fish and olive oil are the base of traditional Ligurian dishes at this restaurant on the town piazza that's jammed with locals.

Locanda Miranda

Via Fiascherino, 92, 19030 Tellaro

☎ 0187.968.130, fax 0187.964.032, locandamiranda@libero.it

€€

The tasting menu is a tour through the specialties of the house, most of which emphasize fresh local seafood.

Varazze

Antico Genovese

Corso Colombo, 70, 17019 Varazze

☎ 019.964.82, info@anticogenovese.it, www.anticogenovese.it

€€

Continuously operated by the same family since 1910, the restaurant today presents a classic, spare dining room where fresh pastas, fish, and meats are served. Cheese list features Italian specialties.

Ristorante Bri

Piazza Bovani, 13, 17019 Varazze

☎ 019.934.605, fax 019.931.713, info@ristorantebri.it, www.ristorantebri.it

€€

Classic Ligurian dishes are presented without frills or fanfare in a nautically inspired dining room or covered terrace on the piazza.

Ventimiglia

Baia Beniamin

Corso Europa, 63, 18039 Ventimiglia

☎ 0184.38.002, fax 0184.38.027, www.baiabeniamin.it

€€€

More than 300 wines from the property's cellar accompany the fine gastronomic dishes prepared at this elegant restaurant on the French border. Reserve for the terrace in summer.

Balzi Rossi

Via Balzi Rossi, 2, 18039 Ventimiglia

☎ 0184.381.32, fax 0184.385.32

Closed last three weeks November, Mondays, Tuesday lunch, Sunday lunch in August

€€€

In the region of the famous caves of the same name is this luxurious Michelin-starred restaurant where dishes combine local ingredients and French/Italian preparations.

Cuneo
Via Aprosio, 16, 18039 Ventimiglia
☎ 0184.231.711
Closed mid-June to first week July, Sunday and Monday dinner March-October, Tuesday dinner, Wednesdays
€€

Classic Italian food served at this popular restaurant in a good, central location.

Vernazza

Gianni Franzi
Piazza Marconi, 5, 19018 Vernazza
☎ 0187.812.228/0187.821.003, fax 0187.812.228,
www.giannifranzi.it

Steps from the sand on Vernazza's tiny and colorful piazza. Trattoria specializes in seafood.

Zoagli

L'Arenella
Lungomare dei Naviganti, 16030 Zoagli
☎ 0185.259.393, fax 0185.259.393
Closed February and Tuesday
€€

Hotel dining room on the cliffs specializes in seafood.

Index